Ch 13, 14.

169-202

vel

A GUIDE TO INSURANCE MANAGEMENT

Also by Stephen Diacon

SUCCESS IN INSURANCE (*with R.L. Carter*)
THE BRITISH INSURANCE INDUSTRY: A Statistical Review (*editor with R.L. Carter*)
THE UK INSURANCE INDUSTRY: Structure, Developments and Market Prospects to 1990

A Guide to Insurance Management

Edited by

Stephen Diacon

Lecturer in Insurance Studies
University of Nottingham

M

MACMILLAN

First published 1990

Published by
THE MACMILLAN PRESS LTD
Houndmills, Basingstoke, Hampshire RG21 2XS
and London
Companies and representatives
throughout the world

Printed and bound in Great Britain by
WBC Ltd, Bristol and Maesteg

British Library Cataloguing in Publication Data
A guide to insurance management.
1. Insurance companies. Management
I. Diacon, S.R. (Stephen R.)
368′.0068
ISBN 0–333–37439–8

Contents

List of Tables

List of Figures

Foreword

A Guide to Insurance Management is designed to provide an overview of the main activities involved in the management of insurance enterprises. It is anticipated that it will be of interest to all levels of management of insurance companies and brokers around the world, and be especially useful for those who wish to obtain a comprehensive understanding of the principles underlying the main insurance company operations.

The international nature of insurance business has been reflected in the nationalities of the contributors, who bring together experience in the management of insurance enterprises from seven countries; Australia (John Pollard), Germany (Walter Karten), Ireland (Henry Ellis), The Netherlands (Hans van Gelder and G.W. de Wit), Nigeria (Samuel Msheliza), the United States (John B. Gragnola), and the United Kingdom. The contributors include people who practice insurance management and those who undertake applied insurance research; they are all known for their writings on insurance issues.

There are very few published texts which concern themselves specifically with the management of insurance enterprises. In one sense this may be no bad thing since it could be argued that there is nothing unique about the management of insurance companies; however, I believe this argument to be spurious. Although it may be the case that human behaviour – and hence the practice of 'man-management' – is just the same in insurance as in any other business, the imperative to demonstrate good quality service to customers (and good quality management to regulators) places special emphasis on the selection, training and motivation of insurance staff. Furthermore, the technical aspects of insurance management (for example in the areas of financial management, underwriting and pricing, reserving, investment, and so on) present problems which are particular to the insurance industry. Even in a discipline as universal as strategic planning, research conducted in the United States by Cummins (1985) and in the United Kingdom by Msheliza (1990) seems to indicate that insurers have special problems in applying the standard techniques. Consequently a book concerned with the specific issues of insurance management, and written by people with expert knowledge of those issues, is long overdue.

The main thrust of professional training in insurance is usually directed towards the needs of the customer, in terms of the types and wordings of the various forms of insurance contract and their legal interpretation. So it is unusual to find a book which concentrates instead on the continuing professional education of insurance managers, and on the needs of the supplier of insurance services. The requirements of the private and commercial buyers of insurance are becoming increasingly complex, so it is appropriate that insurers should pay close attention to ensuring that their staff are well versed in the details of the various insurance products. But the nature of the insurance market is also increasing in complexity as competition intensifies and the supervisory authorities take a more pro-active role in insurance regulation. This book's emphasis on planning and management should be of considerable use to all those involved in managing insurance enterprises in a turbulent environment.

The role of the professional bodies in providing continuing education in insurance management has often been difficult to resolve. Some insurance institutes have provided their members with books of readings which, although based on the general theme of management, are not specifically tailored to the needs of insurance enterprises. Other institutes have decided to minimise their involvement in management education, and have recommended their members to undertake management degrees (such as a Master of Business Administration) which may have no specialist insurance content whatsoever. The impetus for management development must therefore come from within the insurance industry itself, and this book, written as it is by people with significant practical and academic experience, will help to fill the vacuum.

The material in this book can be divided into the two major themes of interest to management: the planning, organisation and future strategy of the overall insurance business; and the operation and coordination of the technical processes involved.

The first three chapters are concerned with the planning and strategy of insurance enterprise in a turbulent environment. In Chapter 1, Samuel Msheliza outlines the main aspects and techniques of the strategic planning and explains how it can be applied by insurers. He finds that strategic planning is underutilised in many insurance companies, but notes that the most successful companies are likely to be those which are able to anticipate the direction of change and plan well ahead to meet the challenges. In Chapter 2, the emphasis is very much on how to implement a strategic plan, as John R. Gragnola discusses his experience of introducing formal planning at Allstate Insurance Company, one of the world's largest insurance groups. Chapter 3 turns attention on a particular issue which will provide threats and opportunities for the worldwide insurance industry – the integration of insurance in the Single European Market; after discussing the likely impact of European integration on the insurance market, Stephen Diacon goes on to examine the main strategic choices facing insurers in the run-up to 1992.

The next three chapters examine the issues of structure and organisation. There is a growing interest in modelling the financial behaviour of insurance companies with new developments appearing almost daily (for example, see Daykin and Hey, 1989). In Chapter 4, Margaret Brown discusses the rationale of model-building with illustrations from ASIR (Advanced Simulation of Insurance and Reinsurance), one of the first such models, ASIR was developed for the Geneva Association as part of its research programme on the use of simulation techniques in insurance. One of the main benefits of the modelling process is the insight it gives to the behaviour (both financial and stochastic) of insurance organisations. The discussion of modelling continues in Chapter 5 as Stewart Coutts and Russell Devitt investigate the factors affecting the financial strength of a reinsurance company. Their explanation of the modelling process is particularly revealing in the understanding it gives of the financial management of insurance operations. Chapter 6 is a little different; it provides a fascinating overview of the division of labour within an insurance company, and discusses the organisational design and managerial control required to execute the necessary tasks. Hans van Gelder notes that in many companies there is often an obsession with control reinforced by the external control exercised by supervisory authorities. However, the pace of change in insurance markets will require companies to decentralise and devolve authority and resource control upon those units where the actual operations and client contacts take place.

The remaining chapters are more concerned with the operation and control of the technical processes involved in managing life and general insurance companies. In Chapter 7, Christopher Nutt (who now runs his own consultancy company specialising in the management of change) shows how to construct a staffing policy which matches the employer's corporate objectives, and goes on to explain how to implement such a policy in an international multi-line insurance group. The discussion in Chapter 8 turns to underwriting as Bernard Benjamin considers the theoretical and practical aspects of the selection of a liability portfolio. After explaining the conditions which influence the acceptance of individual risks in the main classes of insurance, Professor Benjamin shows how an insurer should balance its portfolio of business in order to achieve the primary business objective of profit maximisation, subject to the need to maintain solvency.

The next six chapters are loosely concerned with the costing, pricing, marketing and distribution of insurance products. In Chapter 9, the nature of an insurance company's administrative costs and the basis of cost allocation are discussed with illustrated examples to make the points clear. However, Rodney Young also uses these examples to provide a warning that incorrect cost allocation can lead an insurer to make the wrong decisions in the areas of pricing and branch viability. Chapter 10 provides a more analytic approach to the description and insurance company output, its measurement, and its relationship to administrative costs: the broad purpose of Stephen Diacon's discussion is to warn against oversimplified analyses of cost behaviour in relation to decisions on pricing and the optimal output (and hence size) of insurance companies. In Chapter 11, John Pollard (a leading actuary) undertakes to unravel the statistical complexities of premium rating using simple numerical examples to make his points clear. He shows how the basic calculation of a risk premium can be undertaken, the effects on this of a deductible and of excess of loss reinsurance, and the way in which loadings are added to allow for expenses, contingencies and profit. The treatment of costing and pricing of insurance is rounded off by Walter Karten in Chapter 12 with an analysis of the competitive influences on pricing in insurance markets. Professor Karten discusses the basis of pricing policy, and stresses the need to achieve premium discrimination and avoid the problems of adverse selection.

The marketing and distribution of insurance is then developed in the next two chapters. In Chapter 13, Trevor Watkins and Stephen Diacon discuss the problems involved in marketing insurance services, and the construction of a marketing planning policy to overcome these problems. The distribution of insurance is then taken up by Hugh Cockerell, who looks at the role of insurance intermediaries and their duties, remuneration and regulation around the world.

Chapters 15 and 16 are concerned with the sources and investment of insurance funds. With the aid of carefully worked examples, Professor G.W. de Wit illustrates the source of life and general insurance funds, and discusses the estimation of the various types of insurance company reserve. In the following chapter, Marcus Johnson outlines the main factors to take into account in the investment of life and general insurance funds, placing particular emphasis on the role of the insurer's investment objectives in influencing the structure of the asset portfolio.

The final three chapters are broadly concerned with measuring the success of insurance company performance. In Chapter 17, Henry Ellis takes the regulator's perspective in order to examine the licensing and ongoing monitoring of insurance company operations. He describes the differing ways in which insurance supervisors control entry to insurance markets, and the various philosophies of the regulation of continuing insurance activities. In Chapter 18, Bill Abbott looks at the relationship between solvency and profit in a general insurance company, and discusses the appropriate accounting framework and performance ratios necessary to measure profitability. Finally, in Chapter 19, Sidney Benjamin provides detailed worked examples to illustrate the financial management of a life insurance company, covering the methods of valuation, the emergence of surplus, and the calculation of the value of a life office.

The overall intention of this book is to provide readers with an insight into the main activities undertaken by insurance company management.

Through the efforts of the contributors, I hope that the principles and practice of insurance management will be more widely understood and appreciated.

Nottingham STEPHEN DIACON

References

Cummins J.D. (ed.) (1985) *Strategic Planning and Modelling in the Property-Liability Insurance* (Hingham, MA: Kluwer-Hijhoff Publishing).

Daykin C.D. and G.B. Hey (1989) 'Modelling a General Insurance Company', *Journal of the Institute of Actuaries*. vol 116, pt III.

Msheliza S. (1990) *Strategic Planning in the Insurance Industry*, Discussion Papers in Industrial Economics. University of Nottingham.

Preface and Acknowledgements

In many insurance markets, it is comparatively rare to find either a practitioner or an analyst with a sufficient breadth of knowledge and the time to spare to write a book covering all the main aspects of the management of insurance companies. The practice of technical specialisation among employees in most Western insurance companies often means that only the most senior managers are in a position to overview the whole insurance operation. The obvious solution was to bring together the leading exponents of insurance management to make a book of contributions.

The chapters of this book have been written specially by contributors who are experts, by dint of their experience or research, in the various aspects of the management of insurance operations. Although the book is constructed as a collection of 'tailor-made' contributions, I hope that it will read like an integrated text, and be of interest to a broad spectrum of people working in the worldwide insurance industry.

In acknowledging the help I have received in the preparation of this book, I would like to thank the contributors in particular for the willingness to share their expertise and time. Thanks are also due to Mr Keith Povey for his expert editing, and to Mrs Susan Dunstan for her help in preparing the manuscript.

The editor and publishers would like to thank the following for permission to use copyright material:

Frank Cass Publishers, for an extract from the *Service Industries Journal*;
The Commission of the European Communities, for tables and figures reproduced from *Research on the Cost of Non-Europe* and *European File*;
Gower Publishing Group, for figures from *1992: The European Challenge*;
Christine Ennew and Mike Wright at the University of Nottingham, for tables from their Discussion Paper;
Basil Blackwell, for a figure from the *Journal of Common Market Studies*;
Butterworth & Co. for a figure from *Marketing Financial Services*;
United Trade Press, for an extract from *The Review*.

Finally, although I do not consider it appropriate to dedicate a book of contributions, I would like to acknowledge a debt of gratitude to my colleague Bob Carter, the Norwich Union Professor of Insurance Studies, who has been instrumental in stimulating an interest in the study of insurance among many students at the University of Nottingham.

STEPHEN DIACON

Notes on the Contributors

Bill Abbott is Group Actuary of Legal and General Group plc, the tenth largest insurance company in the United Kingdom. He has published a number of papers in actuarial journals, including 'Financial Aspects of a General Insurance Company' (with T.G. Clarke and W.R. Treen) *Journal of the Institute of Actuaries*, vol. 108, 1981 and 'Actuaries and General Insurance', *Journal of the Institute of Actuaries* vol. 113, 1986.

Bernard Benjamin is Emeritus Professor at The City University, London. During his career he has been Director of Statistics at the Department of Health, Director of Research and Intelligence for the Greater London Council, and Director of Statistical Studies at the Civil Service College. In 1973 he became Professor of Actuarial Science at the City University and subsequently founding Director of the City University Centre for Research in Insurance and Investment. He has held a number of official offices, including President of the Institute of Actuaries (1966–8), President of the Royal Statistical Society (1970–1), Vice President of the International Statistical Institute (1973–7), President of the Eugenic Society (1982–7), and Chairman of the Statistics Users' Council (since 1970). He has published many books and articles, including *The Analysis of Mortality and other Actuarial Statistics* (with H.W. Haycocks), (Cambridge University Press, 1970) and *General Insurance* (William Heinemann, 1977).

Sidney Benjamin is a partner of Bacon and Woodrow, one of the United Kingdom's largest consulting actuaries, and visiting Professor of Actuarial Studies at the City University, London. He has published a large number of papers in actuarial journals, and in 1985 was presented with the Gold Medal of the Institute of Actuaries; he is also Chairman of the Institute's Research Committee. He is a Fellow of the British Computer Society and of the Royal Statistical Society, and a member of the Society of Actuaries Research Committee in the United States.

Margaret Brown has worked as a research officer in the Institute of European Finance and then as lecturer in insurance in the School of Accounting, Banking and Economics, both at the University College of North Wales. She has specialised in the development of computer simulation models of banks and insurance companies, and published her results in journals such as *The Geneva Papers*.

Hugh Cockerell has been Visiting Professor of Insurance Studies at the City University in London since 1971. Prior to his appointment, he was Secretary of the Chartered Insurance Institute for twenty-five years. He was co-founder and is currently Vice President of the British Insurance Law Association. His publications include *Insurance Broking and Agency – the Law and the Practice* (with G.K. Shaw), (Witherby & Co Ltd, 1979), *Lloyd's of London: A Portrait* (Woodhead-Faulkner, 1984) and *Witherby's Dictionary of Insurance*, 2nd edn (Witherby & Co Ltd, 1987).

Stewart Coutts is currently a partner in International Actuarial Consultants having worked previously with Excess Insurance and Bacon and Woodrow. He has published a number of papers in United Kingdom and other actuarial journals, including 'Motor Insurance Rating: An Actuarial Approach', *Journal of the Institute of Actuaries*, vol. 111 (1984). In 1986, he acted as the Convenor of the First International Conference on Insurance Solvency.

Russell Devitt is currently Director of Business Development with the NEL Britannia Group of Companies based in Dorking, Surrey. He was previously Business Development Manager with Pearl Assurance in London. He has published a number of papers on the solvency of insurance companies, in journals such as the *Journal of the Institute of Actuaries*.

G.W. de Wit was head of the research department of the Nationale-Nederlanden N.V. until 1989, when he became Professor of Insurance at Erasmus University in Rotterdam, The Netherlands. He has published many articles applying actuarial techniques to general insurance, and is the Secretary of the Committee of ASTIN. He is also the editor of the series, *Surveys of Actuarial Studies*, published by Nationale-Nederlanden.

Stephen Diacon has been Lecturer in Insurance Studies at the University of Nottingham in the United Kingdom since 1975. He has published numerous books and articles on risk and insurance, including *Success in Insurance* (with R.L. Carter), 2nd edn (John Murray, 1988) and *The UK Insurance Industry: Structure, Developments and Market Prospects to 1990* (Staniland Hall Associates, 1985).

Henry Ellis is Associate Professor of Law and Insurance at the University of Limerick in the Republic of Ireland, and a director of Celtic International Insurance Co. Ltd Galway. He previously worked with the Norwich Union Insurance Group in Ireland and the United Kingdom. He has written several books and many articles on legal and economic aspects of insurance, including *European Integration and Insurance* (Witherby & Co Ltd, 1980) and *Regulation of Insurance in the UK and Ireland* (with J.A. Wiltshire), (Kluwer Publishing Limited, 1986).

John B. Gragnola is currently Vice President of Allstate Insurance Companies – the fifth largest US insurance group – and Director of Allstate Research and Planning Center based at Menlo Park, California. He previously acted as Consumer Research Manager, Director of Research Implementation, and Market Research Director with the same company. He is a frequent speaker at marketing, planning and research conferences, serves on the Board of Trustees of the Marketing Science Institute, and is a past Chairman of the Western Marketing Research Council.

Walter Karten is Ordentlicher Professor für Allgemeine Betriebswirtschaftslehre und Versicherungsbetriebslehre, and Geschäftsführender Direktor of the Seminar für Bank- und Versicherungsbetriebslehre at the University of Hamburg in the Federal Republic of Germany. He is also Studienleiter at the Institut für Berufsfortbildung der Versicherungswirtschaft and the Deutschen Versicherungs-Akademie in Hamburg. He is a member of the Vorstandes des Deutschen Vereins für Versicherungswissenschaften e.V. and the Aufsichtsrates der Central-Krankenversicherungs-AG in Cologne.

Marcus Johnson is currently Managing Director of Premium Management Limited, a firm of investment managers based in London, and is a holder of the Securities Industry Diploma of the International Stock Exchange. He previously worked for Hoare Govett and Alexander Howden Financial Services Ltd. He is a member of the FIMBRA Selection Committee and a past chairman of the London Insurance Economists Group.

Samuel Msheliza is a lecturer in the Faculty of Business Administration at the University of Maiduguri in Nigeria. Since 1987 he has been undertaking research at the University of Nottingham into the strategic management of insurance companies in Nigeria and the United Kingdom.

Christopher Nutt has held a number of senior appointments in UK insurance companies, including Head of Client Services at Abbey Life Assurance Company, and Manpower Services Manager and then Operations and Systems Manager at Sun Alliance Insurance Group. He holds an honours degree in Sociology from London University and a postgraduate diploma in Personnel Management from the London School of Economics.

John Pollard is Professor of Actuarial Studies at Macquarie University, Sidney, Australia. He is the author of many books and articles on actuarial science and statistics, including *Mathematical Models for the Growth of Human Populations* (Cambridge University Press 1973), *A Handbook of Numerical and Statistical Techniques* (Cambridge University Press 1979) and *Introductory Statistics with Applications in General Insurance* (with I.B. Hossack and B. Zehnwirth), (Cambridge University Press 1983).

Hans van Gelder worked for Delta Lloyd in Amsterdam, The Netherlands, before establishing Van Gelder Management Services bv. He has specialised in strategic management, organisation design, personnel planning, budgeting and productivity measurement in insurance.

Trevor Watkins is currently ASDA Professor and Head of the School of Business Studies at Oxford Polytechnic. He has wide experience of both academic research and consultancy in the marketing of insurance and financial services and has recently undertaken work on new product development, marketing strategy, salesforce motivation, and home service in relation to the UK life insurance market. He has published widely on financial services marketing, including *Marketing Financial Services* (with M. Wright), (Butterworths, 1986) and *Marketing Insurance: A Practical Guide* (with N. Dyer), (Kluwer Publishing Limited, 1988).

Rodney Young is Director (Management Services) within the general insurance division of the Legal and General Insurance Group based in London. He is a member of the Institute of Marketing, and holder of the Certified Diploma of Accounting and Finance and the Diploma of the Institute of Marketing.

1 Strategic Planning in Insurance

Samuel Msheliza

1.1 INTRODUCTION

Insurance companies now face many uncertainties. During the 1970s and 1980s, insurance markets have experienced dramatic changes in the hitherto stable environment in which they operate, including greater price competition, deregulation of certain aspects of their operations, the advent and growth of consumerism and the development by large corporations of other methods of managing risk. New sources of competition, such as banks and other financial institutions, now offer services which were traditionally performed by insurance companies. In addition, fundamental changes in the macroeconomic environment create problems which management in insurance have to consider in their long-range decisions.

Management decision-making in insurance companies is still internally focused, with great emphasis on the achievement of efficiency in traditional functions such as underwriting, claims handling, and customer services. This internal focus means that the changes taking place in the external environments are overlooked. The result is that many companies become victims of their environment.

A practical approach to dealing with challenges in the environment is to introduce strategic planning and a growing number of businesses in different industries are adopting this to improve management effectiveness; however, the practice of strategic planning is still relatively new in the insurance industry:

> Whether due to the inherent conservatism in the industry, inflexible and unresponsive organisational structures, lack of planning expertise, or other factors, many companies have been content simply in doing what others in the industry are doing, rather than venturing forth independently to determine opportunities and threats, strengths and weaknesses. (Aylor and Cummins, 1985)

The aim of this chapter is to present the strategic planning process and its major techniques, and to explain how its practice in insurance companies can be improved. The remainder of this chapter is divided into four sections: Section 1.2 defines strategic planning and outlines the benefits to be derived from its practice. Section 1.3 looks at the normative approach to strategic planning and the various steps involved in the formulation of strategy. Section 1.4 discusses the use of portfolio models, and their relevance to insurance management. Section 1.5 gives some results from a survey conducted by the Nottingham Institute of Financial Studies, and a brief conclusion follows in Section 1.6.

1.2 THE CONCEPT OF STRATEGIC PLANNING

Introduction

Strategic planning is the process of reaching and implementing those decisions which significantly affect the company's ability to achieve its objectives. It sets the pattern for resource allocation within the company, in the context of the opportunities and threats in the external environment.

Strategic planning is the development of methods for influencing and controlling or shaping the future of the company, so that management is able to respond quickly to changes in the economic, political and social environment. The process of strategic planning involves a realistic assessment of the internal strengths and weaknesses of the company, the setting of objectives and the creation of action plans for achieving those objectives. Strategic planning should define the range of businesses the company is to pursue, the kind of economic and human organisation it is or intends to be, and the nature of economic and non-economic contributions it intends to make to its shareholders, employees, customers and communities. This is a continuous process taking into account the characteristics and objectives of each company in the context of a continuously changing economic, financial, political and sociocultural market environment.

Strategic planning aims at achieving an effective interaction between the company and all the important aspects of its environment; strategic decisions should significantly affect the company's prospects. Strategical planning is not the same as *tactical planning*, which is primarily concerned with the daily running of the company. Tactical planning is typically made at operational levels, to ensure the smooth running of the company, while implementing strategic decisions. While strategic planning has implications for the entire company, and affects its long-term prospects, tactical plans are supportive of strategic plans, and are short-term in nature.

The need for formal strategic planning by a company emerges as the company grows, necessitating more complex operations. To be an effective management tool, the strategic planning system should be tailored to fit the unique characteristics and needs of a company.

While strategic planning in smaller companies is usually performed by a management committee, it is becoming a common practice for large and especially diversified companies to establish separate units charged with overseeing the strategic planning process. In those companies that have strategic planning units, the units are usually responsible for: collecting and processing required data; modelling the company's performance under different assumptions about the future; preparing planning guidelines and setting schedules; co-ordinating the planning process; and helping with implementation by clarifying any conflicts and confusions which may arise between implementors. In order that strategic planning units provide a viable service to top management, line management must be fully committed and involved in the strategic planning process.

The hierarchy of strategic planning

Strategic planning spans three main levels within a company, incorporating corporate, business and functional strategies. Corporate strategy is the preserve of management at corporate headquarters; business strategy is performed at divisional or business unit level; and functional strategy specifies the strategies for the various departments within divisions. Functional and business strategies are derived from and are supportive of corporate strategies. The lower down in the company a strategy is performed, the more detailed it becomes.

The categorisation of strategy hierarchy is appropriate mainly for a large diversified firm; for smaller companies, strategy may be performed at business and functional levels only. It is essential that strategic planning at the different levels be co-ordinated and integrated.

Corporate strategy is concerned with the type of businesses the company as a whole is in or should be in. It involves the determination of corporate purpose, mission and objectives, which is expressed in the company's desired portfolio of businesses. Any additions to or deletions from the portfolio would be formulated in terms of mergers or divestments. Corporate strategy should address the maintenance of balance in the company's portfolio of businesses by analysing the attractiveness of entire businesses in the light of the strategic characteristics of their markets and their present and potential contributions to corporate profits and growth. The main purpose of corporate strategy is the allocation of resources amongst business units and the determination of the future direction of the company's businesses.

Business strategy deals with the way the business unit (or division) competes in the market it serves. A *strategic business unit* is an autonomous unit with its own external market-place, for which objectives and strategies can be established and executed independently of other business units. The most important criterion for business segmentation is the external market served, rather than production or technical linkages. A strategic business unit should have an identified set of external customers, know which are its main external competitors, and be able to set its own strategies. For an insurance company, strategic business units should relate to the main types of insured (for example, personal, corporate, reinsured) rather than the main types of insurance business.

Business strategy involves setting objectives to be accomplished by the strategic business unit, and establishing action plans and policies for implementation. The strategy should define the unit's strategic posture, its scope in terms of products provided and markets served, and synergies sought in its operations. The essential purpose of business strategy is the delineation of the units – developing their distinctive features in comparison with those of competitors.

Functional strategy is performed at operating levels in the company and is concerned with the way the functional departments contribute to the attainment of business and corporate strategies.

The advantages and disadvantages of strategic planning

Strategic planning is not an end in itself – its purpose is to improve the effectiveness of management. It is the quality of a company's strategy that determines its performance, not how well the process is formulated. We can identify the following benefits of strategic planning:

(a) Strategic planning helps management to reflect upon and assess the attractiveness of the markets they are serving, on the factors determining success in those markets, and on their competitive positions in relation to their major competitors.
(b) Management, by practising strategic planning, is able to formulate explicit objectives, and to resolve conflicts of interest in its operations.
(c) Management can organise a systematic procedure for the collection and analysis of data, thereby analysing and visualising the strategic position of the company both now and in the future.
(d) Through strategic planning management is able to search for new strategic activities such as growth or divestment.
(e) Through participation in the strategic planning process, greater co-operation from lower-level executives and subordinates is achieved for the implementation of the plan, as the process helps them to visualise the strategic importance of their areas of responsibility within the structure of the company.
(f) Strategic planning leads to a more effective means of communicating company objectives.
(g) The strategic planning process is educative: it helps to develop the managerial competence of key members of the company in decision-making and the transformation of objectives into reality.

Some researchers in strategic planning have established that companies practising formal strategic planning have experienced superior performance over those that did not. While the problems inherent in measuring performance are recognised, it appears that it is generally beneficial to practise formal strategic planning.

However a number of practitioners have criticised strategic planning, especially if it leads to over-bureaucratisation and thereby limits management effectiveness. The worry is that strategic planning may promise simple formulae for success which may not be very practical; it may kill creativity in management; and it may appear to be an isolated event within the company when not fully integrated with other management functions.

Most criticisms levelled against strategic planning are concerned with its methods, rather than its fundamental functions. When properly implemented, strategic planning should be flexible and allow for initiative and quick actions to meet challenges arising from the environment.

1.3 THE STRATEGIC PLANNING PROCESS

Introduction

Formal strategic planning usually consists of the following steps:

(a) the definition of the mission of the company and the establishment of statements of objectives to be pursued within the planning period;
(b) the assessment of the external environment;
(c) the realistic analysis of the internal environment, in order to assess the company's strengths and weaknesses;
(d) the development of strategic alternatives, including an analysis of the potential risks and rewards of alternative strategies;
(e) the selection of strategy in view of the given external and internal environmental constraints; and
(f) implementing the chosen strategy and monitoring its success.

Defining mission and objectives

The first step in the strategic planning process is to clarify the principal business of the company, and set objectives to be achieved within the planning period.

A company's *mission statement* describes the fundamental purpose of its existence. It expresses the general objective for the company and provides the guiding principle for the formulation of objectives and strategies; it defines the moral and ethical principles that will shape the character of the company. The statement should be realistic and believable. Its acceptance throughout the company develops respect for and pride in the company and what it stands for.

Mission statements expressing purpose are usually established by the owners acting through the Board of Directors, to provide for the establishment of objectives at corporate and business levels. The mission statement will not be changed frequently, since it is the philosophical basis for guiding thoughts and directions in the company.

In many insurance companies, the mission statement will express commitment to the provision of financial security, underwriting excellence, prudence in financial management and superior investment management.

After defining the principal businesses of the company in the mission statement, objectives to be pursued within the plan can then be set. Thus management may set targets in terms of gross premium income, profits, surplus, expenses, market share and so on. Objectives are set first for the entire company, and then for each of the strategic business units.

Objectives are the foundation-stone of strategic planning: they provide the targets towards which the future operations of the company are directed. Objectives should therefore be easily understood and be clearly stated in measurable terms. They should be achievable in view of the present environmental constraints and company strengths and weaknesses. Clear objectives facilitate teamwork throughout the company by serving as a common basis of reference to guide decision-making at different levels of responsibility. Objectives also provide a basis for measuring performance. The major business objective was traditionally thought to be maximisation of profit, but it is now understood that a company exists to satisfy the aspirations of the various groups that have interests in its operations. These interest groups include owners, managers, insurers, employees, government, and the public at large.

Although objectives are supposed to be rational, in practice the process of setting objectives goes through a political process of bargaining and compromise. Priority in the setting of objectives will depend on the predominating interests. In general, insurance companies appear to pursue multiple and diverse objectives which depend upon whether they are proprietary or mutual companies. Most proprietary insurers have profitability and return to shareholders as important objectives, whereas mutuals are likely to pursue production targets, to achieve low costs and high returns to policyholders. Further discussion of an insurer's investment objectives can be found in Section 16.1.

Assessing the external environment

A company is an open system, which necessitates a continuous exchange and interaction with its external environment. This environment includes the economic, social and political factors applying in the countries in which the company operates, and the competitive factors applying in the company's main markets. The environment in which a business operates changes constantly, presenting opportunities to be exploited and threats to be managed. Environmental scanning is therefore an integral part of the strategic planning process. Since strategies are futuristic, it is important to understand the nature and pattern of the present environment and to forecast how it is likely to change in the future. Many of the factors in the environment (particularly the economic and social ones) are naturally beyond the control of management.

It is essential that a company organises a formal and systematic procedure for the collection and analysis of data about its external environment. The environmental analysis should then forecast changes in the economy that will affect the future of the industry and the company in particular, including: economic growth, unemployment, the volume of foreign trade, inflation, interest rates, taxation, and other government fiscal and monetary policies.

A useful model for analysing the competitive environment is provided by Professor Michael Porter. The model indicates that competition is determined by five groups of forces: the rivalry among existing competitors in the industry, the bargaining power of buyers, the bargaining power of suppliers, the threat of substitute products, and the threat of new entrants (see Porter, 1980). In the United Kingdom the insurance industry has experienced many new entrants and new companies are licensed regularly by the Department of Trade and Industry. Similarly other financial institutions such as banks and unit trust companies have formed insurance subsidiaries. Furthermore many corporate insurance buyers are choosing substitute means of risk financing, such as self-insurance and the use of captive insurance companies. Government-provided pension schemes, medical care and disability insurances via social security programmes also act as substitutes to insurance company services.

In many insurance markets, independent intermediaries and insurance brokers exercise considerable bargaining power on behalf of buyers and this is particularly the case in the London insurance market. The larger the volume of business an insurer company obtains through brokers, the more vulnerable it is to their bargaining power. Some insurance companies have attempted to reduce this dependence by developing their own channels of distribution through forward vertical integration or through organisation of agents. The recent developments in information transmission technology and computerisation present opportunities for insurers to deal direct with major customers.

An insurance company must also analyse the nature of competition among other insurers. The deregulation and abolition of tariff structures in many markets have opened up such markets to more competition.

Companies naturally compete in quality of service as well as in price. In assessing competitors an insurer must identify: who are its present and potential competitors, what products (and varieties of products) they offer, how their products are marketed, what are their market shares, and how vulnerable they are in terms of financial strength, quality of management and staff. Further discussion can be found in Section 2.4.

Assessing internal strengths and weaknesses

Before developing alternative strategies the company needs to appraise its own resources in order to identify its strengths and weaknesses. Such an analysis enables the firm to determine its capability to take advantage of new opportunities and to counter threats from the external environment. Internal analysis will enable the firm to identify its distinctive competence in comparison with its competitors. The usual items to be considered will include the quality and special features of the company products, its distribution system, customer service and goodwill, quality of staff and professional skills, and financial security. Management needs to be very realistic in its assessments.

Developing alternative strategies

Strategies pursued by companies may be grouped into two categories: offensive and defensive. *Offensive strategies* are adopted by management when it wants to pursue growth-related objectives such as increased market share or sales. Typical offensive strategies include concentration on strategies of market penetration, market development, product development, and mergers and acquisition. Integration strategies to control either the sources of supply or the channels of distribution, and diversification strategies and joint venturing are all examples of offensive strategies. On the other hand, *defensive strategies* are usually adopted when management wants to contract the firm's operations, either in view of unfavourable developments in the environment or in order to stabilise its operations in view of its strengths and weaknesses. Examples of defensive strategies are retrenchment, divestment, liquidation and harvesting.

Evaluating and selecting strategies

Although management in different companies will set their own criteria for strategy selection we can synthesise the list of appropriate criteria as follows:

(a) The strategy selected should address the major environmental variables representing both present and future threats and opportunities, as well as the company's own strengths and weaknesses. It should be consistent with the resources available, and within the risk preferences of management. Risk takers are usually more opportunistic, while risk-averse management would tend to be more conservative in their approaches to strategic issues.

(b) The chosen strategy should be clearly aimed at attaining the set objectives. Direct confrontation with stronger competitors should be avoided.

(c) The time dimension for the strategy should be realistic, both in terms of timeliness and the length of time required for implementation.

(d) The chosen strategy should provide for flexibility in dealing with unanticipated environmental changes and with the reactions of competitors. The strategy should allow for contingencies.

(e) The strategy should have the potential for promoting unity within management. A unifying strategy is one that is acceptable to a majority of management staff.

Programming, implementation and control

The final stage in strategic planning is to create programmes for implementation and the assignment of responsibilities. The programmes will be followed by forecasts of expected performance to conform with the targets set at the objectives stage. Budgeting and the preparation of pro forma statements of the expected financial position will then be prepared. The programme will also contain a calendar of events indicating what should be peformed at what times throughout the life-span of the plan.

The plan should also provide for contingencies: since strategic planning deals with future conditions, unexpected situations, such as new government regulations, competitive pressure or new opportunities, are bound to arise. Under such conditions it might sometimes be necessary to revise plans and change strategies. When the environment is analysed, indications can be made as to which factors are more likely to change and the likely consequences of such changes noted. A supplement to the main plan document would be the contingency plans which attempt to answer 'what ifs' for the different assumptions in the plan.

1.4 THE USE OF PORTFOLIO MODELS IN STRATEGIC PLANNING

Introduction

Following the growth in the use of strategic planning by businesses in different industries, various portfolio models have been devised to analyse a company's current strategic position and to identify problems with its portfolio of businesses for future planning purposes. The models provide guidance on the methods for assessing the attractiveness of a market, the strategies for competing in a market, and the development of an optimal group of products to be provided. Recent research in the United States has revealed that 45 per cent of the Fortune 500 firms and 36 per cent of all Fortune 1000 firms used portfolio models in one form or the other; furthermore 75 per cent of large diversified firms were found to be using those techniques.

Portfolio models have a number of advantages:

(a) They are simple and effective in segmenting the firm's activities into a set of well-defined strategic business units.
(b) Portfolio management techniques enable top managers to set appropriate strategies for each strategic business unit, after careful analysis of its needs and potential as represented by the industry attractiveness and competitive position.
(c) The portfolio techniques present a simple visual display of the company's portfolio of businesses, thereby serving as a device for understanding the strategic options open to the company.
(d) Through the use of such models, managers are alert to the strategic importance of their units in the competitive process. The construction of models requires the collection of useful information about competitors, and allows management to anticipate the competitor response.
(e) At the corporate level, these models aid the allocation of resources within the company and are also useful in working decisions on acquisitions and divestments.

The market growth – market share matrix

Developed by the Boston Consulting Group, the growth–share matrix is used to analyse the strategic position of each strategic business unit in the company's portfolio, by plotting them on a four-quadrant matrix. The vertical axis of the matrix measures market growth while the horizontal axis measures competitive position as represented by relative market share (this is the ratio of a business unit's sales to the sales of its largest competitor in the market). Business units are represented in the matrix by means of circles, the areas of which are proportional to their individual contributions to total company sales. The four quadrants are called 'cash cows', 'stars', 'question marks' and 'dogs'. Businesses falling into each of the quadrants received a particular strategic prescription. The matrix is illustrated in Figure 1.1.

Business units falling into quadrant I, and termed 'cash cows', have a strong market position, but are in a mature market experiencing slow

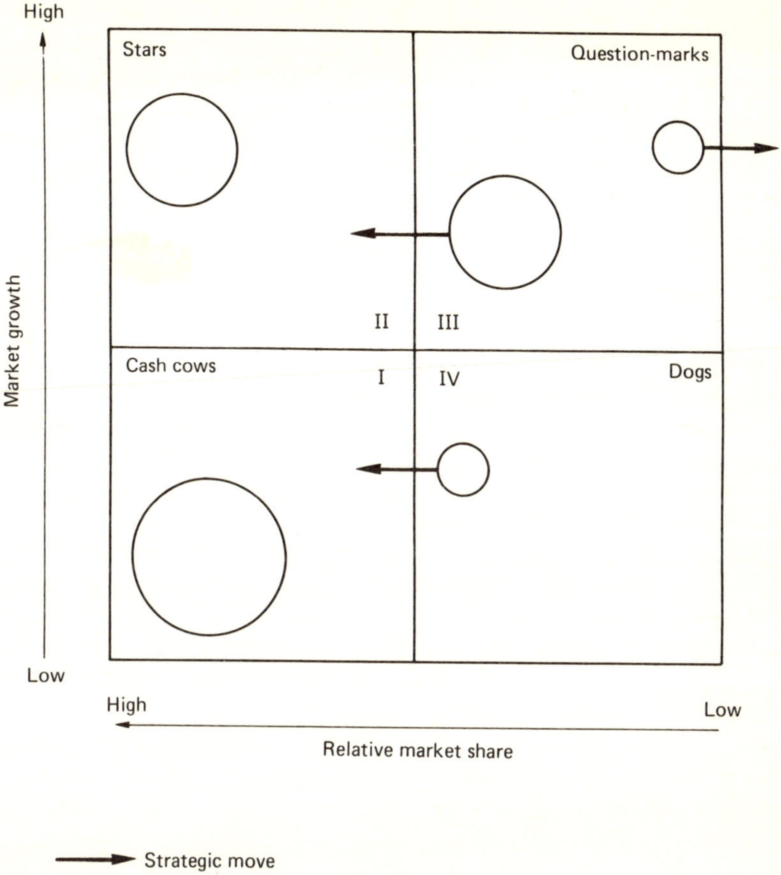

Figure 1.1 Growth–share matrix

growth. Such businesses should be managed to generate cash for the company. The appropriate strategy would be to invest just enough to maintain the market share, while diverting cash from it into other business units that are in growth markets.

The 'stars' in quadrant II have high market standing in high-growth markets. They demand heavy investment to maintain share, and, as the market matures, they could turn out to be the future cash generators.

Business units in quadrant III are dubbed 'question marks' because they do not have strong competitive positions, even though they are in a high growth market. The strategic prescriptions for 'question marks' are either for heavy investment to be committed to them in order to convert them into 'stars' or, if management is not convinced, they should be divested (before they turn into 'dogs').

'Dogs' are business units appearing in quadrant IV: they are operating in low-growth markets, and are in a poor competitive position. Such businesses are cash traps, and should be divested.

The growth–share matrix has been criticised because some products do not fall neatly into one of the quadrants. Furthermore the matrix is based on only two distinguishing factors (market growth rate and relative market share) but, in practice, strategy formulation considers several other factors in the environment, as well as internal strengths and weaknesses.

With respect to insurance, the model has been criticised in that it is based on the experience curve concept which believes that the largest producer with the highest market share has the lowest cost. But, in insurance, market share dominance may not lead to low cost status. In fact large companies may be high-cost producers, owing to maintenance of high-cost distribution systems, and large corporate overheads. High share products may not even be 'cash cows', but rather cash drains as a result of high cancellation rates. Therefore it may not be advisable for an insurer to pursue a large market share just for the sake of converting the portfolio into 'stars' and 'cash cows': the company runs the risk of adverse selection and new business strain.

The market–product evolutionary matrix

Built upon the traditional marketing view of product life-cycles, this strategy concept believes that all products go through a process from embryonic, or introduction, to growth, to maturity and finally to decline or aging, when it is necessary for new products to be introduced to take over from the old. Growth markets provide more opportunities for competition, but in mature markets competition is a 'zero sum game', in which the gain of one company is a loss for its competitor. The matrix is presented in Figure 1.2.

The evolutionary matrix of Figure 1.2 classifies products according to two dimensions: on the vertical axis is the company's competitive position (as judged by its management) which could range from dominant to weak, and on the horizontal axis maturity, which ranges from embryonic to aging. Circles are drawn proportionate to industry sales and the business unit's share depicted by a slice in the circle. Depending on the stage of maturity and the competitive position of the unit, products receive a particular strategy prescription, indicated by the shaded boxes; thus they are products with room to manoeuvre, products whose strategies are cautious and selective, or products which should withdraw to a niche or withdraw completely.

The sales, cash-flow and profit potential of the products would depend upon the stage of maturity and competition in the market. Sales, cash-flow

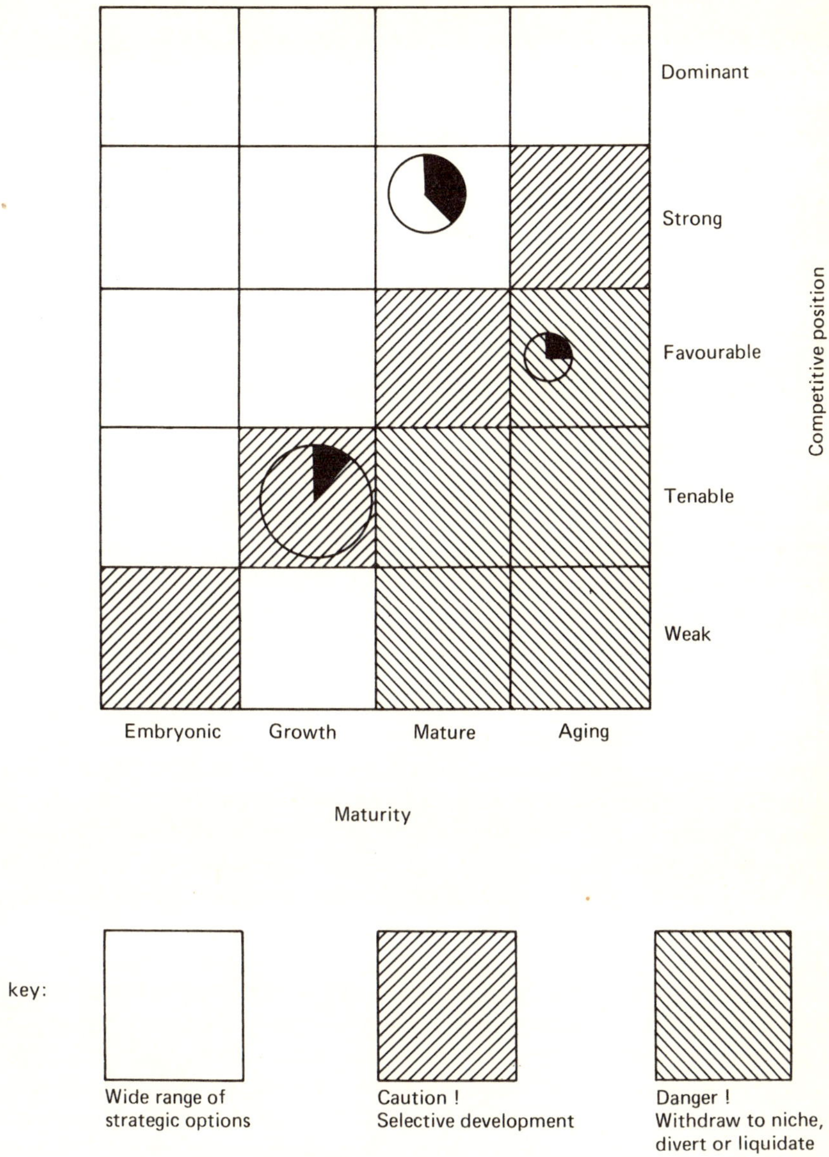

Figure 1.2 Market–product evolutionary matrix

and profits are greatest during the maturity stage, while profits would be negative and cash-flow and sales would be declining during the aging stage. These are presented in Figure 1.3.

In formulating strategies using the evolutionary matrix, it is important that management first categorise their products according to their stages of

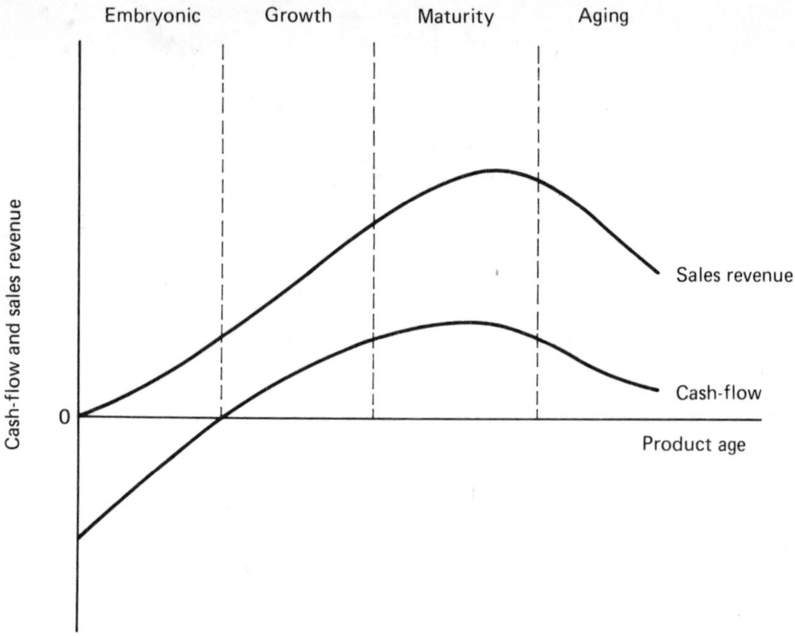

Figure 1.3 Characteristics and strategies of the evolutionary matrix

market growth. Some product lines may be experiencing maturity, while others are in growth stages – the appropriate competitive strategies can then be applied.

1.5 A SURVEY OF UK FINANCIAL FIRMS

Substantial changes in the market for personal financial services in the United Kingdom have been introduced as a result of the Financial Services Act 1986 (which is discussed in more detail in Chapter 14), the Social Security Act 1986 (which restricted the scope of the State Earnings Related Pension Scheme and broadened the range of pensions products and providers in the United Kingdom) and the Building Societies Act 1986 (which allowed building societies to provide a much wider range of personal financial services). A fuller description of the impact of regulatory changes on the market for personal financial services can be found in Wright and Diacon (1988). Preparations have also been set in motion for the expected increase in competition following the finalisation of a single European market in financial services in the 1990s. Suppliers of personal financial services have therefore been forced to adjust their corporate and marketing strategies in anticipation of these considerable structural changes.

Table 1.1 Extent to which different institutions are significant in different service areas in the UK

Services	*Institutions** 1	2	3	4	5	6	7	8	9	10	11	12	13	14	15	16	17	18
1 Current (checking) account	a		b	c		c												
2 Retail deposits	a		b	b		a												
3 Money market deposits/loans	a	a	c	c		c												
4 Eurocurrency deposits	a	a																
5 Offshore banking	a																	
6 Foreign exchange	a		c	c		c												
7 Traveller's cheques	a		c	c														
8 Hire-purchase/consumer finance	a		b	c		c	a											
9 Credit cards	a		c	c		c												
10 House mortgages	b		c	c		a				c								
11 Factories, export credit	a		c	c					a									
12 Leasing	a		c	c				a										
13 Venture capital	a																	
14 Business loans	a		c	c														
15 International lending	a																	
16 Investment in stock market assets	b		c			c								a	a	a		
17 Loan guarantees	a																	
18 Investment and corporate finance advice	a	a															a	
19 Life assurance	c		c							a								
20 Accident insurance (direct) – motor	c		c								a							
21 – employer's liability																		
22 – other	c		c															
23 Reinsurance						c						a						
24 Investment fund management	b	b								b			a					
25 Unit trust management	b	b								a				a				
26 Pension services															a			
27 Securities: underwriting, new issues and placement	a	a																
28 Securities broking	b															a		
29 Money broking																		a
30 Bullion and other commodities trading																	a	

* For key see Table 1.3.
Note: Most large banks undertake merchant banking activities.
Source: Price Waterhouse (1988).

The less restrictive approach to market regulation allowed in the United Kingdom has enabled the development of financial conglomerates, so that financial firms may provide a number of very different financial services: these are summarised in Tables 1.1 and 1.2 (and a key to the notation is given in Table 1.3).

Table 1.2 Proportion of total business of financial institutions accounted for by different service areas in the UK

Services	*Institutions**																	
	1	*2*	*3*	*4*	*5*	*6*	*7*	*8*	*9*	*10*	*11*	*12*	*13*	*14*	*15*	*16*	*17*	*18*
1 Current (checking) account	a		a	a		c												
2 Retail deposits	a		a	a		a												
3 Money market deposits/loans	a	a	c	b		c												
4 Eurocurrency deposits	a	a																
5 Offshore banking	c																	
6 Foreign exchange	c		c	c		c												
7 Traveller's cheques	c		c	c														
8 Hire-purchase/consumer finance	c		a	b		c	a											
9 Credit cards	c		c	c		c												
10 House mortgages	b		b	c	c	a												
11 Factories, export credit	c	c	c	c					a									
12 Leasing	c		c	c				a										
13 Venture capital																		
14 Business loans	a	c	c															
15 International lending	a																	
16 Investment in stock market assets	b		c			c							a	a	a			
17 Loan guarantees	c																	
18 Investment and corporate finance advice	c	a																
19 Life assurance	c		c							a								
20 Accident insurance (direct) – motor	c		c								a							
21 – employer's liability																		
22 – other	c		c								b							
23 Reinsurance												a						
24 Investment fund management	c	a											a					
25 Unit trust management	c	b												a				
26 Pension services															a			
27 Securities: underwriting, new issues and placement	a	a																
28 Securities broking	b															a		
29 Money broking																		a
30 Bullion and other commodities trading																	a	

* For key see Table 1.3.
Source: Price waterhouse (1988).

Some indication of the changing patterns of corporate strategy and strategic planning can be obtained from the results of a survey, undertaken by the Nottingham Institute of Financial Studies, of 264 UK firms which provide personal financial services. The survey focused attention on how firms expected their strategies to evolve over the four years to 1992. The

Table 1.3 Key to Tables 1.1 and 1.2

Institution no.	Description
1	Clearing/commercial banks
2	Merchant banks
3	Savings banks
4	Postal and giro banks
5	Credit unions
6	Mortgage credit institutions/building societies
7	HP finance companies
8	Leasing companies
9	Factors
10	Life insurance companies
11	General insurance companies
12	Reinsurance companies
13	Investment funds
14	Unit trusts
15	Pension funds
16	Stockbrokers
17	Commodities brokers
18	Money brokers
Table 1.1	a = very significant b = significant c = minor significance
Table 1.2	a = large b = medium c = small

survey covered a wide range of UK financial firms, including 64 insurance companies, 46 insurance brokers, 22 banks, 42 unit and investment trusts, 46 building societies, and 27 stockbrokers. A full analysis of the development of the corporate strategy of these financial firms is provided in Ennew, Watkins and Wright (1988).

The questions on corporate strategy were broadly based on the classification provided by Porter (1985) according to competitive scope (broad or narrow) and competitive advantage (cost or differentiation). In the context of the survey, broad competitive scope was represented by strategies entailing broad market coverage, while narrow or focus strategy involved the discovery of a market niche. A cost competitive advantage was represented by a narrow range of (usually standardised) products, while an advantage based on differentiation was reflected in a wide range of products. A summary of the current and future corporate strategies of UK financial firms is shown in Tables 1.4 and 1.5.

The survey results show that 64.3 per cent of financial firms relied on cost-based strategies (narrow product range), the bulk being focused strategies. However, by 1992, 54 per cent of firms expected to shift towards

Table 1.4 Current corporate strategy of UK financial firms

	All firms	*Insurance companies*	*Insurance brokers*	*Banks*	*Unit/ investment trusts*	*Building societies*	*Stock-brokers*
COST FOCUS							
Narrow product range	111	27	11	6	18	20	17
Small number of sectors	(42.0)	(42.2)	(23.9)	(27.3)	(42.9)	(43.5)	(63.0)
COST LEAD							
Narrow product range	59	18	7	3	12	14	4
Large number of sectors	(22.3)	(28.1)	(15.2)	(13.6)	(28.6)	(30.4)	(14.8)
DIFFERENTIAL FOCUS							
Broad product range	52	11	14	5	9	8	2
Few sectors	(19.7)	(17.2)	(30.4)	(22.7)	(21.4)	(17.4)	(7.4)
DIFFERENTIAL LEAD							
Broad product range	42	8	14	8	3	4	4
Broad sectors	(16.0)	(12.5)	(30.4)	(36.4)	(7.1)	(8.7)	(14.8)
Total respondents	264	64	46	22	42	46	27

Note: Figures in brackets are percentages.
Source: Ennew, Watkins and Wright (1988).

a differential strategy by taking advantage of the removal of regulatory restrictions on product ranges. Along with unit trusts and building societies, the majority of insurance companies have adopted cost-based strategies; in spite of some movement towards a broader product range, firms which concentrate on insurance are expected to preserve their narrow product range.

Ennew, Watkins and Wright note that the movement of a large number of firms in the direction of greater differentiation and away from cost-based strategy is bound to increase competition within personal financial markets. With many firms apparently pursuing similar strategies, it is unlikely that all can succeed.

The survey conducted by the Nottingham Institute for Financial Studies also investigated the organisation of corporate planning effort among UK insurance companies and asked about the techniques which insurers use in the preparation of their corporate strategy. Table 1.6 shows that, out of 66 insurance companies surveyed, 19.7 per cent claimed not to operate a formal corporate planning procedure (although more than half of these were in the process of developing one). On the other hand, nearly half the respondents (48.5 per cent) had recently enhanced their existing plan in order to examine new product areas.

The replies to questions about the use of strategic planning techniques are summarised in Table 1.7. In general they demonstrate sparse use of the best-known techniques (product life-cycle analysis, the growth–share matrix, and econometric modelling). The two techniques which are most utilised

Table 1.5 Future corporate strategy of UK financial firms*

	All firms	*Insurance companies*	*Insurance brokers*	*Banks*	*Unit/ investment trusts*	*Building societies*	*Stock-brokers*
COST FOCUS							
Narrow product range	56	10	7	3	10	9	11
Small number of sectors	(22.0)	(16.4)	(16.7)	(14.3)	(25.0)	(19.6)	(44.0)
COST LEAD							
Narrow product range	61	22	7	2	13	9	5
Large number of sectors	(24.0)	(36.0)	(16.7)	(9.5)	(32.5)	(19.6)	(20.0)
DIFFERENTIAL FOCUS							
Broad product range	57	12	11	5	8	11	5
Few sectors	(22.5)	(19.7)	(26.2)	(23.8)	(20.0)	(23.9)	(20.0)
DIFFERENTIAL LEAD							
Broad product range	80	17	17	11	9	17	4
Broad sectors	(31.5)	(27.9)	(40.4)	(52.4)	(22.5)	(37.0)	(16.0)
Total respondents	254	61	42	21	40	46	25

* By 1992.
Note: Figures in brackets are percentages.
Source: Ennew, Watkins and Wright (1988).

appear to be SWOT ('Strengths, Weaknesses, Opportunities, Threats') analysis and brainstorming sessions. However the most striking features of the table are the lack of widespread use of any but the most rudimentary of planning techniques, and the reliance on first finding out what other firms are doing ('Attendance at conferences/seminars') and then copying it ('Imitation of other firms in the sector'): a strategy of the blind leading the blind! A similar survey of 45 UK financial institutions undertaken by Hooley and Mann (1988) reported very similar results; 49 per cent of their sample had either never used or never heard of product life-cycle analysis and the corresponding figure for the growth–share matrix rose to 73 per cent. Conversely, 62 per cent of the Hooley and Mann sample said they used 'strengths and weaknesses' analysis regularly. If the results from both surveys are to be believed, the conclusion appears to be that insurance companies use essentially the same strategic planning techniques as other types of financial firm.

1.6 CONCLUSION

This chapter has introduced the concept of strategic planning and explained the step-by-step approach to the process of strategy formulation. However, as Aylor and Cummins (1985) noted, strategic planning is a comparatively recent phenomenon in the insurance industry,

Table 1.6 Corporate planning in UK insurance companies

Which of the following best describes the organisation of your current corporate planning effort?	*% of sample*
(a) There is *no formal corporate planning procedure*, we simply adapt to day-to-day developments	9.1
(b) We have a formal corporate planning procedure, which is unchanged since its *establishment several years ago*	13.6
(c) We have a *well-established* formal corporate planning procedure, which has recently been enhanced to examine new product areas	48.5
(d) We have *only recently* introduced a formal corporate planning procedure in order to examine new products	18.2
(e) We are developing a formal corporate planning procedure, but as yet it is not implemented	10.6
Sample Size = 66 UK insurance companies.	

Survey administered in Autumn 1987 by the Nottingham Institute for Financial Studies.

Table 1.7 Techniques of strategic planning in UK insurance companies

Technique used in preparation of corporate strategy	*% of sample of 66 insurance companies*			
	Always	*Sometimes*	*Never*	*Null*
Regular market research studies	10.6	54.5	28.8	6.1
'Off the shelf' research studies	6.1	62.1	24.2	7.6
Product life-cycle analysis	10.6	27.3	48.5	13.6
SWOT analysis	21.2	18.2	43.9	16.7
Growth–share matrix	7.6	25.8	51.5	15.2
Econometric modelling of sector	6.1	28.8	54.5	10.6
'Brainstorming' sessions	31.8	47.0	16.7	4.5
Imitation of other firms in sector	10.6	74.2	6.1	9.1
Attendance at conferences/seminars	7.6	72.7	10.6	9.1
Comp. advantage/value chain analysis	22.7	39.4	25.8	12.1

Survey administered in Autumn 1987 by the Nottingham Institute for Financial Studies.

and insurance companies often lag behind other industries in the use of planning concepts. Allstate Insurance Company in the USA is a notable exception, and a description of its planning process is the subject of the next chapter.

Rapid changes are taking place in the environment of many insurance markets and competition – spurred on by deregulation – is becoming more intense. All the indications are that the insurance companies that will win are those which are able to anticipate the direction of change and plan well ahead to meet the challenges. The particular choices faced by insurance groups as a result of the implementation of the single European market are discussed in more detail in Chapter Three.

The necessary conditions for the successful implementation of strategic planning include, first that top management, especially the Chief Executive Officer, must be personally involved and committed to the process. Whether it is devised by a management committee or by a strategic planning unit, a framework must be prepared to get management at all levels involved in the planning process. Secondly, a strategy audit must be performed to define the quality of the current strategy and estimate the future progress of the company if that strategy remains unaltered. Such an audit should consider systems for information processing, the channels of communication, the organisation structure of the company, and the ability and experience of management to perform the strategy formulation.

References

Aylor, C.C. and J.D. Cummins (1985) 'Strategic Planning in the US Property–Liability Industry', in J.D. Cummins (ed.), *Strategic Planning and Modelling in Property–Liability Insurance* (Hingham MA: Kluwer-Nijhoff Publishing).

Ennew, C., T. Watkins and M. Wright (1988) 'Personal Financial Services: An Appraisal of Recent Developments and Research Issues', *Discussion Papers in Industrial Economics*, December (University of Nottingham).

Hooley, G.J. and S.J. Mann (1988) 'The Adoption of Marketing by Financial Institutions in the UK', *The Services Industries Journal*, vol 8, no. 4, October, pp. 488–500.

Porter, M.E. (1980) *Competitive Strategy* (New York: Free Trade Press).

Porter, M.E. (1985) *Competitive Advantage: Creating and Sustaining Superior Performance* (New York: Free Trade Press).

Price Waterhouse (1988) *The 'Cost of Non-Europe' in Financial Services, Research on the 'Cost of Non-Europe': Basic Findings Volume 9* (Commission of the European Communities).

Wright, M. and S.R. Diacon (1988) 'Regulation of the Marketing of Long-Term Insurance', in N. Dyer and T. Watkins (eds), *Marketing Insurance: A Practical Guide*, 2nd edn (Brentford, Middlesex: Kluwer Publishing).

2 Corporate Planning in a Large Insurance Group

John B. Gragnola

2.1 THE BACKGROUND TO PLANNING AT ALLSTATE INSURANCE COMPANY

Someone once wrote, 'The future isn't what it used to be'. This facetious remark contains a serious truth: the changes that are taking place in our world are more disruptive, more widespread and less predictable than they have ever been. As a result, we cannot manage our business unless close attention is paid to what is going on in the world around – in our own and related industries, in world economies, and in society at large. The future cannot be left to take care of itself.

This is not a new perception. Management has long recognised that a company's financial performance depends on planning well in a changing environment. In many companies this is the responsibility of the budgeting department. But budgeting is the tactical part of managing an insurance company. The foundation of budgeting is continuity. Budgeting generally assumes that the business will be run in the next twelve months pretty much as it was run in the last twelve months. Budgeting is not the ideal tool for dealing with long-range change: it does not let you explore alternatives, and it does not help in answering 'what if' questions. For that, you need corporate or strategic planning.

In 1978, Allstate Insurance Company decided that it needed a strategic planning system. The world had become more complex: there were more regulations, more economic instability, more competition, and so forth. The Company had also become more complex, and was active in many businesses – finance, motor club, and of course insurance (property/casualty, commercial and life). Each business had its own problems, its own markets, its own set of competitors, its own regulations, and its own environmental issues.

For these reasons, the Company Chairman decided to revise and modernise the planning procedures. It was decided to establish a new corporate planning process whose purpose was to decide today what Allstate should be in the future. Corporate or strategic planning means anticipating obstacles and identifying opportunities. It means devising strategies and programmes to overcome the obstacles and take advantage of the opportunities. It means preparing ourselves to make things happen our way. The rest of this chapter describes Allstate's corporate planning process as an example of how one large company does it.

Allstate Insurance Company is a wholly-owned subsidiary of Sears, Roebuck and Company, the world's largest retailer. Allstate was organised in 1931, and today it is the second largest writer of property and casualty insurance in the United States. Most insurance premiums come from personal, motor and homeowners insurance, but the company writes a significant and growing volume of commercial insurance. Allstate's life insurance company, although a relatively new company compared to the old-line life companies, is the eleventh largest US producer of new ordinary insurance.

Allstate's strategic planning process was not invented from scratch; there was much preparatory work. We tried to learn from the successes and failures of others, and towards that end we visited leading companies in strategic planning – including Xerox, IBM, General Electric, and AT & T. In addition, we read articles on the subject and we talked to experts and consultants, including people in 'think tanks', such as SRI International, The Futures Group, The Boston Consulting Group, and Harbridge House.

Much was learned from this preparatory work, but our most important lesson was that you cannot transfer a planning system from one company to another without change. Our system had to be tailored to our needs. The system was designed to take into account Allstate's way of doing business, its management style, and its organisation culture. We think our process works well now, but we are sure it will change and improve over time.

2.2 THE ORGANISATION OF CORPORATE PLANNING

The corporate planning process at Allstate contains three levels of organisation: the Corporate Strategic Planning Committee; the Business Planning Units; and the Strategic Planning Division.

There are good reasons for adopting this arrangement. We did not want to centralise the planning function, because we did not want to separate the planners from the doers. Separation would lead to internal confusion over responsibilities. Additionally we did not think that a central planning staff could master Allstate's many complex businesses. Each business operates in a different and rapidly changing environment. Some of yesterday's small businesses have become large businesses in their industries today; others, although small today, have the potential for considerable growth. Because of these differences, it was important that each business manager be responsible for his own plan. But the individual strategic plans do come together at the corporate level for review and consolidation into the corporate strategic plan.

The Corporate Strategic Planning Committee

The Strategic Planning Committee is the top of the planning organisation. The Committee's members are Allstate's most important people – the Chairman of the Board, the President, the Chief Planning Officer, Chief Financial Officer, and the heads of the Business Units. Every employee ultimately reports to one of these men.

The Chairman made it clear when he formed the Committee that its members would have to arrange their busy schedules to make time for planning. The Committee meets regularly – usually monthly – to discuss planning issues, and annually to review and approve or change Business Unit plans. This annual meeting takes the better part of a week. In addition to the formal meetings, Committee members also spend time on other planning-related assignments.

The Strategic Planning Committee has five basic responsibilities. First, it writes the corporate mission and establishes the corporate goals. The mission explains the businesses Allstate is in, while the goals describe what those businesses are to be in the future. Second, the Committee organises and directs the planning process: it sets the timetable, and reviews and approves the plans. Next, the Committee evaluates issues. Issues are the major external trends and events that can significantly affect a company. For example, in 1984, the Committee decided that the main issue was the level of competition in all sectors (since the entire insurance industry was expected to be very competitive throughout the 1980s). Fourth, the Committee allocates the Company's capital and resources. This is its most important function, and can be regarded as the purpose of planning. The Committee, by deciding where Allstate should invest its time, money, and people in effect determines the company's future direction. Finally, the Committee monitors progress. The corporate plans are not documents that gather dust on a shelf. We expect to implement them, so we measure year-by-year achievements.

The Business Planning Units

The next level in Allstate's planning organisation is the Business Planning Unit. A unit is a stand-alone business, with its own markets, products, competitors, opportunities and challenges. Allstate currently has nine such units: personal lines property/casualty insurance, personal life and health insurance, group life and health insurance, commercial insurance, reinsurance, Allstate of Canada, international operations, finance, and the Motor Club. Each unit prepares a five-year plan according to guidelines sent to them by the Strategic Planning Committee.

The Unit's top managers generally write the plan themselves. This is because our planning philosophy dictates that the persons who are responsible for carrying out a plan must be responsible for developing it, and the Unit head knows more about his business than a professional planner could possibly know. An important and often overlooked benefit of this approach is its educational value. The process gives operating managers a good understanding about their unit's place in the company as a whole. It increases their understanding about how outside issues affect their business and, most important, it forces them to think ahead. This leads to better decisions and to better managers.

The Strategic Planning Division

The last level of Allstate's planning organisation is the Strategic Planning Division: a staff group composed of trained professionals in research, economics, finance, planning, insurance and computers. It supports and assists the Strategic Planning Committee's work, co-ordinates Business Planning Unit activities, and consolidates individual plans into the corporate strategic plan.

2.3 THE MAIN CORPORATE PLANNING ACTIVITIES

At Allstate all the main corporate planning functions are undertaken by the Strategic Planning Division.

Economic forecasts

The Division's economists adapt Sears's economic forecasts to its insurance subsidiary's needs. To do this, we keep abreast of the work done by the country's leading economic forecasting services, and develop less likely but possible economic scenarios for the evaluation of their impact on our insurance business.

Research studies

Allstate Research and Planning Center's staff does tailor-made studies that assist in the strategic planning process. The staff includes experts in research in the following disciplines: marketing, personnel, territorial (demographic), actuarial, underwriting, claims and investment.

Industry and competitive analysis

Special studies that consider possible industry directions and analyse the activities of competitors are carried out frequently at the request of planning units.

Diversification/acquisition studies

The Planning Division also examines possible acquisitions. The analysis uses computer models that determine purchase price based on the target company's expected earnings. The calculations include the acquisition's expected effect on Allstate's and Sears's earnings and cash-flows.

Corporate simulations

One of the Strategic Planning Division's first jobs was to develop a computer model of the Allstate Group. The model contains more than 4000 equations and 450 operating ratios and is distinctive in that it links the company's operations to the US economy with 40 economic relationships developed through an exhaustive research programme. The model's output includes a pro forma balance sheet, a profit and loss statement and thirty supporting reports. A ten-year simulation takes about two minutes and costs about $50. Further details can be found in Gragnola (1985).

The model is used in many ways. It can measure the impact of alternative economic scenarios on the Company and assess the impact of management responses to those scenarios. To this extent it is similar to the ASIR model described in more detail in Chapter 4. Our model is used regularly by the investment, marketing, pricing and underwriting departments. For example, it was used to measure the effect of varying the timing and size of motor insurance premium rate increases, and to measure the effect of alternative agency force growth rates. It was also used to test different investment strategies: how much money to put into bonds, stocks, real estate, gas and oil, short-term investments and so forth.

Co-ordination and information

The Strategic Planning Division co-ordinates all corporate planning activities by developing the procedures that guide the planning process, by preparing material for committee meetings, and by consulting with the Business Units. Each year the Division also writes a 'guidelines' book that explains the process, describes important themes in the current effort, and sets the planning calendar. The 'guidelines' book is of great value in a decentralised planning process. The book unifies the separate planning efforts (for example, it describes the planning report format that all units must follow). The Strategic Planning Division then consolidates individual unit plans by putting them into a standard format and sums them into Allstate Group totals at the end of the process.

2.4 THE CORPORATE PLANNING PROCESS

This section reviews the seven steps in the Allstate planning process. They are applied to the overall corporate plan and to each Business Unit plan.

Defining the mission statement

The first step is to define the Company's purpose. The mission statement explains the businesses we are in, or want to be in; it also identifies our stakeholders and describes our responsibilities to them. Stakeholders are groups of people who stand to gain or lose from a company's actions: stockholders, employees, customers, regulators and the general public are all affected.

The stakeholder concept is important to the strategic planning process. We are planning for people who have a vital interest in what we do. For this reason, each unit has to state its goals with its stakeholders in mind.

Allstate's corporate mission is 'To provide those publics, whom we can best serve, insurance and insurance related services that are responsive to need and delivered at the lowest possible cost consistent with a financial return that will insure customer security, corporate continuity, growth, and employee opportunity.'

Our first stakeholder is the general public: 'We will fulfill our social and citizenship responsibilities to the greatest extent possible, consistent with our financial integrity and our high level of corporate ethics'; and the next stakeholder is the customer: 'We will provide high standards of service. We will be a leader in our business.'

After the customer, the next stakeholder is the employee family: 'We will keep our organisation growing and thereby provide additional opportunities for all our employees, regardless of their sex, race, religion or ethnic background'; and another is the shareholder family: 'We will earn a profit adequate to provide the capital to accomplish all these objectives and to pay dividends to our shareholders so they receive a reasonable rate of return on their investment.'

That is Allstate's corporate mission: it defines our business, the people we serve, and our responsibilities to them. It gives us purpose and direction, and is the basis of our company's goals.

Goal formulation

The second step in the process is to formulate goals. Goals are clear statements of what the corporation and business units want to achieve over the next five years: how much growth, how much earnings, and so on. Allstate's corporate goals deal with revenue, profits, dividends to shareholders, surplus and safety, expense ratio, diversification, market penetration, regulatory and social responsibility, customer service, commitment to employees and corporate image. Further discussion on goal formulation, and a comparison of the goals of other insurers can be found in Kaluza (1982).

Each unit is asked to establish milestones on the way to its goals, so that five-year targets can be separated into realistic one-year targets. The first year of a five-year plan ties directly into the annual budget.

Goals take many forms. Some are numerical, some are not; some are specific, some are general. It is important to choose the goals that are pertinent to the Company, and then state those goals realistically. Each business unit of Allstate develops its own goals, and these are not necessarily the same as the corporation's goals. The units may not have the same growth expectations because some are in high-growth areas while others are in mature industries. However the combined unit goals should equal the corporate goals. If they do not, the corporate goals will have to be re-evaluated.

Before formulating goals a review of the present position and past accomplishments should be undertaken. Then ask yourself: am I happy with what has been achieved? Should I try for more in the future?

Environmental analysis

The next step in the corporate planning process is to analyse the environment; this is the world in which a unit expects to operate in the future. Environmental analysis is the foundation for all planning and there is only one certainty: the business environment will change!

Environmental analysis is generally done by a unit's central staff, but, from time to time, the field organisation participates in the effort. Allstate's field organisation consists of the people who sell policies, underwrite them, handle claims and process data, all at the local level. The field organisation's Strategic Planning Committee includes sales managers, controllers and other staff members. The field organisation is in an excellent position to assess the potential of its local market. These assessments have turned out to be the most interesting part of the field analysis. In some cases, the central staff 'expert' did not agree with the field man's assessment. Honest disagreements of this kind are healthy; they air differing views, and ultimately arrive at better decisions.

A unit's environment can be divided into internal and external. The external environment consists of, among other things, the economy, the industry and the competition; the Company itself makes up the internal environment. Both are important in planning for the future.

A study of the external environment should consider the following areas:

(a) *The economic outlook*. Economic variables such as inflation, interest rates, housing starts and motor sales all directly affect the Company's revenues, expenses and losses. The parent group, Sears, regularly prepares a five-year economic outlook, and that forecast is the foundation for Allstate's plans. However, alternative economic outlooks are also formulated to remove the surprise of sudden shifts in the economic climate. At least four alternative outlooks are usually examined.

(b) *The industry outlook*. Each unit develops its own industry outlook, often with help from the Strategic Planning Division. A unit will study how population shifts, and how consumer tastes and expected regulatory changes will change its industry's growth, profitability and capacity.

(c) *The competitive outlook*. Everyone recognises the importance of competitive strategy. Many insurance industries are in a period of volatile change. In America, the legal barriers that kept banks and other financial institutions out of insurance are falling, market growth is slowing down, and competition is ferocious. In this environment, we have to take business from competitors in order to grow, while they try to take business from us. For these reasons, it is important that we know what competitors are doing.

The first step is to identify prime competitors. Too often we look only at traditional competitors; obviously, these are important, but it is not prudent to stop there. New competitors must also be examined: banks, foreign-owned companies, captive insurance companies, and securities brokers, to name a few. Besides the traditional competitors and new entrants, we have to look at the relatively unknown but growing companies: who are they; are they taking market share away from us; why are they gaining on us; what are they doing that is new or different; why cannot we do the same thing? Companies that think that their size and age alone protect them from competition deserve their fates. The nature of the free enterprise system is that it offers companies a chance to succeed, but gives everyone a chance to fail as well.

Obviously, not all competitors can be analysed, but each of Allstate's business units maintains a file on its most important competitors and attempts to answer the following basic questions about each:

Products

- What new products have competitors recently introduced? What major products are they emphasising?
- Can we expect them to expand their product line?
- Do they have a successful product development history?

Distribution

- What are their main distribution channels? Are they changing?

- What is the geographic coverage and quality of these channels?
- How strong are their relationships with brokers and agents?
- Do they use direct mail or telephone solicitation?
- How do they motivate their sales people?

Markets
- Do they have special products and features for special market segments?
- Do they compete on price? On service?
- What is the nature of their advertising? What campaign themes are they using? To whom is it directed?
- Are they serving a market niche?

Financial structure
- What are their expenses ratios, relative to the industry?
- Have they had start-ups, acquisitions, divestitures?
- How much cash-flow do they generate?
- What will their capital needs be in the future?
- How much growth can they support from internal sources?

Organisation and management
- How are they organised?
- Are their operating divisions autonomous?
- What are the Chief Executive's qualities and motivations? (These often provide a clue to the direction a competitor will take.)
- How deep is the management? How flexible and adaptable?

Values and goals
- Do competitors value short-run performance over long-run performance?
- What is their attitude towards risk? Are they likely to enter new businesses early?
- Do they want to be the industry's leader in sales, profits, innovation, reputation?

The answers to these questions will go a long way towards telling how a competitor will act in the future and how it will react to our moves. A conservatively run company will probably avoid head-to-head competition in new markets, but it will fight hard to protect its old markets. Competitive analysis is a lot of work, but it is essential to a company's future.

Similarly the study of the internal environment considers our own Company's strengths and weaknesses, and its resources and abilities. The analysis should include an evaluation of our products, product delivery systems, distribution systems, technological and professional skills, consumer relations, reputation and, of course, management ability. It almost goes without saying that the Company should know its own answer to the questions it asks about its competitors.

Strategies that achieve goals

The fourth step in the corporate planning process is to select the strategies that will achieve the chosen goals. Strategies are a natural outgrowth of environmental analysis as they respond to the economy, the industry outlook and the competitive environment; and in turn they capitalise on the unit's strengths and point out areas of possible weakness. This part of the process requires creativity, because strategies address future as well as present conditions. For this reason strategies depend on experience, creativity and good judgement; they are the heart of the strategic planning process. Strategies are generally active (for example, introducing a new product, or entering into a new market) but they can be passive – sometimes the correct strategy is to change nothing.

A good example of an Allstate strategy involves the rural market. Our environmental analysis showed that Allstate was ignoring rural areas comprising a fifth of the total US market because the people there were too far from the nearest Allstate agent. These agents tend to be concentrated in cities and suburbs, away from the farms and small towns. Moreover these potential customers knew our name through our television advertising and thought well of us. Our goal was clear: to achieve a significant market penetration of the rural market within five years. However the strategy was not clear-cut and there were no large Sears stores in the countryside (many Allstate agents work in Sears stores); we had tried part-time agents in rural communities with little success; and we could not put full-time agents in rural areas because they would have to capture too large a share of those rural markets in order to be profitable. The strategy eventually selected to penetrate the rural market was to use the distribution system already there – the independent agency system.

Programmes to support strategies

The fifth step in the planning process is to develop specific programmes to support strategies. Programmes are action plans: the difference between a strategy and a programme is that the responsibility for a programme can be assigned. Grandiose strategies are often created and discussed over cocktails and dinner, but until the money, people, time and effort are provided, it is all a pipedream. Strategies cannot be implemented without programmes. Planning units are therefore encouraged to include operating managers in the programme development in order to ensure that the plans are viable. We do not want to be told later, for example, that a computer system cannot handle the problem, or that we do not have trained people for the job.

Allstate had to develop several programmes to implement its strategic decision to use independent agents for the rural market. Responsibility was assigned to two people in our marketing department to carry out the strategy; rural markets were identified by using distance and penetration criteria; a contract for independent agents was developed and sales material was prepared to win over independent agents and so on.

The long-range financial plan

The next stage necessitates the production of forecast financial results, including revenue accounts and balance sheets to form a long-range financial plan. The numbers are not simple extrapolations of current operating experience but incorporate the expected impact of new strategies and programmes.

The financial forecast should be the end-product of careful thought about the future: it should be credible and achievable, and should build on the programmes and be compatible with the economic forecast and industry outlook. The plans must be realistic. For example, we do not want plans that show flat growth for the first four years and explosive growth in the fifth. These would be discouraged unless they were accompanied by the necessary manpower build-up and capital investment.

A Business Unit's financial plan depends on its own industry's normal reporting practices. However, at Allstate, each unit prepares a short income statement and balance sheet for each year of the five-year period. These contain the following data: total revenue and growth in revenue, share of market, expense ratio, underwriting income and margin, net income, assets, equity or surplus, personnel count, and return on equity.

Contingency plans

The seventh and final step is to develop strategies which can handle events that could have a significant impact upon a unit's future. Contingency planning is important because it is imprudent not to be prepared for such events. Contingency planning flows directly from environmental analysis. That analysis identifies events that could disrupt the Company's business, and thus overturn existing strategies and plans. Such events could be an opportunity if we are ready, or they could be a threat if we are not.

Each unit develops a list of the important events and issues that require a contingency plan. The list gives the Strategic Planning Committee a broad look at the major threats and opportunities faced by the Company. A contingency plan is five to seven pages long, and contains a brief discussion of anticipated events and the probable strategies to handle the situation. It is not a financial plan.

2.5 IMPLEMENTING THE CORPORATE PLAN

In the first year of corporate planning at Allstate, we set up the process, wrote the corporate goals and mission, designed guidelines, created uniform economic and demographic scenarios and learned how to talk to each other in a new language. The results were encouraging. The second year was easier. A plan was in place, and revising a plan was easier than creating one. Contingency planning was added and synergies were emphasised. Synergies are interactions among units that create value by increasing revenue or by reducing costs (for example selling life insurance to a motor insurance customer is an example of cross-marketing: one form of synergy). In the third year, we stressed accountability and we demanded credible plans and programmes. Progress towards our earlier goals was measured and the goals were revised where necessary. Programmes were also revised, replaced and deleted. In the fourth and fifth years, the planning theme was competition and it was necessary to take a hard look at our industries, at our competition, and at ourselves.

In the sixth year, the process began with a kick-off meeting attended by all business units and by the members of the Strategic Planning Committee. Planning guidelines were presented, and a two-phase review process was introduced. The first phase was concerned with ideas and concepts. In it, each Business Unit identified its most critical goals; analysed its industry, competition, and itself; formulated six to eight major strategies and developed programmes to support these strategies. The phase concluded with a meeting at which each planning unit presented its ideas to the Strategic Planning Committee. Ideas, not numbers, were the principal subject of this meeting and, in the end, there was a general agreement about the industry outlook and the units' key strategies and programmes.

The second phase was concerned with numbers. Each unit produced financial projections that were based on its Phase One ideas. The Business Planning Unit heads presented their final strategic plans to the Strategic Planning Committee, and the result was a blueprint to guide Allstate through the next five years.

2.6 THE BENEFITS OF CORPORATE PLANNING

Allstate and Sears agree that corporate or strategic planning plays a vital role in managing our businesses. Strategic planning and strategic management are often mentioned in the same sentence and there is a growing trend to replace the term 'strategic planning' with the term 'strategic management'. I find no fault with this; in fact I prefer 'strategic management', because that is what you are doing when you implement your plans. Implementation, after all, is the only reason for bothering with planning.

We are often asked whether the planning process is working at Allstate. A list of eight benefits was prepared by management consultants who were asked to evaluate our process and they concluded that planning:

- improves strategic decision-making at the corporate level,
- extends participative management by involving most managers,
- introduces strategic thinking and decision-making within the business units,
- recognises the important issues that affect our businesses,
- forces operational people to think strategically,
- communicates corporate policies and goals to all parts of the organisation,
- increases the understanding of and commitment to the Company's goals, and
- presents a first-class picture of where the Company is and where it is going.

Most managers know how their companies work, so they can rely on their experience and intuition to make important decisions. The corporate planning process augments that experience and intuition – it is a mechanism for managing in a rapidly changing world. Corporate planning makes you answer 'what if' questions. One may ask why we bother to answer these when most scenarios will never come to pass. A chess master will consider dozens of possible lines of play before he moves and he does this even though he knows that eventually only one line can be played. But he also knows that he will win if he continues to examine many lines, even unlikely ones. It is the same with corporate planning – good planners examine many scenarios, even unlikely ones, before they make their recommendations.

Corporate or strategic planning will continue to be an important management tool in the best managed companies of the future. There are few responsibilities more important to top management than to carefully plan their company's future. What could be more important than that?

References

Gragnola, J.B. (1985) 'Corporate Modelling at Allstate Insurance Company', in J.D. Cummins (ed.), *Strategic Planning and Modelling in Property–Liability Insurance* (Hingham, MA: Kluwer-Nijhoff Publishing).

Kaluza, B. (1982) 'Some Considerations on the Empirical Research of Goal Systems of Insurance Companies', *Geneva Papers*, vol 7, no. 24, July, pp. 248–63.

Taylor, B. and J.R. Sparkes (1977) *Corporate Strategy and Planning* (London: Heinemann).

3 Planning for the Single European Market

Stephen Diacon

3.1 INTRODUCTION

The Treaty of Rome effectively created a customs union. Between 1958 and 1968, the six founding members abolished all quota restrictions and duties or tariffs on their internal trade. At the same time they adopted a common external tariff for their imports from other countries. Six other countries, including the United Kingdom, joined the European Community (EC) in the subsequent twenty years. However the abolition of customs duties did not create a single market: there were still considerable barriers to the movement of people, business and capital between the member states of the Community. Those non-tariff barriers, resulting from the fragmentation of the EC market, imposed considerable penalties and costs on its residents.

Consequently, in 1985, the EC summit endorsed the European Commission's *White Paper on Completing the Internal Market*, which set out a detailed legislative programme for creating real home market conditions in Europe by 1993, via some 300 acts to remove non-tariff barriers. These barriers have been classified by Cecchini (1988) into three main types: physical barriers (such as intra-EC border stoppages, customs controls and associated paperwork), technical barriers (including meeting divergent national product standards, technical regulations and conflicting business laws, and entering nationally protected public procurement markets), and fiscal barriers, especially differing rates of VAT and excise duties.

The effects of full integration within the EC arising from the Single European Act 1986 (which enforced the proposals of the 1985 White Paper) have been estimated to produce benefits which will include rises in Gross Domestic Product (GDP) of between 4½ per cent and 7 per cent, a fall in consumer prices of around 5 per cent, and an increase in employment of anywhere between 2 per cent and 5 per cent. A summary of the potential micro- and macroeconomic gains from integration is shown in Figure 3.1.

The purpose of this chapter is to assess briefly the potential impact of the single European market on the insurance industries within the EC and their likely strategic reactions; this is undertaken in four main stages. This introduction examines the impact of the Single European Act and its effect

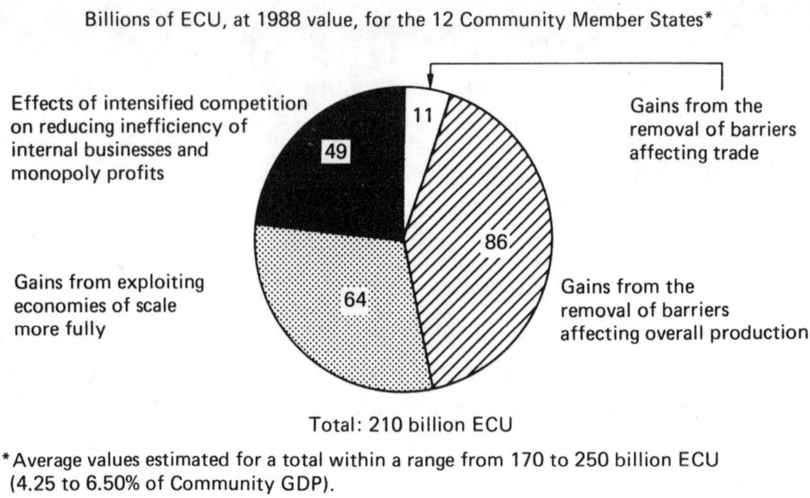

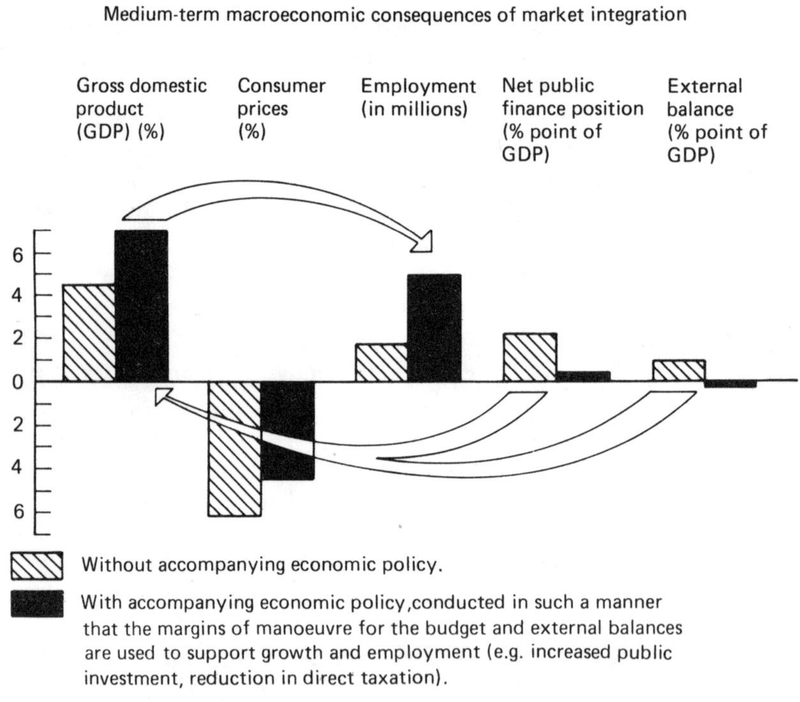

Source: Commission of the European Communities (1988b).
Figure 3.1 Potential gains from the completion of the European internal market – microeconomic estimates

on the insurance industry. Section 3.2 goes on to describe the opportunities and threats for insurers of European integration, and Section 3.3 then analyses the consequent alternative strategic options. Since many of the strategic choices will involve mergers or joint ventures within the European insurance market, these routes are discussed in more detail in Section 3.4. A fuller discussion of insurance company strategies for 1992 can be found in Diacon (1990b).

The Single European Act 1986

By the end of 1992 the European Community intends to achieve a single internal market. The single European or 'internal' market, enshrined in the Single European Act 1986, has been defined as an area without internal frontiers in which the free movement of goods, services, persons and capital is ensured in accordance with the provisions of the Treaty of Rome. The geographical area enclosing the internal market therefore includes the following twelve members of the EC: Belgium, Denmark, Eire, France, Germany, Greece, Italy, Luxembourg, Netherlands, Portugal, Spain and the United Kingdom.

A crucial feature of the Single European Act was the withdrawal of the right of veto that member states had previously enjoyed in the Council of Ministers. The Act introduced majority voting in the Council of Ministers, thus enabling ministers to compromise in the formulation and agreement of policies. The move to majority voting was particularly important in the case of insurance because of the marked differences between EC members (particularly the United Kingdom and the Federal Republic of Germany) in the organisation and regulation of their insurance industries.

Since a common market for goods has already been accomplished, the main impact of the internal market is on services, particularly financial services. Prior to the Single European Act, governments had tended to limit the freedoms of establishment and services (that is, cross-frontier trade) in financial services as a consequence of their attempts to ensure the security and prudential operation of financial institutions. The Act will make possible a fuller financial integration using a minimum co-ordination of rules as the basis for mutual recognition by member states of what each does to safeguard the interests of the general public. The main objective is to establish a single European market in financial services, where a bank can offer the full range of its services throughout the Community and set up branches in another member state as easily as in its own, where insurance can be bought on the most reasonable terms and be valid throughout the Community, and where the market for securities and capital is of a size sufficient to meet the financing needs of European industry and attract visitors from all over the world. Pool (1988) explains that harmonisation is to be guided by the principle of 'home country control', so that the primary task of supervising any EC financial institution will be carried out by its member state of origin (with other members recognising that this control is a satisfactory replacement for the controls which would have operated for a locally established company).

The internal market in insurance services

As far as insurance is concerned, the main aim of the internal market will be to ensure freedom of establishment, freedom of services (to conduct cross-frontier trade in another member state) without the need to establish branches or subsidiaries, and freedom of capital movements throughout the European Community.

Freedom of establishment of insurance companies was secured in 1973 for non-life insurance and in 1979 for life insurance.The Directives harmonised the various rules on supervision and financial requirements, and instigated co-operation between supervisory authorities.

Progress on freedom of services in insurance has been more difficult to achieve. However Fitchew (1988) explains that the Second Non-Life Insurance Coordination Directive, which was adopted in June 1988 for implementation in July 1990, makes important advances in four main areas concerning non-life insurance. First, it provides for some harmonisation of national laws and taxes concerning direct general insurance. In any conflict over which national law should apply to a non-life insurance contract, the choice will depend on the insured's residence or the location of the risk. In those states where premium taxes are levied, the state has the right to charge and collect tax on local risks wherever they are insured. Secondly, the Directive grants the freedom to provide cross-frontier insurance services for large risks in the industrial, commercial and transport sectors. The regulation of such business will therefore be undertaken by the member state where the insurer is established. An important consequence is that commercial buyers will be able to insure risks situated throughout the EC on a global policy. Thirdly, for so called 'mass' non-life insurance risks (purchased by individuals) and for the property and general liability insurance of smaller companies (roughly defined as those with less than 250 employees), member states may continue to require establishment and other controls. However it is intended that measures will be adopted by the 1992 deadline for the harmonisation of freedom of services for mass risks. Fourth, there is to be free access to the EC market for large policyholders and insured parties.

Levie (1988) notes that the progress on freedom of services for long-term business has followed a step behind that of non-life business. Harmonisation of long-term insurance on the basis of 'home country control' is a more difficult issue because of the differences between States in the taxation of savings, the prudential supervision and regulation of local institutions, the variety and complexity of group pensions arrangements (in the areas of insured v. managed, defined benefit v. defined contribution, ease of opting out, the importance of employees' contributions and so on), and social security systems. Inevitably, cross-frontier trade in life and pensions business will involve international capital movements – the subject of separate EC Directives, as described below. An additional complication arises because other types of financial institution may also be involved in the provision of pensions administration, and a consistent treatment across institutions is therefore required.

It is likely that the European Commission will propose a separate treatment for the freedom of services for individual and group long-term insurance. To a certain extent, the problem is more acute for group business because large pan-European employers may want to include all their employees in the same pension arrangement, whereas individual policyholders are more likely to purchase contracts from locally established offices.

The Directive dealing with the freedom of movement of capital within the EC was issued in June 1988, and will be put into effect by July 1990. This will ensure that all EC residents have access to the financial systems of other member states and all the financial products available there, with no restrictions on the transfer of capital between states. It will then be possible for a resident to open a bank account in another Community country, and hence make payments for goods and services (such as life insurance) from a local bank. The 'UCITS Directive' (Undertakings for Collective Investment in Transferable Securities) dealing with the freedom to market unit trust units throughout the EC on a 'home country control' basis was issued in December 1985 and will be in effect by October 1989. This means that savers in unit trusts will be able to participate in any Community country, and trusts (or other forms of UCITS) established anywhere in the EC will be able to sell actively in all member states without needing fresh authorisation in the destination country.

Finally, insurance brokers or independent intermediaries which want to operate internationally will have to register in each of those countries requiring registration.

3.2 OPPORTUNITIES AND THREATS IN THE SINGLE MARKET

The opportunities and threats for the European insurance industry in the integrated single European market arise in three main areas:

- the impact on the macroeconomics of the member states;
- the impact on the microeconomics of insurance buyers; and

– the impact on the microeconomics of the insurance industry.

Whether or not individual insurers will be able to take advantage of the opportunities and avoid the dangers inherent in the threats will depend on the strategies they adopt. This will be discussed in more detail in the next section.

Macroeconomic opportunities and threats

The European Commission (1989) envisages a substantial supply-side improvement in the macroeconomy of the member states of the European Community brought about by improvements in the operation of markets, reduced aggregate prices and improvements in productivity. The result is a possible increase in the level of gross domestic product of each national economy of between 4.5 per cent and 7.5 per cent, with a corresponding rise in disposable income, a fall in interest rates, and an increase in investment and the purchase by firms of capital goods. There will then be corresponding spin-offs for the insurance industry in terms of an increased demand for insurance from all sectors of the economy.

In simple macroeconomic terms, these supply-side benefits enable the aggregate supply of a national economy to be expanded; for example in Figure 3.2 the aggregate supply curve would shift from AS_1 to AS_2. The extent of the resulting increase in gross domestic product for a given economy would then depend on the size of the shift in the aggregate supply curve and the slope of the aggregate demand function.

The macroeconomic threats associated with European integration can also be inferred from Figure 3.2. As well as a rise in output (and associated fall in interest rates), many economies may also experience a fall in the aggregate price level and hence deflation. In some cases there may also be a deterioration in the balance of payments position and/or downward pressure on domestic exchange rates as the rise in incomes sucks in more imported goods and services, while the fall in interest rates reduces capital imports.

A summary of the precise macroeconomic mechanisms that will bring about the expansion of aggregate supply is illustrated in Figure 3.3. Cecchini (1988) examines the macroeconomic effects of the single European market under four headings:

1. *The removal of border controls*. This will lead to reduced prices for intra-EC traded goods and services as a result of the elimination of the excess costs linked to border delays and administrative bureaucracy associated with cross-frontier trade within the Community.
2. *The liberalisation of procurement markets*. The purchases of goods and services by public enterprises, public administration and companies supplying public markets should be achieved at lower prices in the

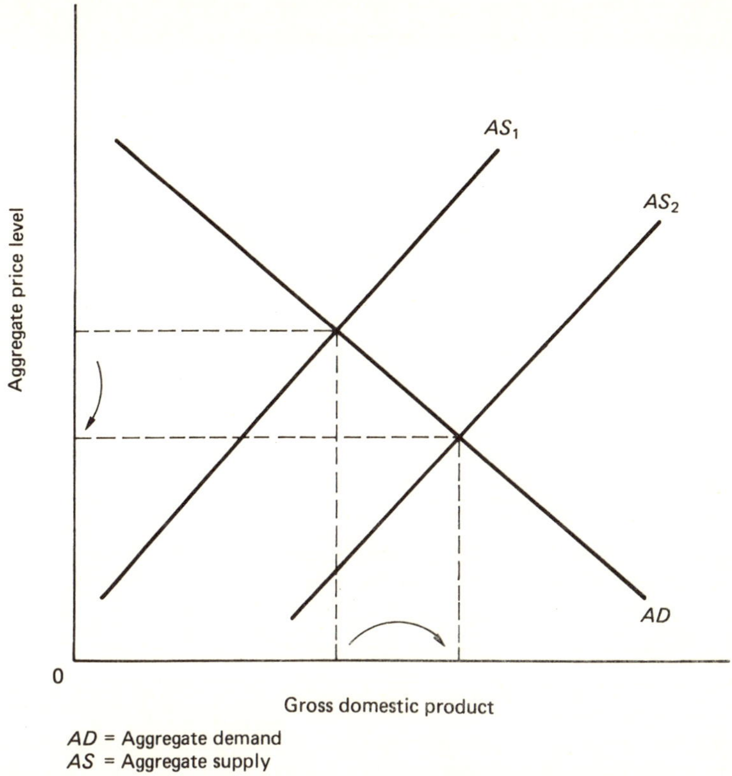

Figure 3.2 The 'supply-side' macroeconomic/effects of the single European market

single market. This downward pressure on prices will result from increased competition within the EC in the supply of such goods and services to governments, as the scope for 'protectionist' public sector procurement policies is to be curtailed.

3. *The liberalisation of financial services*. A single market in financial services should reduce the prices charged by financial firms and hence, for example, the cost of credit and the price of insurance. Thus, although increased competition in insurance markets may force down the premium rates charged on a particular policy, this is likely to be balanced by an overall expansion in premium income.
4. *Improvements in productivity and reductions in business prices*. Business can be expected to obtain improvements in productivity by the more efficient allocation of resources and improved business organisation. Price reductions will also materialise via reductions in unit costs (produced by economies of scale) and increased competition in product markets.

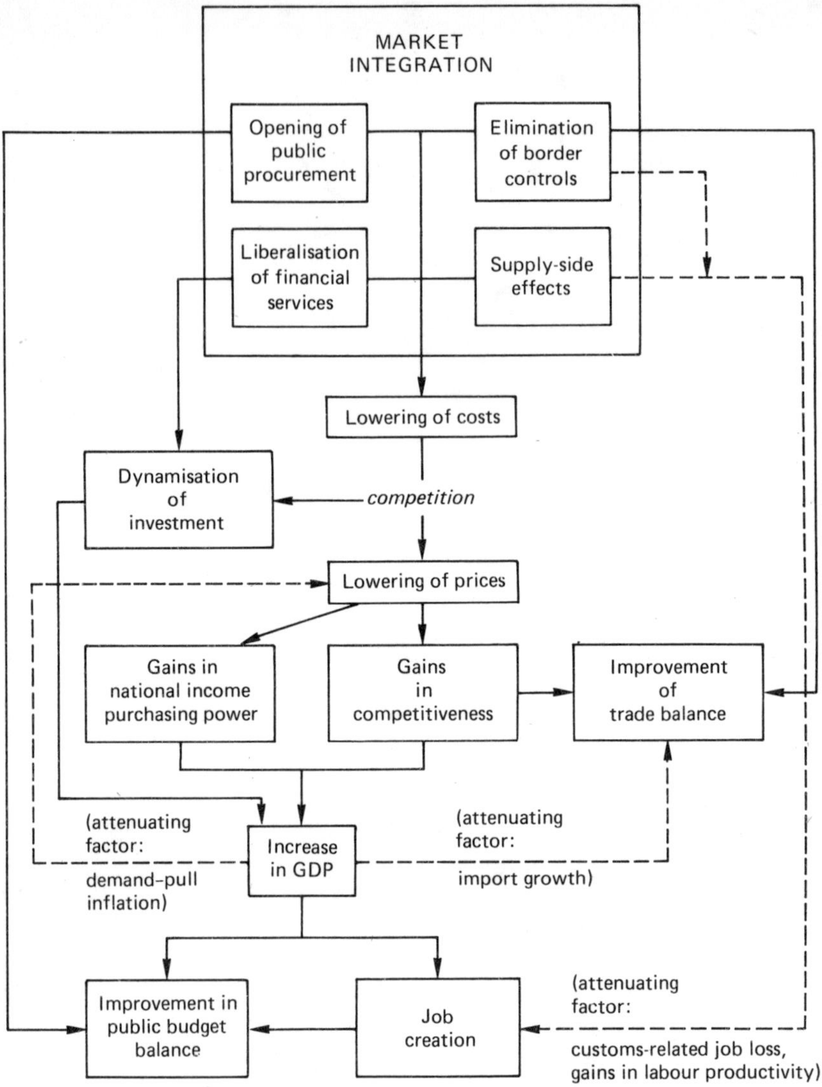

Source: Cecchini (1988).
Figure 3.3 The macroeconomic effects of the single European market

Microeconomic opportunities and threats for insurance buyers

Another aspect of the potential gains to the insurance industry of the single European market is the opportunities and threats experienced by the buyers of insurance, both commercial and individual. The firms and persons which benefit from these microeconomic opportunities can be

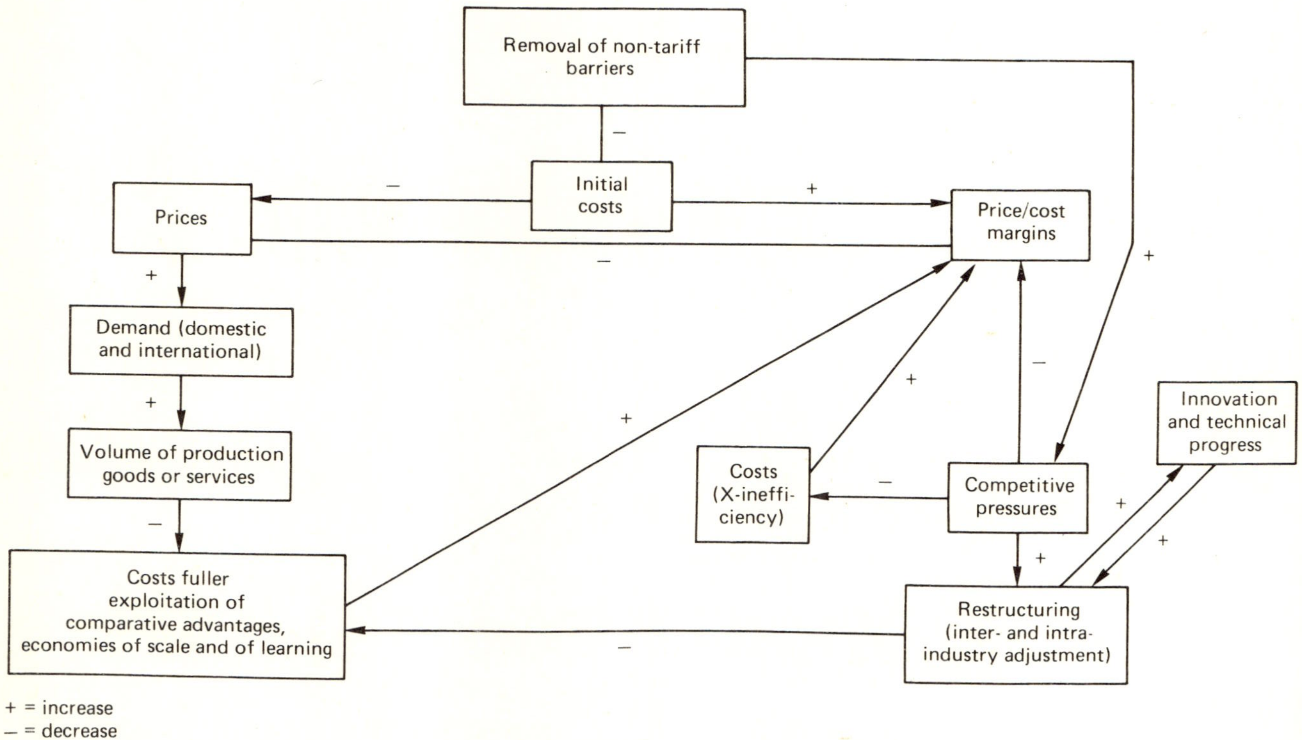

Source: Cecchini (1988).
Figure 3.4 The microeconomic effects of the single European market

expected to alter their demand for insurance coverage, although not necessarily in a beneficial way. A flow chart of the microeconomic effects triggered by European integration is shown in Figure 3.4. Cecchini (1988) notes that three main consequences may be expected from the combined impact of the elimination of non-tariff barriers and the subsequent boost to competition:

1. Reductions in costs. Companies should be able to obtain reductions in costs due to the advantages of economies of scale and improvements in business organisation. The size of the potential reductions in unit costs will vary, however, between industries: for example, it has been estimated that production costs will fall by about 1 per cent for petroleum products, but between 3 per cent and 6 per cent for some sectors of heavy engineering. The consequences for the demand for insurance are uncertain: on the one hand, larger companies are better able to retain their own risks and therefore need less insurance – in fact this may be one of the economies of scale; on the other, an expansion in the business of the insurance buyer as a result of lower unit prices may stimulate the purchase of insurance. The available evidence does not rule out the possibility that an increase in the scale of the insurance buyer will stimulate the demand for insurance.
2. Improved efficiency and lower costs resulting from competition. This factor represents an opportunity for those companies for whom the introduction of the discipline of the market means the removal of inefficient production, the updating of technology and the end to bad management. This will enable them to take fuller advantage of the substantial market opportunities available. On the other hand, companies may no longer be able to enjoy the security and supernormal profits of an element of monopoly power. The issue here is whether increased efficiency and competitiveness of the insured stimulates or discourages the purchase of insurance; unfortunately this issue is largely unresolved.
3. Increased innovation, leading to technological leadership and the development of new products and production processes.

Microeconomic opportunities and threats for insurance suppliers

The single European market poses opportunities and threats for insurers because of the changes in the structure and competitiveness of the various European insurance industries. As discussed in Section 3.1, the eventual completion of the internal market will involve full freedom of services and establishment for insurers authorised to transact business in any member state. Although this process may not have been completed by the end of 1992, the European Commission has indicated a desire to make considerable progress as quickly as possible.

In contrast to many other sectors of European industry, the single market for insurance will actually mean a first opportunity for some insurers to sell throughout the Community, since tariff as well as non-tariff barriers have hitherto been commonplace in many member states. Furthermore European countries differ markedly in the degree of insurance penetration, providing scope for easier business in some of the less saturated regions. Figures produced by Swiss Re. (1988) show that, in 1986, non-life insurance premium expenditure per head of population varied from US $32.1 for Greece to US $563.2 for Germany; similarly the per capita expenditure on life insurance ranged from US $7.4 for Portugal to US $479.3 for Great Britain.

Unfortunately for insurers, the expansion in the market-place for insurance is accompanied by a corresponding increase in the number of competing firms. The balance of opportunity over threat will of course depend on the ability of insurers to respond to the resulting pressures to reduce costs, react to competition, and operate in an innovative manner. The opportunities and threats for insurers resulting from full integration are essentially the same as for other sectors of the economy, although the service element of insurance imposes some constraints on the marketing of business throughout Europe (for example, see Chapter 13). Insurers may benefit from reductions in costs arising from economies of scale and scope: however the existing investigations into the size of such cost improvements have thrown doubt on the existence of substantial scale economies beyond the size of the very smallest insurers (see Section 10.5). Virtually no work has been undertaken within the EC financial sector into the beneficial effects of economies of scope of joint production (that is, synergy), although the recent interest in the concept of the 'financial supermarket' and the growing number of financial conglomerates (in those States where they are permitted) seem to indicate that some companies perceive the presence of such benefits.

In addition, some insurers will undoubtedly benefit from the expansion in the market-place even though it is allied with increased competition: the general argument here is that insurers who are used to operating in a competitive environment will have a head start. For example, Table 3.1 provides evidence of substantial price differentials in various classes of insurance among EC member states. In theory competition should result in a transfer of business to the low-price producers; however, in practice, it appears that consumers are not particularly price-sensitive and one can often find an equally large dispersion of prices within a national market (particularly for individual business). The purchase of insurance is also affected by many other factors (in addition to price) which may be cultural and behavioural in nature: there is thus no certainty that a foreign insurer will be able to break into a local market on the basis of price alone.

Much of the competition in insurance markets is frequently concerned

Table 3.1 Percentage differences in prices of standard insurance products compared with the average of the four lowest national prices*

Name of standard service	*Description of standard service*	*Belgium*	*Germany*	*Spain*	*France*	*Italy*	*Luxembourg*	*Netherlands*	*UK*
1 Life insurance	Average annual cost of term (life) insurance	78	5	37	33	83	66	–9	–30
2 Home insurance	Annual cost of fire and theft cover for house valued at 70 000 ECU with 28 000 ECU contents	–16	3	–4	39	81	57	17	90
3 Motor insurance	Annual cost of comprehensive insurance, 1.6 litre car, driver 10 years' experience, no claims bonus	30	15	100	9	148	77	–7	–17
4 Commercial fire and theft	Annual cover for premises valued at 387 240 ECU & stock at 232 344 ECU	–9	43	24	153	245	–15	–1	27
5 Public liability cover	Annual premium for engineering company with 20 employees and annual turnover of 1.29 million ECU	13	47	60	117	77	9	–16	–7

* The figures show the extent to which financial product prices, in each country, are above a low reference level. Each of these price differences implies a theoretical potential price fall from existing price levels to the low reference level.
Source: Cecchini (1988).

with the control of distribution outlets. The costs involved in breaking into an existing distribution network (or of setting one up from scratch) can be prohibitive, and can be expected to provide a sizeable barrier to entry for insurers wishing to compete in local markets in some classes of business. In view of this, the most likely strategy for an insurer wishing to compete on a pan-Europe basis will be either to acquire an existing local company or to establish a joint venture with another institution. Unfortunately, non-European insurers who wish to establish a foothold in the EC are likely to adopt exactly the same strategy and, as Carter (1988) demonstrates, even the largest European insurers are small in comparison with some American and Japanese companies (see Table 3.2).

A switch to a competitive insurance market will pose problems for some insurers not only because of the usual reasons concerned with the removal of X-inefficiency and the need to allocate resources in a more efficient way (for example, see Figure 3.4) but also because of the problems involved in pricing insurance products and the need to ensure solvency (see Chapter 12). The problems are more severe in those markets which would have been affected by adverse selection had the tariff structure not prevented selection problems in the first place. To give a simple example, Finsinger *et al.* (1985) note that, in the German life insurance market, companies have been prevented from varying their premium rates according to the sex of policyholders and whether or not they are smokers. Similarly Price Waterhouse (1988) explain that UK life offices are the only European insurers which use the mortality experience of insured lives rather than population averages in the calculation of premium rates. Obviously, in these circumstances, non-smoking German women may well prefer to buy their life insurance from British insurers (on a services basis) since they could then obtain substantial discounts. In a single European market without constraints on the way premium rates should be calculated, German insurers will in future need to be more discriminating in order to avoid adverse selection problems in their competition with the British. However German insurers may lack the necessary mortality data to enable them to offer accurate rate reductions to low-risk policyholders, and will have to incur substantial administrative costs in order to collect them.

The ability of insurers to develop innovative products will also depend on their previous experience in doing so. Again it can be expected that those insurers already operating in a competitive environment without regulatory constraints on new product development will have a short-term competitive advantage.

3.3 STRATEGIC CHOICES FOR THE SINGLE EUROPEAN MARKET

The strategic choices facing existing European insurance companies as a

Table 3.2 The world's major direct insurance companies

Company	*1986 Premium Income (US$ million)*					
	Total		*Life*		*Non-life*	
	Gross	*Net*	*Gross*	*Net*	*Gross*	*Net*
American						
Prudential		19 367		17 430		1 937
Aetna Life & Casualty		17 416		10 507		6 909
State Farm		17 473		1 225		16 248
Metropolitan Life		12 871		12 192		679
Allstate		11 080		1 895		9 185
Travelers		9 238		4 024		5 214
American Int. Group		7 740		1 938		5 802
Japanese						
Nippon Life		20 594		20 594		
Dai-Ichi Mutual		13 909		13 909		
Sumitomo Life		12 355		12 355		
Tokyo Marine & Fire	6 129	4 305			6 129	4 305
Yasuda Fire & Marine	4 517	3 122			4 517	3 122
Sumitomo Mar. & Fire	3 105	1 669			3 105	1 669
European						
Allianz Group	9 897					
– consolidated	8 317		3 157		5 160	
Zurich Group		6 221		1 685	5 424	4 536
Royal		5 643		1 027		4 616
Generali		5 093	1 772			3 321
Union des Assurances de Paris	6 033	5 402				
(UAP Incendie-Accidents)					2 654	2 170
(UAP Vie)			1 282			
(UAP Capitalisation)			1 013			
Prudential Corp.		4 783		3 487		1 296
Nationale Nederlanden	4 887	4 388	2 678	2 537	2 209	1 851
Winterthur Group	4 717	4 205	1 672	1 647	3 045	2 558
General Accident		3 540		301		3 239

Sources: *Financial Times World Insurance Yearbook*; Insurance Solvency International Ltd, *International Insurance Profiles; Best's Review* (Life and Property & Casualty editions).

result of the threats and opportunities presented by the single European market fall into three main categories:

1. *Local strategies*, which are concerned with responding to the opportunities and threats presented in the insurer's local market (including the threat of new competition from European and non-European foreign insurers);
2. *European strategies*, in order to take advantage of the opportunities

presented by the single market within the EC on either an establishment or cross-frontier (services) basis; and

3. *Global strategies*, which may be considered as a result of any reciprocal concessions negotiated by the Community (see de Clercq (1988)), or as a means of escaping from the intensified competition within the EC.

Local strategies for European insurers

The strategies available to meet the opportunities and threats in local insurance markets stem from the ways in which insurers approach their markets and structure their internal affairs. As explained in Section 1.5, corporate strategies can be classified according to competitive scope (broad or narrow/focused market coverage) and competitive advantage (cost or differentiation) – a simplified categorisation provided in Section 13.9 ignores the possibility of a broad market coverage (the alternatives then become focused, cost, and differentiation).

A focused strategy involves a creative search for a market niche; van der Merwe (1987) describes this as finding out:

- what customers want,
- how customers compare firms,
- where the competition will come from,
- what segments the firm should aim at, and
- how to balance customer service with profitability.

In addition, a focused strategy for a financial firm must consider the most appropriate distribution system for the selected niche. For example, European non-life offices wishing to aim at large commercial buyers of insurance can be expected to establish branches or contact offices in close proximity to Lloyd's of London (and may even attempt to gain a place on the floor at Lloyd's), utilising the London broker network to distribute their business. Similarly a life office focusing on low-income households (which probably lack bank accounts) would probably have to utilise a direct salesforce. The best example of a focused distribution strategy is the increasing use by many insurers of direct mailshots utilising mailing lists sorted according to the target criteria.

In insurance, a broad market coverage increasingly involves the use of a variety of distribution systems. In the United Kingdom for example, the response of many life insurers to the deregulation enforced in the Financial Services Act 1986 (as described in Section 14.7) has been to select the distribution method most suited to the respective market segment: building societies for mortgage-related life insurance, accountants for personal pensions, consulting actuaries for group pensions, tied salesforces for high net worth households and so on (further details can be found in Diacon

Table 3.3 The changing importance of insurance distribution methods

In distributing your products/service(s) to *final consumers*, how important do you expect *each* of the following methods to be *now* (i.e. 1987) and in *five years* (i.e. 1992)?*

Method	*Score in 1987*	*Score for 1992*
Direct salesforce		
Commission only	1.85	1.93
Salary and commission	1.90	1.89
Direct response advertising	1.61	1.92
Direct mail	1.64	2.08
Building society branch network	1.33	1.44
Bank branch network	1.30	1.31
Insurance company branch network	2.17	2.25
Broker branch network	2.13	2.19
Estate agent – owned	1.13	1.19
Estate agent – not owned	1.29	1.38
Franchising	1.07	1.16
Other independent intermediary	2.11	2.17

* The table shows the score for each method on the scale: 'Very important' = 3, 'Important' = 2, and 'Not at all important' = 1.
Sample Size = 66 UK life and non-life insurance companies.
Source: Diacon (1990).

(1990a)). In many countries, independent intermediaries have been the traditional distribution outlet most appropriate for a broad market coverage.

An indication of the likely developments in the distribution methods of a sample of 66 UK life and non-life insurance companies can be gained from Table 3.3. The high scores for 'Broker branch network' and 'Other independent intermediary' reflect the traditional importance of insurance brokers in the distribution of insurance in the United Kingdom. In examining the differences in the scores between 1987 and 1992, two main features are apparent. In the first place, almost all distribution methods are expected to increase in importance; insurers are therefore predicted to expand the range of distribution channels utilised. Secondly, the biggest increases are forecast for impersonal selling techniques such as 'Direct response advertising' and 'Direct mail', perhaps because it is often presumed that these are one of the most cost-effective methods of distribution; it will certainly be easier to introduce these techniques rather than to start up a broker support division or to recruit and train a direct salesforce.

A strategy of cost-based competitive advantage obviously involves attempts to reduce unit costs below those of competitors. Naturally the strategy of reducing price is only appropriate in those markets where consumers are price-sensitive and can distinguish the prices of competing insurers. In insurance markets, the more price-sensitive consumers are likely to be the following:

(a) Corporate purchasers, who are usually credited with the risk management knowledge and skill to make informed decisions on risk handling and financing. In any case, in an increasingly competitive environment, commercial firms will themselves need to be cost conscious.
(b) Consumers for whom insurance is a 'shopping good' rather than those for whom it is a 'convenience good'. Obviously the former are more likely to utilise the services of an insurance broker, while the latter – who are concerned to minimise the transactions/search costs of buying insurance – may use the most readily available distribution outlet (such as the direct salesman who obtains an introduction). Attempts in some insurance markets to require independent intermediaries to disclose their commission earnings to policyholders (for example in the UK long-term market after 1989) will probably deter the 'convenience'-motivated rather than the 'shopping'-motivated policyholders.
(c) Consumers introduced to the insurer via independent intermediaries rather than more direct means. It can be argued that one of the functions of intermediaries is to evaluate the customer's price elasticity, so that insurers can charge correspondingly lower prices (a practice technically known as price discrimination – see Chapter 12). In some countries the charging of different prices for products distributed in different ways is prohibited.

In insurance, a cost-based strategy does not necessarily involve a narrow product range. It is more likely to be achieved by companies with a low-cost organisational form, appropriate technological support and efficient distribution network. A good example of low-cost organisation is provided by the insurance syndicates operating at Lloyd's of London, which supply insurance with minimal administrative costs (although the costs involved in regulating the market are reducing the syndicate's competitive advantage in this area).

Finally a strategy of differentiation-based competitive advantage requires the company first to position itself so that it is regarded by consumers as different from the competition, and second to give consumers a good reason for wanting to do business with it. As van der Merwe (1987) notes, in services where goods are intangible, customers often buy 'blind' and therefore rely on the firm's brand image.

European strategies for European insurers

European strategies refer to the possible responses by a local insurer to the opportunities presented by the single market within the EC. These

Table 3.4 Motivation for foreign market entry

Reason	%
Seeking greater growth abroad	26.80
Following multinational clients	24.75
Geographical diversification	24.75
Greater underwriting profits	17.86
Other	5.84

Notes: 1. Obtained from a survey of 80 insurers, undertaking 216 market entries. Multiple responses bring the total number of reples to 291.
2. 'Other' include seeking investment in countries with a stable currency, a strong economy, a stable political system, and an experienced insurance market.

Source: Schroath (1988).

strategies will involve insurers in an attempt to sell their contracts to customers in other EC countries, either on a services or establishment basis in order to take advantage of the new market opportunities and gain access to any economies of scale and scope. However, in order to enter a foreign market, the insurer must have specific advantages in order to overcome the extra costs of servicing a distant market in an unfamiliar environment and culture, and be able to compete favourably with the indigenous industry. Bickelhaupt and Bar-Niv (1983) identify a number of reasons to explain why an insurer may want to undertake international operations:

(a) A strong incentive for such business is the internationalisation of trade in goods and services: when businesses move overseas they often want to retain their original insurer in order to obtain an integrated coverage.
(b) Profitability is often greater in some markets than others.
(c) To gain the benefits of large-scale operation, including some element of monopoly power.
(d) To obtain a greater diversification of risks.
(e) To enhance the reputation of the insurer and its management.

Following a survey of 80 international insurance companies which had undertaken a total of 216 foreign market entries, Schroath (1988) analysed the motivation of insurers in undertaking international operations. Table 3.4 shows that the major factors were the desire for greater growth, to follow the business of multinational clients, and to achieve geographical diversification.

Although the main impact of the Single European Act 1986 will be in the area of freedom of services, the most popular integration strategy will probably continue to be physical establishment (although there are a variety of methods for achieving this). This is because many types of insurance product require local servicing and it is generally easier to undertake this from a local base. For example, although Lloyd's syndicates supply insurance around the world on a cross-frontier basis, they have access to the unique network of Lloyd's agents for local servicing and, in any case, syndicates rely heavily on brokers to provide many of the services normally available in-house to an established insurer. Furthermore, many local customers are likely to be suspicious of a foreign insurer which does not have a local office or maintain technical reserves locally. Non-European insurers wishing to gain a foothold within the Community will need to do so on an establishment basis.

The strategic choices presented to an insurer considering European expansion can be analysed using the categorisation outlined by Hood and Young (1987) and reproduced in Figure 3.5. This partitions international strategies according to the degree of control exercised by the 'parent' over the subsidiary, and the extent of geographical concentration. The strategies of the (foreign) subsidiary are then classified in four main ways: marketing satellite – where the subsidiary is mainly involved in distribution and sale rather than production; miniature replica – which is a scaled-down version of the parent; rationalised manufacturer – producing a smaller range of products than the parent; and product specialist, which has the strategic independence to develop new product lines for the local market. Further discussion is provided in Porter (1986).

Global strategies for European insurers

De Clercq (1988) explains that the European Community is determined to maintain a liberal external trading system, and is engaging in a wide-ranging series of trade negotiations in the General Agreement on Tariffs and Trade (GATT) with a view to a worldwide lowering of the levels of protection. However GATT does not cover all international trade, and services in particular are excluded. The EC sees no reason why the benefits of the single market should be extended unilaterally to third countries. The policy instead is to negotiate reciprocal concessions with non-EC countries in order to obtain a mutual balance of advantage. As an illustration of this approach, Part IX of the UK Financial Services Act 1986 gives the Secretary of State for Trade and Industry powers to disqualify or restrict foreign nationals from undertaking investment business in the United Kingdom (as defined by the Act) if the investment, insurance or banking business of UK nationals operating in corresponding overseas countries cannot be carried out on terms as favourable as those applying in the United Kingdom. In a similar way, upon application by a non-Community institution for initial authorisation to transact in the EC, the European Commission intends to check on a case-by-case basis whether similar

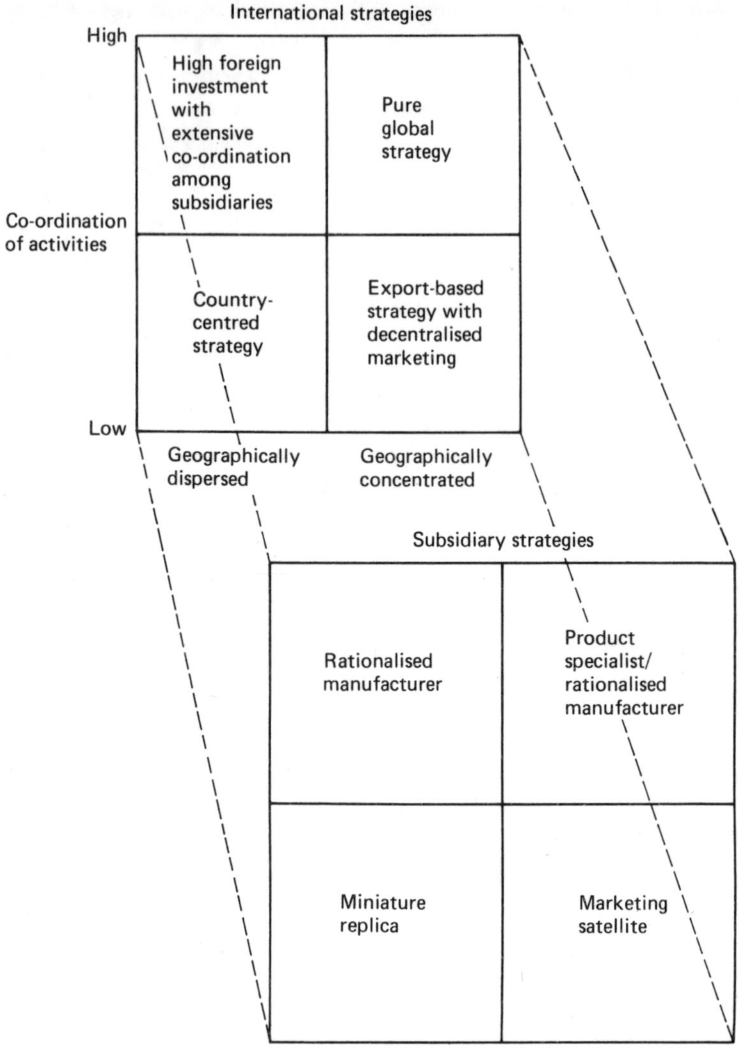

Source: Hood and Young (1987).
Figure 3.5 European and international strategy

institutions from all member states are given the same treatment in the non-Community country concerned. If this is not the case, the authorisation procedure will be suspended until the EC has ensured reciprocity.

The growing importance of the European Community, and the increased attractiveness of its markets for non-EC companies, should therefore ensure that progress is made to liberalise worldwide trade in insurance

Table 3.5 Preferred choice of foreign entry among insurers

Entry technique	%	*Mean success*
Establish a branch office	31.84	6.052
Contract with managing agency	26.85	6.156
Establish a new subsidiary	12.96	6.880
Purchase of existing insurer	12.50	6.666
Joint venture	9.70	5.687
Other	6.15	6.375

Notes: 1. Obtained from a survey of 80 international insurers undertaking a total of 216 entries.
2. 'Mean success' is based on a scale from 1 = least success to 10 = greatest success.

Source: Schroath (1988).

services. Consequently European insurers will have increased opportunity to expand on a global basis. However, if the failure to ensure reciprocal treatment means that non-EC insurers are shut out of the Community, this could have a substantial adverse impact on the operation of the London insurance market.

3.4 IMPLEMENTING STRATEGIC CHOICES: THE ROLE OF MERGERS

In his study of modes of foreign market entry, Schroath (1988) investigated the choice of entry technique selected by 80 international insurers in a total of 216 entries, and attempted to evaluate the success of these various methods. Table 3.5 shows that setting up a new branch office and contracting with a managing agency were the most popular choices of entry. However, when it came to evaluating the success of the various methods, it appeared that establishing a new subsidiary and the acquisition of an existing company were judged by management to be the most successful. The table also shows that, although acquisition or mergers were used in only 12.5 per cent of foreign market entries, they are ranked highly in terms of success. The distrust of the use of joint venturing as a means of market entry confirms the results reported by Cecchini (1988), and highlights the many problems of inter-company link-ups on an international basis.

International mergers or acquisitions are only one aspect of the total picture, since they may also be undertaken on a purely local (national) basis in relation to a company's local strategy. Thompson and Wright (1988) categorise mergers and acquisitions into a variety of alternatives:

(a) acquisition of one independent company by another (usually on the

Table 3.6 Mergers and acquisitions in the European insurance industry

	1984/5			*1985/6*			*1986/7*		
	(a)	*(b)*	*(c)*	*(a)*	*(b)*	*(c)*	*(a)*	*(b)*	*(c)*
National	7	5	1	5	4	0	17	5	1
Community	7	3	0	3	0	0	7	1	1
International	1	0	0	4	0	0	4	5	0
Total	15	8	1	12	4	0	28	11	2

(a) = mergers including acquisitions of majority holdings.
(b) = acquisitions of minority holdings.
(c) = joint ventures.
National = within one EC country.
Community = between companies within the EC.
International = between EC and non-EC company.
Source: Commission of the European Communities (1987).

basis of an agreed bid, although in the United Kingdom hostile bids are more frequent than in other EC countries);

(b) partial acquisition, that is, the purchase of a minority stake;
(c) joint venture, that is, the establishment or purchase of an entity by more than one company;
(d) sell-off (the sale of a subsidiary or division of one company to another);
(e) management buy-out, which is the term given to the purchase of a company or division by the managers and/or employees who run it; and
(f) management buy-in, being the purchase of a company or division by people who are not actively involved at the time, but who subsequently run it.

The role and form of mergers and acquisitions in the European insurance market have been analysed by the Commission of the European Communities (1987) and summary figures are given in Table 3.6. The figures must be viewed in comparison with an estimated 2900 authorised insurance companies in the EC.

The table shows that total acquisitions and mergers of all types rose from 24 in 1984/5, to 41 in 1986/7, with the greatest growth in National (that is, local) mergers including acquisitions of majority holdings. The figures seem to indicate a prevalence of defensive mergers within Community countries, perhaps in preparation for the greater competition of the single market and the diversification of other financial institutions. Over the three years to 1987 intra-EC activity comprised 17 mergers, 4 acquisitions of minority holdings, and 1 joint venture: this seems to confirm the earlier impression that mergers are a preferred medium for implementing international strategies, at least in comparison with joint ventures.

The Commission also publishes a breakdown of type (a) mergers by the size of the insurers' combined premium income: in 1984/5, 9 out of the 15 mergers involved insurers with combined premium income over 1000 million ECU and only 5 involved smaller groups (under 500 million ECU); however, in 1986/7, the position had substantially reversed with 16 out of 28 mergers effected by insurers in the smaller category, and the remaining 12 in the largest. Scarcely any mergers produced groups with a combined premium income between 500 and 1000 million ECU.

Finally it must be noted that, although information on the motivation behind insurance mergers is scarce, studies which have been undertaken of the success of merger activity in general are virtually unanimous in their inability to find any benefits in terms of profitability, efficiency, share returns or market share. Mueller (1988) concludes that the pattern of research findings is broadly consistent with the view that managers undertake acquisitions solely to maintain or increase the size of their firms. Companies merge not because of any synergy between acquirer and acquiree but simply because the acquirer's financial circumstances (in terms of cash-flow and/or share price) are propitious.

References

Bickelhaupt, D.L. and R. Bar-Niv (1983) *International Insurance: Managing Risk in the World* (New York: Insurance Information Institute).

Carter, R.L. (1988) 'Barriers to Free Trade in Insurance', paper presented at *Elaborating a Strategy for the European Insurance Market after 1992* (Rotterdam: De Vlerick School Voor Management) 16 November.

Cecchini, P. (1988) *The European Challenge 1992: The Benefits of the Single Market* (Aldershot: Wildwood House).

Commission of the European Communities (1988a) *17th Report on Competition Policy* (Brussels) pp. 228–41.

Commission of the European Communities (1988b) 'The big European market: a trump card for the economy and employment', *European File*, 14/88, August–September.

Commission of the European Communities (1989) *The Economics of 1992 – An Assessment of the Potential Economic Effects of Completing the Internal Market of the EC* (Brussels).

de Clercq, W. (1988) 'The Impact on the Outside World', *European Access*, November, pp. 10–12.

Diacon, S.R. (1990a) 'Personal Financial Markets', in R.L. Carter (ed.), *A Handbook of Personal Financial Management* (Brentford, Middlesex: Kluwer Publishing Limited).

Diacon, S.R. (1990b) 'Strategies for the Single European Market: The Options for Insurers', *The Services Industries Journal*, vol. 10, no. 1.

Finsinger, J., E. Hammond and J. Tapp (1985) *Insurance: Competition or Regulation?* (London: Institute of Fiscal Studies) Report Series no. 19.

Fitchew, G. (1988) '1992: The creation of an internal market in financial services', *European Access*, November, pp. 7–9.

Hood, N. and S. Young (1987) 'Inward Investment and the EC: UK Evidence on Corporate Integration Strategies', *Journal of Common Market Studies*, vol. XXVI, no. 2, December, pp. 193–206.

Levie, G. (1988) 'Which freedom of services in life insurance?', paper presented at *Elaborating a Strategy for the European Insurance Market after 1992* (Rotterdam: De Vlerick School Voor Management) 15 November.

Mueller, D.C. (1988) 'The Corporate Life Cycle', in R.S. Thompson and M. Wright (eds), *Internal Organisation, Efficiency and Profit* (Oxford: Philip Allan).

Pool, W.E. (1988) 'Directives and proposals affecting the provision of insurance services', paper presented at *Elaborating a Strategy for the European Insurance Market after 1992* (Rotterdam: De Vlerick School Voor Management) 15 November.

Porter, M.E. (ed) (1986) *Competition in Global Industries* (Boston: Harvard Business School Press).

Price Waterhouse (1988) *The 'Cost of Non-Europe' in Financial Services: Research on the 'Cost of Non-Europe', Basic Findings Volume 9*, Commission of the European Communities.

Schroath, F.W. (1988) 'Mode of Foreign Market Entry: An Analysis of the Property and Liability Insurance Industry', *Geneva Papers*, vol. 13, no. 49, October, pp. 361–76.

Swiss Re. (1988) 'World Insurance 1986: Unusual Growth in the Insurance Industry', *Sigma*, no. 5, May.

Thompson, R.S. and M. Wright (1988) *Internal Organisation, Efficiency and Profit* (Oxford: Philip Allan).

van der Merwe, S. (1987) 'Deregulation in Services and the Marketing Challenge', *The Service Industries Journal*, vol. 7, no. 1, January, pp. 24–34.

4 Modelling and Forecasting in Insurance Management

Margaret Brown

This chapter is primarily concerned with computer-based financial models and their application to insurance. There now exists a wide and sometimes confusing variety of models and modelling techniques. This is a consequence of the recent developments in information technology which have made available, at relatively low cost, powerful tools for forecasting and modelling.

While computing power has undoubtedly added a new dimension to the modelling process, it may also obscure the fundamental underlying principles. Using a computer to help plan and control the operations of an organisation may turn out to be a costly mistake or even a complete disaster if the computer model is not understood by management and supplemented by experienced judgement.

The chapter begins with a general overview of types of models, the purposes for which they are used and the assumptions underlying their construction. This puts into perspective the remainder of the chapter, which examines forecasting models and a computer simulation model of general insurance.

4.1 TYPES OF MODEL

What is a model?

For most people, a model normally denotes something specific and concrete. If referring to an inanimate object, a model is assumed to be a physical replica of another object. At the other extreme, a psychologist might say that all conscious human activity is based on implicit models or mental images which are continually being processed and modified by the brain. Such psychological models are constructed from a person's perceptions of the past and present and are related to their objectives for the future.

Most managers and planners would probably agree that a model is any simplified and explicit representation of a real-world situation which has occurred, or may occur in the future, which can be used to enhance their managerial judgement. Such models range from simple financial ratios to large complex affairs requiring a computer and considerable expertise for their implementation.

Iconic, analogue and symbolic models

In iconic models the relevant properties of the system being modelled are represented by the properties themselves, often with a change of scale (as in a model aeroplane), or with a topological deformation (for example a schematic map of the London Underground Railway system).

In analogue models one set of properties is used to represent another set of properties. Important examples in financial management are graphs and histograms; these are analogues that use geometrical magnitudes and location to represent variables and the relationships between them. In general, analogue models are less specific and less concrete than iconic models, but are easier to manipulate, so providing a systematic framework for extrapolation into the unknown or for evaluation of alternative courses of action.

In symbolic models letters, numbers and other types of symbols are used to represent the components of theoretical or real systems and the functional relationships between them. The aim is to express these relationships in such a way that the essential structure of the system being modelled is retained, while at the same time imposing a degree of simplification and idealisation which allows the model to be manipulated. Symbolic models are potentially the most powerful kind of model it is possible to construct; unfortunately they are also the most difficult to understand, and may have only a tenuous connection with reality.

Quantitative and qualitative models

A model is quantitative if it includes measurable quantities and if it can be used to give numerical answers (the 'output' of the model) to appropriately posed questions (the 'input' to the model). The most general type of quantitative model is a symbolic mathematical model in which numerical values can be assigned to a subset of the symbols (the 'parameters' of the model). Numerical values for other symbols (the 'variables' of the model) may then be calculated.

However models of socioeconomic systems have tended to be qualitative rather than quantitative. It has been argued that the intrinsic nature of human activity is such that quantitative models may be inappropriate, since a major problem in quantitative work is the lack of universal standards of measurement for important behavioural variables such as values, attitudes and expectations. The pragmatic approach, however, is to 'quantify the quantifiable' and then supplement the results by human judgement to allow for the qualitative variables left out of the formal mathematical model. For this strategy to be successful, a good understanding of the model's capabilities and limitations is required.

Financial and economic models are the best known forms of quantitative model. Financial models often focus on accounting variables such as balance sheet levels and revenue account items. At first sight these seem to be easily quantifiable, but that is not always the case. For example, 'incurred but not reported' (IBNR) claims may be little more than inspired guesswork for some classes of general insurance and reinsurance.

Of course, one of the aims of modelling is to try to throw light on these problems. However the apparent accuracy of models based solely on accounting principles and historic accounting data may be spurious. Thus no model of claims experience constructed ten years ago could possibly have anticipated the spate of asbestosis claims currently being received by liability insurers.

Economic models must generally attempt to model, in a quantitative form, relationships which are complex and little understood. However, even where there is an abundance of historic quantitative data, the theoretical concepts tend to be qualitative.

Deterministic and statistical models

Deterministic models assume perfect certainty. Unless such models are changed in some way, their output will always be the same, given the same set of inputs. In statistical models, random fluctuations are explicitly taken into account. Statistical packages are then used to construct quantitative statistical models, based on the mathematical theory of probability. The user typically chooses the variables and the structural form of the relationship and the computer then calculates the values of the parameters and the 'goodness of fit' of this model with the data.

Models based on the principles of probability theory are not necessarily symbolic mathematical models. It is possible to construct analogue models which use card shuffling, roulette or spinning wheels or other gadgets to simulate realisations of random events. For example, the progress of a cohort of life insurance policies could be modelled by using an appropriately designed spinning wheel to estimate how many claims are paid in each successive simulated year. This experiment could be repeated many times, each corresponding to a possible realisation of the actual experience of the cohort. These results could then be assembled and their distribution displayed using yet another analogue model, perhaps a graph, or set of graphs.

This process, known as Monte Carlo simulation, is obviously time-consuming, even though the simulation can be speeded up by computerisation.

As the technique is essentially analogue rather than symbolic, it is useful for modelling complex systems or subsystems for which analytical tools or statistical packages are unsuitable.

In recent years the term 'simulation model' has been extended to include not only Monte Carlo simulations but any kind of model which is used to simulate different hypothetical situations. This has led to the concept of deterministic simulations in which different outputs are obtained, from a deterministic model, corresponding to different sets of inputs known as scenarios.

4.2 CREATING A MODEL

It is often said that modelling is as much an art as a science. Like an artist, the modeller has to select those aspects of the real world he wishes to portray and use the materials and tools he has to hand that seem most appropriate. A model, however, is not a static work of art; it should be tested and testable according to the principles of scientific method and superseded or reshaped if found to be inadequate. In particular, the underlying assumptions must be explicitly stated so that users can assess the suitability of the model for their purposes.

If modelling is done internally, modellers and users should be able to collaborate closely. The process of constructing the model may also yield useful qualitative insights into the functioning of the system being modelled.

The process of building a computer-based model is one of deciding on a complete and consistent set of logical rules appropriate for the purpose for which the model is to be used. The process of using the model is one of selecting appropriate data to which the logic is to be applied. This is one of the great strengths of computer-based models, because once the program, or logic, has been stored in the computer, it can be used over and over again for as many different sets of data assumptions as are required.

There are many advantages in using a computer to create a model (such as the high calculation speed, and the facilities to handle large amounts of data and to obtain graphical and printed output). Paradoxically, this computing power may not always be conducive to good modelling. Managers may have to delegate most, if not all, of the model construction process to computer experts, with the consequent very real danger that the assumptions in the model may not be appropriate for the purpose for which the model is intended to be used. It is also possible for decision-makers to be overwhelmed with large amounts of computer output which is difficult to interpret and validate.

Microcomputer technology has enabled managers to construct their own simple models, using modelling packages specially designed for desk-top computers. This trend towards 'do-it-yourself' computer modelling should undoubtedly grow as microcomputers become cheaper and more powerful and as the training of managers expands to include some knowledge of this field.

Selection and simplification

Inherent in all model building are the processes of selecting variables and simplifying the relationships between them. These have the advantage of focusing the user's attention on the important issues, but they are also a source of potential problems: first because important variables may be omitted, and secondly because the process of simplification may give rise to hidden or unnecessary constraints which are not intrinsic to the system being modelled.

In iconic models the results of selection and simplification are usually obvious; for example, it is easy for the user of a road map to decide whether it is sufficiently detailed, accurate and comprehensive for his purpose. But the situation is more complicated in the case of symbolic models. At one extreme, computer-based models may contain hundreds of variables and equations, so that managers may have neither the time nor the technical expertise to evaluate them. At the other extreme, highly simplified models may disguise a whole host of implicit assumptions.

Top-down or bottom-up

This trade-off between complexity and ease of use is related to the degree of aggregation imposed on the model by the modeller, that is on whether the model is 'top-down' or 'bottom-up'. Computer-based simulation models tend to be bottom-up, where the system being modelled is broken down into many smaller subsystems each of which has its own submodel and associated assumptions. This process reduces the risks of omitting an important aspect, or of oversimplifying a crucial relationship. However the linking together of submodels may depend on untested and little understood relationships, and, even if the errors in each submodel are small, their combined total may be large.

Top-down models are based on selected aggregates and their interrelationships, which are often estimated using multivariable statistical techniques. The results may then be disaggregated down to the required detail within the same model, or used as inputs to other models. Many macroeconomic models used for forecasting key components of a country's economy are top-down ones. They depend heavily on economic theory and expert judgement for the selection of the variables in the model and the form of the estimated relationships.

Optimising or 'what if' models

When making decisions for the short term, particularly at the operational level, managers usually have a set of clear objectives and a limited choice of courses of action subject to various constraints. In this kind of situation, it may be possible to construct an optimising model, perhaps based on linear programming techniques, which will calculate numerical values of the controllable variables required to achieve the best possible outcome (an example of linear programming techniques applied to underwriting is provided by Bernard Benjamin in Chapter 8).

In the medium and long term, and particularly at the corporate planning level, it is rarely possible for management to formulate its objectives in precise mathematical terms – a necessary requirement for the construction of an optimising model. The balancing of different and sometimes conflicting aims is usually rather a complex and fluid process which depends on the current state of the organisation and the current and expected economic environment. For example, insurance companies have to weigh the probability of becoming insolvent against the desire for growth in competitive markets, along with a host of other objectives, some of which are in any case not expressible in quantitative terms. Furthermore, uncertainty about uncontrollable important economic variables increases rapidly with the distance of the planning horizon, making it even more difficult to estimate the parameters for the constraint equations in an optimising model.

This is where the 'what if?' simulation model is useful, both for understanding how the organisation or system works and for exploration of possible outcomes, rather than producing the best solution for a given problem. Its function has often been compared to that of a chessboard. First, the 'pieces' are set up in a certain configuration; this corresponds to specifying the initial (known) condition of the system being modelled. Secondly, instructions are provided to determine how each 'piece' moves in each future period. (In a Monte Carlo simulation some of these instructions will have a degree of uncertainty built into them.) Thirdly, the movement of the 'pieces' is then simulated for as many periods as are required – this is called a simulation run. If the simulated environment, or scenario, is changed after a run, this corresponds to a change in the 'shape' of the chessboard.

4.3 MODELS USED IN FORECASTING

Forecasts are essential inputs into any planning or decision-making process. Insurance companies, like all firms which produce goods or services, need sales forecasts (in the form of gross premium income) and estimates of costs (in the form of claims and expenses) in order to make pricing decisions. Insurers also need estimates of investment income. Short-term financing or investment decisions require cash-flow forecasts, while corporate planning requires forecasts of macroeconomic variables such as interest and inflation rates, and assessments of the development of new products.

Forecasting may be based purely on judgement. More often, forecasting methods are a combination of modelling and judgement; they differ according to the type of model used and the degree of importance attached to the modelling component. The majority of short- and medium-term forecasts are based on quantitative models which utilise the information contained in past observations of the system being modelled. These forecasts need to be updated at regular intervals and as new information becomes available. A medium-term forecast for the next two or three years is usually on a quarterly basis while a short-term forecast for the next few months may be on a weekly or monthly basis.

Long-term forecasts may be for any length of time, but in practice most are for up to five to ten years ahead. They are usually on a yearly basis and focus on overall trends and business cycles of several years' duration. They may attempt to predict the effects of future innovations and policy changes at the strategic level. In general, the further the time horizon, the less importance is attached to formal quantitative models, and judgement, combined with qualitative models, plays an increasingly important role. Some useful qualitative modelling frameworks have been developed; these include decision analysis techniques, and the Delphi method for systematically collating individual expert opinions.

All formal forecasting models are based on the assumption that at least some of the patterns of behaviour of a system will continue into the future. This is taken to its logical extreme in models which analyse historical values of the variable being forecast so as to discover underlying trends, cycles and systematic variations, and then project these into the future so that the forecast values are based solely on the behaviour of past values of the series. The best known technique for producing such forecasts uses the method of Box-Jenkins time-series analysis.

The other main method for forecasting uses curve-fitting techniques (usually least-squares or maximum likelihood) to estimate causal models. In such cases the variable to be forecast (the dependent variable) is related to other variables (so-called independent or explanatory variables) which are thought to cause or explain variations in the dependent variable. An appropriate mathematical form for this relationship is chosen, and then multiple regression techniques are used to estimate the value of the unknown parameters from past values of the dependent and independent variables. In the case of single-equation models, the independent variables have values determined outside the model (for example, by the economy) and it is therefore necessary to forecast these first, before predicted values for the dependent variable can be obtained from the model.

Such multiple regression models have been used to predict company sales by product classes. This is often done by a two-stage process; firstly industry-wide sales (for example, total life insurance premiums in a particular territory) are forecast, probably from a regression model including macroeconomic and demographic explanatory variables (for example, see Diacon (1988)). Secondly, sales by the company are forecast. This might be simply on the basis of a time-series which predicts the company's share of total sales or from a causal model which takes future company policy into account. A company's marketing policy may itself be based on the results of a regression model which predicts the sales revenue resulting from different amounts and allocations of resources such as advertising and salespersons.

Regression analysis is a useful and flexible tool which has perhaps not been exploited sufficiently by the insurance industry. The development of microcomputer-based statistical packages will help would-be modellers, but the construction of large econometric models is undoubtedly best left for the experts.

4.4 ASIR: A SIMULATION MODEL OF NON-LIFE INSURANCE AND REINSURANCE

This section describes a computer-based simulation model which was designed and constructed for the Geneva Association as part of its research programme on the use of simulation techniques in insurance.

Aims and concepts

The aim of the project was to construct a flexible 'what if?' financial modelling system which could be used to simulate the results of underwriting different lines of insurance in different territories from the point of view of an insurance company.

A good starting-point for modellers is to ascertain what output is required from a model. In the case of ASIR, potential users were envisaged as planners and managers in insurance companies, and researchers in university or government departments. These various groups would have a wide variety of topics to investigate, ranging from solvency regulations to cash-flow underwriting. The model therefore had to be capable of producing detailed revenue accounts and claims settlement analyses for individual risk classes as well as consolidated results for the company as a whole. A further requirement was that the model should be able to simulate reinsurance from both the cedant's and the reinsurer's point of view.

The model focuses on the money-flows depicted in Figure 4.1. The net result of all the flows occurring in a simulated year is summarised by changes in the balance sheet which represents the state of the company. To

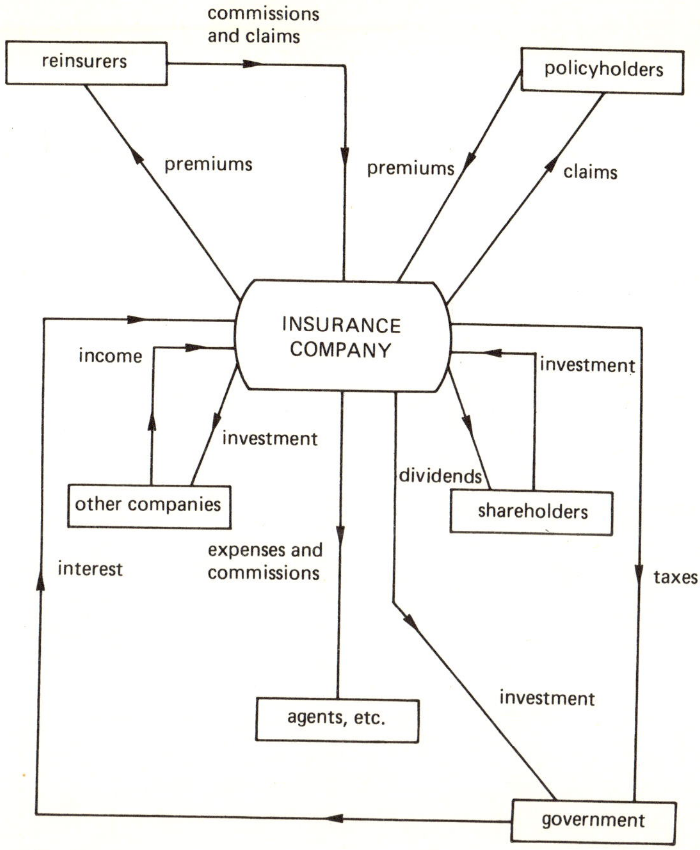

Figure 4.1 Conceptual model of a general insurance company: money–flows

set up a simulation, the user specifies the initial state of the company and the structure of its business. The logical structure within ASIR is shown schematically in Figure 4.2.

One of the main uses of a simulation model is to investigate the effects of different postulated future scenarios. This is sometimes called 'conditional forecasting'. In ASIR, a scenario has two aspects. First, there is the economic environment specified by the user for each simulated territory in which business is transacted. This includes interest and inflation rates and exchange rates. Second, there is the insurance market, which may be different for each simulated risk class. This is subsumed in specifications of premium rates and premium growth which reflect the user's estimates of the combined effects of market forces and company pricing policies.

The major logical assumptions in ASIR are the stability of claims distributions and claims settlement patterns. Risk classes are modelled in some detail, with the choice of either stochastic Monte Carlo or deterministic

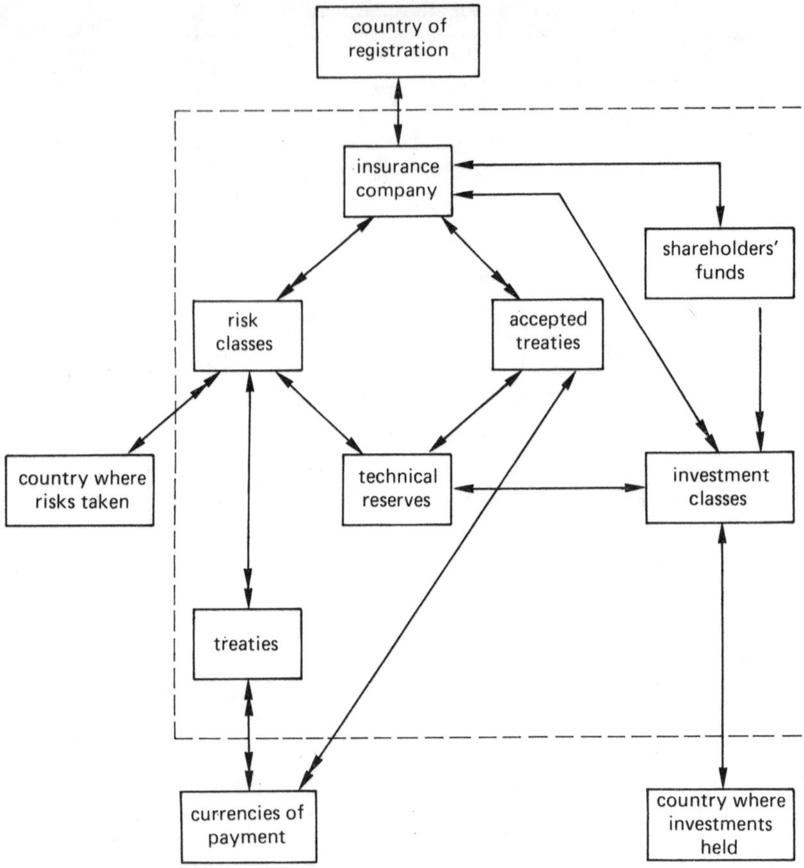

Figure 4.2 Logical structure of insurance company business within ASIR

submodels. Investments are treated aggregatively in a deterministic submodel and the results of investing and underwriting are combined in an accounting framework. ASIR, like most simulation models, requires a large number of data assumptions which have to be prepared and input by the user. The ASIR modelling system, which is implemented on a main frame computer, comprises five separate computer programs, three of which are designed to enable users to create their own data files, which are then input into one of the two simulation programs.

Using ASIR: an example

The ASIR model is described in more detail elsewhere (Brown and Galitz, 1981 and 1982; Brown, 1984). Here, we look at the results of some simulations, and how they were obtained.

Table 4.1 Premium distribution of UK business, 1982.

	%
Motor vehicle	38.3
Property	39.5
Liability	8.9
Accident and health	3.0
Pecuniary loss	8.1
Other	2.2

Source: Carter and Godden (1983).

Table 4.2 'Average' underwriting results for UK business, 1982

	Risk class 1 (motor vehicles)	*Risk class 2 (property)*	*Risk class 3 (composite)*
Claims ratio*	77.9	72.5	79.8
Expenses ratio	26.6	38.3	29.6
Unearned premium reserve	38.7	37.2	36.4
Outstanding claims reserve*	78.7	44.8	171.0
Premium growth over 1981	1.0	8.1	6.0
Proportion of premiums	38.3	39.5	22.2

* denotes a percentage of earned premiums. All other ratios are to written premiums.
Source: Carter and Godden (1983).

These simulations have deliberately been kept at a simple level and do not use the full capabilities of the ASIR system. They should, however, give some indication of how a simulation model can be used as an aid to decision-making in insurance (for a more detailed example, see Brown and Galitz, 1982).

The first set of simulations was created in 1984 to demonstrate how the domestic business of an 'average' insurance company could be simulated. Historic aggregated data was available, in the form of claims and expenses ratios, for five major classes of insurances. They are listed in Tables 4.1 and 4.2, which also give the 1982 premium distribution.

As a first approximation it was decided to simulate an insurance company operating in one territory with three risk classes, corresponding to motor, property, and a composite class comprising the remainder. If more detail was required at a later stage it would be easy to split this third class into two or more classes, using the facilities for editing data files which are included in the ASIR modelling package. Explicit modelling of reinsurance treaties was not included in the demonstration as the data were for premiums and claims net of reinsurance payments.

The bulk of the data assumptions comprised risk class parameters such

Table 4.3 Economic scenarios

	Optimistic	*Probable*	*Pessimistic*
Inflation	down to 3%	about 5%	up to 8–9%
Real growth of premiums	small, positive	zero	negative
Capital appreciation of investments	good	small	negative
Interest rates	down to 5–6%	around 7%	9–10%

as the average time between incurrence and settlement of claims. These were estimated from historical claims settlement analyses. Initial levels of premium rates, expenses and technical reserves were then estimated by extrapolating from the data in Table 4.2. Ratios are not used as direct inputs into ASIR; rather, standard ratios such as claims and expenses ratios are useful model outputs which give some measures of company performance.

The initial state of the simulated company was also based on data giving the distribution of invested assets of British insurance companies at the end of 1982 and on the average level of shareholder's funds (which was approximately 45 per cent of premiums). The minimum level required by EC solvency regulations is between 16 per cent and 18 per cent of premiums and one of the purposes of the demonstration was to investigate what might happen to the solvency margin of the simulated 'average' British insurer under three alternative scenarios (classified as 'optimistic', 'probable' and 'pessimistic') covering the next four years. These scenarios are summarised in Table 4.3 and correspond to the range of predictions which were actually issued by major forecasting institutions at the time.

Although preparing the data files for a set of simulations requires time and effort, running simulations and obtaining results is quick and easy. A number of stochastic runs was made for each scenario. The results obtained for the solvency ratios are shown in Figure 4.3. (A solvency ratio of less than one indicates that the solvency margin has fallen below the EC requirement.) Only four runs are plotted for each scenario, to avoid overcrowding on the graph, but it is clear, firstly, that the effects of the different scenarios are substantially greater than the effects of random variations within a scenario and, secondly, that the fictitious average company is likely to be in severe difficulties if the pessimistic scenario is realised in practice.

Further insight into the effects of the three scenarios is obtained by inspection of the results of the deterministic simulations summarised in Table 4.4. The main reason for the bad results of the pessimistic scenario is the rapidly increasing size of the losses on underwriting which are not compensated by a higher return on investments. In the optimistic scenario, underwriting losses decrease slightly over the four years because of the

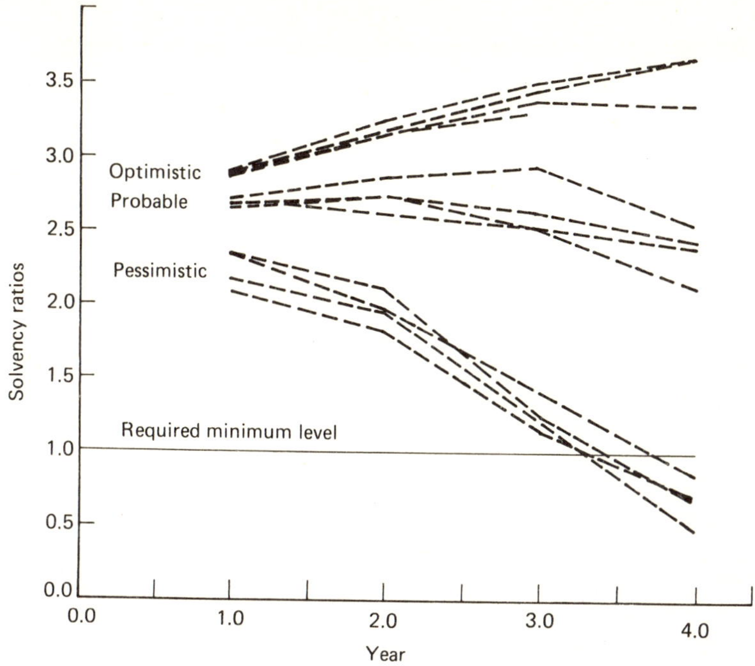

Figure 4.3 Results of sets of stochastic simulations

postulated decrease in inflation rates and the company makes positive total profits; the probable scenario shows a slow worsening trend in all the profits ratios.

An obvious implication of results such as these, for a real insurance company, is that managers need to look closely at the individual risk classes and increase premium rates in those classes which have the worst results. The detailed results produced by the ASIR model can aid in this. Alternatively, if it is thought that the insurance market will not support substantial premium increases, the amount of business underwritten may have to be curtailed in order to cut losses. The various possible options can be simulated easily and quickly using ASIR, making minor changes in the data assumptions.

Of course, decisions depend ultimately on the degree of confidence management have in their macroeconomic forecasts. For example, in early 1984, the pessimistic scenario was felt by some to be unlikely. Subsequently, the balance of opinion swung towards the pessimistic and probable rather than the optimistic scenario. There were also some dramatic changes in the British insurance industry at that time, particularly in the pricing of property insurance and the major insurance companies had announced massive increases in premium rates. Interest rates remained

Table 4.4 Results of deterministic simulations

Profits as % of premiums		*Pessimistic*	*Probable*	*Optimistic*
Underwriting profits	Year 1	−9.6	−8.3	−7.5
	2	−11.7	−8.9	−7.1
	3	−15.0	−9.7	−6.6
	4	−18.3	−10.6	−6.2
Investment income	Year 1	10.8	12.3	13.5
	2	10.7	11.7	12.4
	3	10.1	9.5	8.7
	4	9.9	9.2	8.3
Total profits before tax	Year 1	1.2	4.0	6.0
	2	−1.0	2.8	5.3
	3	−4.9	−0.2	2.1
	4	−8.5	−1.4	2.1

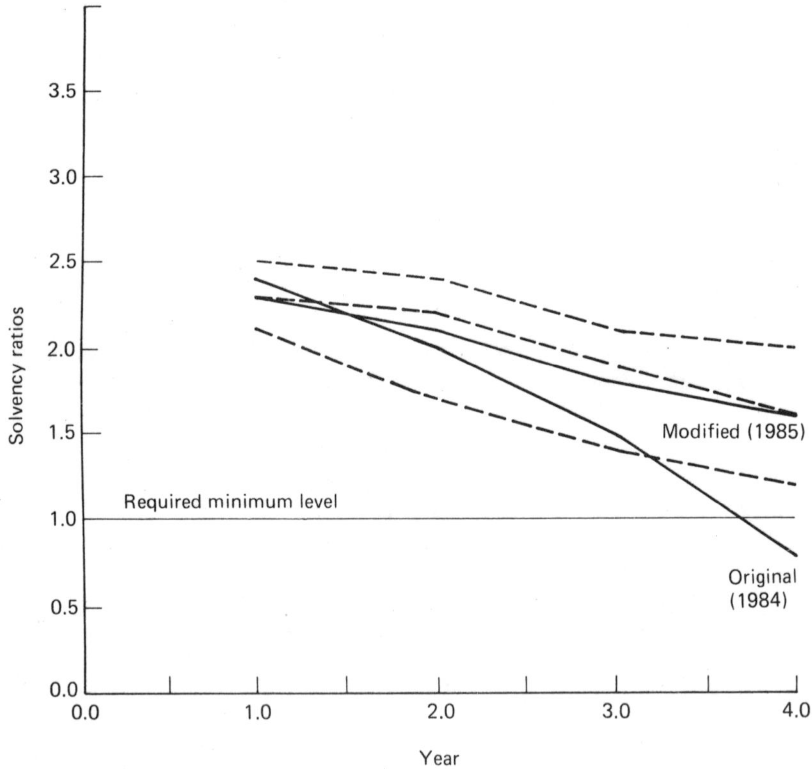

Figure 4.4 Modified pessimistic scenario results compared with the original deterministic results

Table 4.5 Deterministic results for the risk classes in the modified pessimistic scenario

	Loss ratio L %	*Expenses ratio* E %	*Investment ratio I* %	$L+E-I$
Motor Vehicle				
Year 1	78.9	26.4	7.3	98.0
2	80.7	26.7	7.6	99.8
3	81.9	26.5	7.4	101.0
4	84.0	27.0	8.1	102.9
Property				
Year 1	74.2	38.5	4.6	108.1
2	71.2	36.4	4.3	103.3
3	66.4	34.5	3.9	97.0
4	65.2	34.7	4.1	95.8
Composite				
Year 1	83.1	29.7	12.9	99.9
2	85.0	29.8	13.3	101.5
3	87.0	30.0	13.1	103.9
4	88.3	30.1	14.1	104.3

high and had turned out to be higher than expected. The pessimistic scenario simulation was therefore rerun for the 1985 situation, with this extra information incorporated into the data assumptions to see if the changes would be sufficient to alter the downward course predicted by the earlier set of simulations.

Solvency ratios from the modified set of simulations are shown in Figure 4.4, which also includes the deterministic results from the previous pessimistic simulations, for comparison. The new set of results suggested that the premium increases implemented by most British insurers had probably averted the danger of the 'average' domestic insurer becoming insolvent within the simulated time horizon (although the overall trend is still downwards).

It is also useful to look at the results from Figure 4.4 for each risk class separately (Table 4.5). The investment ratio is included as an estimate of the relative contribution of investment income generated by the technical reserves. The property class has a low investment ratio because claims are settled quickly on average and hence the ratio of technical reserves to premiums is low. The composite class, which includes liability classes, has a high investment ratio for the opposite reasons. Even taking this into account, however, it seems that the composite class needs further investigation, as its results in years 3 and 4 are worse than the other two classes. This is where further simulations need to be carried out with the composite class split into liability, pecuniary loss, and accident and health, so that the causes of the losses can be pinpointed.

All these results must of course be interpreted in the light of the confidence, if any, which can be attached to the assumptions which have been incorporated in the model. The value of a simulation model such as ASIR is that it enables these assumptions to be evaluated within a consistent accounting framework. Once the basic logical structure of a simulation model has been set up, it can be run hundreds of times with different assumptions, thus helping users to pinpoint the crucial ones. This method is called sensitivity analysis; it is a flexible and important method of combining the adaptive judgement of the user with the best efforts of the modeller.

4.5 SUMMARY

Modelling is a broad and fascinating topic and there will certainly be further developments in its applications to insurance management. Some important aspects have had to be omitted from this chapter, notably the question of cost. One reason for not attempting to assess the costs of different types of models is the volatility of the computer software market. The price of a computer-based modelling package is out of date almost before it has been put into print.

The major cost of a model, however, may well be the time spent by senior or middle management. This has to be balanced against the possible benefits of using a model. One of the aims of this chapter has been to try to show that there are intangible or qualitative benefits as well as possible tangible quantitative ones. Understanding how a model works is a valuable learning process in its own right. Some of the most successful applications of computer simulation models have in fact been in management training.

Another aspect which has only been touched upon is the need for accurate, complete and recent data if forecasting models are to make any significant contribution to the decision-making process. Financial institutions usually have enormous amounts of data stored on magnetic tapes and it is sometimes difficult to extract the required information in usable form. The implementation of modern database management techniques will help to tackle this problem, which requires close collaboration between modellers and data-processing departments. Some companies are adopting integrated decision support systems which link databases, forecasting and modelling packages with microcomputer terminals.

References

Brown, Z.M. (1984) 'A Guide to the ASIR Model', *Etudes et Dossiers*, no. 78, (Geneva: Geneva Association).

Brown, Z.M. and L. Galitz (1981) 'The ASIR System User's Manual', *Etudes et Dossiers*, no. 52 (Geneva: Geneva Association) November.
Brown, Z.M. and L. Galitz (1982) 'Inflation and Interest Rates: A Research Study Using the ASIR Model', *Geneva Papers*, vol. 7, no. 25, October, pp. 290–320.
Carter, R.L. and A.H. Godden (1983) *The British Insurance Industry: A Statistical Review* (Brentford, Middlesex: Kluwer Publishing Limited).
Diacon, S.R. (1988) 'Economic Forecasting in the UK Life Assurance Market', '*Journal of the Society of Fellows* (London: Chartered Insurance Institute) vol. 3, pt 1, July.

5 Modelling the Financial Strength of a Reinsurance Company

Stewart Coutts and Russell Devitt

5.1 INTRODUCTION

One of the more fruitful applications of computer simulation modelling is in the evaluation of the financial strength (or security) of insurance companies. The difficulty with conventional measures of solvency such as the solvency margin (as discussed in Section 18.5) is that they bear little relationship to the riskiness of the insurer's activities. The model presented in this chapter therefore looks at the effect of possible variations on each of the main elements of an insurance company's cash-flow (or emerging costs). An important feature of this technique is its stochastic nature: the effects of risk and uncertainty are built into the simulation, so that each time the model is 'run', slightly different answers are produced. By running the model a large number of times (normally many hundreds), the overall effect of the variation in each of the many components can be established. It is then possible to evaluate the strength and riskiness of the individual insurer or reinsurer which is being modelled. The model enables the user to quantify the probability that the assets will prove inadequate to meet the liabilities.

The advantage of the modelling approach is to state explicitly the assumptions which are being made and to enable management to explore some of the consequences of alternative strategies. The principal users of simulation models are likely to be an insurer's own management, modelling their own company experience. Insurance and reinsurance brokers and the supervisory authorities may also want to model 'outside' insurers; however there are then substantial difficulties in obtaining sufficient verifiable data. The basic assumptions of the model will also depend on who is modelling whom. For example, insurance management simulating their own company will probably do so on a 'going-concern' basis (that is, on the assumption that the company will continue in business). On the other hand, supervisors may be more interested in a 'run-off' basis (where the insurer is assumed to cease writing new business and existing liabilities are run off and assets sold) in order to determine whether the insurer can meet its existing commitments.

This chapter proceeds in five main sections. First, the general concepts of financial strength and solvency are discussed to contrast the differing views on how the overall health of a general insurance company can be assessed. Section 5.3 then goes on to explain in detail the various components of an insurer's cash-flow, since solvency is really concerned with whether the proceeds of the company's assets (both capital and income) will prove sufficient to meet the liabilities as they emerge. In Section 5.4, we describe how a computer simulation model can be utilised to project future cash-flows and hence analyse financial strength, and a simplified practical example is given in Section 5.5. Finally, some brief conclusions are presented in Section 5.6. Part of this chapter was published in *The Review* (United Trade Press Ltd) and appears with the permission of the publishers (see Coutts and Devitt, 1988).

5.2 FINANCIAL STRENGTH AND SOLVENCY

Introduction

In assessing the financial strength of a general insurance company, some assumptions must be made about the insurer's future operations, and then an appropriate method for determining strength and solvency needs to be selected. The overall objective is to assess whether or not the insurer will be able to meet the commitments it has insured. However the assessment depends on a range of assumptions and can only be stated with a degree of probability.

To a certain extent, it could be said that an insurer is solvent if the supervisory authorities say it is (and allow it to continue in business). Furthermore it has been argued by some (for example, Dickinson and Roberts, 1983; Finsinger and Pauly, 1983) that it is unnecessary for insurers to hold higher levels of capital than the statutory minimum, especially in view of the opportunity costs imposed on shareholders. However insurance brokers and policyholders place considerable importance on the financial strength of an insurer, and company management has the additional incentive of job security to consider.

Winding-up, run-off and going-concern bases

Daykin *et al.* (1987) note that there are three main approaches to the assessment of solvency in relation to the assumptions that need to be made about the insurer's future operations; these are termed 'winding-up', 'run-off', and 'going-concern' and are summarised in Table 5.1.

A winding-up basis values company strength on the assumption that it will cease trading almost immediately. In this case, the court would appoint

Table 5.1 Alternative assessment assumptions for company strength

	Going-concern	*Run-off*	*Winding-up*
In relation to:			
New business	Indefinite	None	None
Expenses	Claims settlement expenses only	All expenses of run-off	All expenses of winding-up
Assets	Market or book value	Market value	Realisation value
Liabilities	Best estimate	Cautious estimate	Best estimate of current value

Source: Daykin *et al*. (1987).

a liquidator to close down the company, sell off its assets as quickly as possible, and transfer its liabilities to another insurer in return for a 'premium' payment. The winding-up basis is rarely used for insurance companies since, in the event of company closure, a run-off of liabilities is generally preferable.

A run-off basis for assessing company strength is the one usually adopted by supervisory authorities. In this case, the insurer would cease to underwrite new business, and the company's assets would be used to meet outstanding liabilities as the resulting claims run off to extinction. The run-off (or 'break-up') basis assumes that the insurer should not be allowed to write new business unless it is solvent for existing business.

A going-concern basis of assessment assumes that the insurer will continue in business, and this is the conventional approach for accounts prepared for shareholders. Administration costs can therefore be spread over future business (instead of being deducted from the value of assets) and there is no need to value investments on the assumption that they will be sold at short notice.

The 'balance sheet' approach to solvency

There are a variety of possible methods for determining the financial strength and solvency of insurance companies. Kastelijn and Remmerswaal (1986) classify the various methods into three main groups: those based on ratios (termed the 'balance sheet' approach), those based on risk theory (which generally focuses on variations in the aggregate claim amount), and 'comprehensive' methods which consider both liabilities and investment yields on assets. The model discussed in sections 5.3 to 5.5 below comes in the 'comprehensive' category. A general feature of the comprehensive models is the use of computer simulation to emulate the random behaviour of many of the important variables affecting financial strength.

Table 5.2 Balance sheet of XYZ Insurance Co. Ltd

Assets	*£m*	*Liabilities*	*£m*
Investments (at market value)	15	Outstanding claims	13
Agents' balances	3	Unexpired risks	3
Cash and deposits	2	Asset margin	4
	20		20

The conventional method of assessing the financial strength of a general insurance company has been termed the 'balance sheet' approach, since it depends on the size of the margin of assets over liabilities as illustrated in Table 5.2. A minimum margin (expressed as a proportion of premium income) also forms the basis for the European Community solvency regulation (as described in section 17.3). Unfortunately the margin of assets over liabilities inherent in the balance sheet approach has no real meaning unless the level of adequacy of the technical provisions (or reserves) is defined and unless the assets can be relied upon to produce the values shown. Similarly, the margin would have to be viewed in the light of the variability of the insurer's assets and liabilities (as discussed in Daykin *et al.*, 1984) and not simply compared with the size of the company's premium income.

The shortcomings of the conventional balance sheet approach to solvency have been known for a long time. The difficulty, however, has been in overcoming them. The balance sheet approach, as shown in Table 5.2, raises several problems.

For liabilities, little information is given in relation to margins; it is not known how cautiously reserves have been estimated or what assumptions have been made in relation to inflation. We probably do not even know whether discounting has been employed and, if so, on what basis. Assets will probably have been included at market value but there must be some question about whether these values are realised when it comes to selling them. There is clearly room for error in the values attributed to both assets and liabilities. Since the solvency margin is the difference between these two figures, any errors in them are compounded. Reinsurance recoveries are included, but how secure are they? The solvency margin or asset margin is disclosed, but will it be adequate for business which the company writes in the future? Individual companies have quite different risk profiles and this is not apparent from conventional accounting statements.

The fundamental problem is that of uncertainty. First, there is variability in relation to claims. This can be classified into the run-off risk and the underwriting risk. The run-off risk is concerned with whether existing provisions are adequate. The underwriting risk is concerned with whether future business will be profitable.

In relation to assets there is uncertainty relating to investment income and realisable value. The risk in relation to investment income is whether in future the company will earn as much as it thinks on its invested assets. The realisable value risk relates to whether the company will obtain what it hopes for when assets are realised.

The balance sheet approach to financial strength is not designed to cope with uncertainty. For example, two general insurance companies may have identical balance sheets and premium income and thus show the same solvency margins. However the insurer whose outstanding claims represent liabilities on a US product liability account and whose assets are invested in the Unlisted Securities Market (USM) represents a very different risk from the insurer which underwrites a UK household property account and invests in government stocks and blue chip equities. We therefore reject the approach as being unsuitable for the assessment of the financial strength of a dynamic insurance company.

Further, in compiling the balance sheet of Table 5.2, the accountant's methodology requires him to insist on spurious precision. He wishes to capture both liabilities and assets in a single figure. This takes no account of the variable nature of these items. Assets and liabilities are stock variables; that is, they attempt to capture in one figure a stream of future cash-flows. This process is analogous to taking an average. While we learn something about the series of figures as a whole, this is at the cost of considerable loss of information. In assessing solvency and financial strength, the real concern is not with the stock variables that appear in the balance sheet but with the associated flows and their interrelationships.

This reasoning gives another definition of insolvency: it occurs when the assets run out before all the liabilities have been met. The conventional definition, which states that insolvency occurs when spuriously precise assets are less than spuriously precise liabilities, is not relevant. Rather we are concerned with cash-flows or emerging costs. The appropriate definition of insolvency is that it occurs when the cash-flows from assets are exhausted before all cash-flows from liabilities have been met. The problem now becomes one of looking at solvency and financial strength on a cash-flow basis.

5.3 MODELLING THE CASH-FLOWS OF A REINSURANCE COMPANY

Cash-flow or emerging costs

So long as there are sufficient assets available to enable all the outflows to be met as they arise, the company will be solvent whatever the balance sheet may show. Solvency can therefore be assessed if the projected future

Table 5.3 The emerging costs of a general insurance company

Inflows	Premium income
	Income from assets
	Reinsurance and other recoveries
Outflows	Claim payments
	Reinsurance premiums
	Expenses and commission
	Tax
	Dividends

outflows and inflows of cash (or 'emerging costs') are identified (as outlined in Table 5.3). Since future cash inflows and outflows are random in nature, it is not possible to assign them fixed values, and some idea is therefore required of the possible variation in the values that cash-flows can take.

A further possible inflow arises if the insurer can obtain additional capital from shareholders in order to prevent insolvency (described by Finsinger and Pauly, 1983, as a 'bailout'): this possibility is ignored in the following discussion.

For inflows of premium income, the future volumes and profitability need to be projected. In the case of assets, we need to estimate future yields and realisations. For reinsurance, the actual amounts recovered in the future must be estimated.

For outflows of claim payments, the future run-off patterns must be realised, and for reinsurance the future cost of protection must be estimated. We also need to know the size of future outgoings for expenses and commission, the company's obligations to the tax authorities, and the dividend payments to be made to shareholders. Having determined all this, a basis for projecting receipts and payments for future years gives a springboard for exploring the effects of uncertainty.

Uncertainties about future cash-flow

The uncertainties caused by variation in future cash-flows are shown in Table 5.4. For claims settled in each future year, there is uncertainty in two dimensions, one relating to amount and the other to time. Future inflation is an additional source of doubt, as is the profitability of future underwriting. The income which can be earned on invested assets in future, the value at which assets can be realised in the future, and the degree of confidence the company has in recovering from its reinsurers should also be taken into account.

Each type of uncertainty identified in Table 5.4 can be represented by a probability distribution to give a range of possibilities and an assessment of how likely each is to occur. This enables the company to simulate alternative sets of scenarios; it can then perform a large number of simulations

Table 5.4 Types of uncertainty about future cash-flows

Claim variability	Run-off risk
	Underwriting risk
Asset variability	Investment income
	Realisable value

and examine the likely pattern of development by following the interactions of the different variables.

Simulation provides a means to explore the effect of changes, examine different strategies, and look at the trade-off between risk and return. Some simulations will give rise to extreme realisations and this provides the opportunity to analyse the combination of circumstances that have led to these realisations and to learn from them. From this, it is possible to obtain a greater understanding of the dynamics of the insurance business concerned. The methodology forces the modeller to make explicit assumptions about the key variables, and the approach can provide some answers to questions such as:

- Is the asset margin adequate for the investment strategy to be followed?
- Is additional capital required for the preferred growth strategy?
- What are the risks involved in developing different types of business?
- Will the company get adequate return on capital invested?

Modelling the reinsurance process requires a number of assumptions to be made on the future volume and profitability of the business written by the reinsurance company; on the probability distribution by time and amount of future claim payments of the reinsurance company; on the structure of the reinsurer's existing asset portfolio; on the decision rules affecting the future strategy for reinvestment and disinvestment; and on future prices and yields on investment.

For direct business, the need to ensure homogeneity of data requires that the insurer's major lines of business are identified and looked at separately. Clearly such a distinction is also essential in the case of a reinsurer. Different currencies produce further complexity. There is also the additional complication introduced by the different types of contract: it is important to distinguish between proportional and non-proportional treaty business, stop loss treaties and facultative as opposed to treaty business, and business written under binding authority agreements may also need to be separately identified.

A specialist reinsurer may need to identify up to 10–15 major groupings that can reasonably be treated as homogeneous lines of business. Not all of the different currencies or types of contract will necessarily occur in each class of business but the number of different segments of business requiring to be analysed separately is still likely to be larger than for a direct insurer. Already it is clear that the process of analysis is of a higher degree of complexity for a reinsurer than for a direct writer.

Turning now to the various components of the emerging costs, the first concern is premium income. It has already been noted that assumptions are required about the future volume of premium income. We need to be able to model the inflow of this income and the period over which it is received (which is typically much longer for a reinsurer than for a direct company). Thus it is necessary to identify the expected payment pattern of the premiums and its variability so that these can be built into the model.

There are also features of the reinsurance contract which can have an impact upon the future inflows in respect of premiums. One example is profit commission: this can be regarded as a refund of premium which is conditional upon the performance of a treaty. For modelling purposes, we need to represent both the timing and the amount of the payment. While the timing may be certain, the amount is variable and the model therefore needs to be sophisticated enough to take account of this conditional decision process.

The uncertainty about future cash-flows in respect of a reinsurer's liabilities, both reported and unreported, exists in two dimensions. There is uncertainty about the amount of payment to be made and about the time at which that payment is made. The degree of uncertainty for either dimension may well be significantly different for individual lines of business.

A particular feature of reinsurance business is the length of the tail, that is, the time taken to run off liabilities. In many cases there will be lines of business with tails as long as 20 years. Furthermore projecting for long periods will lead to a significant increase in the degree of uncertainty.

Another factor which is relatively more important for reinsurers is their own reinsurance protection. Typically, the protection programmes which reinsurers have in place are very much more complicated than those of a direct insurer. As a result it is correspondingly more difficult to assess their impact. In the case of a direct insurer it is feasible to concentrate on modelling results at the net level. In practical terms, this option is not available when looking at the specialist reinsurer. Instead it is necessary to model the gross account first. Then the reinsurance programme must be analysed and modelled separately. Only then can the results of these two exercises be brought together in order to derive the results at the net level. This separation into the two elements of the gross account and the net account is the key to understanding the impact that the reinsurance programme has on the financial strength of the reinsurer.

Inflation and currency fluctuations can also influence the results and financial strength of a reinsurance company. The difficulty here is that both have an impact on the various components of the insurance process in different ways. This creates problems for the reinsurer, by virtue of the fact that these differences are magnified because it is one step further away from the direct insurance contract. Furthermore the paucity of data available to the reinsurer makes it that much more difficult to assess the potential impact.

A further aspect which is peculiar to reinsurance business is catastrophe cover. In this case it is not sufficient, for example, to assume that expected loss ratios can be based on the average of the past five years, because the very nature of the business is concerned with peaks and troughs in loss ratios. The answer may be to build onto the modelling process the assumption that in any period of five years there are likely to be, for example, two bad and three good years. Without an approach such as this it is not possible to assess the potential effects on cash-flow.

The emerging costs approach also requires assumptions to be made in relation to assets. First there is the opening asset portfolio: this will need to distinguish between fixed-interest securities and equity-type investments. For fixed-interest securities, details will be required of the nominal amount held, the coupon rate, and maturity dates if any. For equity-type investments, details will be required of market values at the valuation date, together with current yields and rate dividend.

A set of decision rules defining the reinsurance company's future strategy for reinvestment and disinvestment is also required. These could be relatively straightforward, for example buying or selling in proportion to current market values, or aiming to maintain the initial asset mix. More complex strategies could involve reference to the relationship between liabilities and shareholders' funds or relating the strategy to the performance of the different type of assets. More than one set of decision rules may be identified in order to test the sensitivity of the model to different investment strategies.

Assumptions relating to the models for predicting the income and capital values of the assets are also required. For equity-type investments we require future prices, dividends and yield. For fixed-interest securities the model must enable us to predict the selling price where the security has to be sold before maturity.

5.4 KEY STAGES IN THE MODELLING PROCESS

In any type of modelling there is an inherent conflict. On the one hand there must be a sufficient degree of complexity to ensure that the model gives a reasonable representation of reality. On the other there must be a limit to the complications if the results are to be capable of any meaningful interpretation. A trade-off is therefore required and the right balance will vary from one case to another.

The emerging costs approach requires that the assumptions and models which have been described in the preceding section are combined so that the interaction of cash inflows and outflows can be observed and analysed. The key assumptions which distinguish the reinsurer are those relating to homogeneous groups of business and the ability to model both the gross and net account. The process of observation and analysis can be based on a series of twelve main stages.

Stage 1 Determine the cash inflows for the year in respect of premiums for each line of business. This will relate both to business on the books and to new business and will involve modelling payment patterns which make due allowance for variability and the impact of such factors as profit commission, portfolio transfers, reinstatement premiums and burning costs.

Stage 2 For each line of business generate total gross claim payments for the year, using the assumed probability distribution by time and amount for losses for that line of business.

Stage 3 Determine the aggregate cash flows in respect of the reinsurer's own reinsurance programme, making due allowance for bad debts.

Stage 4 Generate cash inflows in respect of investment income by applying the models of investment yields to the assumed opening asset portfolio.

Stage 5 Aggregate the results of Stages 1 to 4 and determine whether cash-flow for the year is positive or negative.

Stage 6 If cash-flow is positive, the assumed reinvestment strategy is applied. This will lead to a new set of assets at the end of the year. Pass to Stage 10.

Stage 7 If cash-flow is negative determine whether there are assets of sufficient value remaining to meet the payments. If there are, go to Stage 8. If there are not, go to Stage 9.

Stage 8 Apply the assumed disinvestment strategy to arrive at a new set of assets at the end of year. Pass to Stage 10.

Stage 9 Assume sufficient cash is borrowed at some appropriate rate of interest to cover payments for the year.

Stage 10 Determine whether further claims payments are to be made. If yes, return to Stage 1 and repeat for further year. If no, pass to Stage 11.

Stage 11 Record the value of the remaining assets. This can be positive or negative.

Stage 12 Repeat process 1000 times (say) from the start, to build up a distribution of possible values of the strength of the company.

The value of the remaining assets of the company (which is the main output

Table 5.5 The balance sheet for a reinsurance company (£m)

Investments		
Equities	3.00	
Bonds	25.00	
		28.00
Current assets		
Outstanding premiums		2.00
		30.00
Less liabilities		
Outstanding claims		26.88
Solvency margin		3.12

of this process) can be regarded as a measure of the company's financial strength. If it is negative, the company is insolvent. If it is positive, then the greater it is the greater the company's financial strength. The distribution of the possible values of the strength of the company gives an indication of the risk of insolvency. The proportion of cases where assets prove insufficient enables an estimate to be made of the probability of ruin.

5.5 A PRACTICAL EXAMPLE OF SOLVENCY ASSESSMENT

In order to illustrate how the emerging costs approach can be applied in practice to a reinsurance company to assess financial strength on a run-off basis, we need to start with the reinsurer's balance sheet (Table 5.5). We assume that outstanding premiums are reasonable in the following year. Outstanding claims after allowing for reinsurance recoveries will be paid in accordance with the payment pattern shown in Table 5.6.

Written premiums for the following year are expected to be £20m (£15m property and the balance casualty). This level of business is assumed to be constant for two years, after which no more business is written. We expect to receive 50 per cent of the premium in the accounting year in which the business is written, 40 per cent the following year and the remaining 10 per cent in year after.

Total reinsurance premiums payable for any accounting year will be 60 per cent of premiums written for property and 20 per cent of premiums written for casualty. We assume that these are paid, in the year following that in which the business is written.

Turning to claims, the underlying assumption is that the claims incurred for each underwriting year will, in the long run, average 100 per cent of premiums (net of commission) for property and 110 per cent for casualty. However the model introduces random variation in such a way that the actual claim rates will vary around the assumed long-term average.

Table 5.6 The run-off of outstanding claims of £26.88m

Year	*£m*	*Year*	*£m*
1	8.37	9	0.85
2	5.19	10	0.65
3	3.67	11	0.45
4	2.02	12	0.25
5	1.72	13	0.10
6	1.22	14	0.05
7	1.25	15	0.05
8	1.05	16	(0.01)

(Brackets denote a negative figure)

Table 5.7 The claim settlement pattern (%)

Year	*1*	*2*	*3*	*4*	*5*	*6*	*7*	*8*	*9*	*10*	*11*	*12*	*13*	*14*	*15*
Property	15	35	25	15	5	5									
Casualty	1	4	10	25	10	5	5	5	5	5	5	5	5	3	2

Table 5.8 The reinsurance recovery pattern (%)

Year	*1*	*2*	*3*	*4*	*5*	*6*	*7*	*8*	*9*	*10*	*11*	*12*	*13*	*14*	*15*	*16*
Property	7.5	25	30	20	10	5	2.5									
Casualty	0	1	4	10	25	10	5	5	5	5	5	5	5	5	5	2

The claim settlement patterns are expected to be those shown in Table 5.7. Also in the long run we assume that the reinsurance claims recoverable will be equal to the reinsurance claims paid. Again, however, the variation which the model introduces means that this is not necessarily true for any one particular year. The recovery patterns are expected to be as shown in Table 5.8.

The variability inherent in the asset portfolio of a company depends on the nature and distribution of the assets, and the realisable value of many assets will vary from day to day as market conditions change. Following the distribution of assets suggested in Daykin *et al.* (1987), we assume that the reinsurer holds cash, medium-dated Government securities and ordinary shares. The development of the various components of the asset distribution is represented by a series of random processes which generate future scenarios for the values of different types of asset, the income from them, and the corresponding rate of inflation. These time-series processes were developed by Wilkie (1986) from detailed observations on the behaviour

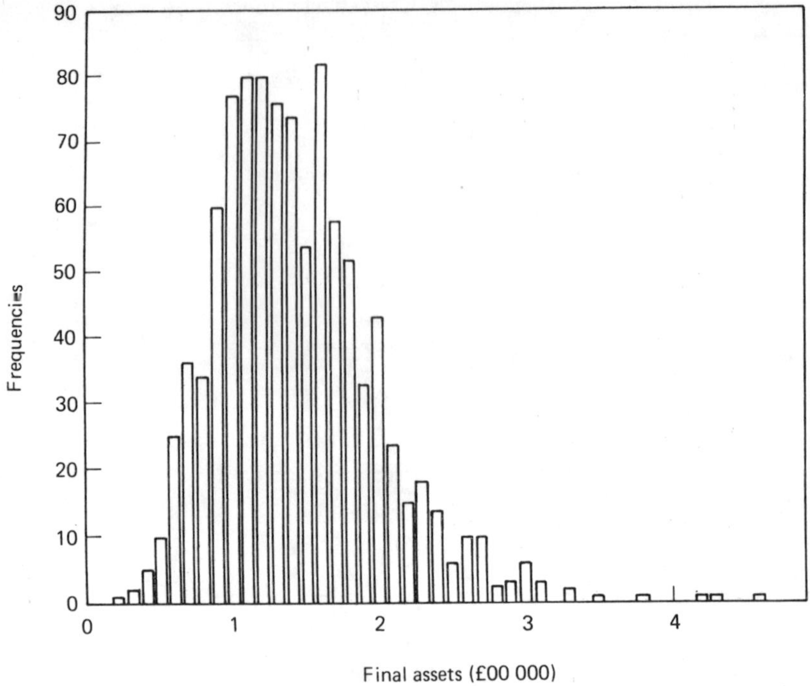

Source: Simulation model results.
Figure 5.1 Final assets after 15 years (in £00 000)

of inflation, interest rates, share dividends and asset yields over a period of 65 years from 1919 onwards.

We can now apply the stages involved in modelling the reinsurance process (as described in the previous section). For each simulation this will generate cash inflows and cash outflows, reinvestment and disinvestment as appropriate, until the liabilities are run off. Each situation will be different, because of the effects of the process of variation at work in the model.

As the previous section indicates, the process is repeated 1000 times from start to finish. This enables us to build up the frequency distribution of the possible values of the strength of the company in terms of the value of assets remaining at the end of the fifteenth year. This is illustrated in Figure 5.1. The histogram enables judgements to be made about the reinsurer's capital strength. The mean or expected value of the remaining assets is a measure of the company's solvency. Broadly, the higher it is, the stronger is the company. The proportion of cases where the remaining assets are negative gives us an indication of the probability of insolvency. The dispersion of the residual values provides a measure of how risky a company is: the wider the range, the greater the degree of risk.

One of the merits of a modelling approach is that it enables alternative scenarios to be explored. Assumptions can therefore be varied and the impact of the alterations assessed on the expected value of the residual assets, the proportion of negative outcomes and the dispersion of the outcomes.

5.6 CONCLUSIONS

The use of the emerging cost approach, in conjunction with a stochastic computer simulation model, has a number of advantages in assessing the financial strength of a direct or reinsurance company. As described in Daykin *et al.* (1987) the technique is very versatile and has great potential for further work in a variety of areas.

The main advantages of the technique can be listed as follows:

(a) It places an obligation on the management to make explicit assumptions about key financial variables.
(b) It gives management a better grasp of the essential financial dynamics of their business.
(c) It provides a method of looking at capital strength, not only in terms of expected results but also in terms of probability.
(d) It lets the sensitivity of financial results to various parameters be assessed.
(e) It facilitates meaningful investigation into such issues as changes in business mix, different reinsurance protection arrangements and different investment strategies.
(f) It enables management to investigate different growth strategies and their associated capital requirements.
(g) It allows management to investigate in advance fluctuations in the market, so that an assessment of the impact can be made.
(h) It permits the effect of investment income on profitability to be appreciated.

References

Coutts, S.M. and E.R.F. Devitt (1988) 'When In Doubt', *The Review*, United Trade Press Ltd, April, pp. 10–12; May, pp. 16–17.

Daykin, C.D., E.R.F. Devitt, M.R. Khan and J.P. McCaughan (1984) 'The Solvency of General Insurance Companies', *Journal of the Institute of Actuaries*, vol. 111, pp. 279–336.

Daykin, C.D., G.D. Bernstein, S.M. Coutts, E.R.F. Devitt, G.B. Hey, D.I.W. Reynolds and P.D. Smith (1987) 'Assessing the Solvency and Financial Strength of a General Insurance Company', *Journal of the Institute of Actuaries*, vol. 114, pp. 227–325.

Dickinson, G.M. and L.A. Roberts (1983) 'Determining an Appropriate Level of Capital for a Non-Life Insurance Company: Some Theoretical and Practical Issues in the UK', *Etudes et Dossiers* (Geneva: Geneva Association) no. 64, pp. 53–83.

Finsinger, J. and M. Pauly (1983) 'Reserve Levels and Reserve Requirements for Profit Maximising Insurance Firms', in M. Beckman and W. Krelle (eds), *Lecture Notes in Economics and Mathematical Systems* (Ulm: Springer Verlag).

Kastelijn, W.M. and J.C.M. Remmerswaal (1986) *Solvency*, Surveys of Actuarial Studies No. 3, Nationale – Nederlanden N.V., May.

Wilkie, A.D. (1986) 'A Stochastic Investment Model for Actuarial Use', *Transactions of the Faculty of Actuaries*, vol. 39.

6 Insurance Company Organisation and Management Structure

Hans van Gelder

6.1 INTRODUCTION

There are over thirteen and half thousand insurance companies operating throughout the world and, although some insurance companies operate only locally, others – particularly those with head offices in the USA and the European Community – spread their activities around the globe. Although the situation varies between regions, on a worldwide basis one-quarter of all insurers are life companies, two-thirds are non-life or general insurers, and something less than 10 per cent are composites operating in both fields.

There is much diversity among insurers with respect to their general economic and market conditions, portfolios, reinsurance contracts, products, technology employed, labour relations, staff skills and cost structures, and the fiscal climate and degree of supervision. Insurers vary particularly in their product range: some are primary or direct insurers and reinsurers, undertaking single-line or multiple-line business. Some insurers cater predominantly to the needs of private consumers, and others direct their attention to industry and commerce, or specifically to agriculture. Some specialise in particular market segments, others are more generalised.

Insurers also vary in their structure: some are set up as mutuals or co-operatives while others are private firms, or limited liability companies, and others are wholly or partially state-owned.

There are also substantial variations in the legal system under which insurers operate. In all countries there is at least some form of governmental supervision, but, as described in Chapter 17, the control differs widely in form and substance. The extent to which insurers may form agreements, tariffs or cartels to control the market also depends on any anti-trust legislation in force.

The objective of this chapter is to discuss the organisational design and managerial control that apply to most insurance companies. The following sections consider first the need for organisations and the factors to take into account in their design and operation, and then go on to examine the special characteristics of the organisation and structure of insurance companies.

6.2 ORGANISATIONS

The pursuit of any objective which requires the execution of tasks that can only be realised through the joint effort of two or more individuals calls for organisation. Organisations are goal-oriented relationships between individuals who, having some objectives in common, form coalitions to further their common as well as private interests. A critical condition is that a complex task can be subdivided into simpler components by the division of labour, that is the appropriate selection of sub-task allocation and the proper co-ordination of activities required. The complete and complex task can then be satisfactorily performed in an acceptable time and at acceptable cost.

Decision-making within an organisation involves the acquisition and allocation of resources in order to produce goods and services at such quality and cost that the organisational goals can be realised. Appropriate organisation is a prerequisite for the successful execution of this process.

Any organisation exists in a precarious and fundamentally unstable equilibrium between the requirements and demands made by its environment and its own ability to fulfil them. An organisation therefore needs to be an open system – a 'living thing' – that adapts and changes with its environment and the changing nature of the threats and opportunities it encounters in that environment. If that environment is stable, then reactive and relatively slow adaptive behaviour by the organisation may be all that is required, but a dynamic and unstable environment necessitates proactive and flexible behaviour, which may be focused by strategic management and the formation of corporate plans (see Chapter 1).

6.3 CONSIDERATIONS FOR ORGANISATIONAL DESIGN

Organisational design is concerned with the creation of relationships and communication patterns among the individual participants and groups of participants (sub-units). This involves the division of labour, the allocation of work, and the co-ordination and control of the subsequent tasks and work activities. The design of a structure to attain the organisation's goals thus involves the solution to two problems: how to perform the division of labour and how to co-ordinate the subsequent tasks.

Division of labour within the organisation is undertaken in two main ways: horizontal specialisation involves division of operational activities by area of knowledge or skill or by market segment, geographical area or product; differentiation of managerial activities such as planning, programming, research and development or marketing leads to vertical specialisation, which is necessary for the co-ordination and control of tasks differentiated under horizontal specialisation.

The organisational structure comprises an allocation of work rules and administrative mechanisms to create a pattern of interrelated work activities which allows the organisation to conduct and control those activities. It is not only a hierarchical allocation of authorities and responsibilities, but encompasses all the managerial and logistic processes that concur in the achievement of the organisation's objectives.

The resulting organisation is an integrated system of logistic (productive and distributive) and management support systems: the organisational structure, the information, and communication and control (evaluation, motivation and reward) systems. The set of work activities to be performed in an organisation is not always specified in advance, except in a most general way. Indeed one of the most important processes in any organisation is the elaboration of the activities and the determination of precisely which activities are going to be performed – when, where, how, and by whom.

Activities within any organisation are of three main types:

(a) *Routine*, where standard procedures of a highly repetitive and routine nature are involved. However the execution and performance of routine activities may still be conditional upon external stimuli involving new information, changed instructions, the progress of time and so on. Once such a stimulus has been recognised it will start the execution of an appropriate course of action, such actions becoming standard if that same stimulus recurs regularly.
(b) *Adaptive*, that is the development of programmes for new activities requiring a standard procedure for day-to-day operation, and the revision of existing procedures. The standardisation of procedures reduces uncertainty, lowers costs, and improves reaction time, predictability, control and productivity. Standard procedures are the organisation's memory.
(c) *Innovative*, involving the search for and selection of new activities to be added to or to replace old activities in order to exploit opportunities and counter threats arising in the environment.

All three types of activities within an organisation are concerned to some extent with decisions. Programmed decision-making deals with the well known, well structured, familiar and highly routine problems, while non-programmed decision-making is concerned with problems which are new, unfamiliar, ill-structured and often important for the future of the organisation. Programmed decisions can usually be made by issuing a set of detailed instructions which specify precisely how the decision should be made. This is impossible for non-programmed decisions because these pertain to new and unknown problems, which are ill-structured and ill-understood.

Decision-making within organisations is not only an extremely important activity but generally a problematic one as well. Information on the set of available alternatives and their chances of occurring is often non-existent or at least hard to come by, and by no means free of cost. Furthermore limited human conceptual and computational capabilities lead to decisions on the basis of extremely simplified models of the world. However the process of decision-making can be rationalised and improved upon through appropriate organisational procedures and the application of relevant technology.

6.4 A FRAMEWORK FOR ORGANISATIONAL CONTROL

The increased size and complexity of industrial, commercial and service organisations has led to the need for greater control. Some control by top management is necessary to ensure that subordinates adhere to policies and translate corporate strategies into action for their own units. Control is also required to co-ordinate the efforts of units so that the joint result is optimal for the larger organisation, and so that units do not take actions that oppose the wishes of top management or transgress their brief, but carry out their tasks in accordance with plans, budgets and schedules. The complex structure and diversified nature of activities and relationships within an organisation require a framework for control. This framework is embedded in the four levels of organisational hierarchy: operational, supervisory, managerial and strategic.

Directly productive processes are at the lowest level of the organisation. At this first operational level, final physical tasks such as claims payment, underwriting and investment are performed, and the organisation's objectives are thereby achieved. In many operational functions, especially those routine ones, workers will have internalised the process of control to such an extent that they perform it almost unconsciously.

The second, supervisory, level of hierarchy controls the activities of workers at the operational level. Decisions are made on the direct supervision, co-ordination and execution of the actual logistic processes. Supervisory staff schedule tasks, personnel, raw materials and components, and assess the machines and tools required. Supervisors should check on completion times, quality of output and the compliance with instructions and procedures; they should also handle contingencies and report on task execution against plan.

At the third, managerial, level, decisions are taken to create the framework within which the former levels of management decision-making operate. Management control is the process of ensuring that resources are obtained and used effectively in the pursuit of organisational objectives. Thus managers should survey the organisation's markets, design its products, services and productive, distributive and administrative systems, and set standards for the performance of such systems. After the performance of lower-level processes has been observed and evaluated, results are fed back into the procedure of goal selection, planning, budgeting and programming to revise the framework within which the lower levels operate. The same information is also reported to higher levels, but generally with different frequencies and levels of aggregation. Horizontal specialisation among management has led to specialised managerial groups that either control one or more not too dissimilar departments at the operational level (line managers), or that have a functional relationship with those departments in which they control a set of similar functional aspects (functional or staff managers).

At the managerial level objectives, policies, guidelines and plans made at the strategic level are translated into goals and targets, plans and budgets suitable for action, implemented and communicated to the operational control level. It is at the fourth, strategic, level that strategy is given form, substance and direction. Strategic management is, or should be, pro-active and outward-oriented and should monitor the environment to detect trends and structural changes, and to spot emerging threats and opportunities.

Each of the levels within an organisation sets objectives, goals, targets and constraints for the layer below. If this is done in an integrated, systematic and rational way, a framework for management and control is provided that enables sub-units within each level to be fully aware of the global strategies and policies for the organisation as a whole. Any problems with communication and co-ordination are also reduced.

Although routine, adaptive and innovative activities are undertaken at all hierarchical levels, the routine activities will tend to dominate at lower levels, while adaptive activities involving the design of systems and procedures will become more important higher up. At the strategic level in the organisation the search for new activities, directions and technologies, which necessitates non-programmed decisions, will require most attention.

6.5 UNCERTAINTY IN ORGANISATIONAL CONTROL

If a task, at whatever level in the organisation, is well understood prior to execution, it can be planned and scheduled in advance. If it is not, then during the actual execution more knowledge may be acquired, leading to changes in resource allocation, schedules and priorities. Uncertainty arises because of a difference between the information required to perform a task and the amount already available. The uncertainty in task performance is a function of:

- the diversity of outputs, products, services, programmes, clients or markets;
- the number of different and specialised inputs utilised;
- the level of goal difficulty or performance required as measured by some efficiency criteria;
- the extent to which these factors may change unexpectedly.

As uncertainty with respect to task execution increases, so does the need for information processing.

The handling of uncertainty in organisations is generally made operational through uncertainty absorption; it takes place when inferences are drawn from a body of evidence and the inferences rather than the evidence itself are communicated and acted upon. Uncertainty absorption replaces uncertainty with certainty equivalents or expectations of performance in the form of standards, procedures, goals, markets, forecasts, budgets, plans and schedules. These are formulated by the organisation's dominating coalition of participants, and are based on the organisation's past goals and objectives, past performance and experience, and the performance of comparable organisations.

A stable and homogeneous environment leads to stable expectations and to well established standards, goals and objectives, and efficient procedures; but a changing environment, and hence uncertainty, poses problems for the appropriate design of the organisation.

6.6 DESIGN STRATEGIES

The design of any organisation is a compromise. Design management has to make trade-offs between present and future requirements, stability and flexibility, efficiency and effectiveness, and task and people. Within an organisation, communication, co-ordination, integration and control are effected by the design strategies adopted. In the first place, design depends on the goals to be established, and the rules, programmes, procedures and hierarchy necessary for their attainment. Other strategies may then be adopted which reduce the level of information that goal-setting procedures require.

Not all design strategies will be cost-effective. The creation of slack resources or self-contained tasks, for example, reduces the need for information processing; but slack resources impair the level of performance by consuming more inputs, while self-contained tasks reduce the specialised skills employed. Investment in improved information systems and the creation of lateral relations increase the capacity for information processing, but the cost of information processing is then increased by the employment of additional employees and equipment.

Goals, rules, procedures and hierarchy

Rules, programmes and procedures form the organisation's 'memory'. They are important co-ordinating and integrating mechanisms that operate well under low to moderate degrees of uncertainty. Many are parameter-controlled and their execution is contingent upon and evoked by external stimuli. In the short run the organisation adapts the parameter values through feedback mechanisms, but in the longer run the structure of the rules, as well as their parameters, is changed. As the organisation encounters new situations it has no ready-made response, and one must be developed which takes into account all the sub-tasks that are affected. This task is handled by managerial positions, arranged in a hierarchy. Hierarchy is employed in addition to rules, programmes and procedures to guarantee an integrated and co-ordinated organisational response.

Goals and targets set a framework within which lower-echelon units can make their own decisions at the points of action where the information originates. This increases the effectiveness and efficiency of decision-making, while ensuring some unity of action. The goal- and target-setting activities take place at various levels in the hierarchy. Managers translate the goals and targets which have been formulated at a higher level into goals and targets for their particular sub-units.

A necessary complement to goal-setting and increased discretion at local sub-task level is the selection of responsible workers. These should have the appropriate skills and attitudes to work more or less independently. Their actions are co-ordinated and constrained by the framework of goals and targets, rather than by explicitly formulated rules, programmes and procedures or by direct intervention and control from the hierarchy.

The violation of planned targets usually requires additional decision-making and hence additional information processing. Exceptions are raised through the hierarchy for resolution, to the first level at which a shared superior exists for all affected sub-units. A decision is then made, and new targets are communicated to the sub-units. In this manner the behaviour of the interdependent sub-units remains integrated. The ability of an organisation successfully to co-ordinate its activities by goal-setting, rules, programmes, procedures and hierarchy depends on the frequency and the nature of violations and the capacity of the hierarchy to handle them.

Slack resources

An organisation can reduce the number of exceptions that have to be referred upwards in the hierarchy by simply reducing the level of required performance. The ratio of inputs to outputs is increased, and relatively more resources are consumed, thus reducing the level of goal difficulty.

These additional resources are called 'slack resources'. Only the intentional creation of slack resources forms a design strategy; in all other cases it is a matter of inefficiency. Reducing the number of exceptions reduces the information-processing load put upon the hierarchy.

Decentralisation of self-contained tasks

Another strategy which reduces the amount of information processed is to adopt a task design requiring less communication and information processing. This often implies a change from a functional task design to one in which each decentralised department has direct control over all the resources it needs to perform its task. Departments or divisions can be created around product lines, geographical areas, projects, markets and so on, each of which contain all or most of the input resources necessary for the task.

Imposed information systems

Organisations can invest in systems which enable them to process more information faster and with higher quality without overloading the communication channels. Improved systems bring information from where it originates to functions higher up in the hierarchy where the decisions are made. Better information processing can lead to improved understanding of problems. Learning is then improved and uncertainty reduced, so that rules, programmes and procedures can be revised and updated. Information-processing capacities can be upgraded by investment in computers, in various man–machine combinations, models, software, and skilled and knowledgeable personnel.

Lateral relations

The employment of lateral decision processes which cut across departmental lines of authority moves the decision-making down to where the information originates rather than bringing the information up to points of decision higher in the hierarchy. Decision-making is then decentralised without creating self-contained groups. In many successful organisations lateral functions which liaise between units have been organised on an *ad hoc* basis to solve problems in the organisation or to initiate new developments.

6.7 DETERMINANTS OF ORGANISATIONAL DESIGN

Organisations are open systems: they communicate with the environment and are affected by it. Thus the behaviour of organisations, and therefore their design, is largely determined by their setting: the environment in which they operate, the technology they employ, their age and size, and the distribution of power.

The operating environment

Operating environments which are simple, stable and homogeneous involve only a low degree of uncertainty. Standardisation of responses to routine stimuli can then be easily effected and there is little need for additional organisational learning. Plans can be drawn up well in advance of task execution, which can be controlled by detailed schedules. There is no need for decentralisation or delegation of authority and there is no need for a sizeable advisory or support staff.

However in complex, dynamic and heterogeneous environments uncertainty increases to extremely high levels. Planning schedules become extraordinarily difficult to draw up and soon become obsolete. The required degree of differentiation among those units that have contacts with the environment is very great and they then become difficult to integrate and control. Information-processing requirements increase enormously; lateral liaison devices have problems in co-ordination and only deliberate policies of decentralisation and creation of organisational slack can bring about a solution. On the other hand, hostile environments may lead to defensive actions whereby organisations centralise their structures temporarily.

Technology

Simple technical systems require no support staff to maintain and run them. Highly complex and sophisticated systems are more difficult to comprehend, require a more elaborate administrative structure and a larger, more professional and specialised support staff.

Powerful groupings of advisory and support staff lead to greater selective horizontal decentralisation of technical decisions (taken for example by a special data-processing department). This requires more integration, information-processing and liaison functions. A very high degree of automation embeds rules, procedures and standards into the machine.

Organisation age and size

Older, larger organisations tend to be more formalistic in their behaviour. The bigger the organisation, the larger the average size of its sub-units and the more elaborate its structure and procedures.

Control requirements

Power factors play a selective role in design. Control of the organisations is loose if the performance of sub-units is considered satisfactory. But stricter control is necessary if change is called for in the lower levels of the organisation. External control tends to formalise structures and leads to centralised bureaucracy.

6.8 THE NATURE OF INSURANCE SERVICES

The primary function of any insurance company is to provide its customers with information services. Taking out adequate insurance cover eliminates or reduces the insured's risk and uncertainty. Claim payments by the insurer will compensate – at least partially – for unexpected losses and expenses. This implies that insureds have less uncertainty about their future wealth and this is the information obtained by buying insurance cover. The output of insurers is analysed in more detail in Chapter 10.

In an insurance contract one party – the insured – transfers some of his uncertainty to another party – the insurer – for a certain fee. These transfers are made operational through the pooling of uncorrelated risks and the spreading among many portfolios of correlated risks. This reduces the variability and thus improves the predictability of portfolio outcomes in contrast to the outcomes of individual risks.

Insurance information services are financial services and insurance is a service industry. Like many other services, insurance has the following characteristics:

(a) Services are intangible. This implies uncertainty for the customer with respect to his expectations. No previous inspection of the product is possible, and difficulties are experienced in assessing its value and utility. For these reasons it is important that the consumer identifies with the company itself rather than with its product.
(b) Production and consumption generally take place at the same time and place. Insurance services are consumed over the cover period, but contact between insurer and insured is restricted to a few instances in which the insurer can demonstrate the value and quality of his service. This service is a process, in contrast to physical products which are the *result* of a process.
(c) Services are transient in nature. Services can only be produced if and when there is demand and there are few possibilities for production smoothing; capacity therefore has to be geared to peak demand.
(d) The quality of services is largely determined by the quality of producer's personnel, and this holds for front-office contact personnel as well as for back-office support.

(e) The role of communication is crucial because of the consumer's lack of information about the service. Personal recommendation is often an important sales message, and, once a sale has been achieved, there is often a long-standing relationship between producer and consumer; indeed buyers of one service may well be potential customers for the supplier's other services. The marketing of insurance services is discussed in detail in Chapter 13.

(f) Differences in service characteristics determine the nature and scope of the relationship between producer and consumer. Knowledge- and skill-based services provide specific knowledge and skills which are often tailor-made for a particular customer. Highly specialised professional services often find unique market niches that provide them with quasi monopolies. Professionals then often succeed in regulating the market and creating barriers to entry. Secondly, facilitatory services, such as those offered by banks, allow customers to take advantage of the supplier's organisations. They generally involve a large number of potential customers, incur high fixed costs, and often enjoy a natural monopoly because of the minimum size required. Finally, contracting-out services, such as insurance brokerage, are ones that could have been provided by the consumer himself, but are purchased because of the economies of scale of the service organisation.

(g) It is extremely difficult to obtain product differentiation in any service to create a unique product advantage for the producer. Often innovation in the service industries can be quite easily initiated, since there are no patents, secret formulas and so on. It is only through process innovation and control of process quality that an advantage can be created.

6.9 ORGANISATION OF INSURANCE COMPANIES

Insurance companies differ from other commercial organisations in certain respects. For example, they do not have research and development problems like the producers of electronics, optical equipment, pharmaceutics or chemicals. They do not need to invest large sums of money in risky and lengthy research and development (R & D) projects whose uncertain outcomes determine the fate of the company. Nor do they face engineering problems on a scale comparable to the aircraft, motorcar or steel industries, although the engineering component is increasing in importance as computerisation develops. Insurers have less problems in funding their operations and new developments, as they are able to utilise the credit extended to them by their customers. Insurers do, however, have problems with personnel owing to the labour-intensive nature of the production process, their funds have to be invested profitably and cautiously, and extensive and stringent book-keeping is required. However important those functions and their accompanying problems may be, insurers only have one real problem, and that is the operation of the insurance market.

Insurance companies developed from small privately-held firms dominated by professionals, into very large publicly-held corporations dominated by management and staff. In the past, the insurance trade was learnt on the job. The professionals largely controlled their own work, assisted by clerks to do the menial work of keeping the books. The services performed were to a large extent knowledge- and skill-based, as the client required extensive advice. Modern-day large insurance companies are generally organised by function with centralisation, detailed division of labour and well-defined authorities and responsibilities. There is often an obsession with control, which is reinforced by the external control exercised by supervisory authorities.

The centralised control inherent in most larger insurers is represented by the size, role and importance of advisory staff in central departments, who design standard procedures, forms, instructions, budgets, plans and schedules and reports. These are used, for example, in underwriting and claims-handling manuals to limit the size and nature of risk to be underwritten by various classes of underwriters, and in deciding the claims to be transferred for handling to specialised central departments. Many exceptions have to be referred upwards to higher and higher levels in the hierarchy.

The functional organisation of most large insurance companies developed to a large extent over the period 1945–75, when circumstances (such as sustained economic growth, and the development of computer technology) were particularly favourable. This has now largely changed. Growth in worldwide insurance markets has slowed considerably. Customers have become more sophisticated and more demanding. Price awareness has put pressure on premium rates, while social and legal developments have increased the frequency and severity of claims. Competition has also become fiercer, putting further pressure on rates. Furthermore another technological revolution is on its way. Advanced information technology will not only make it possible to automate all lines of business, but will link insurers, intermediaries and customers. The latter two will then be able to shop around extensively at very low cost and high speed and, as a consequence, markets will continue to polarise into price and value added segments. The customer, and no longer the product, will become the prime marketing dimension. Insurance companies will acquire a higher degree of technology and will most certainly reduce the number of semi-trained clerical staff that nowadays make up such a large segment of personnel in any insurance company.

Insurance companies respond reactively to competitive challenges by emphasising cost reduction through automation and internal efficiency improvements, and growth through acquisition and merger. Generally this leads to greater central control and a weakening of the peripheral functions. This lengthens lines of communication and, in many cases, results in confusion, strong inward orientation, and a weak strategic definition.

In the future, markets will be characterised by greater dynamism, instability and heterogeneity. Quick and adequate responses and a high degree of flexibility and differentiation among operational sub-units will be required. It will then be necessary to pick up business trends and changes rapidly, through a strong market orientation towards differentiated major sectors and customers. All this can only be achieved by decentralising and devolving authority, resource control and responsibility upon those units where the actual operations and client contacts take place. Operational problems will need to be handled by local units, which should have the necessary resources and authority to accomplish the task. This implies a fair degree of self-containment and a flexible organisation where resources can be shifted from one unit to the other if and when required. In order to respond to multiple pressures without creating a new permanent bureaucracy, insurers will need to develop matrix-type organisations (or adhocracies) where specialists are regularly deployed from their functional base units to temporary problem-orientated project groups.

Market orientation and market segmentation are the ultimate bases for strategy formulation and thus for organisational design. Developments in information technology mean that flexible responses can be formulated to environmental or operational problems. A distinction has to be made between centralisation and decentralisation of control and authority and the geographical concentration of functions and services. Sales, claims settlement, policyholder and agent services are generally distributed or decentralised. A market orientation requires a great deal of autonomy in these parts of the organisation. On the other hand, some functions, necessarily, will have to be centralised and thus concentrated. Strategy design, reporting to owners, governmental authorities and so on will always remain central functions. Whether or not such matters as employee relations, marketing policy or underwriting standards will have to be centralised depends on the organisation's mission and the nature of its choice of market.

The diversified insurance company of the future will have to choose its major market segments carefully. It will not have one overall organisational design that applies to every sub-unit. The organisational structures, procedures, modes of control and information systems for each sub-unit will have to be geared to market requirements and technological opportunities. The challenge of the next twenty years will be to organise and run large corporations as federations of many smaller companies, so as to benefit from the advantages of large and small scale simultaneously. The rapid development of electronic information processing and communication, combined with advances in mathematical modelling, expert systems and artificial intelligence, will offer new opportunities. All routine activities will not only become programmed decisions but will be highly automated as well. Most clerical tasks will be entrusted to the computer, and many 'simpler' decisions in underwriting and claims handling as well. Companies will grant wide authority to the highly professional staff in local units catering to the needs of market niches. Although insurance organisations will retain their hierarchical structure, the hierarchy will not be so pronounced, and the prevailing mode of control will shift from formalised bureaucracies to ones based on shared values and goals.

Recommended reading

Galbraith, J.R. (1977) *Organisation Design* (Reading, Mass: Addison Wesley).
Koontz, H. and H. Weihrich (1988) *Management* (New York: McGraw Hill) 9th edn.
Swiss Reinsurance (UK), *Sigma*, monthly.
van Gelder, H. (1982) 'Organisational Design with Reference to Insurance Companies', Geneva Association, *Etudes et Dossiers*, no. 59, August.

7 Staffing Policy in an International Insurance Group

Christopher Nutt

7.1 INTRODUCTION

This chapter summarises the main considerations and techniques employed in assessing and achieving future staffing needs in relation to corporate objectives, and changes in the market, technology, and employment legislation. Any large, established organisation will have personnel policies which guide decisions concerning its employees. Such policies will cover:

- Responsibilities for decisions about personnel;
- Employee relations, centrally and locally;
- Replacement of leavers and promotees;
- Training, education and development;
- Remuneration.

It takes widespread commercial necessity to change the axioms on which staff decisions are taken, given that most managers will have spent their careers in the insurance industry and will value consistency and certainty. Nevertheless the business organisation needs to martial the efforts of its staff towards its corporate aims and also to take control of critical decisions on staff costs.

Staffing philosophy must be consistent but articulated so as to permit the flexibility to meet the needs of business and its individuals in a changing environment. This requires continuing, penetrating and discerning policy reviews aimed at producing a number of specific, practical courses of action. The strategy for staffing in such an environment is not a scientific one. It is the art of acquiring and deploying staff with sufficient skills and motivation to exert a beneficial impact on the market-place.

7.2 DECIDING ON STAFFING POLICIES

Staffing groups

The first step is to decide at which level to apply strategy. Should this be

Table 7.1 Staffing groups in an insurance company

Jobs – base groups
Clerical staff
Secretarial and keyboard staff
Ancillary non-clerical staff (in various sub-groups, e.g. security)
Professionals and specialists – middle groups
Insurance technical and supervisory management (perhaps sub-divided, e.g. commercial lines, personal lines, life assurance administration, marine)
Sales and sales management (separating life assurance sales)
Actuarial
Computing
Other non-insurance professional and specialist staff (various sub-groups)
Career streams – top groups
Operational management (perhaps sub-divided for branch and head office management)
Project and development management (including marketing)

done at the Group corporate level or, say, within trading divisions? Such structural boundaries may not be the deciding factor. The level may be determined by social and legal matters. Human nature being what it is, people will seek consistency of treatment where they are in social contact unless there are accepted contractual or job differences which govern their employment.

Even if personnel policy is aimed at achieving single status and equal opportunities for advancement, the staffing strategies will nevertheless need to vary between staff groups. The needs of short-term employees are different from those of career staff who, in turn, will fall into a number of occupational and career streams. It is possible for one person to be in more than one group and to change group, but a high incidence of this would suggest that the group boundaries are unrealistic. The following factors map out the boundaries which encompass discrete groups:

- national boundary,
- employer (an insurance group may consist of several legally separate employers),
- job market,
- professional and specialist groups,
- career stream.

The number of separate groups will depend on the number and variety of jobs and their location in relation to each other. Table 7.1 indicates a typical set of groups for a single employer and Figure 7.1 shows a schematic representation of their role in the organisation.

The size and structure of staffing groups is changing. Studies undertaken in the United Kingdom show that developments in information technology

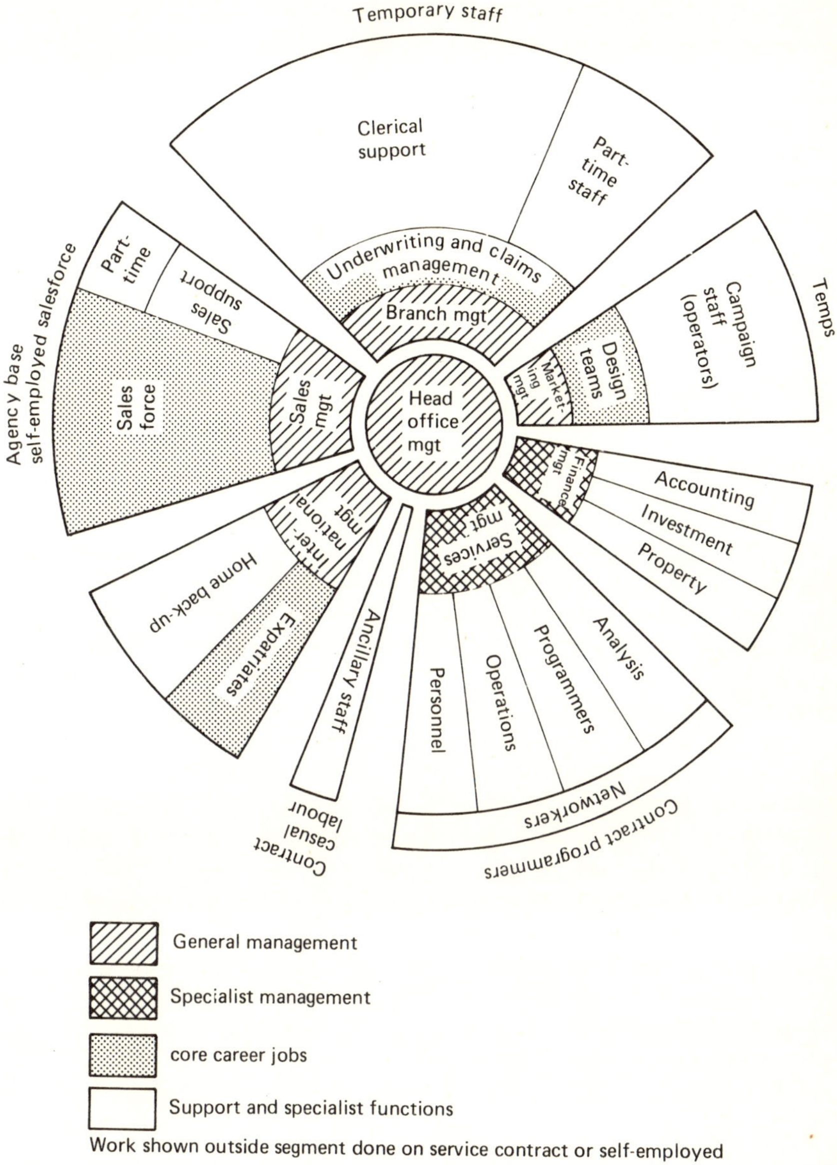

Figure 7.1 Staff segmentation – general insurance company

over the 1980s have considerably reduced the need for low-grade clerical jobs (which were often undertaken by temporary and part-time staff).

In a recent case study of a large UK composite insurer substantial differences in job gains and losses were discovered between the various staff groups (see Table 7.2). The drastic reduction in low-grade clerical

Table 7.2 Composite insurance company: job gains and losses, 1977–85

Occupation	*1977–79*	*1979–85*
Low-grade clerical	−150	−450
Middle- and high-grade clerical	−10	+300
Sales and marketing	+200	+525
Professional (graduates)	+50	+100
Data processing specialists	+30	+70
Total	+120	+545

Source: Rajan (1987).

occupations was not, in fact, achieved by substantial redundancies. This was because the new technology agreements negotiated between UK insurance unions and employers virtually guarantee jobs to existing holders. Instead the savings were achieved by natural wastage and by job loading – the upgrading and enhancing of clerical skills.

Table 7.2 highlights a number of important points. First the emerging job loading resulted in the upgrading of clerical work and a step-increase in the training provision. The repertoire of clerical skills has been enhanced so that on an average day in the case-study insurer around 50 per cent of the clericals had a systems interface and performed at least three of the typical insurance functions (that is, dealing with enquiries, receipt of proposals, underwriting, claims processing, accounts and investment advice). Regular peaks in the clerical workload have now been substantially ironed out, so that the opportunities for part-time work in this company have been practically eliminated and an even spread of work throughout the day on a shift-work basis is now possible. Second, the middle- and high-grade clericals also perform an office-based sales function to the extent that the distinction between them and the field-based sales employees is one of location rather than of the nature of activities. Third, there has been a consistent increase in the number of professional and technical staff due to the growing use of new technology which has extended from specialist to service areas.

The employment impact of the process innovations resulting from information technology is mainly felt in the low-grade clerical occupations shown in Table 7.2. The adverse impact on the lowest clerical group, mainly comprising female employees, is particularly notable. Technology has also facilitated a number of product innovations through either greater flexibility in the conventional product lines or the creation of new ones (particularly in the life insurance). These product innovations have had a beneficial effect on employment in the UK insurance industry, and the main beneficiaries have been the sales and professional occupations, previously occupied by male employees.

Staffing at the corporate level

At corporate level attention should be paid to those top positions which require internationally mobile executives and to certain middle and sales management positions. This requires a policy or commitment to using opportunities for management development and for repatriation and financial assistance for resettlement. It is unlikely that general staff policies need to be consistent in detail across national territories. Depending on employment markets and legislation, similar staffing strategies can be employed if the needs are similar. National employment practices are likely to be the determining factor, although management techniques and controls are now similar in all industrialised and emerging economies; increased standardisation of employment terms and conditions can be expected in the European Community during the 1990s, as labour mobility with the EC increases.

There should be a corporate facility to monitor possible successors for key positions, especially as key executives and senior technical employees are becoming increasingly difficult to retain. It is prudent to ensure that there is an adequate pool of talent, and an understanding of the criteria used to measure progress towards or suitability for the very top echelons.

Staffing at the employer level

At employer level, personnel policies and systems should provide a sound platform from which to initiate a variety of staffing strategies across a broad front. The policies should encompass a range of standard contracts of employment suitable for use in differing job market conditions, and pay and benefit systems which reinforce an achievement orientation. General personnel policies covering all groups will be necessary to facilitate and encourage mobility, and to encourage staff to identify with company objectives. Typical employer level policies would encompass the following aims.

(a) Contracts should encourage the use of temporary and part-time staff for suitable work, control overtime, and provide for flexible retirement by management consent.
(b) Contracts should provide flexibility to set starting salaries according to market rates.
(c) Payment systems should be finely tuned for particular staff groups to fit their career cycle.
(d) Post-induction rewards and planned job placement should be implemented for long-term staff after their initial training, in order to avoid heavy staff wastage at these points.
(e) Salary bands should be wide enough to satisfy the need for progression

within jobs, and to reduce pressure for promotion.

(f) Salary progression should be based on performance assessment against business and organisation needs, with higher salary ceilings for outstanding performers.

(g) There should be assistance with management education and professional studies for defined categories of career staff.

(h) Finally there should be open competition for jobs within the middle groups to encourage mobility and self-development.

Special policies may be required to secure economic resourcing for some groups. For example, incentive payment schemes or commission-based remuneration may be used for specialist salesforces. These may require a new company to be set up with special contracts, and a fresh sales force.

7.3 TACTICAL VERSUS STRATEGIC STAFFING

Once staffing policies have been developed it is all too easy to ignore some of the fundamental aspects of these policies by adopting short-term tactical decisions in the light of commercial pressures. When staffing is decided tactically as opposed to strategically, there are significant costs incurred, both when contracting the work and when expanding.

Problems with contracting staff numbers

The usual responses to contraction are to introduce recruitment bans, early retirement policies and voluntary redundancy. When the company has been recruiting until recently, it will have staff with short service: leaving rates will then be high but variable between occupations. Some jobs most needed may have the highest leaving rates (computing can be one such occupation), and a recruitment ban can result in significant imbalances in the size of staffing groups. Some replacements must therefore be allowed by senior management. In reducing other staff numbers, the cut-back on recruits causes lower wastage rates and total turnover drops accordingly. It therefore becomes more difficult to reduce staff further and the lack of new recruits doing straightforward work is a nuisance.

Early retirement is often considered as an appropriate method of contracting staff numbers, since premature retirees are often those most easily persuaded to leave, and on whom the social consequences will be light. The effectiveness of early retirement in reducing staff numbers is obviously greatest shortly after it is introduced. If it is open to all above the age of 50, a large proportion of employees are likely to be eligible. But early retirement simply brings forward wastage that could be expected within the next few years. Once the option is offered it is difficult to take away again and the long-term effect is to increase early outflow above the age of 50. It may also mean promotion of staff who are insufficiently experienced for senior positions.

The next option for contraction is via voluntary redundancy. A package may be designed to compensate people who decide to leave early, including a lump sum payment together with protection of pension rights. However there may be unforeseen effects: for example, the most immobile group, the 35–50-year-olds, may be attracted by the terms, rather unexpectedly. Those attracted will include people in middle management positions and in the higher ranks of professional occupations. The lump sum payment might just be the capital needed to risk a change. Most importantly, voluntary redundancy schemes are notoriously difficult to control: too many of the best people may leave, even if the scheme requires management approval for each individual.

If none of these options are successful, management will have recourse to what should have been done at the start and consider the business they are in, what its aims are, and how they can best adjust the business to the new conditions.

Problems with expanding staff numbers

The problems of short-term decisions can also be evident in expanding. Market forecasts may cause the management to recruit additional staff so that the percentage of employees with short service will increase and wastage begins to rise. More and more people then have to be recruited, not only to meet expansion plans but to cover the losses from the recruits. Recruitment standards may have to be lowered as the employment market is exhausted. The additional leavers may be wrongly seen as a symptom of increased dissatisfaction, rather than as a normal feature of wastage.

In addition, in periods of rapid expansion the training capacity may well be inadequate. When there are good induction practices wastage levels may be ameliorated, but when staff are not given adequate training and are not sure of what is going to happen to them, wastage tends to be higher.

Thirdly, salary rates may have to rise to attract recruits, with subsequent pressure to readjust the differentials for other staff. Managers may also become less willing to allow their staff to transfer, in the belief that if they release a good performer then the replacement will be inadequate.

Finally, business objectives may be hampered by the continuing staff shortages. Managers will wish to ensure that key departments are relieved and they may therefore augment direct line units with technical support and administrative back-up, in order to help the essential work. The purpose is to release the key staff from administrative chores. However the quality of administration and support work may well be poor during such staff shortages.

Planning for the problems of expansion at the outset would lead to longer-term solutions being adopted, such as the earlier separation of service functions, more considered efforts to improve productivity and the building of an adequate training capacity before it is required.

7.4 THE PROCESS OF STAFF PLANNING

The strategic approach to planning concentrates on deciding the organisation's requirements, and then on how to adjust staffing to match. The three main factors affecting staff planning are: the demand for staff, the rate of loss of existing staff, and the company replacement policy.

The demand for staff

There is a clear need to estimate the number and type of jobs which will be needed over, say, the next five years. However, much can happen over such a period and so 'low', 'medium' and 'high' estimates should be presented. These can only be management 'guesstimates' and will be based on business, organisation and productivity assumptions. The actual number of jobs required will obviously depend on the work volumes and productivity.

The assessment of demand begins with a rigorous questioning of business strategies. It aims to produce a business profile and an associated staffing plan for the future, around which new staffing philosophies can be built. The business profile is communicated to all departmental and functional heads with the instructions to prepare a case arguing for the lowest ultimate level of staffing needed to achieve this business profile. It aims at the ideal distribution of jobs, ignoring the current staffing. By the same token there must be no intention to implement the new establishment overnight. Implementation of the staffing plan should have a reasoned timetable depending on the nature of the changes.

The rate of loss of existing staff

Predicting the rate of staff loss is a complex process but there are four basic outflows: induction losses, losses after training, natural wastage, and retirements.

Induction losses will be reduced by good selection and induction programmes. Losses after training are reduced by the provision of information about opportunities for advancement and by placement counselling prior to permanent job appointments. After the first two years of employment wastage usually reduces. Thereafter the natural wastage typically responds to the level of vacancies in the particular job market. A number of other

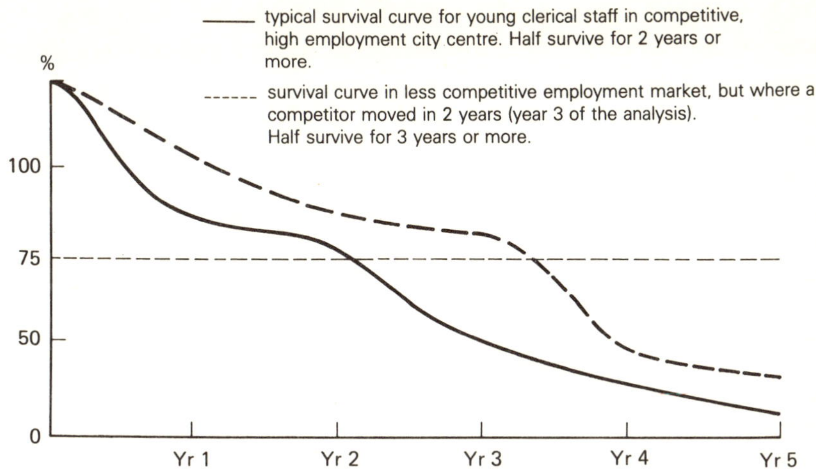

Figure 7.2 The survival curve for employees (showing the percentage of original starters remaining in service at the end of each year.

factors also affect natural wastage, including: occupations (typists switch employers more often than clerks), whether or not employees are in their first job, age, travel to work patterns, and sex. Women in the age band 16–35 generally have a higher likelihood than men of leaving, mainly for domestic reasons. On the other hand, women over 35 have lower wastage rates than men at the same age, although there is a high wastage rate in women returning to work at, say, 35–40, caused by induction wastage.

There are also various kinds of 'involuntary' and company-initiated wastage. Most important of these will be redundancy, including early retirement by reason of redundancy. However unusually high wastage rates should be investigated as they may be symptomatic of poor management or adverse employment conditions.

A crude wastage index can be calculated as follows:

$$\text{Crude wastage index} = \frac{\text{Total leavers in 12 month period} \times 100\%}{\text{Average number employed}}$$

This measure gives no indication of the kind of people leaving and any wastage analysis should also take account of length of service or age. It can be very useful to plot a 'survival' curve for key staff groups, indicating how many of the original staff who joined in a particular year are still in the company after one, two, three years and so on. This can be used to assess the cost-effectiveness of training and give an indication of the likely staff profile of the future. An example is given in Figure 7.2.

Company replacement policy

The staff profile in any part of an organisation reflects the way that people are replaced – the recruitment and selection policy. If it is intended to rely on ready-trained staff from other organisations, then few raw recruits are required for technical jobs. An alternative policy is to recruit trainees and fill jobs at higher levels by promotion. This enables a tight control over the standards of competence by ensuring that a company training programme has been followed and relevant on-the-job experience has been acquired. The recruitment of experienced people will be beneficial, since the recruits will be able to contribute new ideas developed in different circumstances. The gradual aging of the population in many countries must also be taken into account: lower numbers of recruits are available from the education sector and consequently companies may find that retaining of older entrants can be beneficial.

Which policy is best for a particular group or location can be decided by subjective assessment. It is important to evaluate different strategies since they also affect employee relations, the time taken to find a successor, the career prospects on offer, and the types of recruit needed (for example, the percentage of new recruits who are graduates).

There are three types of replacement decisions: first, there is recruitment and selection of new staff; secondly, there are decisions about who to promote, and thirdly, there are transfers involving lateral moves between jobs or between locations. Replacement policy will specify the type of staff to be encouraged or allowed to make these kinds of moves.

When specifying recruitment policies it is important to examine likely constraints. The first and most obvious is whether the employment market has sufficient people of the right experience, skills and qualifications. The proportion of existing staff who are suitable for promotion should be assessed. The geographical mobility of existing staff is a further constraint.

It is also useful to take into account regional and national trends, such as the demographic changes in the numbers of young people entering the employment market, the increase or decrease in the numbers of women available between ages 25 and 45, and the trends towards shorter and more flexible working weeks.

7.5 AN ANALYSIS OF STAFFING POLICIES AND REQUIREMENTS

Qualitative and quantitative analyses of staffing requirements may indicate that different policies are needed as between staff groups. It may become clear that recruitment into some groups is likely to increase even if overall staff numbers are planned to fall. Within a group the numbers at some levels may expand, whilst they decline at other levels. For example, the absolute size of the branch network may be reducing but there could be an increase in, say, the number of agency account managers even within fewer branches. It may be necessary to be prepared for both increased gross inflows of staff and net outflows, depending on market conditions or the timing of a new computer system. Relocation of work may require expansion and contraction simultaneously in different geographical locations. Analyses may help to point out trends for each of the staff groups; more importantly they will signal the levels of demand, wastage and replacement policies which would produce a major problem requiring policy changes.

Career profiles

Figure 7.3 illustrates a career progression diagram for male and female employees based in an insurance company head office. It shows the chances of an individual reaching a certain grade as well as the ages at which different promotions occur. The figure demonstrates the career progression of an imaginary group of 100 employees who join the company in the clerical grade at age 16 and follows their progress via promotion until they retire (although for the sake of brevity the figures cease at age 32). At each age, the figure shows the proportion of those initial 100 by career status, as broken down into clerical, middle manager, senior manager, and top manager grades (on the assumption that they all remain in the organisation).

From the figure it can be seen that by the age of 32 no males remain in the clerical grade. Around 45 per cent of the men who were recruited to that grade (and remain with the organisation) were promoted to middle management before the age of 32, with another 30 per cent getting to senior management, and the remaining 25 per cent were in top management. In this organisation the picture was very different for women, with less than half reaching middle management by age 32, and none attaining senior management. Obviously the company needs to reconsider its selection policy.

The decision matrix

It is useful to see the quantitative effects of various staffing strategies and one way of doing this is to use a decision matrix. In Table 7.3 the aim is to establish university and college graduate recruitment needs based on three wastage rates ('high', 'medium' and 'low'), three possible growth rates in the company's demand for managers ('no change', 'medium growth', and 'high growth'), and three possible replacement scenarios for the relative proportion of non-graduates to graduates (100/0, 70/30, 50/50).

In this example the company has collected data about the current age by

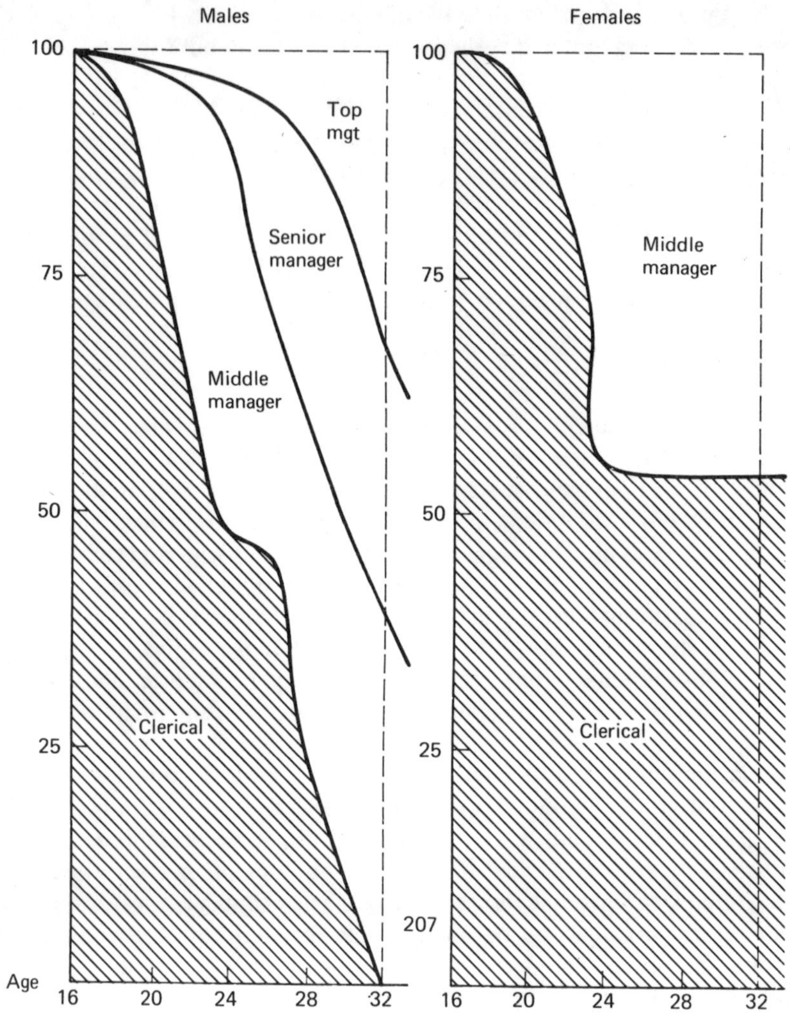

Figure 7.3 Career progression diagram for males and females in an insurance company head office

grade profile of its permanent staff, from clerks to senior managers. Wastage rates have been analysed over the previous five years to produce reasoned high, medium and low wastage projections. It was thought that the number of managers required might be on the increase, so three assumptions were made: one assumed a static number of managers, the others assumed a medium and high demand for managers.

The exercise was designed, firstly, to show that the company did indeed

Table 7.3 Matrix for graduate recruitment

Wastage rate	*Replacement of middle managers*		*Demand for managers*		
	% Non-grads	*% Grads*	*No change*	*Medium growth*	*High growth*
	100	0	(1)	(7)	(7)
HIGH	70	30	8	15	16
	50	50	12	16	20
	100	0	(1)	(4)	(3)
MEDIUM	70	30	6	12	13
	50	50	10	15	17
	100	0	0	0	0
LOW	70	30	3	6	9
	50	50	4	9	10

Notes: 1. This is the matrix used for the head office of a life company employing 480 permanent head office staff, of whom 120 were in middle manager jobs. Graduate recruits could expect to reach middle management within 2–3 years if they stayed.

2. Figures in brackets show that, if no graduates were recruited, the company would need to recruit some experienced managers as replacements for leavers and promotees. There would be insufficient non-graduate staff of the right age and experience to promote.

need to recruit graduates. The matrix of Table 7.3 shows that if the company had a replacement policy intended to replace managers by only non-graduates (that is, the 100/0 rows at each wastage rate) then there would be insufficient staff of the minimum experience and appropriate age range, unless wastage remained constantly 'low' (showing zeros in the appropriate row).

Secondly, the exercise tested the company's intention to appoint about 30 per cent of managers from graduates completing their two-year training programme (the 70/30 rows at each wastage rate). Even with 'high' wastage (both of graduates during training and of all other staff and managers generally) the company would need between 8 and 16 graduates each year, depending on the growth in the number of managers required.

If there was no growth in the demand for managers, would there be too many graduates frustrated by lack of promotion? Assuming that the company recruited 12 graduates, Table 7.3 shows that the company would need to use about 50 per cent of the management vacancies to overcome this problem, if the wastage rate was 'high'. However, if the wastage rate was 'Low', then only four graduates would be required on a 50/50 replacement policy.

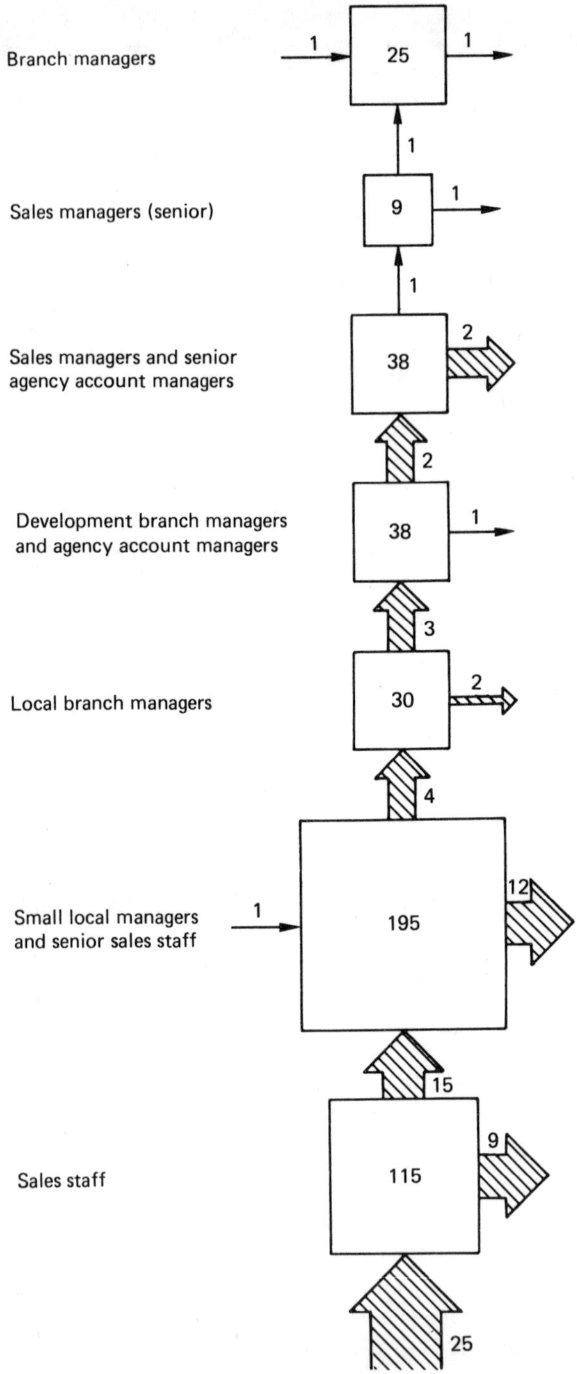

Figure 7.4 Staff system for agency salesforce

Staff group

The important benefit of using staff groups instead of the line organisation is that it enables longer-term decisions to be taken which remain valid against various organisation changes. It is often helpful to represent the staff group diagramatically, as in Figure 7.4, by the use of proportionally sized boxes and arrows representing the way that the group behaves from recruitment to final management level. The boxes indicate the optimal complement of main jobs per level. The flows indicate the number of people recruited into those jobs, promoted into and out of them, and the number of people who leave or are transferred out of the group.

Figure 7.4 shows a staff group expressed diagramatically for a salesforce. The diagram represents a flow system and by entering data based on this system (together with data on age and wastage) into one of a number of available computer models it is possible to project ahead. Again wastage rates can be varied, as can the number of jobs. The results can be used to judge shortages (when extra staff are required to maintain the staff complement – this happens when 'outflows' from the boxes exceed 'inflows', as for example in the case of local branch managers), and promotion bottlenecks (when 'inflows' exceed 'outflows') at each level.

7.6 IMPLEMENTING STAFFING POLICY

The policy base

The general and reliable trends of earlier decades have been replaced by differential and largely unpredictable changes between and within staff groups. A number of strategic steps can be taken to permit continual adjustments as and when required:

(a) Define mission: to ensure that company goals and values are communicated throughout the organisation.
(b) Define responsibilities: identify the level of line manager who is to be held accountable for securing staff productivity and good employee relations and development.
(c) Enhance employee relations: provide efficient communications to inform staff about and gain commitment to business success. Encourage good local staff relations. Provide training in the management of staff relations, particularly on the achievement of high standards and co-operation in change. Build trust between senior management and employees and their representatives. Provide security of employment and protection of individual living standards, except where impractical, as an aid to achieving changes, not as a barrier.
(d) Define replacement: have a carefully researched specific standard of

entry to each of the major staff groups, particularly the key career streams. Have a defined and well-publicised promotion policy. Apart from normal retirement and resignations, the management must have the final decision on out-placements, whether due to illness, incompetence or redundancy.

(e) Provide for training, education and development: have delegated responsibility for skill acquisition among staff who should take personal responsibility for their education and development. Provide central facilities and funding.

(f) Design a remuneration package: use the salary and benefit systems to encourage change, development and mobility – not to secure entitlement by status or longevity. Publicise the general policy on salary scales and relate this to business success.

To implement employee relations, replacement, training and remuneration policies it is necessary to install supporting systems with functional specialists in an advisory role. The policy and systems are normally described in operational manuals for use by managers and in staff handbooks. New systems need to be launched by explanatory briefings or training programmes and maintained by similar means. It is sometimes good practice to have widespread policy consultations in order to gain commitment from the management teams. The managers will then need the means by which to apply policy – a tool-kit.

The staff manager's tool-kit

Companies may find that most if not all the following items become essential to everyday staff management. The application of staffing policy and strategies will be the more effective if the managers are provided with efficient means of staff administration.

The following factors show the main tools required by line managers in a large organisation.

(a) *An organisation chart* showing line reporting relationships between jobs, with the minimum number of reporting levels, and maximum span of control for each supervisor and manager.

(b) *Job descriptions* for each post showing the primary job purpose, the outcomes for which a jobholder will be held accountable, what is done rather than how, and the characteristics of a proficient jobholder.

(c) *Recruitment specification* for each job to define the characteristics of suitable candidates in terms of: experience and qualifications, mental abilities and educational level, social skills, and acceptability to colleagues, seniors and clients.

(d) *Selection methods* which formalise and direct accountability for recruitment, promotion and transfer decisions onto line managers. At least two people should be involved in any decision, aided by selection criteria and selection tests if necessary.

(e) *Training specifications* for new staff which define the standards or objectives to be achieved, the knowledge and skills required, training methods and sources of help, a timetable with target dates, a person or people responsible or managing the programme, and the method of evaluating individual success and the programme itself.

(f) *Planning and review* systems which enable suitable people to contribute to annual plans and budgets, fit personal targets within the plan, and provide periodic information on the work unit's contribution to this, expressed in operational measures or ratios.

(g) *Performance assessment systems* which relate to the above items and help assessors to measure achievements against standards, targets or development goals, and which allow for continuing and formal feedback, and rewards which reinforce success in line with business objectives.

(h) *Psychometric tests* for personnel selection. These involve identifying the nature and demands of the job and then assessing the possible job performance of the applicant. Psychological tests of ability and aptitude are valuable because they are systematic measures covering several aspects of the specific ability or aptitude. For example, a 'verbal ability' test will include items of 'vocabulary', 'deductive reasoning', 'reasoning by analogy' and so on. Comparative data in the form of norm tables (and percentiles) indicate how one individual has performed in relation to others of a similar age, education and so on. Ideally, psychometric tests are designed to be objective (so that scores do not depend on the subjective opinion of the marker), reliable (so that someone who scores high on one day should not score low on the next) and valid (so that, for example, a verbal test actualy measures verbal activity).

Tests can be used for a broad screening of applicants or for detailed assessment of one individual. For selection purposes tests predict the probability of an individual's success in a given situation. Occasionally tests can be used to compare two or more individuals on a specific ability or aptitude. Tests can also be used for training (to identify training needs), promotion (to identify potential in an individual for a different type of job, for example to take managerial responsibility) and counselling, to help individuals recognise and make the best use of their strengths.

(i) *Potential assessment procedures*, comprising a variety of methods, including interviews to establish career goals and to give information about options. It may be useful to arrange off-the-job assessment where the track record is insufficient as evidence. A small number of trained assessors can observe individuals during team exercises or project work.

(j) Managers will be assisted by a *redeployment and redundancy package* which is not skewed unnecessarily in favour of those retiring early, nor recent entrants. The general criteria for selection of redundant employees will normally be set down by national legislation or case law. The company may wish to be more specific in order to achieve consistency and to encourage managers to take care about this when selecting jobholders for normal vacancies. Such criteria should reinforce competence as the main yardstick, but should take account of potential, willingness to be mobile, service and age, as well as personal circumstances.

(k) The following *redundancy procedures* have often been found to be successful: consult representative bodies on the revised organisation and its manning levels in the revised establishment; plan to use wastage, retirement and the lay-off of temporary staff in order to reduce redundancies; control new recruitment in the lead-up to reorganisation; inform staff, then ascertain their preferences regarding job placement, retirement or redundancy; consult representative bodies, then individuals about proposals; warn and then notify individuals affected by redeployment and redundancy after offering job placements to those selected on the published criteria; and offer out-placement and retirement counselling to those leaving, and redeployment and retraining for those switching career streams within the company.

7.7 CONCLUSION

The actual personnel policies of an international insurance group are likely to stem mainly from its history, culture and the practice of its dominant companies (except where imposed by employment legislation or changed through collective bargaining). Customs can become so established and self-evident to employees and managers alike that the policy can only confirm them or adapt them. For example, the sources from which new entrants are recruited may not take account of changes in the social and educational structure. The type of people hired may fit an outdated stereotype but not new job demands. Staff appraisal and promotion patterns may reflect social values rather than performance. Managers may be appointed from a career stream no longer relevant to the core activities of present-day senior management. Pay and status may be based on longevity. Predominant attitudes may reflect a concern with role rather than achievement. It is possible that the management style may protect staff from difficult but important career and employment decisions rather than encourage them to confront difficult choices. It is necessary therefore to pay attention to policy implementation and the monitoring of this policy; not just policy design.

The management of the staffing issues cannot be untangled from business and organisation management, and responsibilities should not be separated. It is likely, however, that the senior personnel specialist will also be able to contribute to strategic thinking and advise on a number of analytical techniques and the systems necessary to implement and monitor the policy.

Reference

Rajan, A. (1987) *Services – The Second Industrial Revolution? Business and Jobs Outlook for UK Growth Industries* (Guildford: Butterworths).

8 Underwriting and the Selection of a Liability Portfolio

Bernard Benjamin

8.1 THE NATURE AND PURPOSE OF UNDERWRITING

The purpose of underwriting is to choose to cover, from all the risks which are proposed to the insurer, those which collectively will be profitable. Essentially, this means that probable claims and the associated handling expenses will be less than the technical reserves held against those claims, so that the proportion of the premium income remaining after providing for these reserves (together with any investment income from the reserves) is available for profit.

Underwriting covers several practical aspects:

- accepting or rejecting risks offered and, in the case of acceptance, fixing premiums and retention (that is, amount of risk not reinsured);
- classifying and rating each risk, establishing the standards of coverage and amount of protection to be offered to each acceptable risk;
- securing a safe and profitable distribution of risks; establishing standards, and rules and procedures to preserve those standards.

To an actuary, the process of underwriting may be one of observation and statistical modelling in order to delineate homogeneous classes of risks, and so to derive a premium structure. Each proposal must then be allocated to the correct class, in order that the probability of loss falls within the sufficiently narrow probability distribution of the chosen class. To the underwriter, on the other hand, this will sound far too theoretical. It ignores the market, that is the fact that insurance contracts have to be sold in a highly competitive world. A judgement has to be made on whether the proposal is acceptable at a price agreeable to the proposer, and only then on class affinity and the appropriate rate to be charged. This judgement is not an automatic result of statistical analysis: it is conditioned by the experience of the underwriter and it is limited by market pressures such as those discussed in Chapter 12.

Although underwriters operate in conditions of uncertainty it is not quite true to suggest that they work without statistical information. Like many managers their decision-making is often intuitive: relying on previous experience and on such explicit information as may be available to conceive a largely informal and unverbalised analysis of options. Often underwriters do not have time to acquire information which is sufficiently complete as to make the options explicit. Because of the pressures of the market, they cannot procrastinate in the hope of avoiding a difficult choice. However information services (whether purely statistical or partly actuarial) can assist underwriters to crystallise their experience and enhance their ability to estimate the losses expected from each category of risk.

The expected or average loss over a period of continued stable conditions will be a product of the expected claim rate and the expected claim size. If, on the average, one in ten of insured buildings catch fire in a year, and if, on the average, the claim for a fire is £100 000, then the expected loss per year is 0.1 × £100 000 = £10 000. This is the average loss; it does not provide any indication of the possible range of fluctuation in loss from year to year – for this probabilities are needed. Risk is measured by a combination of two probabilities in respect of a defined interval of time: the frequency with which claims occur (the claim rate); and the probability that the claim will be of a particular size (although in life insurance, where the sum insured is often fixed, this probability can be left out of account, that is put equal to unity). It is not necessary for the underwriter to be concerned with the mathematics of this risk theory but he should be aware that the calculations, made for the purpose of developing a premium structure, include size as well as frequency of loss, and are therefore true estimates of the expected loss within each class into which a portfolio of risks is divided. Further details are provided in Chapter 11.

As well as estimating expected losses, underwriters must also make some allowance for fluctuations in loss experience. In life insurance, where the claim payment is either fixed or capable of being forecast within fairly narrow bounds, the calculation of the risk premium need not specifically allow for variation in mortality from year to year (since this will usually be small in relation to the normal loadings for bonus, expenses and profit). But in general insurance there can be wide fluctuations in loss experience from year to year, and insurers must set up special reserves to allow for these.

There are two possible approaches to estimation of these random fluctuations in loss experience: mathematically, and by using computer simulations.

In a mathematic sense, the annual claims cost per £ of premium is likely to follow a probability distribution generated by a combination of two other distributions: the distribution of claim frequency (a relatively simple one following a symmetrical curve) and the distribution of claim amount, which is generally a more complex function following a right-skewed curve (that is, one rising rapidly to a peak and falling away slowly to zero). The convolution of these two disributions is an awkward mathematical function to develop but can be approximated.

Computer simulations select randomly from the two distributions (of claim frequency and size) and multiplies the two solutions together as one estimate of annual claims. This process is repeated a sufficient number of times to provide a large number of estimates of total annual claims from which the shape of the distribution can be seen, and from which the parameters of the distribution (such as the mean and variance) can be estimated.

8.2 CLASSES OF INSURANCE BUSINESS

The frequency of claims and the likely range of claim size differ between classes of insurance business. If all general insurance business were lumped together, the range of variation of claim frequency and of amount of claim would be enormous, and the average values (and therefore the risk premiums) would be far too high for motor vehicle insurance and too low for aviation insurance, for example; this would also create the problem of adverse selection discussed in section 12.3. So the types of insurance must be segregated into classes of business that will effectively narrow the distributions (that is, narrow the range of volatility of claim frequency and claim amount).

But of course this is not the sole or even the original reason for making a distinction between different classes of general insurance. The original distinction arose from historical differences in the development of the markets in life, marine, fire and aviation business. In addition, the necessity to develop specialised underwriting experience for aviation as distinct from property insurance, for example, has tended to separate the classes not only by risk consideration but also by underwriting and marketing practices.

Liability insurance

Liability insurance covers the insured against the risk of incurring liabilities to third parties. This kind of insurance is normally divided into two main groups – Employers' Liability, and General or Public Liability – the latter covering many situations where liabilities could arise (such as products liability or professional indemnity). Any liabilities arising from the use of motor vehicles, the use of vessels or aircraft or risk incidental to the construction, repair or docking of vessels and aircraft are excluded from this category. Further details can be found in Carter (1973).

In many types of liability insurance, claims may take very high values so that the distribution of claim amount is liable to be very skewed. Where there has been a criminal act the insurance company may seek to recover money from the culprit, but this is only infrequently successful and even then the recovery is only partial. There is not therefore any serious abatement from such actions of the range of claims.

Marine, aviation and transport insurance

Marine insurance has been defined as 'a contract whereby the insurer undertakes to indemnify the assured in manner and to the extent thereby agreed against marine losses, that is to say, the losses incident to marine adventure' (Marine Insurance Act 1906). The risks to be covered in marine insurances include 'all perils of the sea' (wrecking, stranding, sinking, damage by bad weather or by sea water), fire, violent attack, wilful errors of the master or crew (scuttling, abandonment), war risks or seizure. Marine losses arise in four main areas: hull, liability, freight and cargo.

A ship is insured against total loss or damage in part up to the value stated in the policy. A distinction is drawn between actual and constructive total loss. An actual total loss occurs when the ship is destroyed or so damaged that it is no longer recognisable as the object which was insured, or if the insured is permanently deprived of it. A constructive total loss occurs when the ship has been reasonably abandoned, either in the face of inevitable total loss or because the cost of avoiding total loss would exceed the insured value.

Certain risks such as, for example, indemnity for liability in respect of claims for loss of life or personal injury resulting from accidents, or liability for damage to harbours or for the cost of removing wrecks, are commonly covered not by a marine insurance policy but by mutual insurance between shipowners, who group themselves together for this purpose into Protection and Indemnity Clubs.

Frequently the shipper of goods pays freight in advance and adds the cost to the value of the goods for insurance purposes. On the few occasions when the freight is not to be paid until after shipment, the shipowner has an insurable interest in the freight and can insure it. A claim may arise if the total freight is increased as a result of a reasonably justified diversion of the ship or trans-shipment of the cargo as a result of some hazard on the voyage.

The cargo may be insured either under an individual policy which specifies the goods to be insured and their value, or under an 'open' or 'floating' policy. As in all forms of insurance, anyone proposing to insure the cargo must have an insurable interest in it. Normally the shipper effects the insurance either as principal or agent. Cargo policies are assignable from one person to another (provided an insurable interest is transferred). The policy changes hands with the goods.

The financial risks in aviation are on a large scale and most of the aviation insurance risks are widely distributed among many insurers by means of co-insurance or reinsurance. There are a number of specialist insurance companies and also specialist aviation departments within major insurance companies. Lloyd's has an Aviation Underwriters' Association. There are international conventions governing limits of liability on the part of operations.

Motor vehicle insurance

Motor vehicle insurance covers loss or damage to motor vehicles, and liabilities to third parties, arising out of the use of motor vehicles (but the transit risks covered under marine, aviation and transport insurance are excluded).

Over recent years, there has been an increase in the volume of vehicles on the roads and in the number of people driving. Many of those who drive have limited resources and without the assistance of insurance would be unable to meet their liability to third parties in the event of an accident causing injury or property damage. In most countries the law requires that anyone using a motor vehicle on the road must have, in force, an insurance in respect of this legal liability to third parties, including passengers, for bodily injury.

The most popular form of cover for private cars is a comprehensive policy which provides indemnity for the loss of or damage to the insured's own private car, and liability for injury to third parties (including passengers) or damage to their property. Extra benefits are also commonly included, such as personal accident cover for the insured, payment of medical expenses incurred by injured occupants of the insured's car, and loss of or damage to rugs, clothing or personal effects carried in the insured car (subject to low monetary limits).

Generally, the higher the mileage travelled within a specified period and the denser the traffic conditions, the higher the risk of accident. Insurers therefore require increased premiums if a car is used for professional or commercial purposes rather than if solely for social and domestic purposes or for pleasure. Other underwriting factors include: geographical district of normal use – usually identified by reference to the place where the car is garaged; youthfulness of the driver as an indication of comparative inexperience or carelessness; occupation of driver; and make of car, especially if it is such as may be expensive to repair or is heavier or faster than the average.

An important feature of motor insurance is the provision of a cumulative no-claim discount. The rate of discount increases progressively with each further year free of claim, from perhaps 25 per cent after one claim-free year to 60 per cent after four years without claim. A claim may break this progression. Further discussion of no-claims discounts can be found in Benjamin (1977).

The insurance of commercial vehicles may be limited to the minimum laid down by law, may be for full third party protection, or may be comprehensive. In the latter case the degree of comprehensiveness may be less than for private cars, the extra benefits being rarely provided. A commercial vehicle may be of any shape or size, ranging from a hire car or small van to a motor coach or modern articulated lorry. In which group the vehicle comes and its working conditions (such as long haul over motorways or local delivery in relatively easy traffic) will affect the premium rating. No-claim discounts are given. A special fleet rating may be offered where several vehicles are in single ownership. In this case no-claim discounts are not given but the premium is reviewed each year in the light of the claims experience of the whole fleet.

Pecuniary loss insurance

Pecuniary loss insurance covers risks arising from various sources, including the insolvency of debtors; a failure of debtors to pay their debts when due; or having to carry out a contract of guarantee (for example, to make good a debtor's failure to meet obligations to another creditor). The interruption of or reduction in the scope of business carried on, for example, by some accidental damage to the business premises is also included in this category.

Pecuniary loss insurance also covers fidelity guarantee insurance. This has replaced the old system of personal sureties which an employee in a position of trust used to have to provide as a protection against loss suffered by his employer as a result of the employee's misbehaviour.

Personal accident and sickness insurance

Personal accident and sickness insurance provides cash benefits payable in the event of disablement or death due to accident or to illness. The insurance is normally on an annual contract basis and may vary in scope from benefits for injury by accident only, to benefits arising from an accident or certain specified diseases, to benefits arising from 'accident and all sickness'.

Benefits for accidental death or injury are commonly arranged in a scale of decreasing severity, and are payable regardless of the actual monetary loss suffered by the insured, since such insurances are not contracts of indemnity. Naturally, the insurer would avoid moral hazard by making sure that the level of any periodic payments was not substantially in excess of the normal earnings of the insured. As part of this precaution the insurer would seek information as to all other policies held by the insured with other insurers; the insured would also be required to notify the insurer of any other additional policies.

A medical examination is not required, but the proposal form is searching in respect of the present occupation and of the previous accident, insurance and medical history as well as the insured's present physical condition. The premium rating is related to occupation. Individuals in occupations with a heavy accident risk, such as building workers, attract a higher risk rating than those with only light risk. New proposers over a certain age, say 55 to 60, would not be accepted and renewals at older ages would be discouraged because the risk of accident or illness increases sharply as age 60 approaches, as also does the duration of any temporary disablement.

Property insurance

Property insurance covers the loss of or damage to material property (not including property falling within the scope of marine, aviation and transport insurance and of motor vehicle insurance). The principal peril covered is that of fire, but many policies include additional perils such as engineering failures, or theft. A number of other perils may be covered, such as explosion, riot and civil commotion; malicious damage; damage from aircraft or from articles dropped from an aircraft; storm; tempest and flood; bursting or overflowing of water tanks, apparatus and pipes; impact damage, for example from vehicles. For further details see Carter (1973).

The insurance of the ordinary dwelling is simpler than that of large buildings and business premises. Buildings and contents policies, known sometimes as houseowners' or householders' policies respectively, are combined in a single policy for owner–occupiers. The building policy covers loss of or damage to the building caused by a large variety of perils (see Carter, 1973).

Reinsurance

An insurer will prefer to operate in terms of collective rather than individual risk so that its liability is spread by taking a small share of a large number of risks, rather than take the whole of one large risk which could more than exhaust its resources. Reinsurance is an arrangement between the direct insurer and the reinsurer under which some part of the risk accepted by the direct insurer is passed on or ceded to the reinsurer. By means of reinsurance, an insurer is enabled to accept insurance of sums substantially greater than the maximum he wishes to retain for his own account. Reinsurance is a separate class of business from the ones discussed above because it represents a culling of special risks or parts of risk from all classes of insurance.

Most reinsurance is effected under reinsurance treaties, which are renewable annually, under which some part of the direct insurer's business is automatically reinsured. The reinsurance is either on a proportional or non-proportional basis. In proportional reinsurance, the reinsurer accepts a proportion of each individual insurance, receives that proportion of the premium and pays that proportion of all losses. In non-proportional reinsurance, the reinsurance applies to the whole portfolio of insurance and gives cover to the reinsured in excess of a negotiated cash figure or claim ratio in respect of any one event, or in excess of a negotiated overall claim ratio.

If treaty reinsurance facilities are not sufficient to enable the direct insurer to accept the whole of a risk, he may arrange reinsurance on an individual or facultative basis, but most probably the risk will be co-insured.

8.3 CONDITIONS FOR ACCEPTANCE OF RISKS

The underwriter has to recognise, and must have the information to recognise, those risks which are unacceptable and must therefore be rejected. The reasons for unacceptability will differ from one class to another. For many classes of insurance a bad individual record may justify rejection. It is possible to use statistical methods to give some definition as to what is meant by 'bad' since, if the class insured has been sufficiently narrowed to produce some degree of homogeneity, the risk can be represented by a particular probability distribution. If the recorded accident frequency appears to be outside the range of this distribution, then the underwriter will regard the individual as unacceptable in the particular group in which he is being considered.

Other indications of unacceptability are, for example in motor insurance, a history of traffic violations. In property insurance the underwriter may regard the property as an unacceptable proposition on account of its current condition, the age of the building, the occupancy of the property, or the neighbourhood in general.

In motor insurance, the underwriter will have regard to a number of factors, including the age of the driver (the very young and the very old are especially at risk), the mileage normally driven, gender and marital status, occupational stability, evidence of social maladjustment, evidence of a bad attitude to safety, evidence of a criminal record, or mental incompetency, physical impairment, or addiction to alcohol or drugs.

All this may appear to be common sense but it is so vital to the solvency of the insurer that it has to be a rigorously organised discipline on the part of the underwriter. In a very real sense it is a survival package on the part of the insurer. A more detailed discussion of the acceptability of risks can be found in Berliner (1982).

Reinsurance (and the protection from inordinate loss that it offers) is also an underwriting responsibility. Underwriters should consider, in respect of a particular contract, just how much the company could accept as a direct loss and how much, if the potential loss is greater, should be passed on to the reinsurance market. What is passed on to the reinsurer may turn out later to be profitable business lost, but it may equally be protection against disastrous loss. The reinsurance market has to make a profit to survive, but it is there also to protect the primary insurers.

8.4 PORTFOLIO MANAGEMENT

A general insurance company will normally underwrite several classes of business producing differing underwriting profits (as averaged over a period of time). Because of the differing settlement lags, the investment income generated is also rateably different for each class. These two elements taken together form the operating profit of each class of business. To find the underwriting profit expressed as a percentage of premiums for each class of business, an average over several years is necessary, but care must be taken to observe whether there has been any cyclic feature, in which case the average should be taken over one or more complete cycles. Similarly the averaging should not extend back beyond any year when a marked change of underwriting policy took place.

In assessing the investment income it is first necessary to establish the technical reserves as a proportion of premium for each class of business. The rate of interest to be applied to these reserves needs to be decided. The historic interest earned is of little value as it would be necessary to adjust for realised and unrealised capital gains and losses. It is considered preferable to decide on general grounds the rate of interest to be earned in the future. Such a decision will probably already have been made in the context of corporate planning.

The objective of portfolio management is to arrange the distribution of business among the classes so as to maximise overall profit. It is not simply a matter of transacting all the business in the most profitable class, since a large insurer cannot maintain its premium income by writing exclusively in one class. There might not be sufficient of that class of business in the market and, even if there were, it is unlikely that all of this could be secured in a competitive market without reducing rates of premium and therefore profitability. At the other extreme, it is not possible completely to eliminate an unprofitable class, mainly because of the practice of writing combined or package policies covering all classes, especially in the commercial sector. Even where this practice does not apply, the underwriting department does not have complete freedom of action because policyholders may want insurers to write one class of business (such as property) as a precondition to transacting others. There are therefore constraints on the proportion of total premium income which can be written; on both the maximum and the minimum amounts for each class. A solution to the problem of maximising total profit in the face of constraints can be obtained by using the well-known technique of linear programming.

Linear programming is a mathematical process for maximising (or minimising) a linear objective function of the type:

$$F = a_1X_1 + a_2X_2 + \dots + a_nX_n$$

subject to the constraints on the values that can be taken by the variables X_1, X_2 and so on. In this case, the objective function F represents the insurer's total profits, the variables X_1, X_2 and so on are the premium income in the various classes of insurance, and the constants a_1, a_2, a_3 etc. represent the operating profit expressed as a proportion of premium income for each class. The optimal values of X_1, X_2 etc. are determined by the Simplex Method; this consists of a logical system of matrix algebra by which each step determines the correct next step to take, until finally no further improvement in the objective function can be obtained. At this point the method stops and the optimal values of the variables are produced. The restriction is linear programming to a linear objective function has important implications for the behaviour we are trying to describe. In particular the model implies that a one-unit increase in X_1 will always increase total profit by a_1, no matter how high the existing level of X_1.

The practical value of the Simplex Method is that constraint inequalities (on the behaviour of the variables) can be introduced. By the use of imaginary additional variables (known as 'slack variables') these are changed to equalities giving rise to a series of simultaneous equations. As a result of adding slack variables there are more equations that true variables, so that the usual methods for solving simultaneous equations cannot be used, and an optimal solution is sought which can be chosen either to maximise or to minimise the linear relationship representing total profit.

In the following example based on Coe (1978), the total profit of a general insurance company is assumed to depend on its mix of business among six classes of insurance. The premium income of each class of business (the X_i) and the (predetermined) operating profit expressed as a proportion of premium income for each class (the a_i) are shown in Table 8.1

The linear programming problem is to vary the mix of business in order to maximise the expression:

$$\text{Total profit} = 0.15\,X_1 + 0.26\,X_2 + 0.27\,X_3 + 0.12\,X_4 + 0.10\,X_5 + 0.14\,X_6$$

where the constants (a_i) are the operating profit ratios of Table 8.1. It will

Table 8.1 Current mix of business for a general insurance company

Class for business (i)	*Current class premium income (i.e. X_i)*	*Operating profit as proportion of class premium income (i.e. a_i)**
1	20	0.15
2	26	0.26
3	8	0.27
4	22	0.12
5	14	0.10
6	10	0.14
	100	

* These figures have been predetermined by the insurer's accountants, and show underwriting profit plus investment income on technical reserves as a proportion of premium income for each class of business.

shortly be shown that a rearrangement of the mix of business can increase total profit (which currently stands at 17.36 out of total premium income of 100).

The premium income of each class cannot be varied at will, however, but must satisfy a number of constraints. In the first place, it seems reasonable to assume that there is a limit on the maximum increase in premium income that can be generated for each class: for the sake of convenience, this is assumed to be 10 per cent for all classes (so that, for example, X_1 must not exceed 22, X_2 must not exceed 28.6 and so on). Secondly, the minimum value of premium income for each class will be assumed to be three-quarters of the current level (so that X_1 must be greater than 15, X_2 must exceed 19.5 and so on).

Finally the effect on the surplus of the company as a result of changing the mix of business may also be a consideration. One way of providing for this is to introduce a surplus constraint. It is therefore assumed that, from risk theory calculations or otherwise, it is known that there is a minimum percentage of premium required to sustain a particular class of business (after allowing for investment value fluctuations). Table 8.2 summarises the maximum premium income, minimum premium income, and surplus constraints. It is assumed that the minimum surplus the company requires is 22.5; a change of mix to optimise profit must not then use more capital than the insurer has available. The sum of the capital required for each class (expressed as a proportion of premium income) multiplied by the premium income for that class (X_i) must therefore be less than 22.5.

The linear programme problem described in Tables 8.1 and 8.2 can be solved very simply using a desk-top personal computer, although more complicated problems may require a mainframe. Two sets of solutions are

Table 8.2 Constraints on the mix of business*

Maximum premium income constraints
$X_1 \leqslant 22.0$, $X_2 \leqslant 28.6$, $X_3 \leqslant 8.8$, $X_4 \leqslant 24.2$, $X_5 \leqslant 15.4$, $X_6 \leqslant 11.0$
Minimum premium income constraints
$X_1 \geqslant 15.0$, $X_2 \geqslant 19.5$, $X_3 \geqslant 6.0$, $X_4 \geqslant 16.5$, $X_5 \geqslant 10.5$, $X_6 \geqslant 7.5$
Surplus constraints
$0.25X_1 + 0.27X_2 + 0.62X_3 + 0.08X_4 + 0.08X_5 + 0.27X_6 \leqslant 22.5$

* These figures have been predetermined by the insurer's accountants and actuaries, and show the constraints imposed on the levels of premium income possible for each class (X_i).

Table 8.3 The solution to the linear programming problem

Class of business	*Profit ratio (Table 8.1)*	*Optimal premium income*	
		Without surplus constraint	*With surplus constraint*
1	0.15	22.0 (i.e. max)	22.0 (i.e. max)
2	0.26	28.6 (i.e. max)	28.6 (i.e. max)
3	0.27	8.8 (i.e. max)	6.0 (i.e. min)
4	0.12	24.2 (i.e. max)	24.2 (i.e. max)
5	0.10	15.4 (i.e. max)	15.4 (i.e. max)
6	0.14	11.0 (i.e. max)	8.9
Total premium income		110.0	105.1
Total profit		19.1	18.0
Surplus required		24.8	22.5

shown in Table 8.3: one where the surplus constraint of Table 8.2 is ignored, and the other where it is incorporated. In the latter case, since the total premium income has not been constrained to be less than 100, the company's 'solvency margin' will fall below 22.5 per cent.

Table 8.3 shows that, as expected, in the absence of any constraint on surplus a maximum total profit of 19.1 can be obtained by increasing all premium income to the maximum allowable levels (producing a total premium income of 110 and requiring surplus of 24.8). However the introduction of the surplus constraint produced significant changes: premium income in the most profitable class of business (number 3) switches to the minimum level because it is also the most capital-intensive (with a ratio of surplus required to premium of 0.62). Similarly, premium income in class 6 is reduced below the maximum level since it too requires a high commitment of capital. Total profit declines from 19.1 to 18.0 and total premium income is reduced to 105.1.

Table 8.4 The impact of lower interest rates

Class of business	*New profit ratio*	*Optimal premium income*	
		Without surplus constraint	*With surplus constraint*
1	0.09	22.0 (i.e. max)	15.0 (i.e. min)
2	0.23	28.6 (i.e. max)	28.6 (i.e. max)
3	0.24	8.8 (i.e. max)	7.9
4	0.09	24.2 (i.e. max)	24.2 (i.e. max)
5	0.07	15.4 (i.e. max)	15.4 (i.e. max)
6	0.13	11.0 (i.e. max)	11.0 (i.e. max)
Total premium income		110.0	102.1
Total profit		15.4	14.5
Surplus required		20.5	22.5

If a change in the investment yield is expected, it is useful to be able to calculate whether the optimal mix of business in Table 8.3 will remain unchanged. All that is necessary is to recalculate the profit ratios allowing for the expected higher or lower yields and to substitute the new figures in the objective function. As an illustration, the yield implied in the objective function above has been reduced by 3 per cent. Because of the differing ratios of reserves to premiums by class it is not simply a question of reducing all the profit ratios by 3. Table 8.4 sets out the revised findings; it can be seen that the amount of business to be written is only affected when the surplus constraint is operating.

The new profit ratios in Table 8.4 show that the profit of Class 1 is very sensitive to falls in the rate of interest (the profit ratio declining from 0.15 to 0.09). Not surprisingly therefore, premium income in Class 1 should now be set at the minimum rather than the maximum level of Table 8.3 (when the surplus constraint is effective). On the other hand, Class 6 is insensitive to interest rate changes, so that the fall in interest produces a rise in premium income (from 8.9 in Table 8.3 to 11.0). Total premium income declines as a result of the fall in interest rates when the surplus constraint is introduced, as does total profit.

Instead of using as variables the amount of business by class in a given territory, it is an obvious application of linear programming to use the volumes of business which arise in different operating territories. The constraints will be difficult to determine, but in the first place it will clearly be assumed that it is intended to continue to operate in each territory. In addition to the effect of market conditions on the constraints it will also be necessary to consider the minimum premium income on which the territorial operation remains viable, for example because of overhead expenses.

In the above examples the effects of tax have been ignored, on the assumption that underwriting and investment profits would be taxed at the same rate. When this is so, the optimal solution is not affected, as all the items in the objective function are reduced in the same proportion. If the rates of taxation differ for underwriting and investment an adjustment through the profit factors would seem to cover the situation.

Statistical exercises of this kind do not provide for automatic decisions; they do not absolve the manager from making a judgement and a decision. The inputs to the mathematical models are largely forecasts, although doubtless the best that can be made on the basis of observed trends, and in a competitive market trends can change quite swiftly. The answers from mathematical models are only as good as the forecasts. Although the manager will get good information about trends from statistical analysis, in the last resort he has to decide what forecasts to adopt.

References

Benjamin, B. (1977) *General Insurance* (London: Heinemann).
Berliner, B. (1982) *Limits of Insurability of Risk* (Englewood Cliffs, NJ: Prentice-Hall).
Carter, R.L. (ed.) (1973) *Handbook of Insurance* (Brentford: Kluwer Publishing) (continuously updated).
Coe, L.D. (1978) 'Optimisation by the Use of Linear Programming' (unpublished).
Diacon, S.R. and R.L. Carter (1988) *Success in Insurance* (London: John Murray) 2nd edn.

9 Insurance Company Costs and Cost Allocation

Rodney Young

9.1 INSURANCE COMPANY COSTS AND THE NEED FOR COST ALLOCATION

Most textbooks dealing with costing consider the example of a manufacturing company. The company buys raw materials or components, incurs costs in adding value to them, and sells the resulting products at a price, which, at least in the long run, must cover all costs plus profit margin.

There are many parallels between the manufacturing company's costs and those of an insurance company, but of course an insurance company does not incur raw material costs as such. Instead, the insurer's revenue – its premium income and investment income – must cover three cost components, plus profit and tax. These components are:

claims	(typically 65–80 per cent of premiums)
commissions	(typically 14–19 per cent of premiums)
management expenses	(typically 12–18 per cent of premiums)

The figures in brackets indicate the approximate percentages typical of a large insurance company's non-life business. The claims percentages include claims-handling expenses. All figures relate to gross written premiums.

If an insurance company is to remain competitive, its management must be concerned with all of these cost components. However, while claims and commission will together account for the greater part of the average insurer's costs, they will normally be incurred in respect of identifiable, individual policies. Problems of allocation as such do not arise. It is the ways in which management costs are dealt with which are considered in this chapter. But why should insurance companies take so much trouble to analyse and allocate costs? Clearly costs in general must be kept as low as possible consistent with running the business effectively and providing a competitive service to the policyholder. Why try to determine how much of a particular expense – the chief executive's salary, for example – relates to a particular class of business, or branch office, or even individual policy?

In the case of a small business, producing a single product, cost control may be straightforward enough. The owner knows what costs are incurred and why. He is in a position to judge what costs are higher than they need be and to take steps to reduce them. He knows that all costs must be covered by sale of his product and that his prices must take this into account.

Insurance companies, though, are not small businesses. They are frequently very large ones. They usually have an extensive range of different products, often sold through different divisions of the company, each with its own cost structure. And they spend large sums of money daily on such diverse things as salaries and telephone bills, cars and computer stationery. Responsibility for controlling costs, for setting the prices which must cover these costs and for achieving results, does not and cannot rest with one man. The management of a large company requires different levels of decision-making and accountability to be delegated down throughout the organisation. So, if this diversity of expenditure is to be controlled, and ultimately reflected in the price of policies, careful allocation of costs is essential.

In fact, allocation of costs is necessary for reasons other than cost control and pricing. Much of the effective management of an insurance company depends on knowing what costs 'belong' where. Cost allocation is necessary for:

- Company accounts – the retrospective records of the company's financial results, produced each year for shareholders and others;
- Returns to the supervisory authority – the statutory returns which the company must make for the statutory supervision of its business;
- Management control;
- Management decision-making.

We will examine the importance of insurance company costs under each of these headings, but first we need to consider just what an insurance company's costs are made up of.

9.2 CLASSIFICATION OF COSTS

By item purchased

Claims and commission apart, what does an insurance company spend its money on? The most obvious item of management expenses is staff salaries, which are usually the largest single component of most insurer's management expenses, representing typically 8–12 per cent of gross written premiums for a large non-life insurer. But there are many other types of expenditure, and some of the most important are shown in Table 9.1. Individually, most of these will normally represent less than one per cent of

Table 9.1 Main categories of insurance company expenditure

Staff costs e.g. Salaries, national insurance, pension scheme
Office premises e.g. Property, rents, maintenance, heating, rates
Equipment e.g. Desks, chairs, filing-cabinets, cars
Communications e.g. Telephone, telex, postage
Computers
Advertising and Promotion
Printing and Stationery

premiums, with the exception of premises at around 2–3 per cent. Collectively they may well exceed 5 per cent of premiums.

Current and capital expenditure

Classification according to what the money is spent on is the first and most obvious step in classifying expenditure. It is, however, immediately apparent that Table 9.1 includes two fundamentally different types of expenditure. There are items such as salaries, communications, rents and rates – things which are used up in relation to current activities and are paid for as they are used. These constitute current expenditure. Then there are items such as cars and computers, which have a useful lifetime of several years and which, although often paid for in a single year, continue to contribute to profit for several more years. These constitute capital expenditure.

To charge the cost of capital items against income in the year of purchase could considerably distort profits. It is therefore usual to 'depreciate' such assets – that is, to charge their cost to a capital account in the year of purchase and then to charge out part of the cost each year to the appropriate revenue accounts over the useful lifetime of the asset. A company's depreciation policy – what items it treats as capital expenditure and how it depreciates these assets over subsequent years – will have an important effect on costs allocated each year. It will also affect the way the company's profits emerge year by year.

By spending department

For management purposes it is important to classify costs not just by what the money is spent on, but by whom it is spent and in relation to what activity. Of the items in Table 9.1, salary costs will be incurred by all parts

Table 9.2 Service and operating departments in an insurance company

Service departments/units	*Operating departments/units*
Accounts	UK Division
Personnel	Overseas Division
Computer	Life Department
Property	Fire and Accident Department
Office Services	Marine Department
Investments	Regions
Secretary's Office	Branches
Printing and Stationery	Sales Offices
Marketing Services	

of the company. Most parts of the company will also incur costs in relation to stationery and communications. Other types of expenditure may well only be incurred by particular departments, for example computers by the Computer Department, property maintenance by the Office Services Department.

Of the spending departments within the company, some contribute directly to the profitability of the company by earning premiums. These departments, such as the Life or Marine Departments are sometimes referred to as 'operating departments'. Others contribute only indirectly to profits by supporting, and providing services to, the operating departments. The Computer Department and Office Services Department are examples of such 'service departments'. The costs incurred by the service departments must be divided among the operating departments, since they relate to the running of these departments and will in their turn form part of their costs.

Which are service departments or units and which are operating departments or units will depend largely on the structure of the company concerned, but Table 9.2 gives examples.

Direct costs and indirect costs

Many departments not only have costs which they themselves directly incur in the course of their activities, but also costs which are incurred indirectly on their behalf by other departments and then allocated to them. There is thus a further basis for classification of expenses between direct and indirect costs. Since indirect costs are generally beyond the control of the department to which they are allocated, they are frequently referred to as 'overheads'.

It is important to realise that to some extent the designation 'overhead' is a relative one. To the Life Division, the cost of the Personnel Department is an overhead, while the salaries of the Life Division staff are a direct cost.

To the local Life Sales Office, though, the cost of its own sales staff is a direct cost but that of the Life Division Head Office staff is an overhead.

Fixed costs and variable costs

Finally, costs may be classified as fixed costs, which do not vary with the level of activity, and variable costs, which do. To some extent, fixed costs equate with overhead costs and variable costs with direct costs.

If the Life Division increases or reduces its level of activity some of its costs will automatically increase or reduce. Others, such as salaries, may be capable of being increased or reduced in line with activity. On the other hand, overall Personnel Department costs, some of which will be charged to Life Division, are unlikely to vary much in the short term as a result of Life Division activity.

Once again, it is important to realise that the terms 'fixed' and 'variable' as applied to costs are very much relative terms. In the long run, most costs are variable. Claims and commissions costs are true variable costs. If a company increases its business it will pay more claims and more commission. At the other end of the spectrum, the costs of maintaining the company's head office building are very much fixed costs. Short of moving to a smaller building, there may be little that can be done to reduce these costs if business turns down. Salary costs will normally fall somewhere between these extremes. Over the years, staff numbers can be increased or reduced to reflect business activity. On the other hand, terms of staff employment and statutory redundancy provisions make it virtually impossible to match staff costs to short-term changes in activity. Costs cannot, therefore, be classified simply as fixed or variable for all purposes. Whether a cost is fixed or variable will need to be determined in relation to a particular activity, a particular timescale or a particular management decision.

9.3 BUDGETARY CONTROL SYSTEMS

So far the following expenditure classifications have been identified:

- Classification by type of item purchased,
- Current and capital expenditure,
- Classification by spending department,
- Direct costs and indirect costs,
- Fixed costs and variable costs.

We now need to consider the company's budgetary control system, because it is this which enables costs incurred to be identified by classification.

The question of whether a particular cost is direct or indirect, fixed or variable, is a relative and not an absolute one. Budgetary systems therefore concentrate on identifying: current or capital expenditure; what the money is spent on; and who the money is spent by.

Budgets will normally be split between capital budgets and current expenditure budgets, with some simple rules to determine what goes into which. (Although the basic distinction is the useful lifetime of the item purchased, cost will usually also be taken into account. A pair of scissors may last several years, but the cost is such that few companies would classify such an item as capital expenditure.)

All company expenditure will then be coded, both at the stage when the budget is drawn up and approved, and when the expenditure is actually incurred. Typically, a company's expense codes will fall into two main parts, one identifying who is incurring the expenditure (the location or budget centre code – see 9.3 below) and the other the type of item purchased. The location code may be further subdivided, with the first part of the code indicating, say, a department and the second part the budget

Table 9.3 Expense codings in a typical insurance company

Location Codes		*Expense Codes*	
INTERNATIONAL (446)		ACCOMMODATION	
	Fire and Accident		*Rent and Rates*
446–001	Marketing and Planning	0801	Book Rents
446–002	Agency Administration	0802	Leasehold Rents
446–003	Fire Underwriting	0803	Water Services
446–004	Accident Underwriting	0804	Service Charges
		0805	General Rates
	Marine		
			Building Maintenance
446–010	Overseas Underwriting		
446–011	Home Underwriting	0810	Building Maintenance
446–012	Claims	0811	Plant and Equip. Maintenance
446–013	Administration	0812	Cleaning
		0813	Cleaning Supplies
	Life		
			Heating and Lighting
446–020	Life Underwriting and Dev.		
446–021	Life Actuarial	0820	Electricity
		0821	Gas
	Central		
		0822	Other Fuel
446–030	Accounts		etc.
446–031	Computer		
	etc.		

sub-location within the department. Thus a payment to a newspaper for advertising space might be coded 337–021 1224. Within this code, 337 might identify Life Division, 021 the marketing or advertising section responsible for the payment and 1224 advertising media costs. Table 9.3 gives an example of part of an insurance company's expense coding system. Such a system enables a cumulative total of expenditure by budget location to be maintained, classified by type of item purchased, and compared at regular intervals with the amounts budgeted. Since most companies have computerised their budgetary control systems, cumulative totals can be produced at regular intervals for whatever locations, or combinations of locations, management require.

9.4 COST ALLOCATION METHODS

The company's budget coding system automatically identifies what expenditure is being incurred, what type of item is being purchased and by whom. This does not necessarily establish what activity the expenditure relates to. As we have seen, most operational activities have direct costs and indirect or 'overhead' costs. If we consider a branch office, which may also be a budget centre or location, that branch's direct costs will be immediately identifiable through the budget coding system. However, if the results of the branch are to be assessed, both direct costs and overheads need to be taken into account, because if the company is to be profitable the earnings of the branch must cover not only the expenses of the branch but its proportion of head office costs as well. This raises the question of what that proportion is, for each branch. For example, it may cost £1m per annum to run the company's computer department. If there are ten branches it could be said that this represents £100 000 per branch – that is, £100 000 of the computer department's costs are allocated to each branch as overheads. Suppose, though, that one branch has a premium income of £10m, while another has a premium income of only £2m. Should they be regarded as bearing an equal share of the computer department's costs? Or should these costs be shared, such that the bigger branch has five shares to the smaller branch's one? In these circumstances, to share the computer department's costs equally is clearly less satisfactory than to relate them to the size of the branch, because almost certainly the larger branch will make more demands on the services of the computer department than the smaller. (Technically, where a particular expense is transferred in full to a single department or branch, this is 'allocation'. Where an expense is shared between more than one, this is 'apportionment'. For the sake of simplicity, the term allocation is used throughout this chapter.)

But allocating costs in relation to the branches' premium income may not produce the best answer. The larger branch may be dealing mainly with

Table 9.4 Cost allocation methods

Cost	*Possible basis of allocation*
Premises costs – rent, rates, heating etc.	Floor area occupied by operating unit Staff numbers in operating unit
Telecommunication costs – telephone, telex etc.	Staff numbers Number of policies
Personnel Dept	Number of staff Payroll
Computer Dept	Machine usage Number of policies Number of actions processed Time/cost basis (major development projects)
Investment Dept	Funds managed Investments managed Time/cost basis
Accounts Dept	Number of policies Premium income Number of accounting items handled

e.g. Office premises occupied by Fire and Accicent Dept (35 staff), Life Dept (20 staff) and Marine Dept (10 staff)
Annual rental = £32 500
Basis of allocation, by staff numbers:

Fire and Accident Dept	$£32\,500 \times \frac{35}{65}$	= £17 500
Life Dept	$£32\,500 \times \frac{20}{65}$	= £10 000
Marine Dept	$£32\,500 \times \frac{10}{65}$	= £5 000

larger commercial insurances, with the result that the £10m premium income is produced by only 10 000 policies. The smaller branch, on the other hand, although it has only £2m premium income handles 5000 personal and small commercial insurances. Since each policy has to be processed separately it could reasonably be argued that the smaller branch uses not one-fifth of the computer resources of the larger branch but one-half, and that computer department costs should be allocated accordingly.

If, instead of the computer department, the personnel department had been considered, then the best way of allocating its costs to the branches might be by neither premiums nor policies, but rather by the number of staff employed at each branch. The best method must be arrived at by considering carefully the nature of the overhead, the basis of the relationship between the service department and the operating unit, and other similar factors. Examples of methods of allocating different types of overhead, including a specimen allocation, are shown in Table 9.4.

In fact there is seldom a 'right' answer to the question of how overheads should be allocated. The cost of running the company's computer department is not the sum of the costs of running a separate computer department for each of the branches and to this extent any allocation is artificial. The object must be to find not the right basis of allocation but the most appropriate, and this will vary according to the nature of the overhead.

Depending on the sophistication of the company's budgetary control system, the allocation of overheads may well form an automatic part of the system and of the reports generated. For each location, the reports at the end of each reporting period will show not only the direct costs incurred by that location, but the overheads allocated to it. These can then be compared with budget.

9.5 COST ALLOCATION FOR PRICING

Allocation of overhead costs to operating units enables management to monitor results by operating unit. There are, however, other instances in which results may need to be monitored, either regularly or on an *ad hoc* basis: classes of business (motor, liability, fire, etc.); distribution channels (brokers, part-time agents, etc.); and, importantly, policies. Allocation of costs to policies is important because a policy is the ultimate product which the company sells and by means of which it recovers all its costs. This makes information about costs per policy vital in pricing decisions.

In setting the premium for a particular type of contract – a motor insurance policy for example – a company may assign cost components as follows:

	£
Risk premium (to cover expected claims)	68
Commission (at 10% of gross premiums)	10
Direct expenses (motor department staff etc.)	8
Overhead costs	12
Underwriting profit margin (2% of gross premium)	2
Premium	100

The derivation of the risk premium is discussed in more detail in Chapter 11. The allocation of all direct and indirect costs to individual policies is necessary in order to derive the cost components shown in the above pricing calculation.

The allocation of direct costs

The management expenses incurred directly in relation to the selling, issue and administration of a policy will be mainly staff costs. Allocation of direct costs is therefore primarily a question of the allocation between different classes of business of the salaries, pensions contributions and so on of those staff handling more than one type of policy.

There are various ways in which this can be done. The simplest involves the allocation between classes of business by numbers of policies or gross written premium income. For example, if half the policies handled by a clerk are private car policies, one-quarter are motor cycle and one-quarter are commercial vehicle then the clerk's salary costs could be allocated in these proportions. However, if, policy for policy, commercial vehicle business involves more work than private car or motor cycle, this approach is not very satisfactory. In fact, to achieve any real accuracy it will usually be necessary to adopt some form of work measurement to establish what activities staff are carrying out in relation to each different type of policy and the number and duration of such activities. These investigations themselves are costly and can usually only be justified on an occasional basis, even where the company employs work measurement techniques as a normal method of controlling clerical work. Interim assessments can be made by monitoring the number of actions per class of business – or by choosing one or two of the more significant actions such as new proposals, renewals and claims paid – and then using previously determined work measurements as a basis for the allocation of costs.

Although staff costs make up the greater proportion of direct costs, non-staff costs must also be taken into account. Of these non-staff direct costs some, such as policy documents or sales literature, may be directly attributable to a particular type of policy. Others, such as communications, will need to be allocated using the most appropriate method. This may involve using policy volumes or premiums as the basis of allocation. Alternatively, since staff costs form the major part of direct costs, the best approach is sometimes to allocate non-staff costs in the same proportion as staff costs.

Having allocated direct costs between classes of business, it is next necessary to allocate these costs for each class to individual policies. Similar considerations apply as for the allocation to class of business. It may be sufficient simply to divide total costs by number of policies. However, if some policies are more complicated or require more attention than others this will not give a satisfactory answer. The more complex policies will tend to be those attracting the higher premiums, so the allocation may be improved by calculating an expense factor per £ of gross written premium, rather than per policy. If costs are being allocated as a basis for setting premiums, though, this form of allocation can become dangerously circular. Once again, work measurement may be the only really satisfactory answer.

The allocation of indirect costs

The indirect costs to be met, in part, out of premium income are numerous, and some will be very indirect. Indirect costs will probably include a share of senior management salaries, accommodation costs, personnel department costs, investment department costs and so on. Establishing indirect costs per policy will involve allocation through several different levels; for example, the personnel department costs allocated to, say, the fire and accident department must then be allocated within that department to the different classes of business, and then again to individual policy level. This is perfectly practical, using the standard allocation methods. Frequently allocation of indirect expenses in the same proportion as direct expenses is regarded as the most appropriate method. However there is really no 'right' way of allocating overheads: some methods just produce better answers than others. It may therefore reasonably be asked whether the allocation of a corporate overhead such as the personnel department down to individual policy level produces a result which has any real meaning.

To question the allocation of overheads in pricing is to question the traditional approach to pricing, which involves building up the price to be charged from the various cost components, as illustrated at the beginning of this section. This traditional approach is widely established, not only in insurance but in many other industries. It is as well to recognise, though, that as a method of setting prices in a competitive market this approach has shortcomings quite apart from the artificiality of allocating all costs, however remote, to individual policies.

The main drawback is that before fixed costs can be allocated among policies it is necessary to know how many policies will be sold (or renewed). Yet sales will depend to a large extent on the price which we are currently trying to calculate. Any approach to pricing which starts out with assumptions about the level of sales, and ignores the fact that price and sales volumes are interdependent, cannot be wholly satisfactory. The second example in Section 9.7 examines this problem in more detail and suggests ways of dealing with it.

9.6 THE PURPOSE OF COST ALLOCATION

Costs may need to be allocated for the compilation of company accounts or supervisory returns, for management control, and for management decision-making. These will now be examined in turn.

Company accounts

The main purpose of company accounts is to provide shareholders with a true and fair view of the results of the company in which they have invested. In the United Kingdom, the form of these accounts is governed by the Companies Act 1948–1981 and also, in the case of insurance companies, by the Insurance Companies Act 1982. The Insurance Companies Act requires that a composite company must present separate accounts for its Life and non-Life business. Where, as in many cases, the insurer operates not as a single company but through a number of subsidiary companies, there may be a requirement to present separate accounts for subsidiaries. Some companies may choose to go further in presenting separate results for separate divisions – Home, Overseas, Marine, for example. Even if the insurer does not publish these divisional accounts, they may well have to be produced internally as part of the process of assembling the published accounts.

In recording the company's results, all costs must be taken fully into account. Costs must therefore be apportioned between each of the separate companies or divisions for which published or internal accounts are produced. While there is no statutory regulation of the way costs are apportioned, the auditors must be satisfied that the accounts give a true and fair view of the company.

Returns to the supervisory authority

Within six months of the end of each financial year, all UK insurers authorised by the Department of Trade and Industry (DTI) must provide detailed financial returns on standardised forms. Expenses must be stated separately for each accounting class, such as motor vehicle, general liability or property damage, although there is no requirement to show expenses separately by territory. Within these classes, claims-handling expenses (which are not deemed by the DTI to be management expenses) must be separated out and split between claims arising from incidents occurring during the financial year and prior-year claims. An insurer, therefore, has to isolate claims-handling expenses and to apportion all expenses between the accounting classes. For internal purposes it may also be helpful to split expenses by territory. As with company accounts, the submission to the DTI must be approved by the auditors.

Management control

Many large insurance companies rely on the principle of management by exception to exercise management control. Forecasts are made, plans, including budgets, are produced and agreed and these plans form the basis for monitoring performance. Where performance differs from plan by a significant margin, the manager responsible will be called to account.

The importance of costs in relation to management control is twofold. Firstly, all spending must be budgeted in advance, with the approved level of spending defined as that which will make the optimum contribution to the achievement of the company's objectives, as set out in its plan. Actual spending must then be monitored against budget. For effective control, this monitoring must be related to the cost or budget centre controlled by a manager who makes spending decisions. As we saw in Chapters 1 and 2, the manager responsible for a budget centre should be involved in developing the budget. He will then be responsible for its implementation, that is for ensuring that he achieves his objectives within the level of expenditure authorised by the budget (or, if the company uses a system of flexible budgeting, that any over- or under-attainment of objectives is matched by proportionate over- or under-spending of the budget). This form of budgetary control is an essential part of management control for all departments, both service departments and revenue-earning (or operating) departments.

For operating departments, however, there is a second control mechanism in which costs play an important part. This is the concept of accountability by profit centre performance. For this purpose, profit centres within the company are assessed as far as possible as if they were independent businesses. Operating expenses are set against revenue earned and a 'profit' result derived. (This approach is only really appropriate for operating departments or units because service departments do not directly earn revenue.) A branch office, for example, may well be a budget centre accountable to head office management for its expenditure. It may well also be a profit centre. In this case, the company's plans will include not only budgets but profit objectives for the branch, and profit performance will be monitored against profit objective.

This is not so straightforward as it sounds, because it involves deciding precisely what constitutes profit for monitoring purposes. Ultimately, the company as a whole must take all incurred costs into account in arriving at its published profit figures. But this may not be appropriate for the branch. For example, the branch could be monitored on the basis of premiums less claims and commission, or on these less the direct costs of actually running the branch (salaries, rent, postage and so on). Alternatively an equitable proportion of all head office costs and other overheads could also be taken into account.

Increasingly, insurance companies are using accountability by profit centre performance as a basis for management control of revenue-earning units. Profit centre accountability is seen as a more relevant measure of a manager's performance than, for example, achievement of premium income targets within an agreed budget. For any system of management accountability to work, though, it must be seen by the managers concerned as reasonably fair. This requirement will not be met if many of the important decisions contributing to 'profit' are outside the manager's control. Yet, if profit accountability excludes all costs which in some way are influenced by factors outside the manager's control, it is open to question whether what is left is any longer a meaningful measure of profit.

This is a problem faced by many companies in setting the basis for monitoring the profit performance of managers. There are no easy answers and each company must develop the solution which best suits its purpose. Clearly, though, without careful consideration of what costs are to be allocated and how, the concept of profit centre performance as a basis for assessing managers can easily fall into disrepute. In the case of the branch profit centre referred to, the most satisfactory answer may well be to derive the profit figure after allocation of all costs, including overheads, provided it can be demonstrated to the branch managers that the basis of allocation is fair when comparing one branch with another.

Management decision-making

Routine management control normally operates on the basis of management by exception. But if a manager, or the activity for which he is responsible, is consistently failing to produce the results planned, this may point to the need for reconsideration of the activity in question. Equally, the planning process (which looks at the company's operating environment, the changes in that environment and the threats and opportunities which those changes present, as discussed in Chapters 1 and 2) will frequently require decisions to be made about the action the company must take either to seize the opportunities or counter the threats.

Knowledge of the costs attaching to the activities concerned is usually vital for these decisions, as is the way in which these costs are allocated in examining the implication for alternative courses of action. This can be best seen by considering examples of the sort of decisions which confront insurance company managers and the part that allocation of costs plays in these decisions.

Broadly, management decisions fall into two categories – go/no-go decisions and optimising decisions. In the first category come such decisions as launching a new product, closing an unprofitable branch or computerising a clerical activity. In the second come such decisions as setting standards of service and the staffing levels to achieve them. Also in this second category, and of key importance, come pricing decisions. The examples in the following section consider one decision of the first sort (branch viability) and one of the second sort (pricing a line of business).

Table 9.5 Extract from branch profit report

	Branch A		Branch B	
	£k	%	£k	%
Premium income	5000	100	4000	100
Claims and commission	4500	90	3720	93
Branch salaries and other branch expenses	500	10	560	13
Branch share of HO overheads	400	8	320	8
Underwriting result	(400)	(8)	(600)	(15)
Attributable investment income	300	6	240	6
Overall branch result	(100)	(2)	(360)	(9)

Note: The effect of changes in reserves has been omitted for the sake of simplicity.

9.7 TWO EXAMPLES OF MANAGEMENT DECISION-TAKING

Example one: branch viability

An insurance company writing non-life insurance operates through 24 branches in the United Kingdom. The profitability of all branches is monitored regularly through a sophisticated reporting system which shows not only each branch's premiums, claims, commission and direct branch expenses but also the head office overheads allocated to the branch and the investment income attributable to its business. On the basis of these reports, two branches have been consistently unprofitable. Repeated attempts have been made over the years to improve results, by seeking additional premium income, containing branch expenses and reviewing underwriting procedures. While some improvements have been achieved, they have not been sufficient to bring the overall results into profit. Senior management, having received the latest reports, are now considering closing both branches. These latest reports are summarised in Table 9.5.

On the face of it, both branches are making substantial losses, even after taking into account investment income. There is, however, an important difference. If head office overheads are left out of the calculations, Branch A produces a 'profit' of £300 000 while Branch B still produces a loss of £40 000.

If senior management is satisfied that nothing can be done to improve the results of Branch B then the company will be more profitable without it and its closure will have to be faced (although considerations such as redundancy payments, redeployment of staff, disposal of premises and so on will still have to be taken into account).

Table 9.6 Revenue accounts of EG Insurance Company

	Household *£k*	*Motor* *£k*	*Accident* *£k*	*Total* *£k*
Premium income	2000	3000	1000	6000
Claims	950	1750	660	3360
Commission	300	300	100	700
Direct expenses	150	250	50	450
Overheads	400	600	200	1200
Profits	200	100	(10)	290

Note: The effect of investment income and changes in reserves have been omitted for the sake of simplicity.

Before closing Branch A, however, management needs to consider the effect of closure on total head office overheads. Branch A is contributing to these overheads and, unless total head office costs can be reduced by at least £300 000 following closure of Branch A, the company's overall profitability will deteriorate. Achieving a reduction of this scale by closing a branch is something that many insurers would find very difficult, because the same functions remain to be performed at head office even if the number of branches is reduced. So the company could be more profitable with Branch A than without it.

The decision may still be to close Branch A. After all, it is absorbing company resources for very little return and these resources may well produce better returns if employed elsewhere – in expanding the operations of other, more successful branches, for instance. However, the example illustrates that allocation of all costs to branch level is not necessarily helpful in deciding whether a branch should be kept open or not. This situation is not uncommon with management decisions. The question is not so much 'what is the best basis for allocating costs' but 'which costs should be allocated for the purpose of this decision?' In this case, as in so many others, it is important to distinguish between the costs directly incurred by the unit or activity, and those costs allocated to it.

Example two: pricing a line of insurance business

The E.G. Insurance Company transacts Household, Motor and Accident business. Expenses directly attributable to transacting these classes of business are charged to the revenue accounts. Overhead costs are apportioned between the classes in proportion to premium income, which is judged to be the most equitable method of apportionment for this company. The revenue accounts are shown in Table 9.6. On the basis of these figures, accident business is making a loss. As a result of studying the

Table 9.7 EG Insurance Company: revenue accounts after rate increase

	Household £k	*Motor* £k	*Accident* £k	*Total* £k
Premium income	2000	3000	1070 × 2/3 = 713	5713
Claims	950	1750	660 × 2/3 = 440	3140
Commission	300	300	107 × 2/3 = 71	671
Direct expenses	150	250	50 × 2/3 = 33	433
Overheads	420	630	150	1200
Profits	180	70	19	269

figures, management may decide either that it must stop writing accident business altogether, or that it must put up the rates.

We need not look in detail at what happens if the company decides to stop writing accident business, but the arithmetic is simple. Unless the company can reduce its total overheads in proportion to the reduction in total premiums (which is most unlikely) it will reduce its profits by discontinuing accident business.

Supposing the management decide that accident business must be made to produce the same average profits as Household and Motor (6 per cent of premiums) and they put premium rates up by 7 per cent in order to turn a 1 per cent loss into a 6 per cent profit. What could happen is that the increase in rates makes the company uncompetitive and as a result it loses one-third of its accident business. The figures then become as shown in Table 9.7. Because premiums have changed, the apportionment of overheads has changed. The result is that accident has improved, but not to the extent planned. Household and Motor appear to have deteriorated, and overall profit has been reduced. Clearly, the wrong decision has been taken.

A more satisfactory approach to the problem is to separate expenses into fixed costs and variable costs (that is, those which do not vary with the volume of business and those which do). Broadly speaking, direct costs will tend to be variable costs and overheads will tend to be fixed costs, and they are treated as such in this example. Only variable costs are then charged to each class of business and the gross surplus, or 'contribution', from each class is regarded as part of a pool, from which fixed costs are met. The balance is profit. Reworking Table 9.6 in this way gives the results shown in Table 9.8. Put like this, it becomes clear that each class of business is making a contribution to fixed costs and profits and it becomes easier to examine the consequences of changes in price and volume.

The problem now becomes one of maximising contribution, because, while fixed costs remain fixed, profit will be a maximum when total contribution is a maximum. This is where the relationship between price

Table 9.8 EG Insurance Company: revenue accounts (contribution basis)

	Household £k	*Motor* £k	*Accident* £k	*Total* £k
Premium income	2000	3000	1000	6000
Claims	950	1750	660	3360
Commission	300	300	100	700
Variable expenses	150	250	50	450
Contribution	600	700	190	1490
			Less fixed costs	1200
			Profit	290

and volume comes in. Price is not the only factor influencing the number of policies sold, but it is a very important one. Reducing the premium rates will reduce the contribution per unit, but it will normally increase the number of units sold. Conversely, increasing the premium rates will increase the unit contribution but will normally reduce the number of units sold. The aim of pricing will be to fix the premium rates at the level at which the combination of contribution per unit and total units sold produces maximum contribution overall.

Looking at the example again, it might be estimated that the following changes in accident rates would produce the corresponding (hypothetical) changes in volumes of business:

10% rate reduction	40%	increase in policy volumes
5% rate reduction	33 1/3%	increase in policy volumes
7% rate increase	33 1/3%	reduction in policy volumes
15% rate increase	50%	reduction in policy volumes

If these volume changes were borne out in practice, the effect on contribution would be as shown in Table 9.9. Since at current rates accident business is producing a contribution of £190 000 it can be seen that, provided fixed costs do not change over the volume of business under consideration, contribution is already near the maximum. If anything, a slight reduction in rates will increase contribution a little. Once again, in the case of pricing decisions, the question is not so much how costs should be allocated, but what costs should be allocated, and in this case the vital distinction to be made is between fixed costs and variable costs.

Nevertheless this approach to pricing has clear advantages over the traditional approach, which involves building up rates from a number of components and then adding on a margin for profit. This example, is of

Table 9.9 EG Insurance Company: accident business contribution

10% rate reduction		
Premiums (£k)	1000 × 0.9 × 1.4 =	1260
Claims	660 × 1.4 =	924
Commission	100 × 0.9 × 1.4 =	126
Variable costs	50 × 1.4 =	70
Contribution		140
5% rate reduction		
Premiums (£k)	1000 × 0.95 × 1.33 =	1267
Claims	660 × 1.33 =	879
Commission	100 × 0.95 × 1.33 =	127
Variable costs	50 × 1.33 =	67
Contribution		194
7% rate increase		
Premiums (£k)	1000 × 1.07 × 0.67 =	713
Claims	660 × 0.67 =	440
Commission	100 × 1.07 × 0.67 =	71
Variable costs	50 × 0.67 =	33
Contribution		169
15% rate increase		
Premiums (£k)	1000 × 1.15 × 0.5 =	575
Claims	660 × 0.5 =	330
Commission	100 × 1.15 × 0.5 =	58
Variable costs	50 × 0.5 =	25
Contribution		162

course, an over-simplification of the pricing process and further details are discussed in Chapter 12. In particular:

(a) The changes in volume in the example suggest that competitors have not changed their rates in response but, in practice, the reaction of competitors always has to be considered.
(b) The example treats a class of business as if it were a single, uniform product; in practice, there are many variations.
(c) The approach does not indicate whether the product's contribution is acceptable to the company. Determining whether a particular class or product is making an acceptable contribution is likely to involve some form of allocation of overheads.

9.8 CONCLUSION

This chapter has attempted to show why a proper identification and allocation of costs is vital to the successful management of a large insurance company. To a certain extent, it has been shown that any method of cost allocation tends to be arbitrary. There are no right or wrong methods of allocation, only some which are more appropriate for particular purposes than others. However there are occasions when allocation of all overheads can be inappropriate and can lead to the wrong decision being taken. Furthermore it will be argued in Chapter 10 that the artificial nature of allocation can introduce serious biases in determining factors such as the optimal size of the company and the range of products which should be carried.

Particular care must be taken with cost allocation in dealing with the pricing of a company's products. The traditional approach to pricing (which is discussed in detail in Chapter 12) requires that the cost associated with each policy be reflected in the premium rate on a 'cost-plus' basis. However the examples illustrated have demonstrated the difficulties of that approach and the allocation of all costs to individual policies may not be the right basis for many pricing decisions.

10 Insurance Company Output and Costs

Stephen Diacon

10.1 INTRODUCTION

Many management decisions, especially ones of an economic nature, involve a knowledge of the firm's output. For example, judgements on efficiency, profitability, pricing, advertising and so on cannot be made without reference to an appropriate output indicator. However in insurance, as in many other service industries, no unique measure of output is available because the service that insurers provide to their clients has many different aspects (which in turn vary in importance between the various classes of insurance business). Thus it is perhaps unrealistic to expect to derive a single figure for an insurance company's output. Furthermore many insurance companies are part of multiproduct firms, supplying not only different types of insurance but often other financial services such as banking, housing finance, estate agency or unit trust management. It would obviously be incorrect to attempt to incorporate these other activities into one conglomerate output measure, and yet the cost advantages of diversified firms cannot be ignored. One of the purposes of this chapter will therefore be to argue that it is a serious over-simplification to utilise a single output measure in making managerial decisions.

In practice, many of the key measures of efficiency and performance for insurance companies are made using premium income (that is, sales revenue) in lieu of output. Thus, for example, expense and commission ratios (obtained by dividing management expenses and commissions paid by premium income) are often used to provide an indicator of efficiency. While these have the advantage of simplicity and ease of aggregation, there are a number of crucial problems in using revenue (which, for one-year contracts, is essentially price per unit multiplied by the number of units sold) as a proxy for output. One simple illustration should suffice: if an insurer faces a demand function which has constant unit elasticity, then premium income will remain the same whatever its premium rate (since as premium rates are decreased, this is exactly balanced by the increase in sales – in terms of numbers of policies, say – and total premium revenue then remains constant). So, in this example, an insurer which lowers its premium rates in order to increase sales will do so without increasing premium income: 'output' has gone up (in terms of sales made) but not premium revenue.

The purpose of this chapter is to give an indication of how an insurance company's output could be measured, and then to explore the relationship between output and administrative expenses. The discussion proceeds in four main stages: first, the basic services performed by insurance companies are analysed in order to see what it is that policyholders actually purchase. Second, the use of the conventional measure of output based on premium income, especially in its role as the denominator of expense ratios, is criticised in detail. The third stage discusses an indicator of output that does not depend on premium income but instead attempts to measure the actual services that the insurer performs for its policyholders – this is based on the methodology described in O'Brien (1988). Finally, the important issue of the relationship between costs and output, in terms of economies of scale and scope, are analysed and some indication is given of their importance to the UK insurance industry.

10.2 THE SERVICES PERFORMED BY INSURERS

In supplying an insurance policy, the insurer is providing its client with a number of services or characteristics which form the output of the company. These can be categorised as: guarantee, organisation, investment and advice; the relative importance of these components depends on the type of insurance policy under consideration. Ideally one would want to base the output of an insurer on the number of units of guarantee, organisation and so on supplied (perhaps weighted by some appropriate prices to obtain an output index). However it is generally impractical to do so, and the methodology discussed in 10.4 can only be a rough approximation.

All insurance policies include the following services: guarantee, organisation, investment and advice.

Guarantee

The distinctive feature of insurance contracts is the insurer's guarantee that, subject to his own solvency, valid claims payments will be met. The responsibility for paying for losses covered by the contract is thus transferred from the insured to the insurance pool initially, and ultimately to the insurer's own resources. The insurer's guarantee covers three aspects of the stochastic nature of loss: the frequency and the amount of loss (which cause variation in the value of the insured's balance sheet assets), and the timing of the occurrence (which may cause the insured to experience cash-flow problems). As one might expect, the relative importance of these differs between the various classes of insurance.

In respect of the frequency of loss, many insurance contracts will provide compensation against the risk of one or more loss-producing events occurring during the contract period. In non-life insurance, it is customary to reduce the sum insured or limit of liability by the amount of each claim (thus providing a limit to the number of losses that may be covered in the year); however the sum insured can often be reinstated by the payment of an appropriate premium. In individual life insurance and pensions contracts, only one loss-producing event is usually physically possible in any case.

Similarly, in relation to the amount of loss, cover is often available against the risk of possible variation in the size of loss. Even if a loss were certain to occur, insureds may still want to protect themselves against the occurrence of an unexpectedly large loss. Most non-life insurance contracts are ones of indemnity, where the insurer undertakes to return the insured to the same financial position after the loss as he or she was in immediately before (subject to the sum insured). The majority of long-term insurance contracts, however, are not ones of indemnity and the amount of money to be paid in the event of a claim is predetermined.

As well as protecting the insured from variations in the size and frequency of loss, insurance also provides guarantees against the risk involved in the uncertain timing of the loss occurrence. This arises as, in most classes of insurance, the insurer will pay the claim (and endeavour to do so promptly) whenever the loss occurs during the contract period. Even if the loss was certain to occur, and known in amount, insureds may still wish to protect themselves against a loss which happens at a time when they have insufficient cash-flow to withstand one. Insurance provides protection by ensuring that the insured's cash-flow position is protected from the necessity of incurring unexpected expenditure.

Organisation

The second main function of the insurer is to organise the insurance pool; that is, to organise a group of pool members to join together for the purpose of diversifying their loss experience (so that the losses of the few are borne by the many). The organisation of the pool will involve a number of activities, including: collecting premium contributions and making claims payments; providing accounting and recording keeping; canvassing for new pool members; and investing pool funds (this last being discussed further below). One justification for the existence of commercial insurance firms is that they can organise an insurance pool more cost effectively than could the individual pool members acting on their own.

In general there are two main types of pool: in an *insurance pool* the organiser (that is, the insurer) also provides a guarantee that, subject to his own solvency, all valid claims will be paid. This means that, as described above, the insurer guarantees that, in the event of claims payments exceeding premium contributions, the difference will be provided out of his own resources (free reserves). In contrast, in a *mutual pool* the organiser's sole job is to administer the pool and he provides no guarantee that claims will be met from the existing resources made available by pool members. In the event of claims exceeding premium contributions to a mutual pool, the organiser must turn to the pool members for additional contributions in order to finance disbursements (indeed in such a pool there is no actual need for pre-loss premium contributions at all – all claims could be financed by post-loss calls on pool members).

Investment

In almost all classes of insurance, premium contributions are received by the insurer before any claims payments are made. The insurer therefore has the opportunity to establish a fund out of the premium contributions and invest it over the period until the fund is exhausted through the payment of claims and expenses. In addition to these technical reserves, any authorised insurer offering guarantees will also have free reserves to invest.

It has long been a source of argument whether or not the investment income and capital gains generated by an insurer's technical reserves should benefit the insured. However it is now generally accepted (and has always been so in life insurance) that, provided the funds are invested to match liabilities in the manner described in Section 16.1, the investment gains are attributable to the insured. Since, in some markets, a mechanism may not exist for the return of the benefits of successful investment performance to the non-life insured at the end of the contract, the usual approach will often be to discount premium rates to allow for investment earnings (a practice known as 'cash-flow underwriting'). An exception is the market for automobile insurance in West Germany, where any surplus on the year-end technical reserves in excess of 3 per cent of premium income must be returned to the insureds in the form of *ex post* rebates or dividends (for example, see Finsinger *et al.*, 1985, p. 144).

As will be seen later, the investment earnings on technical reserves may pose a difficult problem in the evaluation of an insurer's output and costs.

Advice

A further service provided by insurers is advice to insureds on risk management, and on the recovery on uninsured losses. Insurers also provide information on the costs of risk handling: for example, without insurance a manufacturer who was considering the installation of a sprinkler system would need to pay for expert advice on the likely savings in fire costs and on the reduction in the risk of a very large fire. But with full insurance cover, all the relevant information needed for the decision is contained in the reduction in fire insurance premium rates quoted by the insurer (irrespective of whether or not these accurately reflect the true reduction in the risk of fire).

10.3 THE PROBLEMS WITH PREMIUM INCOME AS A MEASURE OF OUTPUT

Introduction

Premium income is commonly used to give an indication of an insurer's output, and it easy to see why. The ease with which premium figures can be obtained, and the apparent ability to compare across product lines and companies, means that premium income (with all its faults) will continue to be used in lieu of a more appropriate measure. This is especially the case because there is no other obvious, equally simple and available candidate. Furthermore, even if it was possible to measure the output of one particular class of insurance in homogeneous units (say, numbers of policies sold), there would still be the problem of aggregation across differing classes of insurance business; the usual approach in such cases is to weight the units by their respective prices and sum, thus obtaining something very similar to total premium income.

None the less there are still major problems in using premium income as a measure of insurance company output, and these are particularly serious when attempting to evaluate cost-effectiveness (in terms of scale economies for example). In fact, none of the recent studies into the economies of scale obtainable in insurance cited in 10.5 below use premium income to measure output. In those circumstances where premium income is (and will continue to be) commonly used in practice – for example as an indicator of business growth and as the denominator in expense ratios – it is important to be aware of the deficiencies outlined below.

The problems with premium income as a measure of output arise in two main areas. In the first place, premium income includes items which do not correlate with the services provided by insurers outlined in 10.2 above. In particular, the risk premium component (see sections 11.3 and 12.2) is simply a transfer payment between policyholders and should not be included in the insurer's output. The second area of difficulty arises because premium income is a measure of trading revenue and not output and is therefore affected by the pricing policy adopted by insurers. Only in those (extremely rare) cases where all insurers charged the same premium rate (for a homogeneous product) could premium income be used to accurately reflect output, since differences in premium income among companies would be caused solely by variations in the number of units sold.

Non-correlation of premium income with insurance services

In order for premium income to reflect output accurately it must correspond in timing and amount with the main services provided by insurers – in the form of guarantees, organisation, investment and advice – outlined in 10.2 above. However this correspondence very rarely obtains, and this can give rise to problems not only in judging internal efficiency but also in assessing alternative policy options at a national level (for example, see Price Waterhouse, 1988, section 5). A more detailed discussion of the contribution of insurance to the national economy can be found in Van den Berghe (1984).

The major difficulty with premium income is that, for most classes of insurance, the greatest part of the premium payment is the insured's contribution to the insurance pool. This contribution does not form part of output, but is used by the insurer to effect a transfer payment from those who do not make claims to those who do. The insurer's essential role here is to organise the pool, and it would be a mistake to use a measure which implied that the bigger the pool (in terms of the size of contributions into it) the greater the organisation required. So, for example, suppose insurer A had a household fire portfolio of identical houses each worth £100 000, while insurer B had a portfolio of the same number of houses which were identical to those of A except that they were each valued at £200 000 (because they were located in an area of higher house prices). Obviously, although B's premium income is double that of A, the insurers produce the same output in terms of numbers of policies and organisational services provided.

In theory, therefore, risk premium payments into the insurance pool must be deducted from any output measure based on premium income. In practice the aggregate of risk premium contributions may be unknown, and sometimes claims incurred (that is, disbursements out of the pool) are deducted instead (this is the approach used in the national accounts to obtain the contribution of insurance towards national product). This practice simply introduces further problems by introducing a random term into the output calculation as a result of the variability of claims experience, and causes problems when investment earnings are considered (as described below).

Other problems with output measures based on premium income relate to the timing of that income. For output measured over a calendar year, say, the premium income should obviously relate to premiums earned in that year, and so take account of changes in the unearned premium reserves (as discussed in section 15.5). Unfortunately such reserves are often not separated by class of business. Equally, any claims disbursements deducted (in view of the above comments) should be based on claims incurred rather than claims paid in the year. However in practice the calculation of claims incurred is complicated by the need to include an estimate for outstanding and incurred but not reported claims, and is often further confused by adjustments in outstanding claims reserves relating to claims in previous years.

The treatment of the impact of any reinsurance transactions on premiums and claims should also be considered. Ideally the output of direct insurance and 'outwards' reinsurance business should be treated separately because of their different characteristics and cost structures. However the main issue relates to the purchase of 'inwards' reinsurance: should this be deducted from premium income (to get net rather than gross figures) or not? The answer depends very much on the subsequent use of the output measure: if the purpose is to provide an indication of the value added by the company (which is essential if the outputs of a number of companies are to be aggregated) then premiums net of reinsurance should be used; if however the purpose is give some indication of market presence (perhaps in terms of market share) then the gross figures are probably more appropriate.

The final problem arising because of the lack of correlation between premium income and insurance services occurs over the treatment of the insurer's investment earnings on technical reserves. The crucial issue is whether or not an insurer's investment earnings add to its output. In the UK national accounts, the investment income of life insurers is treated as a transfer payment (so that it belongs to policyholders) and is therefore ignored in the calculation of output. In theory this approach implies that, if risk premiums are discounted for the effects of future investment earnings (as occurs in life insurance and in cash-flow underwriting of general business), then actual premium income will also be reduced by the amount of the discounted earnings, so that output (given by premium income less risk premiums) is unaffected. In practice, if claims payments were deducted in lieu of the (unknown) risk premiums (as described above) then the reduction of premium income by the amount of discounted earnings may not be cancelled out by an equivalent reduction in claims (particularly in non-life insurance): the peculiar position is therefore reached where an increase in assumed investment earnings reduces output. Obviously the discounted investment earnings subsumed in the premium income figure then needs to be added back, to preserve the neutral effect of earnings on output.

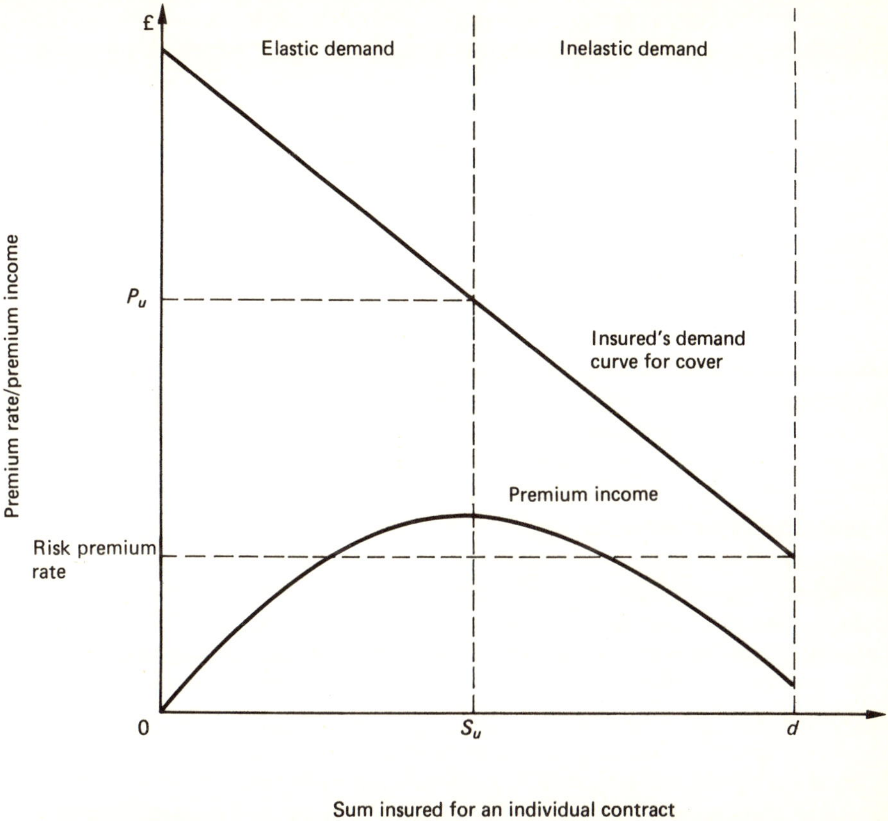

Figure 10.1 The impact of pricing policy on premium income

The impact of pricing policy

The other main problem area involved in using premium income to measure the output of an insurance company arises because premium income is essentially a revenue rather than an output measure. Conceptually the premium income generated from one individual contract is the product of the premium rate (unit price) and a measure of the quantity of insurance coverage required (such as sums insured). If the insured has a downward sloping demand curve for insurance (as one would generally expect) then, at a given risk premium rate, the higher the market or office premium rate the lower the required coverage. Whether or not premium income increases as premium rates rise depends on the price elasticity of demand: the situation is illustrated in Figure 10.1. At premium rates above P_u an increase in premium income can be achieved via a reduction in premium rates (in order to obtain a corresponding rise in the cover required by the insured); similarly at rates below P_u an increase in premium income can be obtained through a rise in unit price (that is, a fall in the cover required). In other words, when demand is elastic premium income and quantity/output move together in response to a price change, but when demand is inelastic they move in opposite directions. Thus, unless the elasticity of demand is always known in advance, it is almost impossible to infer output from the behaviour of premium income.

The position is less problematic if prices remain constant but the demand curve for insurance shifts (perhaps owing to a change in disposable income, advertising, interest rates and so on). In this case a rise in demand (that is a shift in the demand curve to the right) would increase quantity/output and premium income together so long as price remained constant. The same basic results are obtained for the insurer's total premium income when the premiums from a portfolio of homogeneous risks are added together.

The requirement that premium rates should remain constant if premium income is to used as an output measure is rather a restrictive one. In comparing the outputs of differing insurers, it implies that all companies should charge the same price: in a competitive market this is tantamount to the assumption that the market is perfectly competitive (see section 12.4), and this in turn rules out the very possibility of measuring the existence of economies of scale (for example, see Doherty, 1981).

10.4 AN ALTERNATIVE MEASURE OF OUTPUT

The purpose of this section is to describe an output index that does not utilise premium income, but is instead based on the units of service described in 10.2 above: 'although the policies may represent the output, the essence of (life) insurance production is the function undertaken to provide services to policyholders' (O'Brien, 1988). Care must be taken, though, to ensure that it is the output of those services purchased by consumers which is being measured, rather than the input of factors of production or intermediate activities. (For a discussion of the issues involved in measuring the inputs and outputs of the service sector, see Kendrick, 1985).

Although the amount of each service provided by an insurer can be difficult to determine, in many cases it may be better to undertake this imperfect measurement than to use premium income as a proxy for output. Whichever method is selected, it is important that it can be used to give an indication not only of the overall output of the insurer, but also of the company's output in disaggregated individual markets.

If it can be assumed that each policy in a particular class of insurance provides an identical 'package' of the services provided by the insurer (that

Table 10.1 The output of a specialist life office

Insurance service	*Service units*	*Unit cost (£)*
	Year 1	
New business		
New life policies	10 000	110.0
In-force policies		
Sending statements to insureds	80 000	2.0
Dealing with claims	7 000	30.0
Dealing with enquiries/renewals	4 000	5.0
Dealing with surrenders	5 000	50.0
Investment services	80 000	2.0
	Year 2	
New Business		
New life policies	11 000	114.55
In-force policies		
Sending statements to insureds	83 000	2.13
Dealing with claims	7 100	31.97
Dealing with enquiries/renewals	4 636	5.39
Dealing with surrenders	6 000	58.33
Investment services	83 000	2.12

So the increase in company output is given by:

(11 000 × 110 + 83 000 × 2.0 + 7100 × 30.0 + 4636 × 5.0 + 6000 × 50.0 + 83000 × 2.0)
divided by
(10 000 × 110 + 80 000 × 2.0 + 7000 × 30.0 + 4000 × 5.0 + 5000 × 50.0 + 80000 × 2.0).

This gives the ratio 2078180/1900000 which equals 1,09378; an increase of 9.38 per cent.

Source: Based on O'Brien (1988), Appendix 3.

is, guarantee, organisation, investment and advice) then the (gross) output of those services can be proxied by the number of policies sold. Of course, the classes of insurance will vary in the mix of services provided, and for life insurance new business and business in force must be treated separately.

If an aggregated output measure is required (for example, to give total company output), an index of production must be constructed from a weighted sum of the various classes of business. Because of the transfer element included in insurance premiums and the other problems associated with premium income outlined in 10.3 above it is not possible to use prices as weights, and the unit costs associated with each product line must be used instead (as described in detail in Hirshhorn and Geehan, 1977).

Preferably the weights should be derived from industry-wide analyses of unit costs such as that for UK life insurance discussed in Luffrum *et al.* (1986).

O'Brien (1988) attempts a much more scrupulous analysis which is not based on the assumption that each class of insurance has its own particular mix of insurance services. Instead he tries to identify in detail the services or functions provided within each class of insurance (which he terms 'basic service units') and measure these directly. These service units should relate to those 'final' insurance services which motivate the purchase by policyholders rather than any intermediate activity necessary to produce those services. Quantities of the various basic service units are then weighted by the unit costs in their provision to produce an overall output figure for the company.

Table 10.1 illustrates the technique to compute the annual increase in output of a specialist life office, which in the first year services 80 000 existing in-force life contracts at a unit cost of £10 each and 10 000 new life policies at a unit cost of £110. In the second year, the number of in-force policies serviced has risen to 83 000 (an increase of 3.75 per cent) and new business produces 11 000 new life contracts. The increase in company output based on the number of contracts (using first year unit costs as weights) is given by:

$$\{(83\,000\times 10 + 11\,000\times 110)\,/\,(80\,000\times 10 + 10\,000\times 110)\} - 1 = 0.0737,$$

that is 7.37 per cent. Although each new business policy may involve an identical 'package' of services, this is unlikely to be the case for in-force contracts since the expenses incurred in servicing existing contracts are unlikely to be spread evenly over all such policies. Table 10.1 therefore breaks down the insurance service for in-force contracts into more detailed service units and shows that two services in particular ('Dealing with enquiries/renewals' and 'Dealing with surrenders') have increased more rapidly than the overall number of in-force contracts. The more accurate computation of the increase in company output then produces a figure of 9.38 per cent.

10.5 ECONOMIES OF SCALE AND SCOPE IN INSURANCE

Introduction

An understanding of the relationship between a firm's costs and output is crucial. If costs are related to the firm's various outputs then, by selecting appropriate output levels, the insurer can reduce costs to an optimal level which will allow either lower premium rates, higher product performance (in the case of long-term contracts) or greater profits for shareholders. Thus information on cost structures can play an important role in strategic decisions in the areas of company expansion and diversification. In long-term insurance, an insurer with low cost levels will also be able to use this information to demonstrate its efficiency to potential policyholders (who may be comparing the administrative costs of different forms of investment vehicles). For example, following the enactment of the Financial Services Act 1986, life offices in the United Kingdom are required to provide new policyholders with a statement illustrating their cost structures; the available evidence (for example, see Carter and Diacon, 1990, Part C) seems to indicate substantial differences in the efficiency of UK life offices.

Information on economies of scale and scope is also of considerable interest to regulators who may have the job of deciding whether or not proposed mergers between financial services firms are in the public interest. Similarly, in attempting to assess the benefits of European integration, Price Waterhouse (1988) noted that size-related economies would have important implications for the competitive operation of financial markets, and proposed to undertake further work in the area.

The existence of economies of scale and scope

Economies of scale describe the relationship between the output of a single-product firm and the lowest level of cost attainable at that output level. Given the opportunity to plan ahead, firms may be expected to adjust working practices in order to minimise production costs, and hence actually achieve the lowest attainable cost at a given level of output.

The behaviour of this (minimised) cost as output changes has important implications for the success of the firm: for example, if long-run unit costs decline slowly but significantly as output increases then large firms will have a substantial cost advantage over small ones. The presence of these economies of scale could then account for (and justify the existence of) the predominance of large firms in the industry. In those industries where low unit costs can only be obtained at output levels which approach (or even exceed) national aggregate demand there may be some justification for the existence of a natural monopoly. On the other hand, if an industry shows evidence of diseconomies of scale (so that large firms have higher unit costs than medium-sized ones), the existence of large firms is detrimental to the public interest.

The presence or otherwise of economies of scale has implications for the structure of a competitive industry. If economies of scale are important at high output levels then we would expect there to be only a small number of firms operating in the industry. Reversing the argument, the existence of a small number of large firms provides some evidence of the importance of

Table 10.2 An illustration of economies of scope

Company 1 produces 100 of A and 200 of B at a total cost of £140.

Company	2		3		4		5		6	
Product	A	B	A	B	A	B	A	B	A	B
Output	50	100	30	120	70	80	100	0	0	200
Total Cost (£)	75		75		80		90		95	

Economies of scope exist in the output of A and B since the costs involved in producing 100 of A and 200 of B by company 1 (i.e. £140) are less than the sum of costs for any other combination of companies producing the same output; for example summing the costs of companies 3 and 4 gives £155 while the sum for companies 5 and 6 gives £185. Economies of scale also exist because the outputs of company 2 could be doubled at less than twice the cost.

scale economies. Similarly, if an industry has a large number of competing firms (of perhaps varying size) then, if the industry is competitive, economies of scale are unlikely to be very important.

The existence of economies of scope (sometimes known as economies of joint production) gives multiproduct firms a cost advantage over single-product ones. They are said to exist if the cost of producing a given combination of outputs is less for a single firm than for the production of the same combination by a collection of two or more smaller companies. Economies of scope arise when two or more products have joint costs that cannot be perfectly separated and when the marginal cost of producing any one product decreases with increases in the quantities of all other products.

Recent work on economies of scope in insurance tends to treat insurance companies as multiproduct firms; for example the paper by Kellner and Mathewson (1983) regarded Canadian specialist ordinary branch life offices as having four separate (but not independent) product lines (individual life, group life, individual annuities and group annuities). Obviously most UK insurance groups would be multiproduct firms under this definition, since they sell not only insurance (often both long-term and general) but also other financial services products such as unit trusts, estate agency services and housing finance.

The application of economies of scope is illustrated in Table 10.2; they arise in company 1 because it can produce 100 units of product A and 200 of product B at lower total cost than any combination of other companies (such as 3 and 4, or 5 and 6). The figures imply that, if these companies wish to compete with company 1, they must consider some form of merger to obtain advantages of scope. Company 2 also provides some evidence of a multiproduct version of economies of scale since, although its outputs are exactly half those of company 1, its costs are more than 50 per cent of 1's (this is known as 'declining ray average costs' or 'overall scale economies').

It should be noted that no attempt has been made in Table 10.2 to isolate the costs involved in producing A and B separately (by the methods described in Section 9.4). Since A and B are produced jointly it would be a mistake to attempt to allocate costs, and any such attempt would confuse the existence of scope economies. Similarly it would be unwise to try to combine the output of A and B into a unified output index (as described in the previous section) for the same reason.

As with economies of scale, the structure of a competitive industry should provide an indication of the importance of economies of scope. For example, the fact that, in the United Kingdom, nine out of the top ten insurance companies are composites would seem to indicate that there are some cost advantages in being a multiple-line insurer (for further details see Carter and Diacon, 1990, Part A).

The recognition that many financial services firms are multiproduct ones creates problems for the analysis of costs since, on the one hand, it would be a mistake to partition total costs to product lines (because the allocation would be wholly artificial, as explained in Section 9.7) and, on the other hand, the (unpartitioned) total cost cannot be compared with company output (because there is no single measure of that!). These difficulties mean that there is no easy way of assessing the presence of economies of scale and scope for multiproduct firms. Furthermore any attempt to evaluate cost structures which ignores the multiproduct nature of most insurance groups is doomed to failure (especially since the evidence which is available seems to indicate that scope economies are generally more important than economies of scale): this criticism unfortunately applies to the bulk of empirical work on insurance company costs.

There are a variety of possible sources of economies of scale and scope in insurance companies. The main economies of scale are thought to arise via the operation of the law of large numbers in the pooling of insurance risks, and from the spreading of overheads incurred by the central administrative/organisational functions such as computer operations, investment and marketing. Luffrum *et al.* (1986) note that the computer 'system requirements for any office which sells a given range of products is basically the same, and therefore the cost of developing appropriate computer systems – a major factor in the overall computer cost – must, to a certain extent, be of the same order for all offices'. Further discussion on economies of scale can be found in Diacon (1981a; 1981b). The most important economies of scope are likely to arise in the distribution of insurance and other financial services products (since more than one product can use the same distribution network) and in the sharing of marketing information system databases (particularly since the sale of one product provides firms with customer information, as described in section 13.4, which may aid the sale of another to the same client).

Testing for the existence of economies of scale and scope

Very little empirical work has been undertaken which tests for the existence of economies of scale and scope in insurance, or other financial services markets, in a sufficiently rigorous way. The main exceptions are the Canadian studies by Kellner and Mathewson (1983) and Daly, Rao and Geehan (1985) for insurance (although the latter uses a company output index and so ignores the multiproduct nature of insurance companies), and Murray and White (1983) and Youn Kim (1986) for credit unions. Little or no study has been undertaken which considers the broader spread of financial products made available by financial conglomerates.

The absence of satisfactory empirical work can be explained in part by the recent development of the theoretical issues surrounding economies of scope, the problems in obtaining a measure of insurance output, and the practical difficulties involved in testing the relationship between output and costs. All the recent econometric work on the relationship between output and costs has tended to use a translog multiproduct cost function which has the logarithm of total (unpartitioned) company costs as the dependent variable, and the logarithms of input prices and outputs in various combinations as independent variables. An additional complication arises in the estimation procedure which usually involves a system of equations (whose error terms are related in the manner of Zellner's seemingly unrelated regressions) in order to capture the relationship between total cost, input prices and the amount of input factor required in the production process.

In their study of the Canadian life insurance industry, Kellner and Mathewson (1983) found some evidence for certain economies of scope but none for economies of scale. The latter results confirm those obtained by previous, less satisfactory, work. No consistent pattern emerged on the existence of pairwise scope economies however and, in any case, these had disappeared by the mid-1970s, so that more recent entrants to the industry would be less likely to produce a variety of product lines. This conclusion was in fact justified by subsequent experience.

References

Carter, R.L and S.R. Diacon (1990) *The British Insurance Industry* (Brentford, Middlesex: Kluwer Publishing).

Daly, M.J., P.S. Rao and R. Geehan (1985) 'Productivity, Scale Economies and Technical Progress in the Canadian Life Insurance Industry', *International Journal of Industrial Organisation*, vol. 3, pp. 345–61.

Diacon, S.R. (1981a) *Economics* (London: Chartered Insurance Institute, Study-course Number 030).

Diacon, S.R. (1981b) 'Scale Economies in Life Insurance', *Papers in Risk and Insurance* (University of Nottingham) April.

Doherty, N.A. (1981) 'The Measurement of Output and Economies of Scale in Property-Liability Insurance', *Journal of Risk and Insurance*, vol. XLVIII, no. 3, pp. 390–402.

Finsinger, J., E. Hammond and J. Tapp (1985) *Insurance: Competition or Regulation*? (London: The Institute of Fiscal Studies) Report Series no. 19.

Hishhorn, R. and R. Geehan 'Measuring the Real Output of the Life Insurance Industry', *The Review of Economics and Statistics*, vol. 49, pp. 211–19.

Kellner, S. and G.F. Mathewson (1983) 'Entry, Size Distribution, Scale and Scope Economies in the Life Insurance Industry', *Journal of Business*, vol. 56, no. 1, pp. 25–44.

Kendrick, J.W. (1985) 'Measurement of Output and Productivity in the Service Sector', in R.P. Inman (ed.), *Managing the Service Economy* (Cambridge: Cambridge University Press).

Luffrum, G.G., A.G. O'Leary and A.D. Sheddon (1986) 'The Life Associations' Inter-Office Expense Investigation', *Journal of the Institute of Actuaries*, vol. 113.

Murray, J.D. and R.W. White (1983) 'Economies of Scale and Economies of Scope in Multiproduct Financial Institutions: A Study of British Columbia Credit Unions', *Journal of Finance*, vol. 38, no. 2, pp. 887–902.

O'Brien, C.D. (1988) *Measuring the Output of Life Assurance Companies*, paper presented to the Manchester Actuarial Society, 24 February.

Price Waterhouse (1988) *The 'Cost of Non-Europe' in Financial Services, Research on the 'Cost of Non-Europe': Basic Findings Volume 9* (Commission of the European Communities).

Van Den Burghe, L. (1984) 'The Insurance Business: A Macro-Economic Evaluation', in M. Haller and W. Ackermann (eds), *Internationality in Insurance* (Institute of Insurance Economics at the St. Gall Graduate School) Publication Series vol. 14.

Youn Kim, H. (1986) 'Economies of Scale and Economies of Scope in Multiproduct Financial Institutions: Further Evidence from Credit Unions', *Journal of Money, Credit, and Banking*, vol. 18, no. 2, pp. 220–6.

11 Premium Rating: Methods and Problems

John Pollard

11.1 INTRODUCTION

Many factors need to be taken into account in setting the premium rate for an insurance contract. The more important ones, which are discussed in this chapter, are illustrated by the following breakdown of the office premium.

- risk premium: claim frequency
  claim size
  claims-handling expenses
- effect of a deductible
- effect of excess of loss reinsurance
- loading for contingencies
- adjustments for inflation
- adjustments for investment income
- expenses: proportional to premium
  per policy
  overheads
- profit loading
- market forces

The principles involved are clearly demonstrated in the rating of the various personal lines of insurance (householders' insurance, motor vehicle damage and so on), for which adequate statistics are usually available and claims are normally notified and settled with little delay. The same factors need to be considered and the same basic approach to rating adopted in respect of other classes of business, but, for many of these classes, other complications arise which cloud the basic rating routine. Long delays in notification and settlement of liability claims, for example, complicate the compilation of statistics on claim frequency and claim size and the estimation of the underlying distributions for the various liability classes.

Statistical methods are required to assess the risk premium (i.e. that necessary to meet expected claims costs) for a particular line, the effect of a deductible, the effect of non-proportional reinsurances and the loading required for contingencies. The necessary statistical tools are outlined briefly below in Section 11.2.

The major part of the chapter is then devoted to the calculation of the office premium (i.e. that which is actually charged to insureds) taking account of all the main factors displayed above, namely the risk premium, deductibles, excess of loss reinsurance, loadings for contingencies, adjustments for inflation and investment earnings, expenses, profit loading and market forces. Most of the principles involved are demonstrated in terms of a single simple example.

The full rating procedure outlined in Sections 11.3–11.11 below may be applied relatively simply to certain lines of insurance and, with varying degress of difficulty, to other lines. Problems are caused by delays in the reporting and settlement of claims, zero claims, re-opened claims, small data bases, risks which are not homogeneous, and unusual risks. These difficulties are discussed towards the end of the chapter in Section 11.12. If risks are to be underwritten profitably, however, it is essential that all the factors in the basic rating routine be considered, even if practical problems prevent an accurate determination of their effect in many instances.

11.2 STATISTICAL METHODS

Probability theory finds application in almost every area of human activity. For most practical applications, however, fairly lengthy descriptions of the processes being studied are required. Games of chance on the other hand are usually very easy to describe and readily understood. For this reason, they are convenient for introducing and describing the basic concepts of probability and statistics, and we shall make use of them for this purpose now. Intuitively, at least, there would seem to be a great similarity between insurance and a game of chance!

Let us imagine that an unbiased coin is tossed 10 times. We would expect the number of heads to be about 5. Imagine that this experiment is performed many times. We will often get 5 heads. We will also often get 3 heads, 4 heads, 6 heads and 7 heads, and, less frequently, 0, 1, 2, 8, 9 and 10 heads. These results are confirmed in the coin-tossing experiment recorded in Table 11.1, which was performed 100 times. The proportions reported in the table may be represented graphically as a relative frequency diagram, as shown in Figure 11.1.

It is not difficult to show theoretically that the probabilities of 0, 1, 2, . . . , 10 heads when a coin is tossed 10 times are respectively

$$\frac{1}{1024}, \frac{10}{1024}, \frac{45}{1024}, \frac{120}{1024}, \frac{210}{1024}, \frac{252}{1024}, \frac{210}{1024}, \frac{45}{1024}, \frac{10}{1024} \text{ and } \frac{1}{1024}$$

Table 11.1 Number of heads obtained when a coin was tossed 10 times (in an experiment performed 100 times)

Number of heads (j)	*Number of experiments resulting in exactly j heads*	*Proportion of experiments resulting in exactly j heads*
0	0	0.00
1	1	0.01
2	4	0.04
3	13	0.13
4	19	0.19
5	27	0.27
6	20	0.20
7	11	0.11
8	4	0.04
9	0	0.00
10	1	0.01
Total	100	1.00

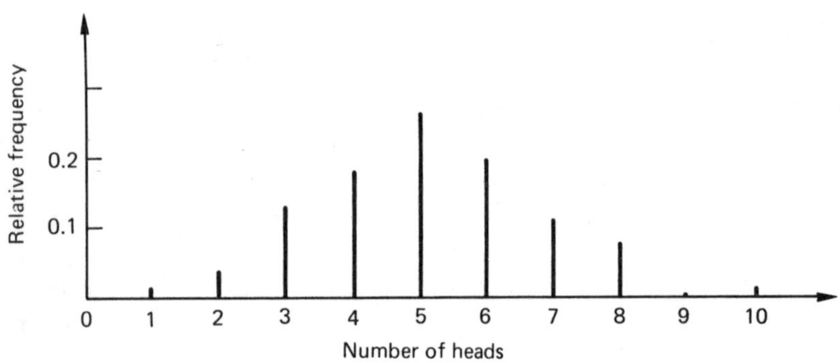

Source: Table 11.1.
Figure 11.1 The relative frequency of heads when a coin is tossed 10 times

These probabilities define a probability (or statistical) distribution over the whole numbers (or integers) 0 to 10, and may be represented graphically as in Figure 11.2. The similarity of Figures 11.1 and 11.2 should be noted. If the experiment reported in Table 11.1 were repeated millions of times instead of just 100 times, the relative frequency diagram and the probability distribution would be indistinguishable. The distinction between the relative frequency diagram, or observed distribution, and the underlying probability distribution is important in general insurance, when the underlying distribution is never known and premium calculations have to be performed using the observed distribution or a distribution based on observed data.

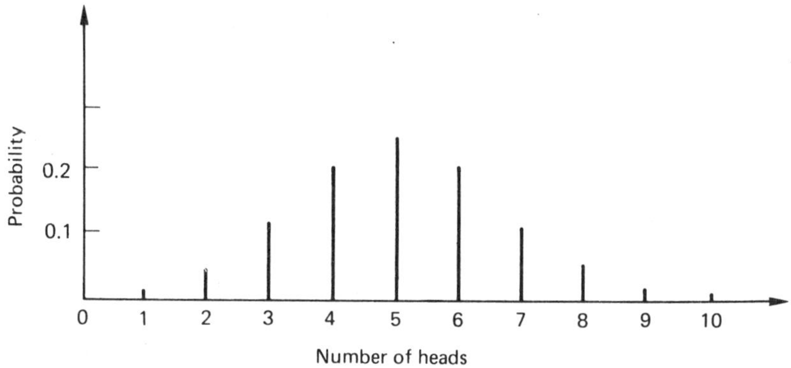

Figure 11.2 The probability distribution of the number of heads when a coin is tossed 10 times

Mean or expectation

It is clear from the calculated probabilities and Figure 11.2 that, if an unbiased coin is tossed 10 times, the probability that the number of heads will lie between 3 and 7 inclusive is very high (about 90 per cent). In other words, we would expect the number of heads to be near a central value of about 5 with a high probability. A convenient measure of this central location is the mean or expectation calculated as follows:

$$\begin{bmatrix}\text{Sum over all possible} \\ \text{values of } j\end{bmatrix} \quad \text{of} \quad \begin{bmatrix} j \times \text{probability of obtaining} \\ \text{value } j\end{bmatrix}$$

In the case of the coin-tossing experiment, therefore, the mean number of heads is

$$\left(0 \times \frac{1}{1024}\right) + \left(1 \times \frac{10}{1024}\right) + \left(2 \times \frac{45}{1024}\right) + \ldots\ldots + \left(9 \times \frac{10}{1024}\right) + \left(10 \times \frac{1}{1024}\right)$$

which turns out to be 5 exactly. The mean or expected number of heads is 5.

Variance and standard deviation

Two probability distributions are shown in Figure 11.3. The distributions have the same mean. It is clear, however, that the first distribution is more widely dispersed. As a result, we would be much more likely to obtain a value well away from the mean with the first distribution than with the second. The variance of a distribution provides a measure of its dispersion. It is usually calculated as follows:

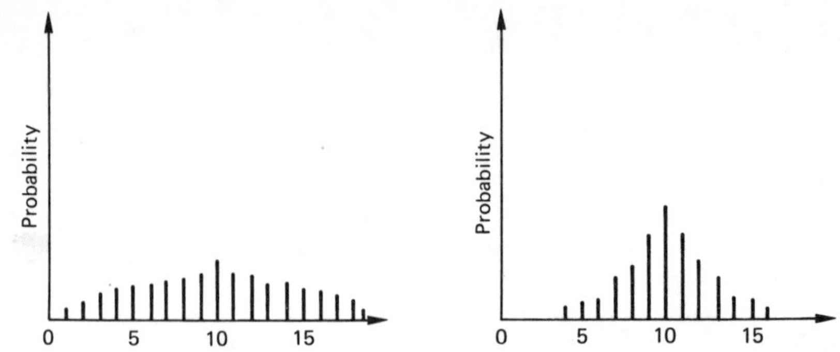

Figure 11.3 Two different probability distributions having the same mean (10)

$$\begin{bmatrix}\text{Sum over all possible}\\ \text{values of } j\end{bmatrix} \quad \text{of} \quad \begin{bmatrix} j^2 \times \text{probability of obtaining}\\ \text{value } j\end{bmatrix}$$

$$\textit{minus} \quad \text{square of mean.}$$

In the case of the coin-tossing experiment therefore, the variance is

$$\left(0^2 \times \frac{1}{1024}\right) + \left(1^2 \times \frac{10}{1024}\right) + \left(2^2 \times \frac{45}{1024}\right) + \ldots\ldots + \left(10^2 \times \frac{1}{1024}\right) - (5^2)$$

which turns out to be 2.5.

When a distribution is concentrated very close to its mean, the variance is very close to zero (that is, there is little dispersion). When the distribution is well spread out, the variance is large. The standard deviation is also often used to measure the dispersion of a distribution and is defined as the square root of variance.

Use of standard probability distributions

There are many standard probability distributions which find application in general insurance (see Hossack *et al.* 1983). Theoretical distributions such as these are useful for the following reasons:

(a) The distributions have convenient and well-known properties which facilitate calculation and analysis.
(b) Each distribution is summarised by a small number of parameters, so that it is not necessary to list all the probabilities of the distribution.
(c) The standard distributions allow one to make inferences about insurance portfolios.

(d) Standard distributions are usually convenient for mathematical manipulation, allowing the development of useful theoretical results.

Whilst, in this chapter, we make little overt use of standard probability distributions and concentrate on observed distributions obtained directly from insurance data, covert use is made of some standard distributions at various stages. The Poisson distribution is an important probability distribution widely applicable to claim frequency data. The methods to be adopted in Section 11.3 for handling exposure depend essentially on properties of the Poisson distribution. This distribution is also assumed for claim frequency in Section 11.6 when determining the loading required for contingencies. The figure of 2.33 standard deviations which also appears in that section is the upper 1 per cent of another standard distribution, the normal distribution, the use of which is justified by an important general theorem known as the Central Limit Theorem.

11.3 THE RISK PREMIUM

Claim frequency and claim size

The risk premium is the premium that would on average exactly meet the expected cost of a given risk, in the absence of management expenses, commission, contingency loadings, profits and so on. To compute it, it is necessary to estimate the claim frequency rate (the expected number of claims per policy per annum) and the mean claim size. The risk premium is the product of these two quantities.

Although risk premiums can sometimes be calculated on a 'rate of payment of claims' basis without separating claim frequency and claim size, these two distinct components should be considered separately if at all possible, for the following reasons:

(a) Premium rates are calculated using recent claims experience data, taking account of trends and other factors which are currently operating and are likely to operate in the future. Some of these factors affect claim frequency and claim size differently. Inflation, for example, will affect claims size, but is unlikely to have much effect on claim frequency (unless there is a deductible which is not exactly indexed to claim inflation).
(b) Only if the claim size distribution is known, can the effect of introducing or varying a deductible, or of varying the retention for non-proportional reinsurance, be properly assessed.

Table 11.2 The distribution of claim size

Claim size range (1) £	*Mean claim in range* (2) £	*Mean claims-handling expenses* (3) £	*Mean cost for claims in range [(2) + (3)]* (4) £	*Number of claims* (5)	*Proportion of claims [(5) ÷ 247]* (6)
0– 250	137	27	164	21	0.085
250– 500	373	32	405	95	0.385
500–1 000	736	59	795	63	0.255
1 000–2 000	1 410	67	1 477	35	0.142
2 000–4 000	3 051	119	3 170	19	0.077
4 000–8 000	5 803	207	6 010	11	0.044
8 000 and over	11 155	298	11 453	3	0.012
Total	—	—	—	247	1.000

Claims-handling expenses

Claims-handling expenses are an essential feature of claims and are best included directly as part of the cost of claims in the calculation of the risk premium, even though this would tend to contradict the strict definition of 'risk premium'.

A numerical example of claim size

In respect of premiums earned during the twelve-month period to 30 June 1984, a general insurer experienced 247 claims for a particular sub-line of business. The distribution of these claims by size is summarised in Table 11.2. Claims-handling expenses are also given. If we assume that claim costs in respect of claims in a given range are concentrated at the mean value for that range, then the distribution of claim size can be represented graphically, as shown in Figure 11.4. The distribution is very skewed, having a long 'tail' to the right.

The mean claim size is

$$164 \times 0.085 + 405 \times 0.385 + \ldots + 11\,453 \times 0.012 = £1228.29.$$

Exposure

So much for the observed claim cost distribution. We now turn to the problem of estimating the claim frequency rate. The 247 claims in Table 11.2 correspond to premiums earned in the 12 months to 30 June 1984. Few if any of the policies involved will have been in force for the exact period

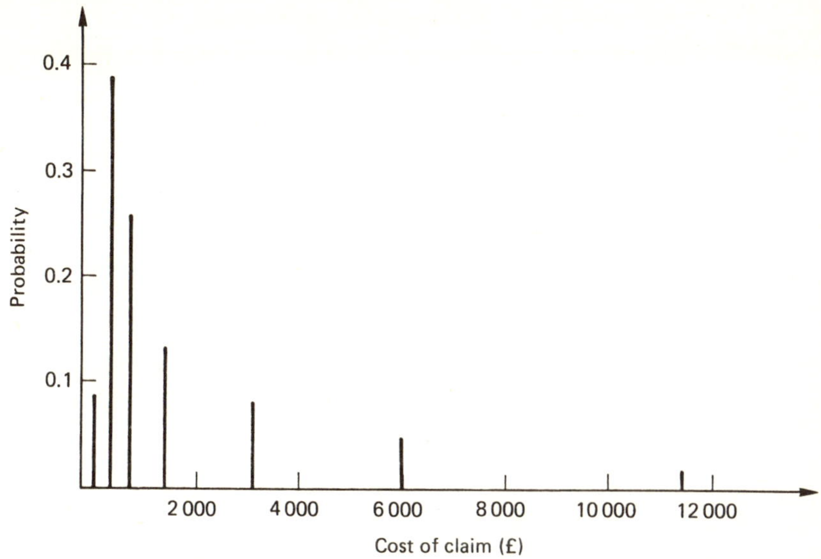

Source: Table 11.2.
Figure 11.4 Probability distribution of claim size

from 1 July 1983 to 30 June 1984. Most will have fractional exposures. The total exposure for the sub-line during the 12 months to 30 June 1984 will be the sum of the individual exposures during that period. The observed claim frequency rate (an estimate of the underlying claim frequency rate) is obtained by dividing the number of claims by the total exposure.

The method used to calculate the total exposure for the sub-line will depend on the record system of the insurer. If the records are maintained within a modern computer system, an exact exposure during the 12-month period for each policy can be calculated and these exposures summed to provide an exact total exposure. Approximate methods which produce satisfactory results are also available, and those methods can be applied to both manual files and computer-based files ('eighths' and 'twenty-fourths' methods, for example).

Numerical example of claim frequency rate

In the case of the sub-line and general insurer under consideration, the exposure data are given in the form shown in Table 11.3, and an approximate method known as a 'census method' can be used. It is apparent that, during the first quarter of the financial year under consideration, an average of about (1876 + 1932)/2 or 1904 policies were in force. These policies contribute 1904 × 1/4 or 476 policy years to the exposure during

Table 11.3 An illustration of exposure

Date	*Number of policies in force**
1 July 1983	1 876
1 October 1983	1 932
1 January 1984	1 949
1 April 1984	1 978
1 July 1984	1 967

* Numbers of policies in force at the beginning of each quarter, 12-month period to 30 June 1984.

the 12-month period. Similar calculations can be performed for the other three quarters, and we deduce a total exposure of 1945 policy years. The claim frequency rate for the sub-line is therefore 247/1945 = 0.127.

Numerical example of risk premium calculation

In the absence of any clearly defined trends in claim frequency or claim size (apart from inflation, which will be accounted for later) the risk premium for this type of contract would be 0.127 × £1228.29 or £155.99.

11.4 THE EFFECT OF A DEDUCTIBLE

The effect of introducing a deductible can only be estimated if the distribution of claim size is known. Let us imagine that, in respect of the sub-line we are considering, the insurer intends introducing a deductible of £250. From the first line of Table 11.2, 8.5 per cent of losses will no longer become claims and the claim frequency rate will reduce to 0.116 (i.e. 226/1945). Furthermore, all losses larger than £250 will become claims of size £250 less than the loss size. The claim size distribution therefore becomes that shown in Table 11.4. With the £250 deductible, the mean claim size becomes

$$155 \times 0.420 + 545 \times 0.279 + \ldots + 11\,203 \times 0.013 = £1080.50,$$

and the variance of the claim size

$$(155^2 \times 0.420) + (545^2 \times 0.279) + \ldots + (11\,203^2 \times 0.013) - (1080.5)^2 = £3\,132\,353$$

The standard deviation of the claim size is therefore £1770.

Once again, the product of the claim frequency rate and the mean claim cost provides the risk premium: 0.116 × 1080.50 or £125.34.

Table 11.4 Claim cost distribution, assuming a deductible of £250

Claim size range (1) £	*Mean claim in range* (2) £	*Mean claims-handling expenses* (3) £	*Mean cost for claims in range [(2) + (3)]* (4) £	*Number of claims* (5)	*Proportion of claims* (6)
0– 250	123	32	155	95	0.420
250– 750	486	59	545	63	0.279
750–1 750	1 160	67	1 227	35	0.155
1 750–3 750	2 801	119	2 920	19	0.084
3 750–7 750	5 553	207	5 760	11	0.049
7 750 and over	10 905	298	11 203	3	0.013
Total	—	—	—	226	1.000

Source: Table 11.2.

Table 11.5 Claim cost distribution, assuming a deductible of £250 and an excess of loss reinsurance treaty with retention £7750

Claim size range (1) £	*Mean claim in range* (2) £	*Mean claims-handling expenses* (3) £	*Mean cost for claims in range [(2) + (3)]* (4) £	*Number of claims* (5)	*Proportion of claims* (6)
0– 250	123	32	155	95	0.420
250– 750	486	59	545	63	0.279
750–1 750	1 160	67	1 227	35	0.155
1 750–3 750	2 801	119	2 920	19	0.084
3 750–7 750	5 553	207	5 760	11	0.049
7 750 and over	7 750	298	8 048	3	0.013
Total	—	—	—	226	1.000

Source: Table 11.2.

11.5 EXCESS OF LOSS REINSURANCE

In the case of the sub-line we are considering, the general insurer intends arranging an excess of loss treaty with retention £7750 (ie there is a deductible of £250 and the reinsurer meets the excess of any loss over and above £8000). Once such a treaty is negotiated, the claim frequency rate will remain unchanged at 0.116. The effects of the treaty on the direct insurer's costs are summarised in Table 11.5 and we see that the mean cost to the direct insurer (net of reinsurance recoveries) will reduce to

$$155 \times 0.420 + \ldots + 8048 \times 0.013 = £1039.48.$$

Thus, knowing the claim size distribution, the likely effect of excess of loss reinsurance can be assessed. Ignoring for the moment the cost of reinsurance, the risk premium becomes 0.116 × 1039.48 or £120.58. For the reinsurance cover, however, the reinsurer charges £15.50 per policy, making the premium the cedant should charge £136.08.

It is worth noting that the variance of the claim size, as far as the direct insurer is concerned, is now £2 429 724, compared with £3 132 353 in the absence of reinsurance. The standard deviation has fallen therefore from £1770 to £1559, indicating the stabilising effect of the reinsurance treaty on the cedant's claim liability.

11.6 LOADING FOR CONTINGENCIES

Let us imagine that the general insurer under consideration expects to write about 2000 policies at the new rates during the 12 months commencing 1 January 1985. The expected number of claims under these policies will be 2000 × 0.116 = 232, and the expected cost to the insurer (net of reinsurance recoveries) will be 232 × £1039.48 or £241 159. The expected total net claims cost to the insurer for all lines is obtained by adding the expected claims cost for the sub-line (£241 159) to those of the other sub-lines and lines, and a figure of £852 960 (say) emerges.

If loss frequency follows a Poisson process, it may be shown that the variability of the claim cost to the general insurer in respect of this sub-line, as measured by the variance of the total net sub-line cost is

$$232 \times (2\,429\,724 + (1039.48)^2) = £814.38 \text{ million}$$

(see Hossack *et al.*, 1983, ch. 8).
This figure is then added to the variances of the claim costs for the other sub-lines and lines of insurance to obtain the variance of the insurer's total net claim cost for all lines, and this turns out to be £8168 million (say). The standard deviation of the total net claims cost is therefore £90 377.

Let us now imagine that the general insurer has free reserves over and above the statutory solvency margin of about £150 000 and that the insurer adds the same risk loading L to the risk premium for all lines, for contingencies. The total risk premium (net of reinsurance premiums) plus contingency loading received by the insurer will then be £852 960 $(1 + L)$. The total funds available to meet claims (other than those required to satisfy the statutory solvency margin) are therefore

$$852\,960\ (1 + L) + 150\,000 = £(1\,002\,960 + 852\,960\ L).$$

The funds available therefore exceed the expected claims cost of £852 960 by £(150 000 + 852 960 L). For the insurer to be 99 per cent certain of being able to meet its liabilities without uncovering the statutory solvency margin, these extra funds available to it must be at least 2.33 times the variability of the total claims cost as measured by the standard deviation. In other words:

$$150\,000 + 852\,960\ L \geqslant 2.33 \times 90\,377$$

(on the assumption that total claims have normal distribution – see section 11.2).

So the loading L must be at least £60 578, which represents 7.10 per cent of the risk premium (£852 960). The risk premium plus contingency loading plus cost of reinsurance is therefore

$$120.58 \times 1.071 + 15.50 = £144.64$$

where, from section 11.5, the risk premium is £120.58 and the cost of reinsurance is £15.50.

11.7 THE EFFECT OF INFLATION

The data upon which the above premium calculations are made are based on claims during the 12-month period ended 30 June 1984, that is, claims which were incurred on average about 31 December 1983 and settled on average (according to statistics available) about 2 months later, (that is, around 29 February 1984). Our aim is to determine the appropriate premium for this sub-line during the 12 months commencing 1 January 1985, these claims being settled around 28 February 1986.

Inflation will affect claims costs, but should not affect claim frequency, if the deductible is adjusted appropriately. Economic indicators suggest that claims costs inflation for the sub-line over the two-year period to 28 February 1986 is likely to be around 12 per cent per annum. The premium for the sub-line should be adjusted accordingly and becomes

$$144.64 \times (1.12)^2 = £181.44.$$

Note that, for this premium to be appropriate during 1985, the deductible and retention level must both be similarly adjusted to £315 and £9725 respectively.

11.8 INVESTMENT INCOME

In the traditional general insurance office, investment income was usually regarded as 'windfall' profit on top of the underwriting profit, the latter being the direct result of insurance operations. With increasing competition in recent years, many insurers have made consistent losses on their underwriting account, but adequate profits overall (once investment earnings are taken into account). Some even take account of their investment earnings now when setting their premium rates (cash-flow underwriting).

The adjustment for investment earnings is not particularly significant in respect of many of the personal-line insurance products, where the period between receipt of premium and payment of claim is relatively short. Nevertheless investment income can be important with some of the longer-tail classes. A loading for profit will be introduced later in Section 11.10.

Since, in our example, the average date a premium will be received during the 12-month period from 1 January 1985 will be 30 June 1985, and claims under these policies will be settled around 28 February 1986, the insurer will have use of these funds for approximately eight months.

Suppose that the recent investment performance of the general insurer, and the current economic outlook, suggest that an investment return (net of taxation and relevant expenses) of about 13 per cent per annum on investible funds is not unreasonable over the next couple of years. To be able to meet its commitments therefore (and make no profit), the insurer would need to charge a premium of

$$181.44/(1.13)^{8/12} = £167.24.$$

In other words, a premium of £167.24, plus investment earnings thereon over an eight-month period, would yield £181.44.

11.9 EXPENSES

Expenses are a major part of the cost of insurance. If the product is to be properly priced, a thorough analysis of costs and expenses is required periodically (as discussed in Chapter 9), and expenses need to be monitored continually. Claims-handling expenses are directly attributable to claims, and were included with claims in the earlier calculation of the risk premium. Investment expenses were handled by using a net rate of return on investments.

The main expenses which now need to be taken account of in the setting of the premium rate are the following:

(a) expenses directly proportional to the premiums charged (e.g. commission), which for the purpose of the example are assumed to be 20 per cent of the gross premium;
(b) fixed per policy expenses (i.e. mailing of renewal notices and so on) which we shall assume to be £10 per policy; and
(c) office overheads, which for the purpose of the example total £450 000.

The share of overheads to be met by an individual sub-line is a management decision. In recent years, the sub-line under consideration has contributed 25 per cent, and this policy is to continue. Furthermore expenses are expected to rise by about 10 per cent per annum over the next few years. Each of the 2000 policies to be written should therefore include the following allowance for fixed per policy expenses and contribution to overheads:

$$[10 + (0.25 \times 450\,000)/2000]\,(1.10)^2 = £80.16.$$

Before incorporating these expenses and the expenses directly proportional to the premium into the premium, it is necessary first to look at the problem of loading for profit.

11.10 LOADING FOR PROFIT

Shareholders' funds of the general insurer amount to £350 000. These funds are currently invested and returning around 13 per cent per annum net. Let us imagine that a reasonable rate of return to shareholders, bearing in mind the risk they run, is 30 per cent per annum (before tax). The difference between the 13 per cent currently being earned on the £350 000 of shareholders' funds and the 30 per cent return sought is $0.17 \times 350\,000$ or £59 500, and this needs to come from the underwriting part of the enterprise. Of the anticipated gross premium income of about £1 200 000, £59 500 represents about 5 per cent.

If all lines are to contribute equally to profits, the premium for the sub-line under consideration must be loaded 5 per cent for profits. In other words, and taking account of the expenses enumerated in Section 11.9, the office premium P for the sub-line must satisfy the equation:

$$P = 167.24 + 0.20P + 80.16 + 0.05P,$$

whence $P = £330$. This premium would then allow:

167	for claims, claims handling expenses, reinsurance and contingencies
66	for expenses proportional to the premium
12	for per policy expenses
68	towards overheads
17	for profit
£330	

and during the 8-month delay between receipt of premium and settlement of claims, the £167 would produce investment income of £14, allowing a total of £181 for anticipated claims, claims-handling expenses, reinsurance premiums and contingencies.

Additional profit will emerge as a result of the contingency loading. The amount involved, however, will vary considerably from year to year, depending upon the claims experience of the insurer.

11.11 MARKET FORCES

The question which now has to be addressed is how competitive the calculated premium is. Would the calculated premium mean for example that little or no business is written (in which case the sub-line would make almost no contribution to overheads)? Can we make the premium more competitive by, for example, reducing the contribution each individual policy makes to overheads and, at the same time, increasing the contribution of another line to overheads? Should the profit loading of 5 per cent be reduced, bearing in mind the fact that a contingency loading of 7 per cent of risk premium has already been introduced, and, in the normal course of events, much of this should emerge as profit?

On the other hand, if the calculated premium is too competitive, too much business will be written, and the office's solvency margin may be endangered. A higher premium might then be charged, allowing a larger per policy contribution to overheads and profits, and a reduction in a less competitive premium in respect of another line.

Many of the factors included in the premium calculation require professional judgement, and a range of possible values is possible for some of them. Conservative assumptions will of course produce higher and possibly less competitive premiums. Without a detailed knowledge of the various factors affecting the premium, the adjustment of a given premium is purely guesswork, and dangerous if discounting is pursued. If the various components of the premium are known, adjustments may be made to it in the full knowledge of the likely effects of the insurer's overall operations. This discussion is taken up in the following chapter.

11.12 PRACTICAL PROBLEMS IN PREMIUM RATING

The full rating procedure outlined above may be applied relatively simply to certain lines of insurance, principally the various personal lines. However practical problems arise even with these straightforward cases, and the problems which arise with other classes can make the application of the full rating procedure very difficult. Nevertheless, if risks are to be underwritten profitably, all the factors described in the above rating procedure must be considered, and the following practical problems tackled.

Zero claims

Zero claims can arise, as a result perhaps of the existence of a deductible, or the fact that a policyholder decided not to pursue a particular claim. If these are not handled correctly, serious biases can emerge in the estimation of the premium. The important thing is consistency! If zero claims are included in the claim frequency count, then they must also be included in the claim cost distribution calculations, and conversely.

Different insurers will handle zero claims in different ways, and there is always the danger that industry data will reflect a mixture of approaches.

Re-opened claims

The temptation to treat a re-opened claim as a new claim must be resisted. Otherwise the claim cost distribution may be seriously distorted and the effects of deductibles and non-proportional reinsurance incorrectly assessed.

Heterogeneity of risk, rating factors and experience rating

In the simple worked example of Sections 11.3–11.11, a homogeneous portfolio of identical risks was assumed. This may be a reasonable first approximation in respect of certain lines, but, for most classes, it is clearly not true.

Policies which are not homogeneous may be subdivided according to one or more rating factors. In the case of motor vehicle damage only policies, for example, the following rating factors might be used: age of policyholder (under 25, 25 to 65, over 65); sex of policyholder; address of policyholder (metropolitan, other urban, rural); use (business, private); modified from manufacturer's specification? (yes, no); garaged at night? (yes, no); and class of vehicle (say 5 levels). While it is theoretically possible to estimate a claim frequency rate and a claim cost distribution for each of the resulting 720 sub-groups, it is clearly impractical to do so. Furthermore, the data available for some sub-groups will be very sparse or non-existent. The practical approach is first to estimate a base claim frequency rate and base claim cost distribution for a common type of policyholder (for example male aged 25–65, driving an unmodified standard family saloon for private purposes only and living in the metropolitan area, where the car is garaged at night). Rating factors can then be used to assess how the calculation of claim frequency rates and claim cost distributions for other sub-groups differ from the base figures. Standard multivariate statistical methods can be usefully employed for this purpose (for example, see Benjamin, 1977).

The use of one or more rating factors will often reduce heterogeneity of risk among policies. Experience rating methods can also be employed to reduce the effects of any residual heterogeneity, although in the case of the no claim discount (NCD) method popular in motor insurance, the improvement is very marginal. A practical approach to the rating of motor vehicle policies subject to NCD would be to rate a couple of important sub-groups at different levels of no claim discount using the full rating procedure demonstrated in Sections 11.3–11.11 above, and then adjust the results using previously determined relativities. When performing these calculations, it is important to remember that discounts applied to premiums affect expense, profit and other loadings as well as the risk premium. Account must be taken of this factor when the rates are set.

The size of the database and credibility considerations

The database upon which the earlier premium calculations are based comprised an exposure of 1945 policy years and (with a deductible of £250) 226 claims. From these data we estimated a claim frequency rate of 0.116 per policy per annum. The sample is relatively small, however, and we could easily have obtained, for example, the observed 226 claims with the same exposure but with an underlying claim frequency rate as high as 0.132 or as low as 0.102. (One does not always obtain exactly five heads when an unbiased coin is tossed ten times!) These extreme values would of course lead to rather different premium rates. So would the high and low estimates of the mean claim size based on the same relatively sparse data. Statistical theory enables us to calculate how large these ranges are, while credibility theory allows something practical to be done.

The general approach is as follows: imagine that we need to estimate a risk premium P. An estimate P can be obtained using the insurer's data for the year ended 30 June 1984. The estimate will be unreliable, however, if the data are sparse – as indeed they are. An alternative approach would be to use collateral data (such as recent industry statistics). An estimate based on such collateral data might be denoted by P_c. Although the collateral data may be extensive, not all of them may relate to exactly the same risk. A trade-off is needed between the estimate based on the insurer's own data for the 12 months to 30 June 1984 and the collateral data estimate. A credibility estimate of the risk premium P is a weighted average of the risk premium according to the insurer's own data (P_I) and the risk premium based on the collateral data:

$$P = Z.P_I + (1 - Z).P_c$$

In assigning a value to the weight or credibility factor Z (which must lie between 0 and 1) account is taken of:

(a) the volume of the one-year data relative to the volume of the collateral data; and
(b) differences between the one-year data and the collateral data.

For further details see Hossack *et al.* (1983, ch. 8).

Delays in claim reporting and settlement

Long delays in claim reporting and settlement are rare for most personal lines of insurance. For these lines, therefore, given an adequate policy and claims record system, it is not intrinsically difficult to calculate exposure during a given recent period and divide the number of claims in respect of policies in force during that period by the exposure, to estimate the claim frequency rate. The claim cost distribution is also readily determined. Once these data are available, the usual calculations may proceed.

In the liability classes, long delays in both claim reporting and claim settlement tend almost to be the rule rather than the exception. Admittedly, the existence of most liability claims will be known within a few years, but in many cases the actual cost may not emerge until a decade or more has elapsed. It is theoretically possible to wait until virtually all claim costs are known, but the resulting data are then of historical rather than practical value.

In classes of business where delays in notification are common, it is still possible to obtain a reasonably reliable estimate of claim frequency within a year or two of the exposure period by the use of a delay table (an example of which is shown in Table 11.6). Such a table needs to be continually monitored and updated. Suppose the period of exposure is the year to 30 June 1984 and the delay table Table 11.6 is judged to be applicable. Then, if the number of claims notified by 31 December 1984 in respect of events occurring in the month of December 1983 is 128, an estimate of the total number of claims in respect of December 1983 is given by 128/0.885 or 145. Treating the other months during the year of exposure, in the same way, we have an estimate of the total number of claims for the year.

The claim cost distribution poses a much greater problem. Sometimes

Table 11.6 Example of a delay table

Number of months since end of month in which claim event occurred	*Proportion of claims (numbers) notified*	*Number of months since end of month in which claim event occurred*	*Proportion of claims (numbers) notified*
0	0.201	12	0.885
1	0.415	24	0.985
2	0.503	36	0.995
3	0.600	48	0.998
4	0.675	60	0.999
5	0.705	72	0.999
6	0.775	120	1.000

claims finalised in a given period are examined. This approach can be very dangerous and should be used with extreme caution, as changes in the amount of business written and in the composition of that business can produce serious biases. Probably the best approach is to allow a couple of years to elapse so that most claims have been notified and many settled, and estimate the outstanding claims on a case-by-case basis (ignoring future claims inflation). Estimates obtained in this manner are admittedly rather subjective, but alternative methods also have their drawbacks.

Claims inflation is a very important consideration in respect of those classes of insurance which are subject to long delays in settlement. While the basic approach of Section 11.7 remains the same, the actual calculations become a little more involved. The same is true of the adjustment for investment earnings.

The assessment of the loading for contingencies

The method demonstrated in Section 11.6 for assessing the appropriate loading for contingencies is an example of the application of risk theory. The method depends on being able to estimate, at least approximately, the variance of the total claim cost to the general insurer.

This is not usually a particularly difficult task in respect of those classes of business when the claims are notified and settled rapidly. Other classes, however, usually pose problems; for example, the determination of the claim cost distribution in respect of a liability class can be very difficult and the results obtained rather subjective. As a result the mean cost of claims, which is required for the calculation of the risk premium, may be rather subjective and the variance of the claim cost even more uncertain.

Premiums must contain margins for contingencies (be they explicit contingency margins, or part of a more general loading 'for profit') if an insurer is to remain solvent in the long term. Margins calculated on a sound scientific basis are obviously preferable to those based purely on guesswork. It is desirable therefore that, whenever possible, the scientific approach be adopted, even if the estimates of variability in claim cost are, to say the least, rather subjective.

New and unusual risks

New and unusual risks might almost be defined as those for which no statistical data are available. The success or otherwise of the rating of such risks must depend upon the experience, skill and judgement of the underwriter. At the same time, all the factors we have discussed in this chapter must be borne in mind (claim frequency rate and claim size, effects of deductibles and non-proportional reinsurances, loadings for contingencies, expenses and profit, adjustments for inflation and investment earnings, and market forces). It would normally be appropriate to include substantial margins for contingencies and profits and to ignore investment income.

References

Benjamin, B. (1977) *General Insurance* (London: Heinemann).

Hossack, I.B., J.H. Pollard and B. Zehwirth, (1983) *Introductory Statistics with Applications in General Insurance* (Cambridge: Cambridge University Press).

12 Competitive Behaviour and Pricing Policy

Walter Karten

12.1 INTRODUCTION TO PRICING

The prices of economic goods result from the meeting of supply and demand in a market. The objective of this chapter is to point out some fundamental aspects of pricing policy from an insurance company's point of view. Following some remarks on price and product in the insurance sector, and a distinction between calculation and pricing policy, a short description of the components of the insurance premium is given. A discussion of the influence of market structure and competition on pricing concludes this chapter.

Product price and product quality

The basic product of an insurance company is protection. The insurer binds itself by contract to make a conditional payment to serve as a compensation for certain economic disadvantages suffered by the insured resulting from an accidental occurrence. The insured event and the contractual obligations are well defined in the insurance contract to determine clearly the nature and extent of insurance protection. Protection for the insured is provided against fluctuations in the amount of possible loss and the frequency of the underlying random events triggering such losses (the insured events). The insured events (and the way of evaluating their consequences) should be closely defined in the insurance contract, in respect of cause (e.g. legal liability), consequences (e.g. material or personal damage), factual relation (e.g. a certain car), region, and time (e.g. a certain policy year).

To evaluate the compensation to be paid following a certain insured event the insurer has to determine the insured value (e.g. replacement value), assess the extent of the loss (for example by calculating repair costs) and assign compensation (taking any deductibles into account).

The quality of the insurance product is determined mainly by the security of the promised payment (which is more or less equivalent to the security of the insurance company), but also by the different kinds of services integrated into the product.

The price of the insurance product is the total amount the policyholder has to pay (the office or gross premium). The relevant amount for the insurer's decision-making may differ, so for example any taxes issued on purchase price would have to be allowed for. In line with Chapter 9 any remuneration to the salesforce is regarded as operating costs.

Product price and product quality are as independent in insurance as they are in other industries. For example, in reinsurance, details about sliding-scale and profit commissions, carry forward losses, cash losses, deposits and interest rates, reinstatements and so on are pricing factors and elements of product design at the same time. Similarly in life insurance the bonus may be looked upon as an increase of future payments or a reduction of premium.

Market price: supply and demand

In a market where buyers and sellers have complete freedom of action the market price results from the concurrence of the decisions of both suppliers and buyers. Their influence has been likened to the blades of a pair of scissors: it is impossible to determine which of the blades cuts the paper. In insurance it quite often seems that the insurer fixes the price, and the potential policyholder either accepts or rejects it. Nevertheless the basic model of a price at the point of intersection of the supply and demand curve is still applicable to insurance markets.

The demand for insurance reflects the price ceilings of buyers, while the supply reflects the price floors of all suppliers in a market. The buyer's price ceiling is defined as the maximum amount he or she is prepared to pay for insurance cover. Assume the owner of a house is worried that the house may be damaged or destroyed by fire. The owner gets an offer of an insurance contract at a fixed premium which gives complete insurance protection. This means that, in the event of fire, the compensation paid by the insurer exactly covers the loss, so that the owner experiences no loss of satisfaction or utility as a result of the fire (assuming that the compensation is sufficient to exactly restore the house and no more). For the certain loss of premium, the insurance company offers to change the risky situation into one of certainty. The price ceiling is that certain decrease in wealth (the premium payment) which is regarded as exactly equivalent (that is, yielding the same level of satisfaction) to the possible but uncertain decrease in wealth caused by a fire.

Such an evaluation of risk is very subjective. Once possible loss events and their associated probabilities have been estimated, the buyer's attitude to risk determines his price ceiling. Only buyers who are risk-averse will pay a premium which is higher than the expected value of loss, and the stronger the risk aversion, the higher the buyer's price ceiling.

The price floor of an insurer can be explained in a similar manner, it being the lowest premium at which the insurer will accept the risk.

However the risk for the insurer does not exist until the conclusion of the insurance contract. The contract will only be accepted by the insurer if the utility of the random amount 'premium less loss, less operating costs' is not lower than the utility of its initial position without the risk. If the insurance company wants to exist in the long run, the expected value of this random variable must be positive, which implies a risk-averse decision on behalf of the insurer. From this equilibrium of utility, theoretically, the lowest acceptable premium for the insurer (the price floor) can be derived. The positive loading for contingencies rises with increasing risk aversion of the insurer.

These basic facts are fundamental for any pricing policy because a contract will only materialise if the price floor of the insurer does not exceed the price ceiling of the buyer.

Pricing policy and the calculation of premium rates

There are two aspects of pricing policy – costing and pricing – and they must be quite strictly separated, although they obviously influence each other. Costing is the provision of information based on computations according to appropriate and functional standards. Pricing on the other hand always implies a decision: its function is the determination of the optimal market price so that the corporate goals are attained in the best way possible.

The determination of the price floor is essentially an exercise in cost allocation. It calls for a sophisticated internal cost accounting system to allocate both claims and non-claims cost (further details are given in Chapters 11 and 9 respectively), although the safety loading is not strictly a contribution to costs. The premium so derived is just an index number for the risk and does not fix the market price in any way.

In most countries, insurers can make their own pricing decisions. Only in regulated markets is the price derived directly from a predetermined formula. However, in some markets, insurers fix their prices in consultation or co-operation with each other (for example, by forming rating bureaux or tariffs); in other countries, this collusive behaviour is limited or even prohibited by anti-monopoly legislation.

Pricing policy is a part of marketing. It is a marketing tool to be ranked alongside the choice of sales programme (product design, product line, service), the use of marketing channels and procedures (employment and remuneration of salesforce or direct selling), and advertising. Therefore a decision on pricing policy should never be made in isolation but always jointly with other marketing instruments, in order to reach an optimal marketing mix (as described in the next chapter). It is obvious, for example, that the pricing policy of an insurer using direct sales technology will differ significantly from that of a company distributing through intermediaries.

Economic literature relates pricing policy to the structure of the market, classified, for example, according to the number of participants and their behaviour. Theoretically, there are two extremes: on the one hand, there is a single firm – a monopolist – having complete control of price, and on the other, the unreal model of perfect competition, where individual suppliers have no say whatsoever in determining price. Between these extremes there is a wide variety of market models, each with an optimal pricing policy.

The markets for industrial and commercial insurance are distinguished by a remarkable heterogeneity of risks and often considerable bargaining power possessed by buyers. The more this is the case, the less is the optimum price determined by the market structure, resulting instead from direct negotiations between supplier and buyer. In such cases game theory shows that a definite price formation is replaced by a bargaining interval between price ceiling and price floor. The result of this bargaining process depends on aspects such as conviction, persuasion, power, intimidation, temptation, discernment and so on.

Finally, pricing policy involves not only the decision on the level of price but also on the premium system (fixed or variable premiums), the terms of payment (annually, monthly) and the criteria and degree of premium discrimination.

12.2 THE BASIS OF PREMIUM CALCULATION

The components of office premiums

The calculation of the gross or office premium is illustrated below:

risk premium
\+ safety loading
\+ expenses loading
\+ profit loading
= gross or office premium
(market price)

The risk premium is the systematic contribution to cover the expected loss payments, the so-called loss costs. Losses are essentially the costs of production to the insurer; they should be calculated according to the same standards and reflected in the premium exactly like other costs. The safety loading is a necessary component in the premium to allow for risk bearing.

The risk premium should be determined according to the principle of equivalence, that is for each individual risk:

risk premium = expected value of losses,

or in case of variable loss-dependent premiums:

expected value of risk premium = expected value of losses.

The principle of equivalence describes how loss costs should be allocated but does not necessarily carry through to the determination of market price. Unfortunately it cannot be applied exactly because precise attribution of loss costs is statistically impossible. The expected value of the losses is a statistical estimator derived from portfolios as homogeneous as possible, but always involving estimation errors. For details of the risk premium calculation, see Chapter 11.

An important aspect of the principle of equivalence is that the monetary amounts (that is, premium and claims payments) are due at different points in time, and interest earnings must therefore be taken into account to obtain a present value at one point in time. The principle of equivalence must then be adapted, so that the expected present value of total premium payments equals the expected present value of the insurance benefits.

The safety loading is not a contribution to costs. In the long run, and on average, it is necessary because, without a safety loading, an insurance company can anticipate with certainty being ruined at some time. The safety loading's function is to cover losses over and above the risk premium and to finance a safety fund which absorbs any fluctuations in claims experience. Theoretically the amount of safety loading depends on the risk aversion of the insurer (in the determination of the company's price floor). In reality, the computation by use of utility functions is too pretentious, and the loading is usually calculated more simply as, for example, a percentage of the risk premium or some proportion of the variance or standard deviation of losses (see Section 11.6).

In practice the calculation of a separate profit loading is unnecessary. There is no definite borderline between the safety and profit loading, since a safety loading not employed to cover excess losses becomes a profit in the income statement. In the reverse case, a profit loading cannot materialise if the losses exceed the risk premium plus safety loading. The profit loading is also sometimes interpreted as a contribution to cover the cost of equity capital tied up in the business. These capital costs should, however, be charged in connection with the loading for expenses, because they are real costs of employing factors of production.

The expenses loading covers all non-claims costs, that is the insurer's expenditure on factors of production (labour, capital and working assets). Expenses such as salaries, commissions, depreciation of equipment, paper and so on are naturally included (and these were discussed in Chapter 9) but reinsurance and the costs of capital should also be taken into account. The cost of reinsurance protection is simply the reinsurance premium minus reinsurance commissions in the case of a proportional treaty, and the average reinsurance premium for non-proportional business. The risk premium for the reinsured part of the risk should be reduced by exactly the same amount as the expected value of losses of the cedant. Thus with both forms of reinsurance, only that part of the reinsurance premium which accrues to the reinsurer as a contribution for expenses and safety loading needs to be taken into account by the direct insurer.

An allowance for the cost of capital in the expenses loading is more problematic. The capital requirements of an insurance company may be subdivided into three categories:

- underwriting reserves (unearned premiums, outstanding claims and other technical services);
- other reserves (for example, provisions for the pension plans of employees);
- equity capital to finance safety funds and other assets necessary for operation.

In some cases, the interest earned on the technical reserves has already been taken into account in the premium calculation (for example in life insurance). However these reserves will usually be positive, and should always be included in a complete premium calculation, since the failure to consider all the insurer's capital costs and investment earnings may lead to false pricing decisions. Similarly the interest on non-technical reserves and on the total equity capital invested should be taken into account to the full amount. As to the interest rate for the equity capital, the rate for risk-free assets on the capital market can be considered, since the risk premium for the shareholder is covered by the safety loading. It is important to include all the capital invested in the operation, not just the assets shown in the balance sheet (such as office buildings, equipment, active debts, cash and so on) because typically there are significant investments made in intangible assets such as sales and office organisation and the prepaid initial expenses for insurance policies.

The influence of investment income

The discounting of premium rates to allow for positive investment income is generally known as 'cash flow underwriting', quite often with a negative connotation. Insurance premiums and investment income both result from an underwriting decision because premiums are usually (but not always) received in advance of the corresponding claims payments, and can thus be invested. Consequently, a reasonable judgement on the profitability of an underwriting decision can only be made on the basis of all costs incurred and all earnings obtained.

An assessment of the attributable investment earnings should be made very carefully because the different premium components contribute very differently. The risk premium is available as a source of earnings until any claim is paid; that is, on average, half an insurance period plus the average period for claims settlement (which varies according to the class of insurance and the type of loss). On the other hand, the greater part of the operating expenses (especially commissions) fall due immediately after the premium payment and do not contribute at all to investment earnings.

The best way to include interest in the premium calculation is to discount to the moment of premium payment, using the realised average yield on investments. To the extent that payments for claims and operating expenses are directly dependent on changes in the value of the money, the expected inflation rate should also be taken into account.

Cash-flow underwriting is not a danger to market prices: it merely reduces the cost of premium rates. It is important, however, to calculate correctly the costs of capital, any inflationary effects, and also for the risk of drastic changes in interest rates.

12.3 COMPETITION AND THE PREMIUM CALCULATION

Pricing policy is the goal-oriented determination of a premium in the market (or rarely, the acceptance of a premium offer from the buyer's side). This is generally done by a long-term fixing of general premium rates, which is nothing else but a price-list for certain risks and types of policies. But deviations are possible, and for commercial risks a pragmatic and short-term bargaining policy often occurs. In case of mutual insurance companies which are committed to non-discrimination against their members, a policy of generally applied premium rates is required, with no individual bargaining.

A premium policy, of course, is mainly concerned with the premium level. The optimal level is always a compromise between a high premium offering a high profitability per policy but with a low turnover, and a low premium supporting the sales volume but resulting in unsatisfactory profits. A special problem of insurers arises from the repercussions of the pricing policy on the existing portfolio. For unregulated premiums, the effect of price increases is typically attenuated and delayed, whereas price reductions for new business work through to the portfolio pretty quickly, even to long-term policies.

Modifications in the terms of payment (e.g. annually or by instalments) or in the basis for premium assessment (e.g. by sum insured, type of risk, features of the risk and so on) are of secondary importance for a pricing policy. However they serve to reduce market transparency and make it more difficult for consumers to compare prices and give insurers an opportunity for non-price competition.

The introduction of variable instead of *ex ante* fixed premiums (e.g. experience rating and premium refunds) is of special importance to pricing policy. Any kind of experience rating which ties the premiums to the individual loss experience always has at least three effects which determine its expedience:

(a) Risk transfer. The technical risk of the insurer is partially transferred to the insured because the premiums fluctuate according to the random course of the losses. This is particularly beneficial if the net risk premium is based on an unreliable estimate of expected losses.
(b) Coinsurance. A rate increase following a loss means that the insured has paid a part of that loss.
(c) Premium discrimination. In a portfolio of individual risks with a heterogeneous loss expectation but a homogeneous premium rate, experience rating leads to an approximation of the premium appropriate to each individual insured.

Premium discrimination and the principle of equivalence

Premium discrimination is the practice of graduating the market premium according to the principle of equivalence, so that the premium paid by individual insureds reflects the claims that each is likely to make on the insurance pool. This may be achieved in three ways: (a) by varying the premium according to recognisable characteristics of each insured (i.e. the rating factors of section 11.11); (b) by using experience rating, where the premium depends on the individual's own past loss experience; or (c) by retrospective (or retroactive) rating where, by offering premium refunds or levying additional charges, the premium depends on the individual's loss experience over the duration of the existing contract.

The alternative to premium discrimination is to charge each insured an average or pooled premium irrespective of recognisable differences in the loss expectancy. This will involve a systematic redistribution of income from policyholders with lower expected losses to those with a higher loss expectation. For example, in West Germany private health insurance premiums are charged according to the insured's age and sex, whereas in the national health insurance scheme they are based only on per family income: this is an intended redistribution of income.

Premium discrimination can, of course, only be applied to the gross or office premium because a breakdown of the components of market price (as illustrated in Section 12.2) is not usually available to the buyer. The practice of premium discrimination does not necessarily imply that the gross premium has to be proportional to the individual's expected losses, because the charge to cover general costs and insurer's profit may not be proportional. The transition to the average or pooled premium takes place when the deviations from risk proportionality can no longer be justified by reasonable allocation of the general costs.

It should be stressed that the economic term 'price discrimination' has the opposite meaning to 'premium discrimination'. Price discrimination means offering homogeneous products in separate markets for varying prices, whereas premium discrimination means varying prices for varying products (risks) in the same market. Price discrimination relies on the insurer's ability to segment markets and charge different prices in each segment: this process is discussed in the next chapter.

There are a number of general reasons in favour of the process of premium discrimination:

(a) Premiums are independent of the composition of the portfolio. With an average or pooled premium in a heterogeneous portfolio, a variation in the structure of the portfolio entails a variation in the average premium, even if there is no change in the individual risks.
(b) A differentiated premium offers incentives for loss prevention and facilitates reinsurance.
(c) It avoids the dangers of adverse selection (or antiselection) in insurance markets. This is discussed in more detail below.

Adverse selection in insurance markets

Adverse selection in an insurance market can occur when the insurer does not enforce premium discrimination, and does not distinguish between policyholders with differing loss expectancies. The problem may arise because of asymmetric information: insureds know their own loss expectancies but insurers do not. The implications for competitive insurance markets when insurers cannot apply premium discrimination are discussed in more detail in Rothschild and Stiglitz (1976).

Suppose that, in motor third-party liability insurance, married car-owners have a claims frequency of 0.125 (i.e. 125 per thousand) and unmarried owners 0.225. Assume that there are only two insurers in the market, initially with an equal market share. Insurer A charges premium rates which distinguish between married and unmarried owners, while Insurer B charges an average or pooled premium. If there are 6000 married car-owners and 4000 unmarried ones, the pooled premium charged by Insurer B will be (6000×(0.125) + 4000×(0.225))/10 000, i.e. 0.165 per

Company A (50% Market Share)

Premium Revenue	Expected Losses
Married: 3000 x £125 = 375 000	0.125 x 1000 x 3000 = 375 000
Unmarried: 2000 x £225 = 450 000	0.225 x 1000 x 2000 = 450 000
£825 000	£825 000

Company B (50% Market Share)

Premium Revenue	Expected Losses
5000 x £165 = £825 000	0.125 x 1000 x 3000 = 375 000
	0.225 x 1000 x 2000 = 450 000
	£825 000

Figure 12.1 Initial position

£000 of insurance cover. Thus, if every car-owner buys £1000 of insurance cover, Insurer A will charge premiums of £125 to marrieds and £225 to unmarrieds, while B charges £165 to all. The initial position is outlined in Figure 12.1.

If the market were perfectly competitive policyholders would react to the price differentials, so that all married car-owners would be insured by A, and the unmarried ones by B. The accounts for the following period are shown in Figure 12.2.

The result of the failure by Company B to apply premium discrimination is a deficit of £240 000: this will force B to charge prices which discriminate between married and unmarried car-owners. The process of adverse selection is more serious when the insurers are unable to distinguish between high-risk and low-risk policyholders: in such cases a competitive insurance market may be unstable (for example, see Cummins *et al.*, 1983).

In reality, of course, the adjustment process illustrated in Figure 12.2 does not happen immediately or completely. The effect of adverse selection works more strongly the more competitive the market. Any intentional deviation from the differentiated premium can only be attained by selective interference with the market (for example by supervision or a cartel).

In practice, the operation of adverse selection is limited by the extent of competition and by the difficulty in verifying the statistical differences between different policyholders. It can also become increasingly costly to handle very differentiated premium rates.

Company A (Married Car-owners Only)

Premium Revenue		Expected Losses
Married:	6000 x £125 = 750 000	0.125 x 1000 x 6000 = 750 000
Unmarried:	0 x £225 = 0	0.225 x 1000 x 0 = 0
	£750 000	£750 000

Company B (Unmarried Car-owners Only)

Premium Revenue		Expected Losses
Married:	0 x 165 = 0	0.125 x 1000 x 0 = 0
Unmarried:	4000 x 165 = 660 000	0.225 x 1000 x 4000 = 900 000
	£660 000	£900 000

Figure 12.2 The effects of adverse selection

12.4 PRICING POLICY IN INSURANCE MARKETS

The guiding principle of modern competition policy is no longer the static concept of perfect competition (which implies the so-called 'graveyard-peace'), but the dynamic process of workable competition (for example, see Pritchett and Wilder, 1986). In a permanent sequence of innovation and imitation, as is generally known, such competition performs the following functions:

- optimal allocation of narrow resources;
- optimal supply of goods and services;
- income allocated according to the market performance.

Since selling precedes production and working on stock is impossible, insurers cannot employ output as a parameter of action. For example, it is not possible for an insurer to throw 10 000 cheap homeowners' policies onto the market simply in order to utilise spare capacity. Insurance products typically need considerable explanation and consumers are often initially unaware of their need for cover. These factors explain the predominant position of agent or broker services in many insurance markets, with pricing policy of secondary importance.

Formulating a pricing policy can be relatively complicated because, quite frequently, insurance markets tends to be unbalanced, so that a price

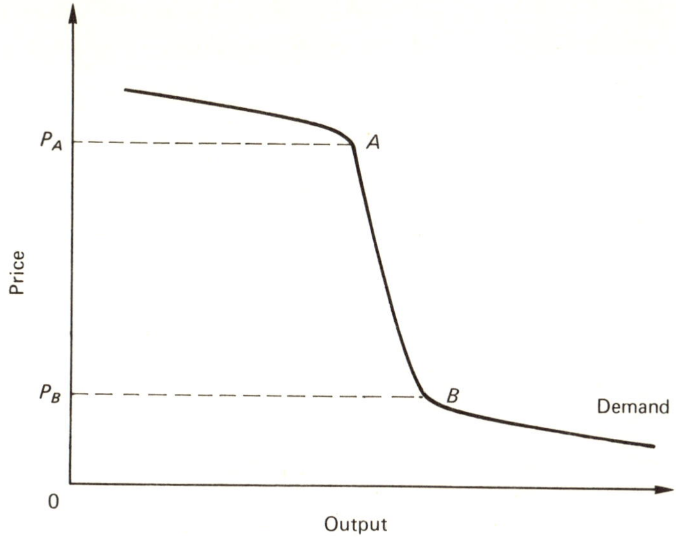

Figure 12.3 Monopolistic competition in insurance

reduction (caused for example by increased supply) does not automatically settle down in a new equilibrium once marginal sellers have departed from the market. This is because of the delayed and randomly disturbed feedback between low premium rates (and hence trading losses) and the highly flexible capacity of insurance companies. It usually takes years before an insurer recognises, via the trading losses experienced, that the premium level is too low. If an insurer is eliminated from the market, the quantity of insurance supplied is not necessarily reduced, since the remaining suppliers typically dispose of enough capacity to satisfy the total demand at once.

Insurance markets are generally imperfect, and examples for the whole spectrum of markets can be found. Monopolistic (polypolistic) competition is characterised by many suppliers with relatively low market shares and a low market transparency – this is typical of many private insurance markets. In this case the supplier is often confronted with a demand curve with an interval of relatively inelastic demand (see Figure 12.3).

Figure 12.3 shows a relatively inelastic demand between *A* and *B* where sales are not responsive to changes in price. Only when price rises above P_A, or falls below P_B, does the insurer experience significant changes in demand. In this case, pricing policy is a tool of secondary importance in marketing. Instead, the insurer will try to intensify consumer preferences and reduce market transparency in order to raise the inelastic interval above his price floor, and to enlarge and stabilise it. The pricing policy within the interval *A–B* can be oriented towards the monopolistic profit maximum, which does not necessarily imply a price close to P_A.

In private insurance markets there are also segments of well-informed consumers. They have a good knowledge of the market, develop only a few preferences and are very price-sensitive. Insurers will therefore attempt to charge these consumers lower prices, while simultaneously charging higher rates to less price-sensitive buyers. As this practice is not allowed in many countries, insurance companies often establish subsidiaries for direct selling with a higher premium level.

Insurance markets for commercial business, on the other hand, typically have more of an oligopolistic structure. Although sometimes the number of suppliers is not much smaller than in private insurance markets, only a small group of larger and specialised companies is relevant for competition. The buyers, possibly through brokers, have a good knowledge of the market and a significant negotiating power. The reactions of competing insurers are often interrelated: any marketing activity, especially variations in price, create counteractions or adjustment reactions by competitors. Therefore price theory can only derive optimal pricing policies under certain (mostly unrealistic) behavioural assumptions. Such oligopolistic markets tend to follow two alternative tendencies: firstly 'peaceful' coordinated behaviour among competitors (especially in saturated markets with no or slow expansion) involving arrangements such as cartels, rating bureaux or pricing leadership; alternatively there always exists the possibility of destructive competition by predatory price-cutting.

An active pricing policy by a single oligopolist may become completely ineffective: a rate reduction does not attract additional business, because the competitors follow suit – similarly, a rate increase may result in a loss of market share because the competitors do not follow. Oligopolistic price-cutting usually has only losers and no winners.

For most insurers a pricing policy of pacifism and adaptation is advisable, supported by advertising, product design and so on. Only clearly verifiable cost advantages and statistically persistent differences in the risk (expressed by the expected loss) may justify premium reductions. This is particularly true for special and very large risks, where the estimation of the expected loss is rather unreliable. In this situation underwriters tend to make concessions which frequently could be described as a victory of hope over experience and the opposite of a rational pricing policy.

Price formation in cartelised markets and direct price regulation by the supervisory authority more or less eliminate a managerial pricing policy. Marketing will therefore concentrate on other marketing tools, so far as they are not also regulated (for example, product design or remuneration of the salesforce). An indirect pricing policy is often utilised to evade the regulations: examples include the reduction of a cartel premium by manipulating the risk assessment, and an indirect rate reduction by offering concessions on non-cartelised policies of the same insured. In case of government-controlled prices, a 'clever' cost allocation may have an influence on the prices. Further discussion of the effects of regulation on insurance markets can be found in Finsinger *et al.* (1985).

References

Cummins, J.D., B.D. Smith, R.N. Vance and J.C. VanDerhei (1983) *Risk Classification in Life Insurance* (Hingham, MA: Kluwer-Nijhoff Publishing).

Finsinger, J., E. Hammond and J. Tapp (1985) *Insurance: Competition or Regulation?* (London: Institute for Fiscal Studies) Report Series No. 19.

Pritchett, S.T. and R.P. Wilder (1986) *Stock Life Insurance Company Profitability and Workable Competition*, Huebner Foundation Monograph No. 14.

Rothschild, M. and J.E. Stiglitz (1976) 'Equilibrium in Competitive Insurance Markets: An Essay on the Economics of Imperfect Competition', *Quarterly Journal of Economics 90*, pp. 629–49.

13 Marketing Insurance Services

Trevor Watkins and Stephen Diacon

13.1 THE MARKETING OF SERVICES

This chapter introduces the concept of marketing and examines the contribution which marketing can make within the insurance industry. The discussion proceeds under five main headings: firstly the special problems and strategies of services marketing will be examined, leading next to a discussion of the role of marketing in insurance. Sections 13.3 to 13.5 then describe the main components of the marketing process: demand analysis, market research and marketing mix. Further consideration is given to three key features of the marketing mix in sections 13.6 to 13.8, and the chapter concludes with a brief discussion of marketing strategy.

The most important feature of marketing can be simply stated as a customer orientation – this should pervade the entire insurance organisation. The art of marketing involves the application of available marketing tools and techniques to meet consumer needs profitably. Successful marketing requires firms to research the insurance requirements of their customers, to design products which meet those needs, to decide how to distribute those products, and to persuade the customers to buy. The application of these activities must, of course, be co-ordinated in an overall marketing strategy.

The growth of marketing as a business function began with fast-moving consumer goods such as soap powder and breakfast cereals. However the application of marketing to services, rather than goods, needs to take account of their special characteristics. The distinctive feature of a service is that it is performed on a particular person's behalf in order to change that person's condition, or the nature of his property. Four basic characteristics of a service are generally identified: intangibility (that is, it cannot be seen, felt and so on), inseparability of production and consumption (that is, a service does not exist until it is used by consumers), heterogeneity (since the quality of a service varies considerably in its performance), and perishability (that is, it cannot be stored or saved). The marketing problems that can result, and the possible solutions available, are outlined in Table 13.1. In a survey of the problems of marketing services, Zeithaml *et al.* (1985) concluded that the characteristic of services which caused the

Table 13.1 The unique features, problems and solutions in services marketing

Unique service feature	*Resulting marketing problem*	*Marketing strategies to solve problems*
Intangibility	– services cannot be stored	– stress tangible cues
	– cannot protect through patents	– use personal more than non-personal sources
	– cannot readily display or communicate services	– increased reliance on word-of-mouth communications
	– prices difficult to set	– create strong organisational image
		– use cost accountancy to help set prices
		– engage in post-purchase communications
Inseparability	– consumer involved in production	– emphasise selection and training of personnel in contact with customers
	– other consumers involved in production	– manage consumers
	– centralised mass-production difficult	– use multi-site locations
Heterogeneity	– difficult to standardise or maintain quality	– replace individual service with organised pre-planned systems
		– alternatively, customise services
Perishability	– services cannot be inventoried	– use strategies to cope with fluctuating demand
		– make simultaneous adjustments in demand and capacity to achieve a closer match

Source: Adapted from Zeithaml *et al.* (1985).

greatest difficulty was the large possible fluctuation in demand by service customers. The strategies suggested to cope with the problem of fluctuating demand included relying more on part-time staff and overtime; calling directly on customers; and taking care of existing customers and allowing others to wait.

Similarly Carter *et al.* (1986) note characteristics peculiar to financial services which have a major impact on the marketing strategies adopted. In the first place, there are often substantial exchanges of information between supplier and customer prior to the sale. Information is required by insurers because the service they provide depends on the nature and circumstances of the insured. Consequently insurers, and other providers of financial services, frequently possess a considerable degree of information about their customer's income, employment, wealth, family and so on. Secondly, most financial institutions essentially make promises to pay their customers a sum of money in the future. Since it is difficult for customers to assess the likelihood that these promises will in fact be met, government regulation and supervision of financial institutions is not unusual. Thirdly, a firm's ability to perform a financial service depends on its customer's confidence in its ability to provide the cash when so required, and trust in its proper stewardship of the customer's assets.

13.2 AN INTRODUCTION TO MARKETING PLANNING

Figure 13.1 shows a simplified view of the role of marketing within an insurance company. In order to profit from customer orientation, an insurance company must understand the needs of its customers. In many insurance markets, insurers effectively have two levels of customer: the independent intermediary and the final consumer (the insured). In order to complete a successful sale via an independent intermediary, insurers must make their product acceptable to the broker or consultant and also make it attractive to the insured. Only then, when the insured is offered a choice by the intermediary, is he likely to opt for that insurer's product. There can, of course, be tremendous variation in the type of insured – from comparatively ill-informed individuals to large, highly sophisticated commercial insurance buyers.

Understanding of the customer (both intermediary and insured) can be achieved by market intelligence which should be used to evaluate the range of services that could be offered to identify market opportunities. Each such opportunity should be considered as a potential new product. The planning process should also involve some form of market testing on intermediaries and/or policyholders in order to fine-tune the product specification, and to plan the marketing communication approach, the distribution strategy and the price.

At the same time, some forecast of demand for the new product is required in order to estimate its likely profitability. The marketing plan should then be complete with profit, sales and cost targets and an assessment of how sales will be achieved, using a choice of the available marketing tools and techniques.

The final stage involves the synchronisation of sales, distribution, promotion and pricing strategies. The balancing and fine-tuning of this marketing mix is the essence of marketing practice. An outline of this whole process is shown in Table 13.2 on page 216.

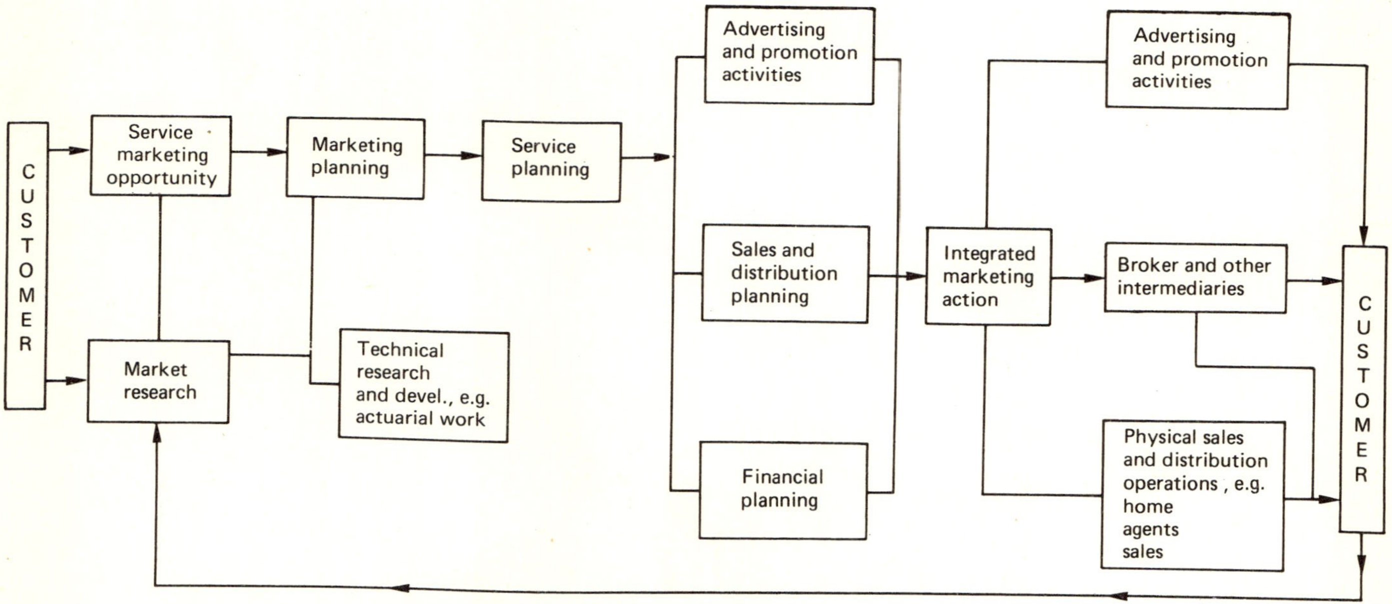

Source: Watkins and Wright (1986).
Figure 13.1 The marketing process

13.3 DEMAND ANALYSIS

The two basic questions to be answered from an insurance company marketing point of view are: why do people buy insurance, and how do consumers choose which company (and, if appropriate, intermediary) to buy from? Some of the main economic and other factors influencing a consumer's demand for insurance are discussed below, but a further examination of corporate insurance purchases can be obtained in Main (1982).

At the macroeconomic level there are a number of indicators which are important influences on the total market size. For personal insurances these include the level of disposable income, the saving ratio for different income levels, employment levels, the rate of inflation, expenditure levels on various goods and services, levels of home ownership and indebtedness, car ownership and holiday expenditure. For corporate customers, relevant macroeconomic indicators include the level of business activity, the number of new business registrations, and the values of net capital stock.

At the microeconomic level the competition for personal savings forms a major economic influence on the demand for life insurance. The determination of the total amount that will be spent from the consumer's budget on insurance will be influenced in part by the level of that income but also by competing demands for the funds by other forms of personal savings (for example building society accounts, bank deposit accounts, National Savings, and shares).

The purchase of an insurance contract involves many other influences than mere economic ones, including:

(a) *Compulsory insurance requirements*, both statutory and contracted.
(b) *Fiscal matters*, which are often important in both long-term insurance for individuals and non-life insurance for corporations.
(c) *Perceptions of risk and attitudes to insurance*. There is a substantial body of evidence that people do not rank their perceived risk in the 'statistical' order of riskiness and that these perceptions of risk have an important impact on their willingness to purchase insurance. A notable feature is the disinclination of many people to insure against low-probability disasters.
(d) *Previous experience of losses* and of the purchase of insurance.
(e) *Family life-style*. Market research agencies tend to segment many consumer markets by family life cycle characteristics tempered by income and occupation influences. The four main stages are: dependent (mainly under 24, living in the family home); pre-family (mainly under 35, established separate household but with no children); family (under 65, with one or more children in the home); and late (all adults whose children have left or are over 35 and childless). The measure-

ment of life-style (known as psychographics) often involves other psychological subdivisions of these basic categories (aggressive–submissive, independent–dependent and so on). A recent development in this area is the ACORN classification developed in the United Kingdom. ACORN (A Classification of Residential Neighbourhoods) uses 39 types of housing clustered into 12 groups to classify all housing in the United Kingdom. For example, Group D, 'poor quality older terraced housing', covered 4.5 per cent of the 1981 UK population, whereas Group J, 'affluent suburban housing', accounted for 15.9 per cent. By adding further population characteristics to the ACORN classification, valuable insights can be gained into a range of market segments of high potential value to insurance markets for household policies.

(f) *Sociological factors*, for example cultural and sub-cultural influences, family and work-group influences, social class and reference group influences can all affect household purchasing of insurance. Because corporate purchasing decisions are made by individuals or committees, these types of influence are carried over into the organisational environment and influence purchasing behaviour.

13.4 MARKET RESEARCH

Market research is the process whereby marketing managers obtain market intelligence as an input to their decision-making. There are two types of market research: desk or secondary research, which uses information already published for other reasons, and primary research, which involves collecting specific information. Most market research projects are a mixture of the two. Obviously, it is less expensive and quicker to use data which is already available than to collect new information. As market research always involves balancing accuracy against cost, this is a significant consideration. The design and implementation of primary research is a specialist area best left to market research agencies.

The most important consideration is to identify accurately the information required. This necessitates a careful appraisal of the marketing decisions to be made and the information required for these decisions.

Sources of information

Insurance companies and brokers have the potential benefit of a rich seam of customer information – the proposal form. The exact information will vary according to the specific proposal form, but typical examples of data which could be available for marketing use include: name and address of customer, postcode and telephone number, occupation (and, from this, social class), age, marital status, place of birth, medical history, house type and ownership status, ownership of specific consumer durables, such as freezer, car details; (for business customers) type and location of business, value of stock, profits, payroll and so on.

Secondary information may also be obtained from competitors. Whilst it is difficult to approach competitors directly for information, their Annual Report can give useful leads as to future intentions. Another source of information is trade journals, which will often give early indications of sales successes or forthcoming new products. Trade bodies, such as the Association of British Insurers and the British Insurance and Investment Brokers Association in the United Kingdom, are other possible sources of summarised data. For international information an invaluable source is *Sigma*, published monthly by the Swiss Re.

In addition much secondary information can be obtained from government publications. The Census of Population and Production data can be used to identify market potential, growth rates and macroeconomic influences. In the United Kingdom, reports like The Family Expenditure Survey, Social Trends and Economic Trends are other easily available sources of socioeconomic and demographic data.

In an attempt to persuade advertisers to use their media vehicles, all the media owners publish a vast array of data relating to their audiences. These data cover not only media accessibility but also socioeconomic data, attitudinal and consumer-durable ownership data. The obvious application is in advertising campaign planning, but other uses are also feasible.

Finally, from time to time, syndicated market research studies are undertaken and sold 'off the shelf' to interested parties. These can be on the impact of particular events, on specific attitudes or on particular market segments, and may or may not be relevant to market intelligence needs. Other studies are conducted on a regular basis with a panel of respondents, the reports being available to subscribers.

Sources of PRIMARY information

Secondary sources can be supplemented by trade gossip, feedback from salesmen, agents, complaints analysis, exhibitions and conferences, and a range of other low-cost sources to add to the understanding of buyer behaviour. In many cases, however, specific information will be required, in which case primary sources must be used. The company must then decide: how to specify and interpret terms of reference and objectives for the research; what to ask – questionnaire development; who to ask – sample size and structure, sampling procedure; how to contact respondents; how to ask for information – self- or interviewer-completed questionnaires, dichotomous (yes–no), polychotomous (multiple–choice) or open-ended questions; short or in-depth interviews; how to analyse the resultant data – which statistical methods to use; how to interpret the results in terms of the original terms of reference; and how best to present the findings, with appropriate recommendations. A typical market research process, having answered the above questions and decided on the best approach to each issue, will proceed as follows:

(a) Identify marketing opportunity or problem – leading to information needs specification and terms of reference.
(b) Face a 'make or buy' decision – has the organisation sufficient resources and expertise to carry out the project in-house; if not, which outside agencies should be approached?
(c) Develop and issue a specific research brief – this should put the opportunity or problem in the context of the company's marketing situation. It should identify the type of information needed, the relevant population to sample, the level of accuracy required and, of course, budget and time constraints.
(d) Receive and evaluate research proposals. Evaluation should take into account a variety of considerations such as cost, research design, professionalism and value of money.
(e) Select and hire an agency. A formal agreement with the chosen agency is recommended, to avoid disagreements later. This should cover the detailed issues such as sample size, methodology, progress reports, cost payments, presentation requirements and time limits.
(f) Execute the research plan with agreed progress checks.
(g) Report on the findings. The major part of the report will be the results, the results analysis and interpretation, and conclusions and recommendations. There should also be a re-statement and interpretation of the terms of reference, and a methodology section appended (with technical matters such as sample selection, questionnaire and details of statistical techniques used). Results should be clearly tabulated, with a commentary on the major points. The highlights of the report should be incorporated into an executive brief at the beginning of the report. An oral presentation of the findings is an opportunity for the client company to interrogate the agency on the report.
(h) Finally, evaluate the results, specifying any necessary follow-up research. The need for follow-up work can often be avoided by clear thinking at the outset of the process. The specification of information requirements should be in terms of the marketing decisions to be made, rather than in terms of a 'nice-to-know' basis.

13.5 THE MARKETING MIX

Once an identification of the information requirements, in terms of the

Table 13.2 Elements of the marketing mix for insurance companies

Product Planning
Product lines to be offered – qualities, design, detailed contents, etc
The markets to sell – to whom, where, when and in what quantity
New product policy – research and development programme
Branding
Selection of trade marks and names
Brand Policy – individual or family brand
Sale under private brand or unbranded
Pricing
The level of premium rates to adopt
The margins to adopt – for the intermediary market, for direct sales
Channels of Distribution
The channels to use between company and consumer
The degree of selectivity amongst brokers and other intermediaries
Efforts to gain co-operation of the independent intermediary market
Personal Selling
The emphasis to be placed on personal selling and the necessary organisation to sell direct *vis-à-vis* intermediary market
Advertising
The amount to spend – the emphasis to be placed on advertising
The desired product image and corporate image
The mix of advertising to independent intermediaries and to final consumers
Promotions
The use of special selling plans or devices directed at or through independent intermediaries
The form of device for consumer promotions
Servicing
Providing after-sales service needed to intermediaries and to final consumers (e.g. renewal and bonus notices, direct mail offers)

Source: Schwart (1965) pp. 389–90.

marketing decisions, has been made the next stage is an analysis of the major marketing decision variables which are relevant in insurance marketing planning. Although these are considered individually, the art of marketing lies in integrating the individual components into an effective composite programme.

Table 13.2 shows the elements of the marketing mix which need to be combined to provide a unique selling proposition (USP). The USP is the special quality being offered by the company which is not available elsewhere – the company's best attempt at meeting customer needs profitably. In the consideration of the individual elements of the marketing mix, the main emphasis will be placed on product policy, promotional policy and distribution policy (sections 13.6 to 13.8), as pricing policy was considered in detail in Chapter 12.

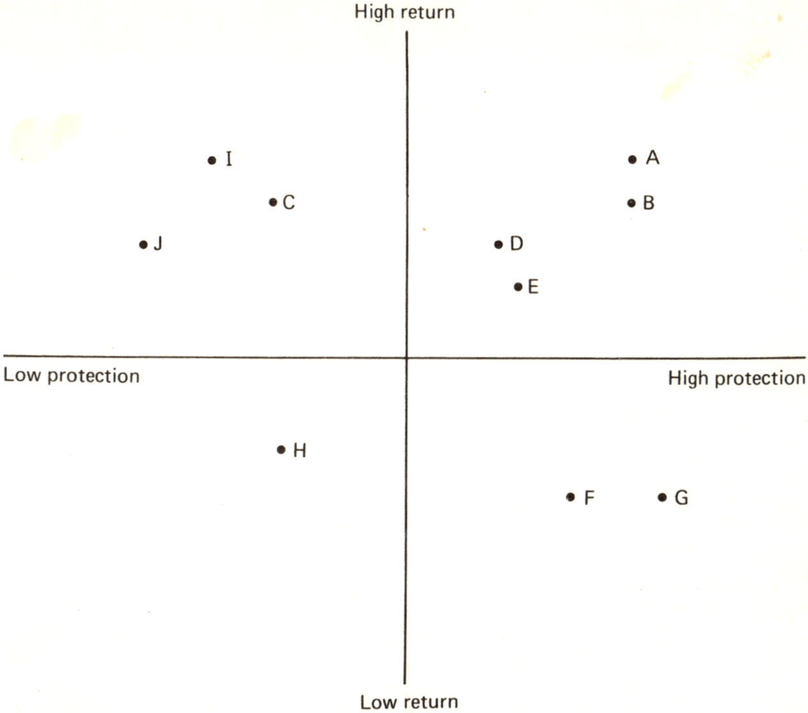

Figure 13.2 Gap analysis for life insurance products

13.6 PRODUCT POLICY

After identifying customers' needs for underlying motivations towards insurance, the company must construct a range of products which appeal to the customers in some special or unique way which differentiates the company from its rivals. Three aspects of product policy will be considered: new product development, the determination of product range, and market segmentation.

New product development

The process of spotting gaps in the market should be customer driven, but this is difficult because of the highly competitive nature of many aspects of the insurance industry. One approach which not only generates ideas but assesses consumer preferences is 'gap analysis'; this involves four main stages. First is an identification of the product market by ascertaining which products consumers perceive as having the same uses. Secondly comes a representation of these products in a multi-dimensional space with 'actionable' dimensions or attributes (that is attributes which can be connected to product characteristics and which are therefore useful in product development). The third step is to construct a model of consumer choice between existing products.This involves relating the distance between products in the attribute space to individual preferences. This relationship or model may then be used to predict how an individual would react to a new product concept. Finally the model is used to search for new product ideas. A simple example for life insurance is shown in Figure 13.2.

Suppose consumers perceive the existing life insurance products (A–H) on only two dimensions (the level of investment return and level of protection offered). If they are asked to rate existing products on these dimensions, then, by averaging responses, the perceptual map in Figure 13.2 could result. If, in addition, the concept of an ideal product is tested on consumers in the same way (and found to be point A) the distance between each product and the ideal product in attribute space is a measure of preference.

In this example, the gap around the ideal point (A) represents a possible new product idea. If consumers could be persuaded (by promotions) to perceive the new product (B) as having that particular combination of attributes, then, as it is close to the ideal, consumers might be expected to prefer it to existing products.

Further development of new product ideas would require assessment by the actuarial department, price setting, development of a promotional platform for the launch alongside further testing on consumers, and the definition of the technical issues involved in the product specification. The product definition and associated costs must be seen in the light of the proposed target market.

Before the product can be launched further market testing is desirable. For consumer goods this is most often done by test marketing. This usually involves launching the new brand into a limited area, usually a regional television area. This ensures that the company has the correct marketing mix while offering the opportunity to fine-tune the level of the marketing variables. With a consumer good it is relatively easy to withdraw from the market if all is not well. With an insurance product, commitments in terms of policies taken out have to be honoured, perhaps for years ahead. This can add substantial costs to the test marketing decision (although these will of course be less than those incurred if a 'faulty' product is launched without test marketing). Nevertheless the use of a test market is still advisable (for example by offering the product in one region only) to assess reaction. The length of the test market may need to be considerable to cover not only the normal renewal period (at least one year for annual contracts) but also a further period in order accurately to assess claims

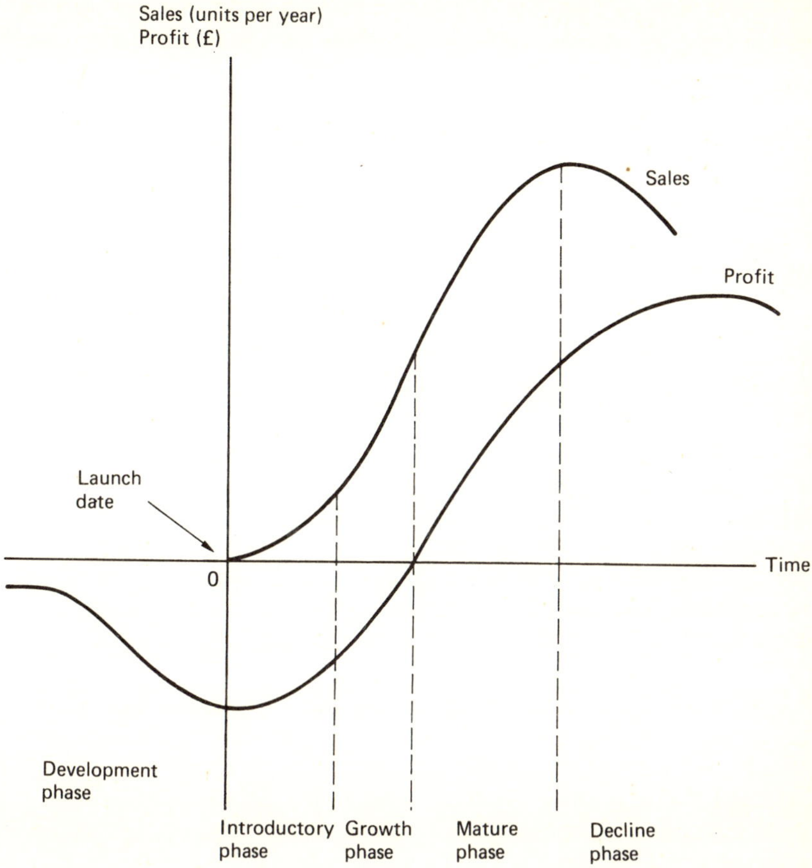

Figure 13.3 The product life cycle

experience. Another great danger of test marketing is that competitors are informed of the imminence of a new product, giving them extra time to produce their own version. As always, the test marketing decision involves balancing benefits against costs – the major benefit is avoiding an expensive failure from a subsequent national launch.

The launch of a new product is the culmination of marketing planning and requires the co-ordination of various activities, such as liaising with intermediaries, and promotional activities, such as sales aids, advertising, packaging, and brand creation. The product must be presented to the market for critical evaluation by customers, intermediaries, commentators and competitors. Using market research in the development process is one step towards ensuring that the new product is well received.

Product range determination

The concept of product life cycle may be a useful tool in analysing the suitability of the existing range of an insurance company's products and is illustrated in Figure 13.3. During the development phase the project generates losses as investment of time and effort, often extending into years, accumulates. From the launch data, sales are made, slowly at first, as time is needed for the promotional effect to percolate through to the target market. The speed of the sales growth will be influenced by market size and by the attractiveness of the new product to the target market (along with the level of awareness and interest generated by promotional activity).

This introductory phase usually involves a loss as sales effort (including training costs) is high and heavy promotional expenditures are often necessary. As awareness levels increase, it is hoped that a growth phase follows, when sales rise at an increasing rate. It is at this stage that alert competitors, sensing a successful new product, may be enticed into the market, depending on the barriers to entry. For existing insurance companies there are generally low barriers to entry into perceived profitable associated product fields (except when specialist technical or sales staff are required, when the product imposes substantial technological requirements or when large marketing expense levels need to be incurred). Increasingly, competition from other financial services suppliers is likely to be a threat in the personal insurance markets.

The mature stage is reached as sales start to level off (as all potential new buyers are exhausted and sales stabilise at the repurchase rate). Typically for insurance products this stage lasts a long time, and these traditional, profitable products will form the mainstay of a company's sales income. In customers' minds, the company and the product are now well-established and it may be difficult to alter these established images.

Eventually sales will decline as the product becomes outmoded and superseded. In this final stage, the product can still be profitable, appealing mainly to habitual, traditional buyers with little need for promotional support. Eventually sales fall to an uneconomic level and the product is withdrawn from the company's range.

In many markets, products in the mature or decline stages can be rejuvenated to give a boost to sales. In the UK car market, for example, Ford Motor Company revamped the Cortina four times, each time giving a boost to sales. Similarly for existing insurance products, new features could be added to give an additional promotional appeal.

The value of the product life cycle concept is in being able to analyse objectively the company's product range. From a profit and a cash-flow viewpoint, the range should include a sufficient number of profitable sellers in the late growth and maturity stages (i.e. the 'cash cows' of Chapter 1) which will enable the development of new products to be financed.

Equally, if too high a proportion of the range is in the decline (or 'dog') stage, the image of the company may be adversely outmoded: it may be perceived as old-fashioned and out of touch with modern needs.

Market segmentation

Market segmentation is a systematic attempt to choose the most important sectors of the buying population, and then to design brands, products, packages, communication and marketing strategies around them. This segmentation may be by age, purchase reason, benefit, sagacity grouping, geographical or indeed any other relevant factor. The product range should then reflect the different segment needs.

In conjunction with the product life cycle, segmentation can provide another form of analysis of the product range decision. The aim is to provide a profitable mix of products, each of which can be justified not merely on its own merits but also as an integral part of the structured range.

13.7 PROMOTIONAL POLICY

Once a suitable product has been designed, promotion must be used to contact potential customers and to persuade them to buy it. An integrated promotional policy should have, as a common goal, a communications theme or image which the promotion aims to generate in the minds of consumers. Promotions policy must harmonise with the other elements of the marketing mix in order to produce a composite brand or company image. An insurance company may use a variety of promotional elements, but we will concentrate on advertising, direct mailing, sponsorship and personal selling.

Promotional policy should use the most cost-effective tools to meet communication goals within the marketing strategy. The allocation of funds for advertising rather than sponsorship, direct mail or personal selling must be justified in terms of the alternative uses of such funds. This implies an estimate of advertising effectiveness – which is fraught with difficulties. Off-the-page response rates in terms of coupons returned, policies sold and premium income generated can be calculated, but the returns from a company image-building campaign are almost impossible to quantify. Nevertheless the company must allocate funds between competing promotional methods to optimise returns.

Advertising

Whilst the media advertising budget of most insurance industries is small compared with some of the large consumer goods industries, it is nevertheless an important form of promotion. Although some of advertising expenditure is directed by companies to final consumers, much is also directed at independent intermediaries. Insurance brokers also advertise, but usually on a limited scale.

The types of available media each have particular features with respect to insurance advertising. Television enables an appeal to be dramatised in sound and vision, conferring a social legitimacy on the advertised product. This medium is particularly effective in heightening people's awareness of the impact of fire, theft, death and so on. It has long been recognised that the ease with which people can imagine or recall to mind the consequences of an event substantially influences their reactions to it (this has been termed the 'availability heuristic'). Newspapers enable topical, detailed copy to be transmitted in a retainable form and are particularly useful for 'off-the-page' direct response for personal insurance contracts such as life and motor insurance. Magazines have a longer retention, greater use of colour, and higher credibility than many newspapers; because of their elective readership they are particularly suitable for corporate or brand image building. Trade magazines are often the most effective way of advertising to insurance intermediaries. The low audience size for radio, cinema and poster advertising makes these media more suitable as a back-up to a major medium to extend a campaign.

A number of stages are involved in providing a logical framework for the creation of an advertising campaign. Because of the complexities of the process it is usual to use specialist advertising agencies to undertake the creativity and media-buying functions even if the entire process is not sub-contracted (the steps in hiring an agency are similar in principle to those outlined in Section 13.4 for hiring a market research agency). There are six main stages in the launch of an advertising campaign.

First the target audience and their media accessibility must be identified. This is vital as it influences the likely response to the presented message. Identification can be in terms of any relevant factors discussed in Section 13.3. Secondly, a specific advertising message must be created which can be directed at the target audience. This needs to be done in relation to the promotional objective (which, for example, may be to increase awareness, increase the level of interest in the product, increase sales, increase repeat sales, create a particular brand image, or create a particular company image). Thirdly, the most effective media to reach this audience must be selected. This reflects the type and structure of the message and audience characteristics as well as the available media and their costs, characteristics and audience size. Next, the campaign must be scheduled to provide the best timing, frequency and impact, given the promotional objectives. At that stage the advertising budget must be fixed. In an ideal world the size of the advertising budget should be balanced against the specific promotional objectives. In practice the advertising budget may be set as a proportion of actual or expected sales or on a 'what can be afforded' basis. Finally, the success of the campaign must assessed. However, because of the great difficulties involved, relatively little attention is directed at examining the effectiveness of advertising expenditure.

Direct mail

Direct mail is an increasingly important promotional tool for insurance companies. Existing customer records (or those of a newly-acquired subsidiary, such as an estate agency, for example) are utilised to provide a marketing list which can be used to sell extra services to existing customers. Although response rates often tend to be below 3 per cent, this may still be enough to make the exercise highly profitable. The advent of low-cost microcomputer-based word processing systems linked to high-quality printers has enabled sophisticated personalised letters to be produced. Split sample experiments can be used to assess, for example, the increase in the response rate obtained by using free gifts or special offers. The advantage of direct mail is that the cost per response and cost per sale are low when compared to media advertising, and the timing can be matched to individual consumer needs. However the use of direct mail requires an efficient computer-based marketing information system to provide the necessary details of customers, so that the relevant products can be selected.

Sponsorship

Commercial sponsorship of sporting and cultural events has grown very rapidly in recent years, and this growth rate shows no signs of falling off. In the United Kingdom, insurance companies are often at the forefront of this booming industry, sponsoring cricket, swimming, table tennis, horse racing and a host of other sports and arts events. The UK company Cornhill Insurance plc reportedly found that its name awareness rose from 2 per cent in 1977 to 21 per cent in 1982, primarily as a result of its sponsorship of English test cricket. However Gillette Industries plc ended their sponsorship of cricket in part because their market research showed that consumers no longer associated the 'Gillette Cup' with the company's products.

In marketing terms, sponsorship can be seen as a form of marketing communication. It stands alongside media advertising, personal selling, public relations and other forms of sales promotions as a method by which insurance companies can 'speak' to potential customers. It is unrealistic to expect a direct link between sponsorship and increased sales; instead the main objectives are communication, customer/intermediary relations, and public relations. The type of event to be sponsored should match the desired image of the insurance company. For example, the image of 'solid dependability', 'protectiveness' and 'traditional values' (which might appeal to those seeking insurance contracts) should fit the type of events which the insurance company sponsors: cricket, tennis, golf and athletics, as well as national orchestras and other arts events, are likely to provide such image links, whereas motor racing probably would not. All these advantages are enhanced by media coverage of sponsored events.

Personal selling

Personal selling is an expensive promotional activity but one which can be highly effective with good sales training and sales aids. Personal selling should be seen as part of the overall marketing strategy; indeed the marketing strategy should pre-sell the product, making the personal selling task easier. There are a number of possible selling methods involving face-to-face contract. Independent intermediaries play an important role in many insurance industries. In addition tied agents will sell the products of one insurance company only, often on a commission-only basis. This can lead to 'high-pressure' techniques of selling to boost commission earnings. Finally company salesforces may contact final users as well as intermediaries, often on a salary plus commission basis. The product and company knowledge of employees should be thorough, as their role is essentially an ambassadorial one. The salesperson will have a direct impact on the way the company is perceived by clients.

The sales role is vital to a company. It is important that it is not misused to benefit short-term earnings at the expense of longer-term sales by being over-zealous in presenting products to potential buyers. In many countries, governments have passed laws to regulate the way in which insurance (particularly life insurance and other financial services) is sold. These are discussed more fully in the next chapter.

13.8 DISTRIBUTION POLICY

The insurance company is faced with a number of strategies to market its products to final consumers. It can use independent intermediaries, its own direct salesforce, an independent direct salesforce (if regulations allow), direct mail, direct response advertising, or a mix of some or all of the above strategies. The discussion here will focus on direct versus intermediary marketing approaches and the benefits and disadvantages of each will be considered. Further details can be obtained in Dyer and Watkins (1988) and Diacon (1990).

Direct marketing

The major advantage of direct marketing is control over the marketing channel to the final customer. This enables the company to instigate marketing initiatives without the need to elicit the support of independent intermediaries. Skilful sales training backed by appropriate sales aids can be used to maximise the impact of a direct sales presentation of the company's products. The control of the sales programme should enable the company to present its products to potential customers effectively.

Direct mail or off-the-page response advertising saves sales staff costs but means that standard products must be presented in a simple manner to maximise response. Complete reliance on this system leaves the company vulnerable to postal and/or newspaper disputes. Also the communication is one-way only, unlike face-to-face presentations, which allow interaction, discussion and persuasion as part of the sales process.

Intermediary marketing

Marketing in a competitive environment to independent intermediaries requires the insurance company to offer a professional, efficient service which will enable the intermediary to operate effectively. Companies must first offer good products which appeal to the intermediary's customer mix, and which an independent intermediary can recommend in preference to the contracts of competing insurers. The technical efficiency of insurers is also important: the back-up service provides quick and accurate answers to an intermediary's queries. This increasingly involves the use of computer-based links. Furthermore the commission structure adopted by the insurer (or the industry in general) must reflect the difficulty involved in servicing particular contracts and the profitability of these for insurers.

In terms of the promotional policy to be adopted, an awareness amongst intermediaries of the name and reputation of the insurance company will naturally help to pre-sell policies. Similarly, personal relationships built up over time between the company and the intermediary (whether by telephone, post or personal contact) and backed by good-quality sales literature can be an important boost to sales of the company products. This can be further enhanced by a trade-push promotional campaign. Demand-pull promotional campaigns (which are aimed at making consumers specify a policy by company name) must direct consumers to intermediaries, otherwise conflict can arise if the insurer attempts to bypass intermediaries and sell direct.

13.9 MARKETING STRATEGY

As a component of corporate strategy, marketing strategy is concerned with the appropriate positioning of the company's products in the competitive market-place. The purpose of such strategies is to achieve the company's corporate objectives (as outlined in Chapter 1).

In general, insurers can adopt one of three main approaches to their marketing strategy: cost leadership, differentiation, and focusing. The strategy of cost leadership requires insurers to provide a range of insurance (and other financial services) at unit costs (and hence premium rates) which are lower than those achievable by competitors. Differentiation occurs when insurers attempt to be unique in respect of one or more characteristics of value to customers (for example, security or good investment performance). In a focused strategy, insurers identify specialist or target market segments which will be competed for to the exclusion of other segments, utilising the cost or differentiation strategies outlined in Chapter 1. A more detailed discussion can be found in Diacon (1985, pp. 52–9) and Carter, Chiplin and Lewis (1986, ch. 3).

Finally, recent research indicates that, in the United Kingdom at least, financial institutions are becoming more marketing orientated. In a survey of 45 institutions, Hooley and Mann (1988) noted that, over the previous five years, there was a significant shift in the business orientation and marketing approach of UK financial institutions. For example, 53 per cent of institutions described their current strategic emphasis as 'market-driven', whereas the corresponding figure for five years before was 2 per cent.

The increasing proportion of the sample surveyed by Hooley and Mann claiming to be market-driven is also reflected by a change in the marketing approach of the financial firms. Almost 80 per cent of institutions now describe their approach as one of market orientation (that is, they place major emphasis on prior analysis of market needs, adapting products to meet these as necessary): for five years before, the figure was 2 per cent. Similarly, in describing the situation for five years previous, 82 per cent of companies categorised their marketing approach as one of product orientation (that is, they provided a range of traditional products for whoever wanted to purchase): the recent percentage has fallen to 11 per cent. These figures corroborate the results of a recent survey of insurance companies, banks, and building societies (Davison, Watkins and Wright, 1989) which indicates that around 83 per cent of institutions describe themselves as having a marketing function which, in the majority of cases, is undertaken in a separate department.

References

Carter, R.L., B. Chiplin and M. Lewis (eds), (1986) *Personal Financial Markets* (Oxford: Philip Allan).

Davison, H., T. Watkins and M. Wright (1989) 'Developing New Personal Financial Products – Some Evidence on the Role of Market Research' *International Journal of Bank Marketing*.

Diacon, S.R. (1985) *The UK Insurance Industry: Structure, Development and Market Prospects to 1990* (London: Staniland Hall Associates).
Diacon, S.R. (1990) 'Personal Financial Markets', in R.L. Carter (ed.), *Handbook of Personal Financial Management* (Brentford, Middlesex: Kluwer Publishing Limited).
Dyer, N. and T. Watkins (eds), (1988) *Marketing Insurance: A Practical Guide*, 2nd edn (Brentford Middlesex: Kluwer Publishing Limited).
Hooley, G.J. and S.J. Mann (1988) 'The Adoption of Marketing by Financial Institutions in the UK', *The Service Industries Journal*, vol. 8, no. 4, October.
Main, B.G.M. (1982) 'Business Insurance and Large Widely-Held Corporations', *Geneva Papers*, vol. 7, no. 24, July, pp. 237–47.
Schwart, G. (1965) *Science in Marketing* (New York: Wiley and Sons).
Watkins, T. and M. Wright (1986) *Marketing Financial Services* (London: Butterworths).
Zeithaml, V.A., A.B. Parasuraman and L.L. Berry (1985) 'Problems and Strategies in Services Marketing', *Journal of Marketing*, vol. 49, Spring, pp. 33–46.

14 Intermediaries and the Agency System

Hugh Cockerell

14.1 THE LEGAL ASPECT OF INSURANCE INTERMEDIARIES

Intermediaries play a prominent, often a dominant, part in insurance. They fall into two main categories: those appointed by insurers to sell and service insurance contracts on their behalf, and those used by the buyers of insurance to help them obtain cover. Insurers describe all intermediaries as 'agents', but the law distinguishes the two categories: it regards those in the first category as agents of the insurers and those in the second as agents of the insured. This distinction has important legal consequences.

In the United Kingdom, the law regards as an agent anyone who is mandated by a principal to act on his behalf within the scope of the authority given by the mandate. This may extend to entering into a contract on his principal's behalf. Such a contract will then bind the principal and may be enforced by him as if he had entered into it himself.

On occasion an agent may play a dual part as agent for both insured and insurer. For example, an insurance broker, whose prime function is to obtain insurance on a proposer's behalf, may be empowered by an insurer to issue cover in its name. In issuing such cover the broker acts as the insurer's agent and binds the insurer. Where anyone acts as the agent of both parties there is the possibility that their interests will conflict. The law raises no objection to dual agency provided both parties have given their informed consent to it.

An example of the difficulty that may arise through the use of agents is seen in the matter of disclosure of material facts. A proposer for insurance is under a duty to tell the insurer of all facts that he knows or ought to know which would influence the mind of a prudent insurer in deciding whether to grant the insurance and, if so, on what terms. A failure to disclose may entitle the insurer, on learning of it, to avoid liability under the insurance. If the failure to disclose was a failure on the part of the proposer's agent (an insurance broker, say) the failure is attributable to the principal and the insurer may avoid liability. The proposer may then sue his agent for damages. If, on the other hand, the material facts were disclosed to the insurer's agent, they are deemed to be within the knowledge of the insurer. The insurer cannot therefore avoid liability, though it may be entitled to damages from its agent for his negligent performance of his duty.

14.2 TYPES OF INTERMEDIARIES

There are two main categories of insurance intermediary: those appointed by the insurer to help in providing its services, and those advising buyers of insurance. The pattern of insurance intermediaries varies widely between countries, for reasons of history and geography, and between classes of insurance within countries.

The first category of intermediary covers those persons appointed to sell and service insurance on the insurer's behalf. These may be subdivided into:

(a) individual salespersons;
(b) firms, who may or may not have insurance as their principal business, and who represent insurers in a given locality (sometimes with exclusive rights to do so); and
(c) persons thought likely to be able to introduce buyers by virtue of their business or social connections. Prominent among the introducers are those whose principal occupation is likely to bring them into contact with people at a time when they need insurance (for example, solicitors, accountants, travel agents, building societies and motor dealers).

The second category includes independent intermediaries acting for those seeking to buy insurance. These include insurance brokers, being independent persons who hold themselves out as expert in advising on and placing insurances; or others, sometimes styling themselves insurance consultants or financial advisers, who perform a similar independent function.

The terms of the UK Financial Services Act 1986 require the 'polarisation' of intermediaries involved in the selling of or advising on 'investment' business. Exactly what constitutes an investment is defined very precisely to include shares, options, unit trust units, futures contracts and most types of long-term insurance. Polarisation requires that intermediaries involved in investment business must either be fully independent advisers or representative of just one company (that is, tied). Introducers of investment business must thus either become tied agents of only one investment company or introduce clients to an independent intermediary.

14.3 DUTIES OF INTERMEDIARIES

The duties of an insurance intermediary vary between the simple and the complex. For investment business governed by the UK Financial Services Act 1986 the duties also vary between the two categories of intermediary. At the simple end of the scale an intermediary may be concerned only with effecting a single policy on instructions from a client who, it may be, even designates the insurer (this is sometimes known as 'execution only' business). In more complex situations the client may rely on an intermediary for advice on all his financial needs and for consequent action.

The intermediary must begin by examining the client's circumstances and current insurance arrangements to see whether these arrangements could be improved by amendments to cover, elimination of overlaps, filling gaps or transferring cover to insurers offering a better deal. The client's risks should be analysed to see whether any can be eliminated or reduced and whether insurance is the best financial treatment for the residue. It may be necessary to advise the client to take safety precautions or, in the case of property, to obtain valuations so that property is covered for its current value.

Once an insurance programme is agreed an independent intermediary or broker also needs a knowledge of the market for insurance to enable him to recommend suitable insurers. The financial solidity of insurers is a prime consideration. Policy terms and premium rates are then negotiated with the insurers.

The intermediary should check each policy when it is received to ensure that it correctly reflects the cover required. He should make clear to the client the extent of the cover, the conditions that must be complied with, and the need to keep the independent intermediary or insurer informed of changes in the client's business that could affect his need for insurance. Insurances need to be reviewed at least once a year before renewal. Clients must be reminded when renewal premiums are due.

Independent intermediaries commonly receive and forward notifications of potential claims and negotiate settlements on behalf of their clients. Often this is done without charge, but if a charge is to be made the client should be informed of this at the outset. Many offer additional services, such as detailed advice on risk management or risk improvement, or the administration of pension schemes.

In many classes of general insurance an insurance broker may be authorised by insurers to grant immediate cover on their behalf. With large risks he may need to put together a consortium of insurers, going outside the domestic market.

14.4 REMUNERATION OF INTERMEDIARIES

Almost always intermediaries are paid by the insurer rather than by the insured. The payment usually takes the form of commission calculated as a proportion of premium income (although salesmen employed directly by insurers may also be paid a fixed salary). The practice of remunerating intermediaries by commission is open to the objection that intermediaries acting for the insured will not seek low premium rates because their remuneration will fall with the premium. But, if the insurance market is competitive enough, the intermediary may then lose the business to a competitor who quotes a lower premium rate.

No doubt a system of remuneration by fees paid by the insured would be open to less objection, but so far such a system has not gained much ground (except in some areas of commercial insurance purchases). Fees are particularly appropriate when the intermediary is asked to report and advise on a client's insurance requirements without an undertaking that any insurances recommended will be placed through him; or where advice is sought on, for example, risk management or safety precautions in which the intermediary may be expert and where the adoption of the recommendations may lead to the discontinuance of or a reduction in the insurance carried.

In a market where the commission rates paid by insurers are determined entirely by competitive forces, the following behaviour is likely to result:

(a) Insurers will compete for business by offering higher rates of commission. This process will continue until the higher premium rates that will inevitably result act as a sufficient deterrent to insurance buyers (although in many insurance markets, buyers are not particularly price-conscious).
(b) Insurers will be indiscriminate in granting agencies; the *reductio ad absurdum* is the payment of commission to someone who brings in only his own insurances (the own-case agency, as it is known).
(c) In market segments where buyers are more price-conscious, intermediaries may pass on (that is, rebate) some of their commission in the form of discounts. However, in countries where insurance agents have a strong political lobby, the rebating of commissions has been forbidden by law. This does not apply in the United Kingdom.

Excessive commission rates may be regarded as contrary to the public interest (particularly when consumers are not particularly price-conscious). Therefore, in countries where consumer protection is strong, commission rates have sometimes been limited by legislation. For example, in the United Kingdom the commission rates on life and pensions business paid to independent intermediaries were initially controlled by so-called Self-Regulatory Organisations. However, following the recommendation of the Office of Fair Trading, this commission agreement was disbanded in 1990, on the grounds that it was anti-competitive.

Insurance companies in a market often seek to limit commission rates by agreement among themselves (although such action may fall foul of anti-cartel rules and other legislation designed to protect consumers from the abuse of monopoly power). Enforcement of such limits has proved difficult and is liable in the long run to break down, especially when new companies are seeking to force their way into the market. An example in England and Wales was the Life Offices' Association (LOA) which for many years prescribed a series of maximum commission rates for life insurance and pensions contracts. The LOA was driven to abandon its scheme in 1981 because some member companies began to resign in order to protect themselves against depredations by outside competitors.

14.5 INTERMEDIARIES IN THE UNITED KINGDOM

A brief history

The so-called agency system of British insurance has been anything but systematic. It developed freely to meet the needs of policyholders in each class of business without much governmental control. History offers the key to its development, which has varied from class to class.

In marine insurance (historically the oldest class) the need for insurance brokers was felt from early times because, where anyone wanted insurance, it was necessary to seek out a number of individual underwriters who would accept the risk offered each for himself and not one for another. The broker had not only to find suitable insurers but also to prepare the policy, obtain the signatures of the numerous underwriters concerned and, if a loss occurred, collect the appropriate proportion of it from each. The broker system has persisted at Lloyd's and now extends to all classes of insurance undertaken in the Lloyd's market.

In fire insurance, companies anxious to extend the geographical spread of their business began in the eighteenth century to appoint local agents, often tradesmen, who accepted proposals offered in their locality and administered the local contracts. The tariff system whereby nearly all insurance companies charged agreed rates meant that there was little scope for insurance brokers until Lloyd's underwriters entered the fire insurance market on an independent basis in the 1870s. The companies did not encourage the activities of brokers, fearing that rate-cutting would result.

In life insurance, too, brokers came late on the scene. For insurances necessitated by financial transactions such as mortgages, insurers relied in the main on agents such as solicitors and bank managers who were privy to the transactions and were therefore able to recommend the companies they represented. With the advent of industrial life insurance, sold to small weekly wage-earners, insurance companies found it necessary to appoint large numbers of salesmen collectors to canvass for business and collect the premiums weekly or monthly. Such business offered no scope for insurance brokers. It was not until the 1930s, with the coming of group insurance and pensions business involving substantial premiums, that brokers began to become a significant force in the life market.

Table 14.1 Market share of insurance brokers in the UK domestic market, 1979

Class of insurance	*Brokers' share (%)*
Motor	52
Other non-marine	76
Marine and aviation	94
Ordinary life	(20–25)
Pensions	(80–85)
Industrial life	0

Source: British Insurance Brokers Association, 1982.

The development of accident insurance, notably employers' liability and motor, led insurance companies in search of the business to multiply the appointment of part-time agents, such as motor dealers. For example, the Royal Exchange Assurance, although established in 1720, had less than 600 agents in 1850. By 1900 the number had risen to 5000 and by 1912 to 15 500. The rapid rise in car ownership after 1945 led to the birth of so-called 'High Street' brokers with shops selling principally motor insurance.

It remains true, however, that brokers have been most successful in penetrating insurance markets where they have concentrated on insurances with substantial premiums, and the insurances of businesses in particular. A study undertaken by Kitcat and Aitken for the British Insurance Brokers' Association showed brokers' market share of the various classes of insurance as differing widely (see Table 14.1). The UK intermediary system today is best understood by considering separately the operations of Lloyd's and of the insurance companies.

Lloyd's of London

All insurance at Lloyd's is transacted on behalf of individual underwriting members, who numbered over 33 500 in 1988. Each member belongs to a number of underwriting syndicates of his choice. There are over 350 such syndicates. Every syndicate has an active underwriter to whom the underwriting is entrusted. When he accepts a risk for his syndicate he binds its members. A syndicate is not a partnership however; each member accepts only a stated proportion of any risk and receives that proportion of the premium. A member is not liable in any circumstances for the proportions accepted on behalf of any other member.

Active underwriters sit in the Underwriting Room. Only brokers approved by the Council of Lloyd's, known as Lloyd's brokers, have access to the Room, where business must be transacted. There are some 260 Lloyd's brokers but a hundred of these are subsidiary companies.

A broker wishing to place an insurance prepares details of it on a printed form known as a slip. He shows the slip to an underwriter, choosing one who has the reputation of being a leader in insurances of the class concerned. If the underwriter is disposed to accept a share he initials the slip and applies his syndicate's stamp, at the same time recording on it the percentage of the risk accepted for the syndicate and the rate of premium. The broker then shows the slip to other underwriters, one by one, until he has sufficient acceptances to enable him to complete the insurance. The underwriter binds his syndicate for its percentage by his act in initialling. Equally the broker binds himself to pay the premium even if he is unable to collect it from the insured. By a legal fiction the courts regard the broker as a principal in his dealings with the underwriter who must therefore sue the broker and not the insured for any unpaid premium. Once the insurance is completed it is the broker's task to prepare the policy. This is submitted to Lloyd's Policy Signing Office with the slip, where it is signed on behalf of all the Lloyd's underwriters concerned. Premiums are paid and claims settled through a central accounting procedure.

It falls to the broker to report and negotiate settlement of claims. Until recent years brokers were often asked by underwriters to obtain an assessors' report which the broker then forwarded to the underwriter. Difficulties about this procedure came before the High Court in 1969–70. In two cases where claims were disputed and the insured had to sue the underwriters for payment, the insured sought to obtain from the brokers a copy of the assessors' report, on the ground that the brokers were their agent and ought therefore to give them every help. The court held that in obtaining the assessors' report the brokers were acting as the agent of the underwriters and were not entitled to provide copies to the insured. But judges were critical of the dual agency involved which gave rise to a conflict of interest. As a result of judicial criticism of the procedure brokers have been made aware of the undesirability of having assessors' reports routed through them.

The cases drew attention to the somewhat incestuous relationship that had long existed between brokers and underwriters at Lloyd's. It had often happened in the past that prominent underwriters (such as Angerstein at the beginning of the nineteenth century and Cuthbert Heath at the end) functioned as both underwriters and brokers. Nowadays the active underwriter in charge of a syndicate's underwriting no longer also acts as a broker, though many directors of Lloyd's broking companies and some senior employees are also underwriting members of Lloyd's (known as Names). That is, they provide some of the capital in which an underwriting syndicate's business is based, but they are not permitted to function as active underwriters.

Lloyd's underwriting agencies perform one or both of two functions. As members' agents they recruit the underwriting membership of Lloyd's and manage the Lloyd's affairs of individual members, recommending what syndicates the member should join. As managing agents they manage the affairs of one or more underwriting syndicates, including the appointment and dismissal of a syndicate's active underwriter. For their services they receive fees from the underwriting members concerned, plus a share of the syndicate's profits.

The report in 1980 of a working party (the Fisher Report) appointed by Lloyd's drew attention to the potential conflict of interest that arose when insurance brokers owned or controlled managing agencies which operated underwriting syndicates. As brokers, their duty was to obtain insurance for clients on the most advantageous terms. As the operators of syndicates, their interest was to maximise the profits from underwriting. The appointment of active underwriters for the syndicates they owned or controlled was in their hands. There was a danger that they would put pressure on the syndicate to underwrite risks contrary to the underwriter's better judgement, or to write business at rates below those he would offer to other brokers, or to give high commissions, or settle claims on terms that he would otherwise not agree. Alternatively brokers might have been tempted to place business with the syndicates they controlled though better terms were available elsewhere. The Fisher Report concluded that logic pointed to a complete divorce between Lloyd's brokers and managing agencies, and this has been brought about. Thus the Lloyd's Act 1982 provided that, by 1987, Lloyd's brokers must have divested themselves of their interests in managing agencies. However brokers remain free to control members' agencies.

Since 1964 the underwriting of motor insurance at Lloyd's has departed from the general pattern described above. It was found impracticable to insist that all proposals for the millions of potential clients should pass through Lloyd's underwriters to the Room. Motor underwriting syndicates have therefore been allowed to set up offices (like miniature insurance companies) to service policies and claims. Their offices are permitted to correspond direct with non-Lloyd's brokers (provided that they are sponsored by a Lloyd's broker who, in return for an overriding commission, accepts ultimate liability to the underwriters for payment of premiums).

A report from a government-appointed committee in 1987 (the Neill Report) recommended that Lloyd's own regulation of Lloyd's brokers should be tightened up and that the same standards should be applied to all firms. It also proposed that Lloyd's brokers should be subject to periodical re-registration. Other areas to be the subject of consideration and possible regulation by the Council of Lloyd's were indicated, namely:

(a) how the Lloyd's practice of brokers acting for underwriters in connection with the investigation and settlement of claims by the brokers' clients could be reconciled with brokers' duties to their clients so as to avoid potential conflicts of interest; and

(b) whether the continued ownership or control by brokers of members' agencies was open to abuse and, if so, how such abuse could be avoided by regulation.

Insurance companies

Insurance companies adopt a wide variety of strategies in the employment of intermediaries. At one extreme two old-established UK life offices have followed a consistent policy of paying no commission and have therefore attracted little or no business from brokers (although they are no doubt hoping that the 'best advice' requirements of the Financial Services Act 1986 will change this situation). At the other extreme, a number of recently formed companies sell only through brokers. In the sale of marine, aviation, general non-marine business risks, and reinsurance all insurance companies tend to follow the Lloyd's pattern. Each company has an underwriting room of its own in the vicinity of Lloyd's where slips are submitted by brokers who follow the lines of Lloyd's practice, except that insurance companies prepare their own policies. Many large insurances are split between Lloyd's syndicates and companies. In marine insurance the broker is liable to an insurance company for the premium in the same way as he is to Lloyd's underwriters (whether this is also true for non-marine insurance has not yet been tested in the courts).

Large composite insurance companies with a network of branches also appoint many thousands of agents such as solicitors and building societies. These companies undertake comparatively little direct selling of general insurance, except to persons who approach them direct (such as those responding to an advertisement). Appointment of agents is in a standard form which sets out the periods of credit, if any, allowed to the agent, the rates of commission on various classes of business, the power, if any, of the agent to issue temporary cover on the company's behalf, and the right of the company to terminate the agreement. A so-called cash agent is not given any credit and the insurers require the premium before they will accept the risk.

Personal life insurances are sold in various ways, discussed more fully in Chapter 13. The sale of industrial life insurance is monopolised by each company's field force of salesmen–collectors. Their remuneration, whether expressed as salary or commission, is closely related to the amount of business they bring in. Ordinary life insurance is sold partly through part-time agents who are in some business other than insurance, partly through a company's own direct salesmen, and partly through insurance brokers and financial consultants. The duties and obligations of each of these has now been clarified by the Financial Services Act 1986 (see below). Some companies specialising in industrial life insurance are averse to dealing through brokers or part-time agents at all. Others will accept insurances, notably pensions business and insurances primarily of investment type (such as capital bonds) through brokers. Credit to intermediaries is not customary in life insurance.

14.6 REGULATION OF INTERMEDIARIES IN THE UNITED KINGDOM

In the past, insurers have been free to appoint what intermediaries they choose and to remunerate them how they will. This freedom has been under attack since the early 1970s when the Vehicle and General Insurance Company (which was primarily a motor insurer and owned a chain of insurance brokers) failed in 1971. Discontent was also caused when a number of life insurance companies, which had been largely supported by brokers, got into financial difficulties after the property values crisis of 1973–4. At that time the only regulation of brokers was exercised by the Committee of Lloyd's over Lloyd's brokers and by three professional bodies over their respective members, membership being optional. These bodies, and Lloyd's, joined in promoting the Insurance Brokers (Registration) Act 1977, with government support. The regulation of intermediaries involved in investment business was further strengthened by the Financial Services Act 1986 – see 14.7 below.

The 1977 Act created an Insurance Brokers' Registration Council (IBRC) consisting mainly of insurance brokers elected by brokers. The Council has the duty of preparing and maintaining a list of individual insurance brokers and a register of corporate insurance brokers. For individuals, certain qualifications by way of education or experience are required and the Council must be satisfied as to a person's character or suitability. Lloyd's brokers are entitled to automatic enrolment. Only persons or companies registered by the Council are entitled to style themselves 'insurance broker', 'reinsurance broker', or the like. The Council has made rules, approved by the Department of Trade and Industry, which establish a code of conduct, lay down accounting and business requirements, provide for professional indemnity insurance, and establish a disciplinary procedure.

In 1987, the Council was given permission to establish itself as a Recognised Professional Body (under the requirements of the Financial Services Act 1986) for the purpose of regulating the behaviour of brokers for which investment business forms only a small proportion of their total business. Brokers who transact a large proportion of investment business are generally regulated by the Financial Intermediaries, Managers and Brokers Regulatory Association (FIMBRA) (under the 1986 Act) whose rules and requirements are typically more stringent than those laid down by the IBRC.

Brokers' code of conduct

The Insurance Brokers' Registration Council established a Code of Conduct which was intended as a guide to insurance brokers as to their professional conduct, but is not necessarily comprehensive. Except in investment business, acts of negligence will be dealt with by the courts rather than the IBRC, but the IBRC acknowledges that gross or repeated negligence may amount to unprofessional conduct. For investment business, the IBRC must operate under the guidelines established by the Financial Services Act 1986.

The IBRC Code enumerates three fundamental principles. First insurance brokers shall at all times conduct their business with the utmost good faith and integrity. Secondly insurance brokers shall do everything possible to satisfy the insurance requirements of their clients and shall place the interests of their clients before all other considerations. Subject to these requirements and interests insurance brokers shall have proper regard for others. Thirdly statements made by or on behalf of insurance brokers when advertising shall not be misleading or extravagant.

Accounting and business requirements (non-investment business)

The Accounts and Business Requirements Rules arising from the 1977 Act provide that brokers must have and maintain a working capital of not less than £1000, being an excess of assets over liabilities. Moneys received in connection with (non-investment related) insurance transactions must be paid into a separate 'insurance broking account' which shall be used only for payments to an insured or an insurer in connection with the broking business or for the purchase of approved short-term assets, the withdrawal of brokerage and, eventually, any surplus on the account. The broker's audited accounts must be submitted annually to IBRC, together with certificates signed by the broker and a qualified accountant stating that there have been no material breaches of the rules relating to the account.

Lloyd's brokers are exempted from these rules on the basis that they are regulated by the Council of Lloyd's, which imposes requirements at least as stringent.

Professional indemnity insurance

The Indemnity Insurance and Grants Scheme arising from the 1977 Act provides that practising insurance brokers must hold insurance against liability for negligence, errors, omissions, dishonesty or fraud and claims for loss of money or property resulting from dishonesty or fraud on the part of employees or partners. There must be a minimum limit of indemnity of £250 000. This is increased, where brokerage earned in the previous year exceeds £83 333, to three times the brokerage earned, with a maximum of £7.5 million.

It will be appreciated that an insurance against liability does not indemnify a broker against the consequences of his own dishonest or fraudulent conduct, as opposed to that of an employee. Nor does it provide for failure of the broker to pay what he owes, for example claims collected on behalf of a client. The requirement for insurance is therefore supplemented by a grants scheme to compensate individuals against loss in connection with a United Kingdom insurance arising out of the negligence, fraud or other dishonesty of brokers or their failure to account for moneys received. The grants scheme is administered by the IBRC and financed by a levy on brokers (other than Lloyd's brokers).

Disciplinary procedures

The IBRC has a disciplinary procedure with suitable safeguards for persons against whom a complaint is made. The ultimate, indeed the only, sanction is its power to erase a name from the register or list of insurance brokers, whereupon the description 'insurance broker' or the like can no longer be used. There is, however, nothing to prevent the business concerned from continuing to operate as insurance consultants or insurance advisers, so long as it can find insurers willing to pay it commission.

An overlapping jurisdiction is exercised by the British Insurance and Investment Brokers' Association, a professional association to which many though not all insurance brokers belong. Also the Council of Lloyd's exercises jurisdiction over Lloyd's brokers who need its approval if they are to carry on business at Lloyd's.

There is an Institute of Insurance Consultants for non-broker intermediaries but membership of that body is voluntary. It has no jurisdiction over non-members. Its members have no monopoly of the appellation 'insurance consultant'.

Codes of practice for non-broker intermediaries (non-investment business)

In 1988 the market association of insurance companies in the United Kingdom (the Association of British Insurers (ABI)) published a revised code of practice for all intermediaries other than brokers, and the companies undertook responsibility for enforcing this. The main conditions were as follows:

(a) ABI members established standard criteria for the appointment of all general insurance intermediaries who are not registered brokers. There are stringent rules for the appointment of these as agents, disclosure of the agent's status, selling practices, and handling of clients' money.

(b) All intermediaries are required to disclose their status to prospective clients before embarking on any business, so that the client knows who is responsible for the agent's conduct.

(c) All ABI members require their non-broker intermediaries to hold professional indemnity insurance.

(d) All clients will be made aware by ABI members of the protection afforded by the code.

Further details of the code can be found in Carter (1973).

The behaviour of non-broker intermediaries in transacting investment business is now controlled by the provisions of the Financial Services Act 1986. A code of conduct for company representatives, incorporating many of the above-mentioned points and others has been produced by the Life Assurance and Unit Trust Regulatory Organisation under its powers given by the Act.

14.7 THE UK FINANCIAL SERVICES ACT 1986

The Financial Services Act 1986 set up an elaborate machinery of self-regulating organisations with compulsory membership for institutions providing investments or investment advice. It does not apply to investments made for the purpose of becoming an underwriting member of Lloyd's.

The Security and Investments Board oversees other organisations such as:

- the Life Assurance and Unit Trust Regulatory Organisation (LAUTRO);
- the Financial Intermediaries, Managers and Brokers Regulatory Association (FIMBRA);
- various Self-Regulatory Organisations (SROs) for professional persons such as chartered accountants, solicitors, actuaries, and insurance brokers not registered by FIMBRA.

Life insurance companies are obliged to join LAUTRO, which regulates their conduct of business and the conduct of their representatives whose remuneration must not be biased towards the sale of particular contracts. LAUTRO lays down a code of conduct for company representatives and also initially specified maximum rates of commission (although these were formally abandoned in 1990). There are also rules about product disclosure and advertisements. Projections of future benefits payable are regulated and a table of surrender values must be supplied. Purchasers of life insurance must be given the opportunity of withdrawing from contracts even after they have signed a proposal.

FIMBRA is the body which regulates life insurance brokers and consultants who must also observe its code of conduct. Insurance brokers are already regulated by the Insurance Brokers' Registration Council, so membership of both FIMBRA and IBRC will be required unless the broker's involvement in life insurance is only a minor part of its business. Exemption from membership of FIMBRA is also available to solicitors (i.e. attornies), chartered accountants, and actuaries where giving investment advice is not their main business. In such cases their professional bodies will act as SROs. Acting as an investment adviser entails an obligation to obtain details of a client's circumstances and to give 'best advice', except in one-off transactions where a client specifies the policy to be bought (known as 'execution only' business). Further details of the Financial Services Act and its impact on the distribution of life insurance can be found in Wright and Diacon (1988) and Carter (1990).

14.8 INTERMEDIARIES IN THE UNITED STATES

The development of intermediaries in the United States followed a different pattern to that in the United Kingdom. Insurance companies in the nineteenth century found that they could expand only by appointing agents with exclusive rights to obtain business for them in some state or territory. The pattern has differed for life and general insurance.

Insurance agents in US life insurance

Selling has been based on individual agents who usually act for one company only. They are supervised by a general agent in their area or by a branch manager of an insurance company. The general agent recruits and trains the agency force and draws a commission on the business they get. Some agents specialise, for example, in business life insurance or pension plans. The underwriting is done centrally by the insurance company. Agents may employ persons, known as solicitors, to seek business for them.

Insurance agents in US general insurance

General insurance has been sold traditionally by the independent agency system. An insurance company appoints a general agent with exclusive rights to sell for it in a given territory. The general agent is usually a company specialising in insurance and is given wide powers, often including the right to bind the insurers for many classes of business and to handle claims. The general agent commonly represents a number of companies (sometimes as many as 30) and owns and controls the policy records. If an agency is terminated it may be expected that the agent's business will be placed with another insurer.

The general agent may employ sub-agents and persons (known as solicitors) to solicit business. As insurance is separately regulated in each US state the general agent may be given statutory powers, for example to countersign all the policies issued by a company in his state, as a guarantee that state requirements have been complied with.

Since the early 1950s the independent agency system has been challenged by the exclusive agency system. Here the agent is appointed by an insurance company or group of companies to work for it alone. The company retains the ownership and control of policy records. This facilitates direct billing of the insured by the company. Large companies with exclusive agency systems have made considerable inroads into the business of independent agency system companies, especially in automobile and other personal lines and they now transact around half such business.

The late 1980s saw some blurring of the distinction between the two systems. Some companies now operate both. Some exclusive agents may be given a right to the goodwill of their business or be allowed to place insurances, where necessary, with outside companies.

US insurance brokers

As in the United Kingdom, US law distinguishes between an insurance agent, as acting for the insurer, and a broker, as acting for the insured; however, in practice the distinction is not so clear-cut. Many independent insurance agents are also licensed as brokers. They may, for example, place part of a property insurance with the companies they represent and act as a broker in placing the rest of the risk with other insurers. Even where an agent is not formally a broker he will by no means limit his concern to the insurers he represents. It is in his interest to do the best he can for the insured as well because he owns the goodwill in the insured's continuing support.

However good agents may be in this respect many insureds feel the need for independent advice on their insurance and brokers flourish even though, in many cases, they have to deal with insurance companies through their general agents. Often brokers specialise in the requirements of particular businesses. Large and multinational companies are particularly in need of insurance and safety advice. The United States is the home of the so-called alphabet brokers, known by their initials, such as A & A (Alexander and Alexander) and M & M (Marsh and McLennan), placing business all over the world.

A special species of US broker is the excess or surplus lines broker, which is concerned with finding a market for insurance that cannot be placed (or at least cannot be placed economically) in the state where the business originated. Most of Lloyd's US business comes through this source. Usually some legal formalities have to be complied with before an insurance can be placed outside the state and brokers will fulfil these requirements. Reinsurance brokers are also numerous and active.

The regulation of US intermediaries

Each US state has its own regulatory statutes for intermediaries. Some states issue licences freely on payment of a fee, but more commonly some check is made on the apparent honesty of the intermediary and a test administered of his insurance knowledge. Tests vary in quality from the nominal to those requiring a written examination after a course of study lasting many hours. On the whole they are no more than a low hurdle.

There may be separate requirements for agents and brokers, and solicitors of business on their behalf. Within these categories, there can be separate tests for those concerned with life, health and multiple line insurance. A broker, for example, may hold a licence valid for life insurance transactions only. In a few states insurance consultants also require a licence.

Generally agents are licensed to represent only insurers who are permitted to do business in their state. Many states have countersignature laws which require all policies issued by an insurer to be countersigned by a licensed agent resident in the state. Sometimes, however, states have surplus line laws which permit specially licensed agents to represent unauthorised insurers where cover is not available at a competitive price from insurers licensed in the state. Insurance commissioners have wide powers to check fraudulent or unethical practices such as misleading advertisements, misappropriation or twisting. Twisting consists of persuading a policyholder (to his disadvantage) to discontinue a life policy and effect a new one. Sometimes state laws require that premiums be kept in a separate bank account: where this is so, it is an offence to do otherwise.

Often so-called 'unethical practices' include rebating, that is the sharing of commission between the intermediary and the insured. However it is hard to see how a ban on rebating can be considered a consumer protection measure: it seems rather to be designed as protection for agents. Agents collectively exercise a strong political influence and legislation is often framed with an eye on their interests.

There is machinery for the insurance commissioner to receive and investigate complaints against agents or brokers. He exercises jurisdiction over them and may caution, fine or suspend them, or even withdraw their licence after due process.

As so often occurs in the United States, the quality of the licensing provisions varies from the more or less effective to the notably ineffective. New York State has always been prominent in the regulation of intermediaries and its example is often copied elsewhere.

14.9 INSURANCE INTERMEDIARIES IN OTHER COUNTRIES

The pattern of insurance intermediaries varies from country to country. Some countries, such as France, continue to rely a great deal on local agents who represent given insurance companies in an area. A few, notably Luxembourg, have not allowed insurance brokers to operate at all, though in Luxembourg they are now permitted to handle insurance for large industries. Brokers tend to be weakest where premium rates are strongly controlled, either by the state or by tariff associations of insurers.

Many countries have licensing systems for insurance agents and brokers and regulate commissions. Sometimes commission rates vary with the status of the intermediary and take into account the extent of the work done by the intermediary. Licensing systems vary in efficiency. In some developing countries they may be no more than nominal.

Life insurance works mainly through tied intermediaries remunerated largely by commission. Japan pioneered the use of postmen or postwomen for the sale of life insurance to the mass market. Elsewhere, in less developed countries, life insurance tends to be underdeveloped among the mass of the people; where brokers operate they concentrate on pension schemes, group life, and provide for the needs of the country's comparatively small middle class. Constant inflation and, particularly in Moslem countries, religious objections to life insurance, militate against the development of life insurance for the masses, so that intermediary systems remain undeveloped.

References and recommended reading

British Insurance Brokers Association (1982) *British Insurance Broking: A Statistical Report by Kitcat and Aitken* (London: British Insurance Brokers Association).

Carter, R.L. (ed.) (1973) *Handbook of Insurance* (London: Kluwer Publishing Ltd) (continually updated).

Carter, R.L. (ed.) (1990) *Handbook of Personal Financial Management* (London: Kluwer Publishing Ltd) (continually updated).

Wright, D.M. and S.R. Diacon (1988) 'Regulation of the Marketing of Long-Term Insurance', in N. Dyer and T. Watkins (eds), *Marketing Insurance*, 2nd edn (London: Kluwer Publishing Ltd).

15 Sources of Funds and Estimation of Reserves

G.W. de Wit

The first part of this chapter deals with the necessity to set aside free reserves and technical provisions. In the second part, the methods of calculation and estimation applied to determine the size of the technical provisions will be examined. The determination of the actual amounts of the free reserves will be discussed within the context of the solvency problems (see Chapters 18 and 19).

15.1 THE SOURCES OF INSURANCE FUNDS

Just as with any other business, an insurance company must be able to follow the development of its operations. One of the major reasons for preparing regular financial reports is to meet this need for information. For this purpose, the continuous course of the company's operations is divided into discrete periods of time and the state of affairs at a specific point in time (at the end of a period) is determined.

The representation of the state of affairs at a specific point in time, usually in the form of financial statements and other figures, depends on who requires the information and its purpose. Several different types of reports can be distinguished: financial reports must be submitted to supervisory authorities annually or biannually; other reports must be published for shareholders; financial statements must be submitted to the tax authorities; and finally internal reports may be required for the company's own planning decisions.

Each of the above reports will vary in their contents. For example, a supervisory authority, having the primary task of monitoring the solvency situation, will naturally lay down more conservative and prudent requirements with respect to the valuation of the technical provisions. A good illustration of this is found in the United States, where the annual accounts to be submitted to the Insurance Commissioner are drawn up in accordance with the Statutory Accounting Principles (SAP), whereas the annual accounts required by law must be on the basis of the Generally Accepted Accounting Principles (GAAP). The Insurance Commissioner is primarily interested in solvency, while the GAAP annual account must provide a

Table 15.1 Insurance company balance sheet

Assets	Liabilities	
	Capital Free reserves	Shareholder's equity
	Technical provisions Other liabilities	Liabilities (debt)

truthful representation of the company's operating results (not provided in the SAP annual account).

An insight into a company's state of affairs can be obtained from the balance sheet. On the credit side one finds the capital resources. The credit side is shown in a simplified form in Table 15.1. For the purpose of reporting, the continuous course of the company's operations is usually divided into periods of one year, although for internal reporting shorter periods are also used. The technical provisions included in the balance sheet are in fact a result of this division of time. Insurance business does not take place just within the bounds of one year. For example, part of the premiums received is earmarked to cover risks in the following financial year, and a number of claims will not be (fully) settled at the end of the financial year. Therefore an insurer will have to reserve funds. For certain classes of insurance an annual accounting period may be too short; as will be shown, in such cases it is necessary for the insurer to establish further reserves (see Section 15.3 below).

The dividing line between the shareholder's equity and the liabilities, in the balance sheet of Table 15.1, is not clearly definable. When the balance sheets of insurance companies in differing countries are compared it can be seen that there are various ways of appending certain 'items' under the headings of free reserves or technical provisions. This particularly applies to reserves and provisions for equalisation and catastrophic losses: in Germany, for example, it has been decided that the so-called *Schwankungsrückstellung* was not to be accounted for in the equity, but in the liabilities (see Section 15.8). In the United Kingdom, however, there is no obligation to establish an equalisation reserve, but the supervising authority encourages companies to set up reserves to cover exceptional fluctuations (which can either be part of the technical provisions or part of the company's free reserves).

In the following sections, attention will primarily be focused on two specific balance sheet items: the free reserves and technical provisions. However these items are only a part of the balance sheet and should not be considered in isolation, but in relation to the other balance sheet items. This is necessary in order to obtain a correct (cautious) valuation of the technical provisions, a correct valuation of the assets, and a correct presentation of the volume of the company's equity in relation to each other.

15.2 FREE RESERVES

The shareholders' equity consists of share capital (or equivalent capital from mutual funds and public corporations) and free reserves. Together, they must guarantee the company's solvency.

The EC Directive for insurance companies (which will basically follow the fourth EEC Directive on Company Law of 25 July 1978) will, when implemented, probably prescribe the following breakdown of the shareholder's equity on the balance sheet (unless national legislation requires that a particular item should come under another heading):

- subscribed capital;
- share premium account;
- members' funds;
- revaluation reserve;
- reserves:
  (i) legal reserves and reserves for own shares (in so far as required by national legislation),
  (ii) statutory reserves provided for by the Articles of Association;
- undistributed profit (profit and loss brought forward);
- financial result after tax if the balance sheet has been drawn up before profit appropriation, that is, profit and loss for the financial year.

15.3 TECHNICAL PROVISIONS

The technical provisions are characteristic of an insurance company's report. They represent the obligations of an insurer to the insureds and the other beneficiaries of insurance contracts. Therefore the technical provisions, also referred to as technical reserves, do not form part of the shareholder's equity. The calculation of the technical provisions is only one aspect of what is involved. It is equally important that these provisions are covered by carefully evaluated and adequate (suitable) assets.

The estimates of technical provisions are mainly based on experience. Estimates should be made only with the utmost caution. Insurance business is based on a relationship of trust, primarily because the policyholder has to make his payments in advance. Consequently the technical provisions must be sufficient to cover future requirements under all circumstances. The insurer must be able to meet his obligations at all times.

Legislation in the EEC countries

The first co-ordination directives of the European Community (in 1973 for non-life insurance and 1979 for life) made it obligatory for companies to establish adequate technical provisions. The amounts of such provisions are determined on the basis of rules enacted by the government concerned or, in the absence of such rules, in accordance with the country's customary practice. The second co-ordination directive of the European Community in 1976 comprised a number of basic minimum requirements which must be satisfied in the calculation of the non-life technical provisions.

Methods of financing claims payments

The manner in which claims payments are financed is closely tied up with the formation of provisions. Basically, there are two methods of financing claims payments: the pay-as-you-go system and the capital-funding system. Under the former, the insurer's expected total premium revenues and expected expenditures in any one year are equal, while under the capital-funding system the expected revenues and expenditures are only equated over the whole term of contract. In cases where the incidence of claims remains constant during the entire term of contract, both forms of financing amount to the same thing (and, in the case of the capital-funding system, no capital will accrue in these circumstances). In cases where the incidence of claims increases during the policy period, for example because of rising mortality rates as age increases, financing via the pay-as-you-go system implies that the premium rates must be changed each year to meet the changed risk (for example, in life insurance the premium is then dependent on the age structure of the portfolio). In contrast financing via the capital-funding system means that the premium rates remain constant and capital will in fact accrue so that the excess amount paid on a premium during the first years, together with interest accrued from capitalisation, will precisely offset the deficit on the premium in later years.

If premium rates are to be maintained at a constant level, insurance contracts which cover risks with claims incidence increasing with time should be financed by means of the capital-funding system. Application of the pay-as-you-go system for financing insurances where the risk increases with time implies that the factor causing the increase in the risk (for example, individual age) is not included in the calculation of the premium (see de Wit and Eeghen, 1984). An example of the use of pay-as-you-go for financing an increasing risk is found in the Netherlands for medical expenses insurance. The attendant dangers of this have been recognised and the supervisory authority has made it obligatory for insurers to establish a so-called 'provision for increasing age'.

Mathematical provision

In the case of capital-funding, the premium is higher than the risk in the early stages of a contract. Part of the premium is then necessary to cover the future when the claims incidence is higher than the premium. Naturally this part of the premium must be reserved, and this is the mathematical provision. (For insurances which include a savings element, this saving part is also reserved in the mathematical provision.) Generally speaking, the mathematical provision can be defined as the amount which is needed, combined with the premiums to be received in the future, to meet the obligations.

In the EC countries, reporting of the so-called mathematical provision (also sometimes known as life insurance business provision) only applies to life insurance (of which disability insurance forms part in some countries) and medical expenses insurance (in Germany). For non-life insurance, the actuarially calculated provisions for annuities are accounted for under the heading of loss reserves. In the case of life insurance, the provision must be calculated annually by an actuary in accordance with approved actuarial methods.

The technical bases for calculating mathematical provisions in life insurances are mortality, interest and costs. In disability insurance, in addition to these three elements, disablement, rehabilitation and disability mortality also play a role. Medical expenses' insurance also has its own technical bases.

The so-called 'liability for future policy benefits' in the United States (GAAP) is based on the following technical bases: expected investment yields, mortality, morbidity, terminations and expenses. The basic elements relating to guaranteed policy payments are also included. The bases of calculation in the successive periods are grounded on the expectations applicable at the time of commencement of the insurance contract (and thus in general, they are not the same as those for the premium calculation). They include explicit margins for unfavourable deviations, contrary to the practice in the EC countries.

Provisions for unearned premiums and unexpired risks

Generally the premium payment term will not coincide with the financial year. This implies that not the entire premium received can be considered as earned income at the end of the financial year. The part of the premium which is to cover the risk and costs in the following year needs to be reserved as provision for unearned premiums.

The 1976 EC directive prescribes a 'pro rata temporis' method of calculation. Statistical methods may be applied if these produce approximately the same results. When the nature of the risks is such that the 'pro rata temporis' method fails to reflect the claim requirements, then this may be deviated from. Commission may be deducted. In the GAAP system (United States) the premium is considered as being earned for the contract period in proportion to the amount of insurance protection offered. In practice, this means that it is time-proportional, except in a few cases where the insurance protection decreases in accordance with a predetermined scheme.

In EC countries, besides the provision for unearned premiums, additional amounts must be reserved for risks to be incurred in the following financial year if the 'pro rata temporis' reserved amounts (and any premiums still to be received) are likely to be insufficient to cover claims and costs. Under the GAAP system a similar provision must be made to cover unexpired risks in the case of a premium deficit.

In a number of countries, such as West Germany, the United Kingdom, and the Republic of Ireland, the provisions for unearned premiums and unexpired risks are very often shown in the balance sheet as two separate items, while in other countries they are combined into a single item in the balance sheet.

Outstanding claim reserve

At the end of the financial year, part of the claims will not have been (completely) settled, either because they simply have not yet been paid or owing to their complicated nature (for example, on grounds of liability) or for other reasons. A claim reserve needs to be set aside for the claims which relate to the current financial year, and it involves both claims arising in the current financial year to be closed and those still outstanding for previous financial years. Outstanding claims reserves comprise two main components: a provision for reported but not (fully) paid losses, and a provision for claims as yet unreported but actually arising before the end of the financial year (the so-called 'incurred but not reported' (IBNR) reserve).

According to the 1976 EC directive proposal, the provision for reported claims must, in principle, be determined on a case-by-case basis. Nevertheless statistical methods are permitted if they result in an adequate provision in view of the nature of the risks involved. In practice, there has been a gradual shift towards the use of statistical methods: the IBNR provision is determined on the basis of past experience, taking into account the probable development of loss payments.

Claim settlement costs are included in determining the claim reserve, whether these costs are of an internal or external nature. The provision made for claim settlement costs must be sufficient to settle all claims without calling on premiums from following financial years.

With respect to interest, it has been suggested within the EC that, with the exception of the obligations calculated on an actuarial base, no reduction may take place with respect to the interest allocated to the claim reserve (although member countries may permit a reduction, provided that it is calculated on an actuarial basis).

In the United States, in accordance with GAAP, the claim reserve is based on the estimated final cost of settling claims (including the effects of inflation and other economic or social factors). Records of past experience are used, adapted to present developments.

Combined provisions

In a number of countries, several classes of business are permitted to establish one combined provision instead of the two separate provisions for unearned premiums and outstanding claims. In such cases, for each underwriting year (the year in which the insurance contract is signed or the risk has started) a fund is formed, consisting of all premium payments from which the commissions and loss payments are deducted and to which investment returns are added, other costs being subtracted. Such combined provisions are not closed at the end of the underwriting year (and thus there is no determination of profit), but are kept open over a number of years. After this period, the claim reserve is determined in the manner described above.

Equalisation reserves

The object of this provision is to equalise fluctuations in the annual claims requirements which are borne by the insurers themselves (that is, after deduction of reinsurances). This provision is based on the principle that, although premiums received in a class of business over a long period of time may cover all losses and costs, the equalisation of premiums and claims within one financial year is often not possible. Thus, if an insurer considers the surplus obtained in favourable years to be a profit (which may then be distributed to shareholders), the funds will be insufficient to meet his obligations in subsequent unfavourable years. Therefore, in classes of business which are known to be subject to considerable fluctuations in loss experience (after subtraction of reinsurance), insurers may set up an equalisation reserve. This provision, together with the premiums, must be sufficient to cover the expected losses and costs in the long run. The equalisation provision is thus a technical provision and as such forms no part of the shareholder's equity.

In actual practice, the equalisation provisions differ from country to country. In West Germany, for each class of business (with the exception of life and medical expenses insurance) the decision on whether or not to set up an equalisation depends on the statistical characteristics of the risk. If such a reserve must be established, the amount and construction are also determined on a statistical basis.

In France, Denmark and Italy, equalisation provisions are obligatory for certain classes of business (in France this relates to risks arising from natural forces and liability risks arising from environmental pollution; in

Denmark to hail and storm insurance; and in Italy to hail, credit and surety insurance). In the Netherlands, equalisation provisions can be made for classes of business dealing with hail and storm, credit and surety insurance. In the United Kingdom no provisions are made for normal fluctuations: insurers are, however, encouraged to reserve funds to cover exceptional fluctuations – these reserves can be in the form of (equalisation) provisions or can be part of the free reserves. Also in other countries, insurance companies set up equalisation reserves to cope with exceptional fluctuations in loss experience to allow, for example for the possibility of catastrophic losses.

The 1976 EC directive proposal stipulates that equalisation provisions must be established for classes of business dealing with credit insurance, hail and frost damage, and for storm damage risks, and other natural catastrophes when these risks fall under the hail and frost damage classes of business.

Provisions for nuclear risks

The object of this provision is the equalisation in nuclear insurance. Again this is based on the idea that, over a longer period of time, the premiums must cover losses and costs. Nuclear risks are extreme risks. Losses seldom occur, but if they do arise, they are likely to be of considerable magnitude. To cover such events, the premiums received in other years will be needed. Equalisation cannot possibly be achieved in the short period of one year. Therefore a provision for nuclear risks is a technical provision and as such forms no part of a company's equity.

The establishment of a provision for nuclear risks is obligatory and is classified as a technical provision in Germany (as a special item within the equalisation provisions and replaces *Schwankungsrückstellung* for this class of business), in France and Italy (as part of the equalisation provisions in those countries), and in Denmark. Companies in the Netherlands, Belgium and the United Kingdom have a free choice in the matter of establishing a provision for nuclear risks and it is not stipulated whether these provisions form part of the free reserves or part of the technical provisions.

Other technical provisions

Other additional technical provisions are obligatory in some countries:

- provision for large aviation risks (Germany and France),
- provision for the return of premiums (Germany and France),
- provisions for cancellations (Germany and France),
- provision for unused premiums for suspended insurance (Germany and Luxembourg).

One technical provision which has not been mentioned is the 'provision for the benefits of policyholders'. This provision consists of amounts allocated for payments to policyholders as required by law, articles of association or company plans, including premiums to be restituted to policyholders on a contractual basis. When profits arising from the valuation of insurance contracts have not been fully allocated, the unallocated surplus is included in the provision for policyholders.

15.4 THE ESTIMATION OF RESERVES

The preceeding sections described the most common technical provisions. Sections 15.5 to 15.9 focus attention on the determination of the size of these provisions. Here the emphasis is not on theoretically advanced methods (details of which can be found in van Eeghen, 1981) but on relatively simple and practical methods of estimation and calculation.

Mathematical reserves – some comments

The mathematical reserve in life insurance can be approached from two points of view. On the one hand, the mathematical reserve can be seen as the received premiums remaining after addition of the interest and deduction of the payments already made (the retrospective consideration). From the other point of view, the mathematical reserve is the amount that must be available (together with premiums and interest yet to be received) to cover the future payments (the prospective method). If the actual mortality rate follows the mortality table precisely, and if the actual interest generated is equal to that taken into account in the premium calculation, then both methods produce precisely the same result (the administrative costs not being taken into consideration in this case). However this situation will not arise in practice. The prospective method is often preferred because the mathematical reserve will then be sufficient to meet the obligations. The occurrence of a mortality loss will not affect the mathematical reserve and any excess interest arising can be allocated to profit.

The bases of calculation for life insurance with respect to premium and mathematical reserve are mortality, interest and costs. Setting aside some exceptional situations, calculations using a lower interest rate produce higher mathematical reserves. In general one can say that an insurer who reckons on generating the least interest works most safely. The influence of the mortality table is more difficult to substantiate. Lower mortality rates have no singular effect on the total mathematical reserve, since in practice the reserve comprises a mixture of insurances providing a benefit payable in case of survival and those paying a benefit on death.

As far as expenses are concerned, various methods have been developed for calculating the mathematical reserve. These methods are based on certain views on how administrative costs should be accounted for in the operating result; two such methods, the net premium method and the Zillmer method, are discussed in section 19.2.

In many cases the premiums for life insurances are guaranteed, that is to say fixed for the whole premium paying term. At the time an insurance contract is effected, the insurer must make as good an estimate as possible of the future expenses in order to determine the expense loading in the premium. In practice, faced with the inflation of costs, the expense loadings determined in the past often appear to be too low. It is very difficult, and sometimes impossible from the viewpoint of competitive considerations, to estimate the correct expenses over a period of thirty years or more and to introduce them into the premiums. Cautiousness with respect to the expense bases is therefore recommended.

15.5 ESTIMATING THE UNEARNED PREMIUM RESERVE

The unearned premium reserve in non-life insurance consists of the parts of the premiums received which are to cover risks (and costs) in the following financial year. The starting-point for the calculation is the annual gross premium income. The unearned premium reserve must first be reduced by the commission costs and other acquisition costs since these relate to the current financial year. The commission, for example, will generally be paid out directly on receipt of the premium, irrespective of whether or not part of the premium relates to the following financial year.

In the past, a number of approximation methods have been developed for the determination of the unearned premium reserves in order to eliminate a great deal of work. These approximation methods are all based on the fact that the due dates of the premiums on individual insurances are more or less equally distributed over the year. Nowadays it is no longer an insurmountable problem to calculate the unearned premium reserve separately for each policy, even for a large portfolio of insurance policies with varying premium paying terms and due dates, and then to add the results together.

The 40 per cent method

With this simplest of the approximation methods, the due date for the payment of premiums for all policies is assumed to be in the middle of the reporting period (normally a calendar year). In this case the reserve amounts to one-half of the written premium, which must be reduced, however, by the commission cost. It is then assumed that the latter absorbs (on average) 20 per cent of the gross premium, so that the unearned premium reserve amounts to 40 per cent of the written premium.

The 24ths method

When the assumptions underlying the 40 per cent method (of an equal distribution of the premiums over the year) are not satisfied, it is desirable to use a more accurate method. The unearned premium reserve can instead be determined on the basis of the written premium (less initial commissions and other acquisition costs) in separate quarters (1/8 system) or in separate months (1/24 system). In the 24ths method, the due date of a policy is assumed to be in the middle of the due month. In the case of an item subject to annual payment and a due day in March (say), 5/24 of the premium is reserved; this part of the premium will have to cover risks in the following year. The premiums for all policies with the same premium payment term and the same due month can then be added together and the reserve for this can then be determined at once. The unearned premium reserve is derived by adding up the results of the various premium payment terms and due months.

As an example, consider a fictitious portfolio consisting of eight policies, all issued in 1986. Table 15.2 comprises the necessary data. The total written premium income for 1986 amounted to 3720 and it is assumed that the commission is 20 per cent of the gross premium. The 40 per cent method results in an unearned premium reserve at the end of 1986 of 1488 (that is, 0.4×3720), the 24ths method gives 1276 (that is, $0.8(600 \times 1/24 + 480 \times 5/24 + \ldots + 480 \times 23/24)$, while calculation on a day-by-day basis (using 730ths) gives an unearned premium reserve of 1249.

In general, in the case of an equal percentage reduction for costs, the 40 per cent and 24ths methods are more accurate, the closer the due dates are to the middle of the year (40 per cent method) or month (24ths method). In the cases where the due dates are highly concentrated in the second half of the year or in the second half of a month, these methods will result in unearned premium reserves which are too low.

15.6 ESTIMATING LOSS (OUTSTANDING CLAIMS) RESERVES

The estimation of the loss reserve is a complicated matter. Non-life insurance is very heterogeneous and comprises highly diverse classes of business. The loss reserve for different types of insurance must be estimated as accurately as possible. A good estimate of the loss reserve is of great importance in obtaining an accurate operating result and an accurate premium level, and in making the right company policy decisions.

Table 15.2 The estimation of unearned premium reserves

Insured	*Annual premium (in 1986)* £	*Frequency of premium payment*	*Next due date*	*24ths reserved*	*730ths reserved*
1	600	monthly	11. 1.1987	1/24	21/730
2	480	quarterly	17. 3.1987	5/24	151/730
3	480	half yearly	15. 2.1987	3/24	91/730
4	480	half yearly	23. 5.1987	9/24	285/730
5	360	yearly	1. 4.1987	7/24	181/730
6	400	yearly	15.10.1987	19/24	575/730
7	440	yearly	1.10.1987	19/24	547/730
8	480	yearly	19.12.1987	23/24	705/730

The estimation of loss reserves involves making pronouncements about the future based on past experience. Loss settlement is not a closed process which stands by itself but a process which is subjected to environmental influences. Thus, in estimating the loss reserve, all the variables affecting the loss frequency, the amount of loss, and the loss development pattern must be taken into account, including:

- the dynamic nature of the insured risks;
- the claim-handling procedures and the claim department's organisation and practices;
- the external variables; variables may have either a continuous effect on frequency or claim amount or on both (for example, inflation) or exercise a one-off 'shock' effect (for example, changes in legislation).

The loss reserving process takes place in three main stages. The first involves the collection of data and the establishment and building up of a database. Second comes the analysis of the data, and finally the estimation of the loss reserve on the basis of these data. The building up of the database requires full attention, for this is the cornerstone of the loss reserve analysis.

Case estimation of outstanding claims

The 'individual case estimates' method is based on the premise that for each open claim there is an individual estimate available of the final payment on this claim. The (net of reinsurance) 'individual case reserve' consists of this estimated value of the claim minus the payments already made on the claim. The total net case reserve is the sum of these individual cases reserves. The assumption of the individual case estimates method is that the claim department can accurately evaluate a claim. When a large number of claims is involved, over-reserved and under-reserved claims will tend to balance out and the case reserve will be acceptable as long as there is no bias in the individual estimates.

The 'correct case reserve for bias' method estimates the reserve for reported claims by applying a correction factor to the case reserve. It is assumed that the percentage bias in the current case reserve is equal to the percentage in the previous reserves. The correction factor can be determined by comparing previous case reserves with the actual payments on the claims concerned. Assume, for example, that, at the end of 1984, the estimated case reserve for the year of origin 1984 amounted to 18 000 and that the payments actually made in the years 1985 to 1988 inclusive amounted to 16 000 (by which time all the claims have been settled). The correction factor would then be 16/18 = 0.889. When, after checking the consistency of the correction factor over a number of years, it appears that the factor is realistic and the case reserve for the year of origin 1988 is 22 500, then the correct case reserve will be 0.889 × 22 500 = 20 000.

Estimating the IBNR reserve

The reserve for incurred but not reported claims is usually estimated as a certain percentage of a selected basis which may be written premium income, the number of claims reported, net or gross case reserve, or the number of open claims. It is assumed that the developments in the number and/or amount of IBNR claims run parallel with the changes in the selected base.

One method of calculating the IBNR reserve has been produced by Tarbell (1971). The starting-point in the calculation of the 1988 reserve is the total amount of claims incurred no later than the end of 1987 but not reported until 1988. This figure is then scaled up or down to allow for:

- any change in the number of reported claims in 1988 (in comparison with 1987);
- trends in the average incurred cost per claim; and
- an allowance for the claims which take more than twelve months to be reported.

The run-off triangle

A practical and meaningful manner of presenting data on the development of claims up to 1988 is shown in Table 15.3. The row numbers (1985, 1986 and so on) in this matrix indicate the year of origin of the claim (that is, the year in which the policy was written), and the column numbers gives the development year. The $C_{i,j}$ can denote a variety of factors including the number of claims in each development year, the average or total claims

Table 15.3 A run-off triangle (for current year 1988)

Year of origin	*Development year* 0	1	2	3
1985	$C_{1985,0}$	$C_{1985,1}$	$C_{1985,2}$	$C_{1985,3}$
1986	$C_{1986,0}$	$C_{1986,1}$	$C_{1986,2}$	x
1987	$C_{1987,0}$	$C_{1987,1}$	x	x
1988	$C_{1988,0}$	x	x	x

payments, or the corresponding cumulative figures. For example, if the number of claims in each development year was being analysed, $C_{i,j}$ would denote the number of claims arising in year $(i + j)$ from business written in year i. The 'x' values can then be estimated on the basis of the data of the run-off triangle. The method of presentation offers the possibility of analysing both the loss development horizontally across a row (i.e. by year of origin) and the trends in loss costs vertically down a column (i.e. by development year).

A projection of the unknown values 'x' is made on the basis of the historic data presented in the triangle. Projection methods always assume a stable pattern over time. Whenever there is a question of instability, care must be taken that methods sensitive to these unstable patterns are not used. Two main estimation methods may be distinguished: those based on the development of the total loss involved and those based on a separate analysis of the loss frequency and the average amount of loss per claim.

To illustrate how the run-off triangle can be used to estimate loss reserves, assume that all claims are settled within five years. Table 15.4 shows the run-off triangle for the current year 1988 with the $C_{i,j}$ figures indicating the value of cumulative total claims payments, thus $C_{1984,3}$ (= 38.9) denotes the total claims paid on 1984 business, up to and including 1987.

Figures in the first row of Table 15.4 show that, out of total claims paid of 39.1 for 1984 business, 59.34 per cent (i.e. 23.2) are paid in 1984, 86.45 per cent have been paid by the end of 1985 (i.e. 33.8), 95.40 per cent by the end of 1986 (i.e. 37.3) and 99.49 per cent by 1987. The ratios of the cumulative amounts paid in successive years (for year of origin 1984) are known as the 'development factors' M_j. Thus, for development year 1, $M_1 = 33.8/23.2 = 1.457$. Similarly $M_2 = 37.3/33.8 = 1.104$, $M_3 = 38.9/37.3 = 1.043$, and $M_4 = 39.1/38.9 = 1.005$.

Table 15.4 Run-off triangle for cumulative claims totals

Year of origin	*Development year* 0	1	2	3	4
1984	23.2	33.8	37.3	38.9	39.1
1985	25.8	37.3	42.9	45.6	x
1986	22.1	30.3	30.7	x	x
1987	35.9	43.0	x	x	x
1988	34.9	x	x	x	x

An estimate of the loss reserve for the years of origin 1985, 1986, 1987 and 1988 can be made exclusively on the basis of the run-off pattern of the first year of origin (1984). The expected ultimate total loss for each year of origin is calculated by multiplying the 1988 cumulative total for that year of origin by the successive developments factors for all outstanding development years. For example, for 1986 business, the cumulative total paid by 1988 (i.e. 30.7) is the position at the end of the second development year: to obtain the estimate of total losses resulting from 1986 business, this must be multiplied by the development factors for the third and fourth development years (i.e. M_3 and M_4). This calculation is shown in column (*c*) in Table 15.5. A full run-off matrix using this method is shown in Table 15.6. Deduction of the claims already paid produces the estimated total loss reserve for 1988 (i.e. 32.41). When the loss reserve is estimated in this way, use is made only of data relating to the development of the first year of origin and the information relating to later years is disregarded. It is assumed that the run-off pattern will be stable over time and random deviations from this stable pattern are not corrected.

An analysis of possible trends over the various years of origin can also be of importance. A vertical analysis of the run-off triangle in Table 15.4 gives a comparison of the data in the same stage of development (for example, one year after the occurrence of the claim). Thus any increase or decrease can be highlighted in losses paid at comparable points in time in the development process of the successive years of origin.

The chain-ladder method for estimating loss reserves

Once again take as starting-point the run-off triangle with cumulative claim

Table 15.5 Calculating the loss reserve for 1988

Year of origin	*Losses paid up to 1988 (a)*	*Product of development factors (b)*	*Estimated total loss (c) = (a) × (b)*	*Estimated loss reserve for 1988 (d) = (c) − (a)*
1985	45.6	M_4	45.83	0.23
1986	30.7	$M_3.M_4$	32.18	1.48
1987	43.0	$M_2.M_3.M_4$	49.76	6.76
1988	34.9	$M_1.M_2.M_3.M_4$	58.84	23.94
				32.41

Table 15.6 The complete run-off table

Year of origin	*Development year* 0	1	2	3	4
1984	23.2	33.8	37.3	38.9	39.1
1985	25.8	37.3	42.9	45.6	45.83
1986	22.1	30.3	30.7	32.02	32.18
1987	35.9	43.0	47.47	49.51	49.76
1988	34.5	50.85	56.14	58.55	58.84

payments. In the chain-ladder method, the development factors are determined on the basis of the loss development in all past years of origin and not just the 'completed' one (i.e. 1984 in Table 15.4). The run-off and the ultimate total loss of the current and preceding years of origin are then estimated as before by means of these development factors. The method is based on the assumption that the development of loss payments over the years has exhibited a stable pattern (apart from random fluctuations). The estimation of future cumulative loss payments is achieved by first estimating the development factors M_j, and then using these to estimate the cumulative loss payments $C_{i,j}$.

In the preceding section, the calculation of development factors depended only on the progression of 1984 business; in the chain-ladder

Table 15.7 Run-off table using chain-ladder method

Year of origin	*Development year* 0	1	2	3	4
1984	23.2	33.8	37.3	38.9	39.1
1985	25.8	37.3	42.9	45.6	45.83
1986	22.1	30.3	30.7	32.36	32.52
1987	35.9	43.0	47.04	49.58	49.83
1988	34.9	47.12	51.54	54.33	54.60

Table 15.8 Estimated loss reserves based on chain-ladder method

Year of origin	*Estimated total loss*	*Losses already paid*	*Estimated total reserve*
1984	39.10	39.1	—
1985	43.83	45.6	0.23
1986	32.52	30.7	1.82
1987	49.83	43.0	6.83
1988	54.60	34.9	19.70
			28.58

method, the calculation also includes information on the (incomplete) development of later years of origin. The development factor for development year j (M_j) is calculated by dividing the sum of the figures $C_{i,j}$ in $_j$th column of the run-off triangle by the sum of the corresponding figures in the preceding development year (i.e the $(j-1)$th column). Note that since the $(j-1)$th development year will always have one more item than the jth column, the last element in the $(j-1)$th column is omitted from the summation.

The estimated total loss for each year of origin is then obtained, as before, by multiplying the most recent cumulative total by the successive development factors for all outstanding development years. The loss reserve at the end of the current year is then the sum of the cumulative

Table 15.9 Estimates of combined provisions (for underwriting year 1986)

	1986		*1987*	
Position at the end of the previous financial year		—		56 750
Premium	95 000		8 400	
Commission	(14 250)		(1 260)	
Claims	(24 000)		(33 000)	
Balance		56 750		(25 860)
Position at the end of the financial year		56 750		30 890

totals of all years of origin, less the claims already paid. For example, consider the run-off triangle in Table 15.4: the four development factors are now:

$$M_1 = \left(\frac{33.8 + 37.3 + 30.3 + 43.0}{23.2 + 25.8 + 22.1 + 35.9}\right) = 1.350$$

$$M_2 = \left(\frac{37.3 + 42.9 + 30.7}{33.8 + 37.3 + 30.3}\right) = 1.094$$

$$M_3 = \left(\frac{38.9 + 45.6}{37.3 + 42.9}\right) = 1.054 \qquad \text{and}$$

$$M_4 = \left(\frac{39.1}{38.9}\right) = 1.005$$

The run-off triangle can be completed to form a rectangle by making use of these development factors, to give Table 15.7. For example, the figures for year of origin 1987 are obtained as follows:

$$C_{1987,2} = 43.0 \times M_2 = 47.04$$

$$C_{1987,3} = 47.04 \times M_3 = 49.58$$

$$C_{1987,4} = 49.58 \times M_4 = 49.83$$

When, at the end of 1988, all claims have been fully settled, the loss reserve amounts to 28.58, as shown in Table 15.8.

The chain-ladder method is based on the assumption that the run-off pattern remains stable over the years. This assumption is no longer valid when the development pattern is influenced by external or internal

Table 15.10 An illustration of three-year accounting (for 1988)

	Underwriting years				
	1985 and earlier	*1986*	*1987*	*1988*	*Total*
Position at end 1987	22 050	30 890	55 300	—	108 240
Premium		1 000	14 000	124 000	139 000
Commission		(150)	(2 100)	(18 600)	(20 850)
Claims	(6 700)	(18 000)	(70 800)	(27 300)	(122 800)
To P/L acct	(2 150)	(5 640)	—	—	(7 790)
Strengthening	—	—	31 600	—	31 600
Position at end of 1988	13 200	8 100	28 000	78 100	127 400
Loss reserve required	13 200	8 100	28 000	—	

changes. For variations of the chain-ladder method and for more advanced methods of determining the loss reserve, see van Eeghen (1981), Peterson (1981) and Taylor (1985).

15.7 DETERMINATION OF THE COMBINED PROVISIONS

In a few classes of business the unearned premium reserve and the loss reserve are combined into one provision. In such cases, all payments are kept in the accounts per underwriting year (the year in which the policy is underwritten or the risk has commenced). For each of the underwriting years, a fund is formed and maintained open for a certain number of years. During this period all premium payments relating to that particular underwriting year are deposited in the fund and all commission and claim payments are made from this fund. Returns on investment may also be added and expenses subtracted from this fund.

Suppose for example that in 1986, with respect to the underwriting year 1986, the premiums received amount to 95 000, the commission to 14 250 and the claim payments to 24 000. In 1987 the amounts for the underwriting year 1986 were 8400 in premiums, 1260 for commission and 33 000 for claim payments. The calculation of the fund with respect to the underwriting year 1986 at the end of 1986 and 1987 respectively is shown in Table 15.9.

Suppose that each underwriting year is held open for three years so that the underwriting year 1986 is closed at the end of 1988. The loss reserve is determined (very often on a case-to-case basis) for the outstanding claims (including IBNR). If the balance of the fund is greater than the required loss reserve, the difference can be transferred to the company's operating result. In Table 15.10 (in which the loss reserve for the underwriting year 1986 is estimated at 8100) the profit released at the end of 1988 is 5640.

In the case of the closed underwriting years, the loss reserve for the still outstanding claims will be calculated anew. The difference between this and the available fund for the respective underwriting years will then be taken as profit or loss.

When it looks as if the fund with respect to a particular underwriting year is going to be insufficient to cover commitments then it must be strengthened. The amount required is roughly estimated (an accurate estimate of the loss reserve is not possible at this time). The fund is then supplemented to the required amount from current financial year resources. This situation is illustrated in Table 15.10 for the underwriting year 1987. The position of the fund for the underwriting year at the end of 1987 is (3600), that is: 55 300 + 14 000 − 2100 − 70 800. A rough estimate shows that 28 000 will be needed as a loss reserve, so an amount of 31 600 (i.e. 28 000 + 3600) must be added to the fund and this constitutes an interim loss for the company.

The total fund for a certain class of business is the sum of the funds for unclosed underwriting years, the loss reserve for the underwriting year yet to be closed, and the loss reserve for the closed underwriting years. In our example the fund thus amounts to 127 400 at the end of the 1988 financial year.

15.8 *SCHWANKUNGSRÜCKSTELLUNG*

In West Germany the rules regarding equalisation provisions were formalised in law in 1978 (further details can be found in Karten, 1980). For each class of business, with the exception of life and medical expenses insurance, it is determined separately whether a *Schwankungsrückstellung* is to be established. It is obligatory to set up a *Schwankungsrückstellung* (or 'fluctuation reserve') if:

(a) The average premium earned (for own account) for the last three years preceding the financial year amounts to over DM 250 000; and
(b) the standard deviation of the loss ratio for the observation period (which is usually 15 years preceding the financial year) amounts to not less than 5 per cent; and
(d) the sum of the loss ratio and expense ratio is greater than 100 per cent at least once during the observation period.

Thus *Schwankungsrückstellung* is required when there are considerable fluctuations in the class of business. When one of these conditions is no longer satisfied, the provision must be phased out within five years.

The maximum size of the *Schwankungsrückstellung* is normally set at 4.5 times the standard deviation of the loss ratio, multiplied by the earned premium for own account in the financial year. When the average loss ratio is smaller than a 'borderline loss ratio' of (0.95 minus the average expenses ratio over the previous three years) a deduction is applied of three times the difference between the two ratios, multiplied by the premium earned. Each year 3.5 per cent of the maximum amount applicable that year is added, independent of the occurrence of above average or below average losses (this is the so-called 'interest addition').

When the loss ratio for the year is below average, then an addition to the *Schwankungsrückstellung* is made of the difference between the actual losses paid and those expected (so that a 'good' year is used to build up the provisions). However, when the year's loss experience is above average, then this 'excess' is withdrawn from the *Schwankungsrückstellung*. If the average loss ratio is smaller than the borderline loss ratio, a smaller amount will be withdrawn.

15.9 SIZE OF THE PROVISION FOR NUCLEAR RISKS

The purpose of this provision is the equalisation of losses in nuclear risks insurance. However, contrary to the *Schwankungsrückstellung*, the fluctuations in the annual claims requirements cannot be used as a basis, since the number of losses incurred is far too small. Therefore only flat-rate methods are used to determine the size and build-up of the provision for nuclear risks. The calculations can be based, for example, on the technical result, the amounts insured for own account, or the annual premium.

References and recommended reading

Eeghen, J. van (1981) 'Loss Reserving Methods', *Surveys of Actuarial Studies, No. 1* (Rotterdam: Nationale-Nederlanden, N.V.).

Karten, W. (1980) 'The New "Schwankungsrückstellung" in Annual Statements of German Insurers – An Application of the Theory of Risk?', *The Geneva Papers on Risk and Insurance*, no. 17, June.

Peterson, T.M. (1981) *Loss Reserving – Property/Casualty Insurance* (London: Ernst & Whinney).

Tarbell, T.F. (1971) *Incurred But Not Reported Claim Reserves*, Proceedings Casualty Actuarial Society (58) pp. 84–9.

Taylor, G.C. (1985) *Loss-Reserving* (Amsterdam: North-Holland).

Wit, G.W. de and J. van Eeghen (1984) 'Rate Making and Society's Sense of Fairness', *ASTIN Bulletin*, vol. 14, no. 2, pp. 151–64.

16 The Investment of Insurance Funds

Marcus Johnson

16.1 INVESTMENT OBJECTIVES

Introduction

The aim of this chapter is not to make readers into investment experts but to allow them to understand when looking at the asset portfolio of an insurance company why it is structured the way it is and what the major constituents are there for.

Investments are bought in the hope of achieving added value in the form of capital gains or income, and in a general sense not only insurance companies but all investors share this objective. Where the investors are corporate rather than individual these general requirements have specific limitations placed on them. It is generally the case that the appropriate investments for an investor can only be determined by reference to the source of the money available for investment and its intended end use. For insurance companies the sources of their funds are either their shareholders or their policyholders, and their ultimate use is to pay claims to policyholders or dividends to their owners. Mutual companies have of course only their policyholders' funds available but, for the purposes of this discussion, the policyholders' surplus which will be retained by the company for the foreseeable future can be regarded as analogous to shareholders funds' in a proprietary company.

Matching

There is an important difference between the investment objectives of a life office and that of a non-life (property and casualty) business. In life insurance the product sold to the consumer is determined by the investment opportunities which are available; there is therefore a direct link between the contracts underwritten and the investments bought. This link is usually described as 'matching', and matched liability and asset portfolios have been the first and main investment objective since the beginning of the life insurance industry. Each liability accepted can be defined with reasonable accuracy and if, say, a contract is issued which has an expected length of 15 years, then the insurer is able to match the promised pay-out by purchasing a fifteen-year bond.

In non-life insurance, the objectives of companies vary much more widely. In recent years the importance of investment income to the survival of most major non-life companies has become so great that much more attention is now being paid to their investment portfolios. Matching is still probably the prime consideration in a general sense but, whereas a life office has a measure of certainty attached to its liabilities, a non-life insurer has considerable problems with the occurrence, size and timing of its liabilities. This makes a matched investment portfolio a difficult concept to apply in non-life insurance. Companies may nevertheless adopt matching as an objective, and attempt to define their liability portfolios accurately so that these are capable of summarisation in sufficient detail for an appropriate asset mix to be maintained.

Solvency

The second major investment objective for all insurance companies is the maintenance of solvency. There are important differences between life and non-life companies in their solvency calculations: the former usually value their future liabilities at present values using market-related discount rates, whereas the latter often use no discount rate at all (but add amounts due today and amounts due in ten years together as if they were of the same value). This has an important impact on the respective investment policies: as we will see later, life offices, especially ones in the United Kingdom, can hold long-term bonds appropriate to the term of their policies (without risking their solvency) much more easily than non-life insurers.

A related investment objective is that of maintaining solvency, as defined by regulatory authorities. On many occasions regulatory authorities impose idiosyncratic methods of solvency calculation which may have little to do with an insurer's actual ability to maintain itself in business. Since regulatory authorities have the power to put the company out of business, solvency as defined by regulators is just as important in business planning as the company's true solvency position. Solvency regulations will often limit the quantities and qualities of particular assets or classes of assets which may be counted in the assets of an insurance company. They may thus force investors into particular investments – indeed in some countries regulations are so strict that the investment portfolio is effectively determined by the regulatory authorities (a more detailed discussion can be found in Section 17.3).

Profit maximisation

Another overall objective of both life and non-life insurers is profit maximisation. In life insurance this is interpreted slightly differently because with-profits policies distribute much of the investment earnings. The objective is thus to be seen to have produced returns which make policyholders happy, or to be able to promise returns which will make selling policies easier. The life office needs results which it can advertise, and this may mean keeping several different investment funds so that, at any one time, at least one should have a relatively good record of performance. This is now particularly important for UK life offices as the Financial Services Act 1986 requires independent intermediaries to recommend insurers on the basis of 'best advice'.

In non-life insurance profit maximisation is also subject to the so-called 'agency problem' as the company management may well have much shorter-term horizons than their shareholders. Long-term profit maximisation can then suffer in the search for short-term profits, for example by allowing investment gains and losses sometimes to be treated as current income and sometimes to be ignored. The objective of profit maximisation is then subject to qualifications – but few insurance entities will admit to them. The management of insurance companies may pursue investment policies to further personal or corporate design unconnected with investment returns. They may use investments to back up marketing campaigns or to cement business relationships.

In the United Kingdom particularly insurance companies qualify their pursuit of profits with 'social' or political aims. This can be regarded as a form of long-term profit maximisation, or as part of a public relations budget, and only has marginal effects on behaviour.

16.2 INVESTMENT MARKETS

Introduction

In economic terms investment is the application of goods or services to a purpose which will produce a future income of goods or services, and has a counterpart in a decision to postpone consumption. The financial counterpart of such economic investment involves the issue of promises to finance consumption at some future point if the investor provides money today. There are many ways in which investment can be financed, but the most important are fixed interest ('bonds'), equity share capital ('stocks'), and real assets such as property. The boundaries of these classes are not fixed, and there are sub-categories within them, but the important characteristics of bonds is that the return is independent of the trading results of the enterprise which issued them (except in the case of default), whereas the return on equity instruments varies with the performance of the issuer. Real assets are another important category within many insurance investment portfolios: property is the largest category, but a variety of other tangible assets ranging from gold to works of art or vintage cars may also be found.

Fixed-interest securities

In recent years the largest source of bonds has been government-issued debt, although a hundred years ago the main borrowers would have been industrial and commercial companies. In the United States and United Kingdom, securities issued by the government commonly carry a fixed redemption date and a fixed coupon. Maturities extend to about 30 years in both countries, and large quantities of new debt have been issued in recent years. The markets for government securities are highly liquid, and billions of pounds or dollars can be invested over a relatively short time in most maturity ranges. The secondary market is very liquid and prices in £ or $10 million of bonds would be fairly normal. Both governments have a very high credit standing and are considered good for their commitments under almost all circumstances. This liquidity and creditworthiness means that government paper provides a measure by which other investments are judged in both countries.

In the United States there are two further important categories of fixed-income securities: corporate bonds and pass-through mortgages. A sophisticated rating system exists for the former which enables credit judgements to be made on whole portfolios in a consistent manner. The market for corporate bonds varies considerably between different issuers, and even for the largest and highly-rated issuers price would usually be available in only a fraction of the size of the government market. Smaller and lower-rated issuers trade 'by appointment only'. There is a wide spectrum of fixed income issuers, and it is important to emphasise that, although they carry lower risks than other forms of asset, the price of fixed-income securities will move sharply if interest rates change. Furthermore there are substantial credit risks outside the government sector.

A fixed-income bond encapsulates in its market price the future value of an income stream and a redemption value, and its market price will fluctuate as perceptions of future interest rates change. A thirty-year bond issued at 100 to yield 10 per cent would fall in price by about 10 per cent if its yield were to rise to 11 per cent. In any portfolio of non-government bonds, it can reasonably be expected that a proportion will fail to meet their commitments; therefore a higher yield is required by holders to compensate them for possible losses. If the market's perception of the likelihood of default changes, then the margin of the yield premium over government securities of a non-government fixed-income bond will also change. Investors which follow rigid rating systems deceive themselves if they consider these avoid loss through credit risks: by the time the borrower is downrated (triggering a sale on their portfolio) the price at which they will sell will have already reflected a readjustment.

At the boundaries of the bond markets there are investments which are in some respects closer to equities. Such instruments as 'floating rate', 'index-linked' and 'convertible' bonds are increasingly coming to form part of most investment portfolios. The return on all of these may vary considerably in either real or nominal terms. Convertible bonds are a combination of a conventional 'fixed interest' bond and an equity option. They are, depending on the conversion terms, normally either valued as an equity or as a bond. They are very popular with Japanese issuers in the Eurobond market and provide a dollar-denominated stake in Japanese companies for many investors.

Floating rate and index-linked bonds are a response to high inflation and high interest rates. The return on such bonds is adjusted in line with short-term rates and inflation indicators respectively. Over a period, the real return on such bonds is much more stable than on any other class of financial asset and they have found a home in many portfolios for this reason. In addition, floating rate instruments can offer a degree of protection against large changes in portfolio valuation – which is very useful for solvency-regulated organisations such as banks or insurers. The only problem for most holders of such paper is that neither the UK nor US governments currently issue floating rate debt, and only the United Kingdom issues index-linked. This means that, although valuation risks can be reduced, higher risks of default must be accepted. To a certain extent the value of the 'hedge' can be questioned, as the same conditions that call into question the value of conventional bonds (high inflation and interest rates) will also put many of the issuers of floating rate paper under financial strain.

The bond market contains many other instruments and such is the pace of development that exciting new instruments of one year can be forgotten the next. Zero coupons, stripped bonds and interest rate swaps all enable investors to customise portfolios to their precise specifications. There are now major markets on which bonds can be bought and sold for future delivery and options to buy or sell can be traded. Many institutions use these new markets to increase or stabilise the yield on fixed-interest portfolios.

Equities

Markets in equity instruments are even more diverse than those for bonds. Investment portfolios can entirely consist of household names (for example, most of the constituents on the Dow Jones Index would be familiar to most people) or they may be invested in smaller companies. The vast majority of larger companies are listed on the Stock Exchanges (or in the United States on the OTC (Over The Counter) market run by the National Association of Securities Dealers). The returns on equities are less predictable than in the fixed income markets. The dividends paid can move extremely sharply over a short period of time, even in the largest companies. The prices at which stocks trade in the stockmarkets are subject to extremely large fluctuations, and not only individual securities but, as the crashes in October 1987 and 1989 showed, the general level of equity prices can also move extremely sharply and rapidly.

Despite the fluctuations, equity markets have produced, in both the United Kingdom and the United States, returns which are consistently above the rate of inflation and also above the return on government securities. To a long-term investor, returns on a diversified portfolio of equities in almost any period this century will have been substantially higher than an investment in bonds. This is mainly owing to the higher inflation rates which occurred in the 1920s, 1950s and 1970s. If the trend of the 1980s towards lower inflation continues for the next 30 years, then the future return on bonds will compare much more favourably with that on equities. A diversified portfolio of equities is likely, over any long period of time, to perform as well or badly as the business sector of the economy in which its constituents are active, and therefore it is a 'real' rather than 'monetary' asset over a period of time.

As well as shares in individual enterprises, there are also vehicles available for buying a share in a range of investments (for example mutual funds, unit trusts and investment trusts). Many investors in recent years, especially in the United Kingdom, have begun to use 'index funds' where a manager tries to mimic the performance of a specified index. In addition traded options exist in most major stocks to buy or sell at specified prices on specified future dates. Futures contracts in market indices enable investment managers to increase or decrease risk in a portfolio without changing the actual holdings.

Equities are more unpredictable in essence than bonds over any short period, and all the modern techniques of computer analysis and risk control cannot prevent sharp movements in value from day to day. This means investors need to look at them over a long time horizon, making them most suitable for long-term funds, especially those with real liabilities.

Real assets

Property and other tangible assets are also hedges against high inflation, but tend to be relatively unmarketable; they are thus more appropriate for long-term investors. Many real assets require a high level of expertise to maintain and administer, and therefore the yield has to be proportionately higher to cover the cost involved. Assets such as gold, works of art and other tangibles are rarely found in institutional investment portfolios: they do not have a yield, they may incur storage and insurance costs, and over long periods of time they are likely to perform considerably worse than most other investments. However they are the ultimate hedge against loss in real values and are therefore particularly useful in hyper-inflationary situations where no monetary asset acts as a store of value.

Large insurance companies frequently invest heavily in property development since, over time, the yield on shops and offices is likely to keep pace with inflation. They can do this successfully because they are large enough to maintain a specialist estate management staff. In a larger portfolio, no single property should be able to put the portfolio at risk, therefore there is a minimum size below which even long-term funds cannot prudently invest directly in property. However many investment vehicles allow the smaller investor access to the property market, principally unit trusts and property companies in the United Kingdom, and Real Estate Investment Trusts in the United States.

16.3 INVESTMENT PRACTICES

Life insurance

In many cases, life companies are selling an investment product, and this has led to a preponderence of long dated fixed-interest securities in their portfolios. They will, in addition, frequently have equities and property within the life fund and the amount of these investments will depend on the philosophy of the office concerned and the proportion of with-profits business it is writing. The larger life offices are among the largest operators in the respective investment markets (only pension funds are of a comparable size or bigger) and this gives a certain inflexibility to their investment behaviour. Large investors are 'locked in' to their investments by size and have effective discretion only over the investment of new cash-flow.

Major life offices maintain large investment organisations which have specialist departments for particular investment areas, and thus even new cash-flow has institutional barriers tending to push it into the existing investment markets. In recent years there has been a trend in both the United States and the United Kingdom towards international diversification as a way of increasing the range of possible investments. This has mainly affected the equity and property markets as there has been no shortage of available government fixed-interest bonds in either country.

Non-life insurance

Non-life insurance investment portfolios vary much more widely between insurers, from being invested wholly in bank deposits to being placed wholly in Eurodollar medium-term fixed-interest stocks. The smaller insurers vary most in their investment practices, with many relying on outside investment managers. Larger companies usually have more well-thought-out practices, but these still vary considerably from company to company.

In the United Kingdom the non-life funds of the major composites have about half their money in the fixed-interest market, a quarter in equities and one-eighth in property. Comparable companies based in the United States have a larger preponderance of bonds in their portfolios. This is the result of a differing accounting treatment which allows the bonds to be carried at cost-related value in financial statements. There is a much larger range of credit risks in such bond portfolios and in most cases they have longer maturity profiles than their UK equivalents. This same accounting treatment means that, whereas the major UK composites tend to actively manage their fixed-interest portfolios to improve the returns, their US equivalents are frequently prevented from doing so by considerations of the short-term consequences on operating results. This same factor, it should be noted, leads to substantial over-estimation of assets by US insurers in a period of rising interest rates, without any compensating under-estimation at a time of falling interest rates if the companies sell their bonds to realise gains.

16.4 INVESTMENT CONTROLS

Traditional methods

The objectives of insurance companies can only be met by subjecting the management of asset portfolios to the same sort of controls as are usually imposed on the underwriting of liability portfolios. There is a need to maintain solvency and limit the adverse consequences of fluctuations in value, while achieving high returns. The response to the need for investment controls is one of the fastest developing areas in the investment management industry, and what can be considered as 'best practice' is rapidly changing. The ability of modelling techniques to simulate many possible scenarios allows a much more sophisticated approach to investment control.

Traditional controls on the behaviour of investment managers have been achieved by imposing quotas – quantitative controls on the amount that could be put in particular classes and types of investment. Companies would preserve liquidity by, for instance, stipulating that 50 per cent of their investments should be in government-backed securities. They would guarantee their survival from fluctuations in market values by stipulating that, for example, 10 per cent of the fund should be in property, 20 per cent in equities and 20 per cent in bonds beyond 10 years. These quantitative guidelines achieve the objective of limiting valuation risk in an acceptable manner but usually suffer from inflexibility, and achieve a degree of permanence once prescribed.

Modern methods

Modern techniques of risk measurement and quantitative analysis allow the use of a 'tariff' system which, instead of applying fixed proportions to each type of investment, applies differing weights depending on the riskiness of the investment and allows an overall quantum of risk which can be related to solvency, shareholders funds, regulatory constraints and so on. Such techniques allow the management of an insurance operation to decide what fluctuations in value it would find acceptable within an accounting period, and to constrain their investment managers appropriately.

A model by which an insurance company could control risks would consist of a maximum possible loss (MPL) determined with reference to statutory solvency requirements or desired minimum solvency levels, and a maximum interest rate (MIR) at which it was desired that solvency be maintained. The MIR can be determined by reference to historical highs and is in essence a policy decision by the company; it refers to the rate of interest on government bonds and can be translated into appropriate price changes for any other financial instrument. The MPL becomes the determinant of the risk which can be taken into the investment portfolio, the MIR the policy input. A conservative company might choose a high MIR to ensure survival under the most adverse circumstances, whilst a more adventurous company might hope to maximise investment returns by choosing a lower figure.

The model does not allow any greater predictability of return or remove any of the investment uncertainty on particular classes, but it does allow judgements to be made about capital movements. The longer term the insurance account the less short-term fluctuations matter, indeed in a conventional with-profits life fund, year to year fluctuations should have virtually no impact on the shareholders or policyholders. If discounting of reserves becomes accepted practice for the majority of non-life companies, then similarly it can be expected that any move in interest rates reducing a fluctuation in investment values will have a compensating counterpart on the liability side, due to the use of a higher discount rate for future liabilities. A move to revaluation of liabilities in line with present values would make matching a much more practical proposition for property and casualty companies in the United Kingdom. Matching is currently more practical in the United States, where investments are carried at book cost related values (and therefore neither assets nor liabilities need be revalued) but currently Department of Trade and Industry regulations for the UK insurer look at market values for solvency purposes. For management and pricing decisions it is clear that present valuing of both assets and liabilities is the only rational method of assessing the company's balance sheet, but such an approach is often unpopular with auditors. In the United States the Tax Reform Act 1986 made the practice of discounting universal for taxation purposes, and in the United Kingdom the Inland Revenue has been holding discussions with the insurance industry since the beginning of 1985 with a similar aim.

16.5 THE INFLUENCE ON INSURANCE OF INVESTMENTS

The earlier parts of this chapter have concentrated on the ways in which insurance liabilities affect the investment assets of the insurer. There are, however, several ways in which the investment assets influence the insurance liabilities, particularly in premium rating and policy design. These influences have been traditional and obvious in the life insurance industry but in recent years they have become more prevalent in property and casualty markets.

To a certain extent the practice known as 'cash-flow underwriting' (which is usually a pejorative term) is a class of investment-determined insurance transaction. The latter phrase, when used as a term of abuse, normally implies that non-life underwriters accept business at any price purely to achieve the investment income. There is a thin line between this practice and designing premium rates so that the combination of underwriting and investment result gives a satisfactory return to the equity holder on the capital provided. On 'long tail' non-life business it would be foolish not to take account of the investment income in setting premium rates, and increasingly policies are designed to take account of the fact that a pound or dollar today is worth more than a pound or dollar in a year's time. An extreme case of such influence on policy design is seen in the area of funded reserve transfers, where effectively the 'tail' of an insurance company is transferred to another for a consideration which reflects the present value of the future liabilities. The claims which the reinsured can make under this policy are in many ways similar to those of the same party buying a long-term investment. In the future such close relationships between underwriter and investment manager seem likely to become more common. Fast calculations and communication will allow insurers to co-ordinate their underwriting and investment portfolios better than they have in the past.

The essence of the proper relationship between the asset and liability portfolios is that the former should be controlled in the full knowledge of the latter. The traditional attitude of insurers (which was to take risks on underwriting, not on investments) is still valid but it needs qualifying with appropriate definitions of what constitutes an investment risk. It is in this area that future development is likely to concentrate and it is possible that in future managers of insurance companies will be both able and willing to run the business as a whole, co-ordinating assets and liabilities in a consistent manner.

Recommended reading

Peasnell, K.V. and C.W.R. Ward (1985) *British Financial Markets and Institutions* (Englewood Cliffs, NJ: Prentice-Hall International).

Wise, A.J. (1987) 'The Matching of Assets to Liabilities', *Transactions of the Faculty of Actuaries*, 40 pp. 18–63.

17 Government Regulation of Insurance Companies

Henry Ellis

Exact details of laws regulating insurance companies may vary from country to country, but they typically follow the same pattern. First, legislators prescribe a licensing system controlling access to the national insurance market. Usually unlicensed insurers are also forbidden from transacting business. Secondly, the regulatory authority is given special powers to enable it to monitor the trading activities of licensed insurers. The more important of these 'ongoing' regulatory powers usually takes the form of financial and accounting requirements. The licensing and control of insurance companies are discussed in detail later on, but first a short rationale for the general regulation of insurance companies is necessary.

17.1 THE REASONS FOR REGULATING INSURERS

Protecting consumers

Controlling and managing an insurance company involves custody of large sums of money belonging to policy claimants, beneficiaries, policyholders and shareholders, among others; this is particularly true in the case of life insurance companies. The financial collapse of an insurance company can involve serious political repercussions. The insolvency of a life insurer can be particularly traumatic. As a result of such a financial failure, many policyholders or their dependents could lose the benefits of their life's savings at a time when they were too old to make alternative pension or other arrangements. Accordingly, government control or regulation of life insurers (which may be part of a wider concern for investor protection) has often been stricter than the supervision of non-life insurers, extending to matters such as approval of premium rates (and, as a result, lowering, if not altogether eliminating, price competition within a national market).

Obviously the rationale underlying government regulation of insurers is the prevention of insolvencies amongst insurance companies. Virtually all governments seek to ensure that insurance companies operating within their national market are financially sound and transact business in a responsible manner. Governments regulate insurance companies, not primarily to limit their numbers, but to protect the interest of claimants and members of the public who have bought policies.

Typical insurance transactions involve pre-payment of a premium in respect of an unsecured contingent promise by the insurer. The insurer's promise may be contained in a policy which is expressed in highly technical legal language not easily understood by the 'average consumer'. The consumer's position is further exacerbated because much insurance business is transacted on standard contract forms and rates, over which there is often no individual negotiation. Accordingly, when regulating insurance companies, governments often attempt to ensure a sense of fairness in the contractual relationship between the insurer and the insured, by taking powers of approval over insurance contract forms.

The extent of policyholder protection embraced by the approval of contract forms as a licensing condition can often be minimal (particularly in common law countries.) The applicant insurer is usually licensed to use the standard package of contract terms already in use by other licensed insurers in that market.

In some countries (such as the United Kingdom and Australia) concern has been expressed at the possible unfair operation of insurance contracts, particularly in relation to the disclosure of material facts and warranted information. Consequently proposals have been made to reform 'unfair' contract terms, making them more in the favour of individual policyholders. In the United Kingdom, this concern resulted in the adoption by members of the Association of British Insurers and by Lloyd's syndicates of the revised Statements of Insurance Practice issued in 1986.

Regulation of reinsurers

Insurance companies themselves purchase reinsurance protection, often from specialist reinsurance companies. But generally government regulation of insurance companies does not extend to include these reinsurance companies. This is because direct insurance companies should be qualified to assess the security offered by a reinsurance company and many specialist reinsurance companies may be domiciled in a foreign country.

An exception to the general rule is provided by the United Kingdom, where reinsurers are regulated on much the same basis as direct insurers. The UK regulatory authority feels that many insurance companies writing direct business may be heavily dependent upon financial protection from specialist reinsurers to whom they have ceded business. Not surprisingly the UK government would like to see the practice of regulating specialist reinsurers used more widely.

Some governments (for example in certain states in the United States) whilst not officially regulating reinsurers, may exercise indirect control by treating the ceding insurer as an intermediary. Governments then either prohibit regulated insurers from dealing with reinsurers that have not been recognised or refuse to give credit for reinsurances ceded to unapproved reinsurers when valuing the direct insurers' reserves.

Regulation in federal jurisdictions

In unitary states it is clear that the one government is responsible for controlling the activities of insurance companies operating within its national market. However, in federal multi-governmental countries, which authority has the responsibility for regulating insurers?

In Australia, for example, action following the Australia Law Reform Commission's report on consumer protection is being taken by the federal government. The federal government is the authority for regulating the solvency of insurers operating in the states of Australia. However, some state government regulatory authorities may impose additional regulations on insurers in respect of certain classes of business. In Canada the primary objective of insurance company regulation (that is, prevention of insolvency amongst insurers) is also the subject of federal laws implemented by the federal government, but the jurisdiction over insurance is divided so that provincial legislation caters for such matters as fairness of insurance contract conditions. There is a high degree of uniformity amongst provincial insurance laws in Canada and these are co-ordinated by the Association of Superintendents of Insurance of the Provinces of Canada.

Although the responsibility for regulating insurers in the United States (unlike Australia and Canada) is a matter for the individual state governments there is a certain amount of uniformity in all individual state laws. This desirable and necessary uniformity has been fostered by the workings of the National Association of Insurance Commissioners (NAIC). Achievements of NAIC include the development of several standard accounting forms of submission by insurers to the various state individual regulatory authorities.

The European Community is not a federal association of countries. However, by means of Council of Ministers' Insurance Establishment Directives, the laws regulating insurers (both non-life and life) in each independent member state are being co-ordinated and harmonised.

17.2 LICENSING REQUIREMENTS FOR ENTRANTS TO INSURANCE MARKETS

In general persons wishing to transact insurance business in a national market are required to have an 'establishment' there, either by forming a new company with its head office within the state or by setting up a branch office. In either case, countries will not usually permit the starting up of a new insurance company or a branch operation without the applicants first obtaining an insurance license or authorisation.

Clearly obtaining an insurance authorisation is a condition precedent to entering a national insurance market. The conditions which must be fulfilled by applicants to qualify for the granting of a licence can be classified under the broad headings of legal, financial, accounting, technical and economic.

Legal conditions for licensing

The first legal condition for the authorisation of insurers concerns the corporate form of the new enterprise. The high amount of initial share capital required to start up an insurance enterprise generally places it outside the scope of both wealthy individuals and unincorporated associations. Accordingly authorities commonly require an insurer to be an incorporated company. The most common forms of licensed insurance corporations are the limited liability, joint stock and mutual companies. However exceptional forms of business organisations (such as a syndicate of Lloyd's underwriters) are sometimes allowed to transact insurance business.

Secondly, in addition to prescribing an acceptable form of business organisation, some governments also enforce restrictions on company ownership. For example, in the United States, over half of the individual states have insurance licensing provisions precluding the authorisation of any insurer that is owned or controlled by a foreign (or indeed any) government. In Australia proposals by foreign nationals to establish a new insurance company must show substantial net economic benefits to Australia or, where these net economic benefits are likely to be insignificant, must involve an effective partnership between national interests and the foreign investor in the ownership and control of the company concerned. Canada, too, has special rules relating to the licensing of foreign insurers. However the term 'foreign insurer' in Canada means a company that is neither Canadian nor British.

In Western Europe the main objective of the Treaty of Rome (which established the European Community) is the liberalisation of trade. Consequently some barriers to market entry based solely on nationality have been removed, particularly in the establishment of new insurance companies. Following implementation of the 1973 non-life and the 1979 EC life insurance establishment directives, the phrase 'national' company effectively means a domestic or EC member state company within the European Community. Insurers now enjoy the legal right to enter other member state national insurance markets, either by establishing a branch or starting up a new insurance company there.

An insurer domiciled in a state outside the European Community is termed a 'third country' insurer in the EC non-life and life insurance establishment directives. In the United Kingdom, legislation implementing these directives styles insurance licence applicants from third countries as 'external' applicants. As external applications are based outside the EC, the conditions of licensing applied to them are more onerous than those applicable to Community-based applicants. For example, the UK regulatory authority will not issue a licence to an external applicant unless it is a corporate body (entitled under the law of the state where its head office is situated to carry on the class of business for which it is seeking a licence). External applicants must also appoint a general representative resident in the United Kingdom. A general representative must be a UK resident or company with its head office in the United Kingdom. External applicants must also deposit a prescribed amount with the Accountant General of the Supreme Court, and maintain assets in the United Kingdom of such value as directed by the regulatory authority. The UK regulatory authority will also have to be satisfied that any director, controller, manager, main agent or general representative is a 'fit and proper' person to hold their position.

Thirdly, some regulatory authorities may insist on submission to them of a corporation's memorandum of association (or at least a summary of the objects clause contained in it) before a licence is granted. Governments may refuse to grant an insurance licence unless it is clear that the company intends to confine its trading to insurance business and directly related activities such as investment. In the United Kingdom an insurer is statutorily prohibited by the Insurance Companies Act 1982 from carrying on any activities other than, or in connection with, or for the purposes of, its insurance business.

Fourthly, in most states an insurer will not be licensed to transact both life and non-life insurance business. The United Kingdom used to be a notable exception, but the practice of licensing new composites has now ceased, following the implementation of the 1979 EC life insurance establishment directive. Specialisation offers protection to life policyholders by ensuring that assets representing their funds are kept separate and distinct from assets representing non-life policyholders' funds.

Finally, the authorities may also monitor insurance contract terms by inspecting proposed policy forms. These forms may have to be submitted by applicants with their business plans. The 1973 and 1979 EC insurance establishment directives provide for the submission by applicants of a 'scheme of operations' to the appropriate regulatory authority, containing the general and special policy conditions which they propose to use.

Financial conditions for licensing

It is clear that the basic objective in regulating insurers is to see that they remain solvent. This aim is usually implemented at the licensing stage by prescription of a minimum share capital to ensure adequate initial financial resources.

The minimum share capital required to start up a new insurance company is invariably far in excess of any amount required to incorporate an ordinary commercial trading company. For example, it has now been agreed within the European Community that all newly licensed life insurers should have a minimum capital of 800 000 European Currency Units (ECUs), while new non-life insurers should have a minimum share capital of 400 000 ECUs. However it is worth remembering that, in a large competitive insurance market, brokers' security committees may not be too impressed with a new entrant which possesses only the bare statutory minimum amount of share capital.

In addition, initial guarantee deposits may also have to be made, although this form of security is tending to be seen as mainly appropriate for the establishment of branch operations by non-national insurers.

Accounting conditions for licensing

The regulatory authority may wish to obtain confirmation that the initial capital has been subscribed. As evidence it might require an initial Balance Sheet, or perhaps merely a certificate showing that the share capital has been paid up. Similarly the regulatory authority will want to satisfy itself that the capital base of the proposed insurance company is sufficiently high to support the amount of new business which it intends to write. Accordingly, the business plan will usually include projections of the estimated expense of installing the administrative services and the organisation for securing business and also of the financial resources intended to cover these. In addition projections may be required, for the first three financial years, of the expenses of management (other than costs of installation) and in particular of current general expenses and commissions, premiums and claims, and the financial resources intended to cover underwriting liabilities and any prescribed solvency margin.

Technical information for licensing

It is usual for applicants to furnish information dealing with the nature of the insurance risks which the company intends underwriting, the premium rates which it proposes to apply for each class of business and its guiding principles as to reinsurance (including the company's maximum retention per risk or event, after all reinsurances ceded). More mathematical information will often be required from applicants for life insurance licences.

Economic consideration for licensing

The licensing requirements discussed above are necessary to monitor market entry with a view to protecting policyholders against the risk of an authorised insurer becoming insolvent. However the granting of an insurance licence to a non-national applicant may be made conditional on the reciprocal treatment of the country's own insurers in the applicant's home state, for reasons of economic protectionism.

17.3 THE REGULATION OF LICENSED INSURANCE COMPANIES

Licensing restrictions exist primarily to prevent unsuitable companies from obtaining access to national insurance markets. Obviously the regulation of insurers must then extend to the monitoring of their trading activities once they have been licensed.

An insurance company's need for financial resources will tend to increase with new business expansion. To avoid a licensed insurer over-stretching its initial capital base, most governments prescribe the maintenance of a reasonable ratio of surplus assets to premiums. The most important 'on-going' regulations are therefore financial and prescribe the levels of solvency margins and technical reserves, and the bases for valuing the assets representing these reserves. Only licensed insurers who are able to meet mandatory financial tests are allowed to continue trading without intervention from the regulatory authority.

Solvency tests

In general, there are three levels or indicators of solvency for licensed insurance companies. Firstly, insurers must be able to demonstrate that they possess a sufficiency of assets to cover their underwriting liabilities; this level of assets is equivalent to the technical reserve requirement. If an insurer's assets do not cover technical reserves then it will be unable to pay its trading debts and will actually be insolvent. Most governments have the right to intervene in such a situation, including the ultimate power to initiate winding-up proceedings.

Secondly, given the political importance attached to maintaining the solvency of insurers, most governments do not wish to be confronted with the imminent insolvency of one. Accordingly, a 'buffer' of 'free' reserves is often prescribed, to be maintained by insurers over and above the level of their technical reserves. This 'buffer' is styled a 'margin of solvency' in the United Kingdom and can be defined as the excess of the value of a company's assets over the amount of its liabilities, that value and amount being determined in accordance with the applicable valuation regulations. In the United Kingdom, it would amount to approximately 18 per cent of the premium income of a non-life insurance company (for further details, see Carter, 1973).

The third solvency test is a concept based on EC legislation: this is the idea of a minimum guarantee fund. The prescribed minimum guarantee fund is initially akin to a minimum capital requirement. It must amount to a specified amount or one-third of the amount of the solvency margin, whichever is the higher. Once an insurer is transacting business, its minimum guarantee fund will therefore usually amount to one-third of its margin of solvency.

The valuation of liabilities

In many countries rules are prescribed for the valuation of underwriting liabilities (and the assets representing them). In the United Kingdom, for example, non-life insurers must calculate their underwriting liabilities in accordance with customary market practice. Underwriting liabilities include reserving for unearned premiums and claims (both outstanding and incurred but not reported). There are more precise formulae for the calculation of insurers' solvency margins and minimum guarantee funds.

In Canada, life companies are required to demonstrate that they have assets sufficient to meet their future liabilities. The most important component of these liabilities is the actuarial valuation of an insurer's obligations to its policyholders (styled the 'policy reserve' in Canada; also known elsewhere as 'mathematical reserve'). The actuarial valuation takes into account the probability of death at each age and makes allowances for compound interest. Until recently, Canadian legislation stipulated that only certain interest rates and mortality tables could be used by insurance companies in computing required policy reserves. However insurance companies can now apply to the federal Superintendent of Insurance to use reserve bases different from those specified in legislation. The interest rates used in the valuation of the policy reserve are significantly lower than the interest rates prevailing in the market. The effect of using low interest rates is to overvalue a company's liabilities. In this way the company is obliged to maintain a policy reserve larger than is likely to be required to meet its obligations.

Within EC member states, the concepts of technical and mathematical reserves, margins of solvency and minimum guarantee funds are used in the calculation of life insurers underwriting liabilities and general solvency levels.

In American states, technical reserve calculations are usually prescribed in great detail for life insurance liabilities. For non-life insurers state codes often provide for a minimum reserve in relation to specific classes of business, such as auto liability.

Choice of covering assets

Some governments allow insurers more freedom of choice in the investment of assets representing their 'free' reserves than those representing their underwriting liabilities. This attitude is reflected in the 1973 EC non-life insurance directives. These allow member state non-life insurers complete freedom of choice in the investment of assets in excess of those representing the technical reserves. However, the technical reserves must be covered by equivalent and matching assets localised in each country where business is transacted. This would mean, for example, that a Dutch insurer transacting business in the United Kingdom would have to hold sterling assets (technical reserves) equal to its sterling liabilities.

Under federal legislation in Canada, only certain types of investments by life insurance companies are allowed. Even within a class of investments there are further restrictions with regard to quality and quantity. Assets can be invested in Canada bonds and those of certain other countries, as well as in provincial, municipal and public authority bonds. Subject to certain conditions, assets may also be invested in corporate bonds, debentures, preferred shares, real estate mortgages and real estate. In general, these investments are to be in Canada or in another country where the company is doing business. The rationale for these rules is to ensure solvency by limiting the degree of risk in the important investment portfolios held by insurance companies. The tightest restrictions are on the riskiest assets, namely common or ordinary shares.

The main limitation on investment of assets in life funds by Australian insurers is that one life office may not invest in another (whether directly or indirectly) without court sanction.

State insurance codes in the United States generally set out strict guidelines for the investment of assets, both in classes of assets that are admissible and in limits on specific types of asset. These restrictions usually apply to assets representing technical reserves, as well as to those representing capital and surplus. In fact some states impose stricter standards for investment of assets corresponding to the statutory minimum capital or surplus (free reserves). This is a different regulatory philosophy to the European approach. The latter recognises the function of technical reserves as the primary fund for insurance claims, as compared with the secondary 'guaranteeing' function of the free reserves. Accordingly, in Europe, insurers generally enjoy wider freedom of investment of free reserves than their counterparts in the United States.

The supervision of insurance managers

Of course, the guarantee element in the free reserve presupposes that the technical reserves are adequate: if not they constitute a very weak foundation on which to build a margin of solvency. Accordingly regulators are aware that solvency margins can never replace the basic soundness of an insurance operation emanating from good management (that is, realistic underwriting, pricing and reserving, allied to a prudent investment policy).

In view of the importance of management, some authorities insist that insurers notify changes in controlling shareholders, directors, chief executives and managers.

In their 'Report on Insurance Contracts' of 1982, the Australian Law Reform Commission were not satisfied that the benefits of screening insurance managers on the UK lines would outweigh the administrative cost involved. They recommended instead that the Life Insurance Commissioner and the Insurance Commissioner should have power to order an insurer not to appoint or replace any director or manager found guilty of certain offences.

Administration and enforcement of 'On-going' regulations

The regulatory authorities monitor observance of financial requirements by checking accounts and returns compulsorily submitted to them (at least) annually. The accounting forms to be submitted by insurers usually comprise revenue, profit and loss and balance sheet, together with specified additional information. All such accounts must usually be certified by a director, and include an auditors' report. In the case of life insurers an actuarial investigation or certification may also be required.

If the regulating authorities find that an insurer's assets do not exceed the statutory 'free reserve' level, they have powers to take appropriate action, for example by ordering an injection of additional capital, or prohibiting the writing of new business. Ultimately, if it happens that the asset level is insufficient to cover even the technical reserves, the authority will normally have the power to initiate winding-up proceedings.

In the United Kingdom, a special guarantee fund to compensate policyholders of an insolvent insurer was set up by the Policyholders Protection Act, 1975. It is financed primarily by levies on licensed insurers, both non-life and life. In addition to paying (usually 90 per cent of) claims of insolvent insurers the Policyholders Protection Board also has discretionary powers to assist insurers in financial difficulties.

If government regulation of insurers is strict, it will lower the likelihood of an insolvency and therefore lessen the need for a guarantee scheme. Conversely, the need for a 'claimants' safety net' increases where the regulatory environment is liberal.

17.4 REGULATION AND INTERNATIONAL INSURANCE TRADE

The idea of licensing implies exclusivity in the context of national insurance markets so that unlicensed insurers cannot trade within them. However in some national markets foreign insurers may be able to write business even though they have not obtained a licence to set up an establishment there. This type of market access is often styled 'freedom to provide insurance services'.

The strict regulation of insurers in national European insurance markets has made those markets most difficult for foreign insurers to enter. Furthermore, because of variations in law and administrative practices, the same type of insurance cover was often 'packaged' differently in the various national markets. Thus geographical division of the international European market was accompanied by 'product' differentiation between the individual national markets. This scenario did not make individual markets very attractive to foreign-based insurers which were unable to offer insurance 'products' different to those available from domestic insurers. As a result, insurers wishing to enter a national European insurance market usually did so by taking over, or merging with, a domestic insurer.

The 'protected' national insurance markets of continental Europe were the very antithesis of the models envisaged in the Treaty of Rome. Articles 52 to 58 of the Rome Treaty provide for the gradual abolition of restrictions on non-national Community persons entering national member state markets and starting up a subsidiary company or branch operation there. The non-life insurance establishment directives of 1973 introduced the 'free trade' provisions of articles 52–58 for the benefit of non-life insurers. The 1979 life insurance establishment directive did likewise for life insurers.

There are a number of practical effects arising from implementation of these freedom of establishment directives within European Community member states. Firstly, Community nationals now enjoy the legal right to enter any national member state insurance market, either by starting up a new subsidiary company or by deciding to trade there by means of a branch operation. Secondly, the licensing requirements to be met by Community applicants have been standardised. If an applicant meets these common EC market entry requirements then it *must* be granted the licence by the regulating authority. Thirdly, the classification of non-life and life insurance business within each member state has been standardised. This development in product homogeneity benefits consumers in national markets and further encourages the liberalisation of international insurance trade.

Yet another practical effect is co-operation between member state governments in monitoring the solvency of EC-based insurers. Unlike the situation in the United States, an EC insurer's global solvency is controlled by only one agency – the regulatory authority of its 'home' member state. Finally, the EC insurance directives provide for access to member state national markets by non-EC-based insurers. However there are special licensing conditions for such 'third country' applicants.

Freedom of establishment gives European Community-based insurance companies rights of access to foreign member state markets. However such access is subject to being licensed and having local representation. Under the economic freedom of services, neither establishment nor prior authorisation is envisaged.

In respect of insurance business, freedom of services means giving European Community-based insurance companies the right to sell insurance in foreign member state domestic markets, without firstly having to set up a subsidiary or branch operation there. Equally, it means the freedom for Community citizens to buy an insurance policy from any authorised Community insurance company, whether established in his own member state or not.

Freedom of services exists for reinsurers and insurance intermediaries. Some member states permit trading into their domestic market for non-life insurance risks by way of freedom of services: other member states do not. To overcome this divergence in law and practice, directives have been promulgated permitting access to all or most member state markets for coinsurance and defined 'large' non-life insurance risks.

A directive in 1978, aided by the decision of the European Court of Justice in case no. 205/84, introduced freedom of coinsurance services for Community non-life insurance companies. However the coinsurance services freed were limited to very large risks. A directive permitting the introduction of freedom of services for large non-life insurance risks was promulgated in June 1988. The directive only applies to certain categories of large industrial and commercial risks, including property, pecuniary and liability insurances when the policyholder (company) satisfies two out of the three criteria: 500 employees, or an annual turnover of 24 million ECUs, or an annual balance sheet total of 12.4 million ECUs.

Eight member states must ensure that the directive comes into force on 1 July 1990. Transitional arrangements will delay full implementation in Spain, Portugal, Greece and Ireland, thereby slowing down penetration of these national markets. A second and reduced threshold for large risks is to be introduced with effect from 1 January 1993. From that date the three property, pecuniary and liability insurances thresholds are to be virtually halved.

Further evidence of the political will to create a common European Insurance market of 320 million 'consumers' (generating about one-quarter of the world's total premium income) is the two draft directives of December 1988 containing proposals to liberalise certain motor and life insurance services.

References and recommended reading

Carter, R.L. (ed.), (1973) *Handbook of Insurance* (Brentford, Middlesex: Kluwer

Publishing Limited), (continuously updated).
Ellis, T.H. (1980) *European Integration and Insurance* (London: Witherby & Co Ltd).
Ellis, T.H. and J.A. Wiltshire (1986) *Regulation of Insurance in the UK and Ireland* (Brentford, Middlesex: Kluwer Publishing Limited), (continuously updated).
Kimball, S.L. and W. Pfennigstorf (1981) *Regulation of Insurance Companies in the US and the European Communities: A Comparative Study* (International Insurance Advisory Council, Chamber of Commerce of the United States).
Mathewson, G., R. Wither, C. Campbell and T. Gussman (1983) *Regulation of Canadian Life Insurance Market: Some Issues Affecting Consumers* (Ottawa: Canadian Bureau of Consumer and Corporate Affairs).

18 Profit and Solvency in General Insurance

Bill Abbott

18.1 TECHNICAL AND INSURANCE PROFIT

It is possible to compute the profit gained by an insurer on an individual policy. This is sometimes referred to as the 'technical profit' and consists of the excess of premiums collected over claim amounts paid and any expenses specific to that policy. It is, in reality, a contribution to the profit of the insurer, to which should be added the contribution from the investment return on the cash-flow generated by that policy, less the contribution from non-specific expenditure. Where the policy is subject to reinsurance there may be further non-policy-specific items (such as profit commission), which should be taken into account before an overall picture of profit can be established. As defined, this technical profit can only be established after the period of exposure to risk is over and after the last claim payment has been made.

The accounts which keep the closest to this concept of technical profit are those maintained by the syndicates at Lloyd's of London. Policies have to be grouped together for practical purposes, and this is done by category of business and by underwriting year (where the underwriting year is the calendar year of booking the policy). Apart from any subjectivity involved in the categorisation of the contracts, factual records can be built up of the technical profits as they develop for each underwriting year.

An insurance company may follow the Lloyd's accounting system in this respect. Alternatively, as part of its internal management accounts, a company may be able to group policies according to the calendar year of their inception (or renewal) and follow the claims and specific expenses on these policies through to produce a technical profit on a policy-year basis. A further variant would be for the company to construct rating-series profits based on policies beginning in a particular period (typically that between two rate increases). Such a basis has the advantage of indicating any possible selection effects of rate increases.

'Insurance profit' is a term which has been introduced to indicate the insurer's total incremental profit arising from writing insurance business. Unlike technical profit, insurance profit can never be quantified on a factual basis even in the ultimate. Non-specific items have to be attributed by one rule or another. Expenses incurred in a year may need to be

Table 18.1 Balance sheet as at . . .

	Investments
plus	Net current assets
less	Technical reserves
equals	Shareholder reserves

Table 18.2 Revenue accounts for the year ended . . .

	Written premiums
less	Claims paid
less	Expenses (including commission)
less	Increase in technical reserves
equals	Underwriting result

Table 18.3 Profit and loss accounts for the year ended . . .

	Underwriting result
plus	Investment income
equals	Gross reported profits
less	Taxation
equals	Net reported profits
less	Dividends
equals	Net retained profits

identified (for example, as between claims-handling costs and others): where underwriting year statistics are being maintained, these expenses have to be attributed to an underwriting year or to a category of business (but see the discussion on the problems of cost allocation in Sections 9.5 to 9.7).

The cash-flow generated by successive tranches of insurance business is invested in assets which cannot normally be identified with any specific tranche of business. These assets will also probably be merged with those provided by the insurer as capital to support the insurance operation. Even if identifiable registers of assets covering technical reserves are maintained, the investment return on these assets cannot automatically be associated with the cash-flow, as the shareholders' capital may have had its income-earning potential depleted. However it is possible to devise some rules for the attribution of an investment return to the cash-flow (in a similar manner to the allocation of non-specific expenses).

The insurance profit for an underwriting year cohort can be viewed as the discounted value of the cash-flow generated. This requires a degree of subjectivity in the treatment of non-specific expenses and investment return. Since insurers cannot wait for the last claims to be paid, they have to make estimates. For premium rating purposes it is obviously important to have an estimate of the insurance profit as soon as possible. Unfortunately the sooner the estimate of outstanding items is made, the less reliable is the estimate of profit.

The Lloyd's market distributes profit to the syndicate names at the end of the third year of the underwriting year; thus the profit distribution for the 1986 underwriting year will be determined on its closure at 31 December 1988. This provides a natural point for releasing profit, although a loss would have to be supported where assessments of the open year position may indicate. However the estimate of the outstanding liability at the three-year point is unlikely to be correct, and may be covered by reinsuring it into an open year account, or externally. Records of the ultimate experience of a cohort to extinction may show a very different experience from that declared at the three-year stage.

No assessment of profit is complete without taking tax effects into account. Sometimes the shape of the accounts may be determined by the need to achieve tax efficiency. As a general point, underwriting year and similar statistics require a lower degree of subjectivity than the measures described below. All measures of profit will contain some degree of subjectivity through categorisation, the attribution of non-specific expenses, the timing of profit reporting, and the estimation procedures utilised.

18.2 ONE-YEAR ACCOUNTING

The accounting framework

Some insurance companies are able to follow the concept of funded accounts, releasing profit on closure after three years but taking up identifiable losses on open years. This is especially true for those companies operating close to Lloyd's in the London market and for the marine and aviation business of UK companies. However accounts prepared on a one-year basis are more usual. Tables 18.1, 18.2 and 18.3 illustrate typical formats for balance sheets, revenue accounts, and profit and loss accounts. A revenue account separate from the profit and loss account is shown, although this practice may vary from one country to another. The terminology used is also by no means standardised.

The revenue account of Table 18.2 may be recast as:

	Written premiums
less	Increase in unearned premium reserve
less	Claims incurred
less	Expenses, including commission
less	Increase in other technical reserves (if any)
equals	Underwriting result

where 'claims incurred' equals claims paid plus increase in the outstanding claim reserves, where technical reserves are the sum of the unearned premium and outstanding claim reserves.

The link between the profit and loss account and the balance sheet is completed by the following schedule, which assumes that investments are valued at market value and that there is no provision for any contingent tax liability arising from market appreciation:

	Shareholders' reserves at start of year
plus	Net retained profits
plus	Increase in market value of investments
equals	Shareholders' reserves at the end of the year

To this accounting framework must be added a set of guiding accounting principles. These vary from one country to another, and possibly even within a company, since accounts may be prepared for the shareholders, supervisory authorities, taxation authorities, and for management. The two most common accounting principles concern whether the insurer is viewed on a going-concern or on a break-up basis (these are often identified with the perspective of the shareholder and of the supervisor respectively). In practice there may be some blurring of the issues: for instance, a break-up basis should cover liabilities arising from redundancy payments if an insurer went into immediate liquidation. Another instance would be the adoption of different claim-reserving principles where the break-up accounts might be considered as requiring a greater degree of prudence.

The interpretation of an insurer's accounts must depend on recognising the guiding accounting principles utilised. There is a growing trend towards standardisation of these principles, either in compulsory statements of generally accepted accounting principles or of voluntary codes of recognised good practice. Inter-company comparisons of profitability and of security are plagued by the lack of standard principles. Even where standard principles exist, the interpretation of these principles and the practice may vary from one insurer to another. However some degree of standardisation can be expected among insurers in the European Community once the EC directive on insurance company accounts has been implemented.

An insurance company which prepares its financial accounts on a one-year accounting basis is not obliged to keep separate underwriting years for distribution purposes. The annual accounts are designed to show the profit which accrues in the year, recognising revenue and costs as they are incurred and not as the money is received. Profits, if identifiable, may be released at the end of the underwriting year. It should be noted, however, that the one-year system has the capacity to provide technical reserves on a very prudent basis at the end of the underwriting year. In consequence an underwriting strain (that is, a temporary loss, which is later reversed) may emerge.

Accident-year statistics

The revenue account shows an *underwriting profit* which is equivalent to a technical profit diminished by non-specific expenses. The technical profit (given perfect and exact estimations) would equate with the technical profit relating to an *accident-year cohort* which follows through the experience of claims originating in a given year: these arise from the policies exposed to risk during that year, with that exposure being measured through earned premiums. In comparison with policy-year accounts, there are two further points of movement away from a factual basis, through the identification of claims to a particular year, and through the calculation of earned premium.

For accident-year statistics, claims have to be identified by their year of origin. For many claims (such as those relating to a motor accident) this is a simple and indisputable fact. For other claims, such as those associated with an industrial disease, there may be problems relating to the attribution of a date of origin. This is a potential source of error, not only in accident-year statistics but also in policy-year statistics.

The accident-year statistics relate claims to 'earned premiums'. The concept of earned premium is easy to follow for annual policies where the exposure to risk is spread evenly over the policy year. The annual premium can be apportioned *pro rata* to the period of exposure in each year. With the advent of computers this is normally on an exact basis, but some companies still retain the traditional grouping by month, quarter or even year of risk (leading to the $\frac{1}{24}$, $\frac{1}{8}$ and $\frac{1}{2}$ rules of Section 15.5).

However there are arguments for saying that, for some policies, exposure throughout a given period is not even. For example, *ceteris paribus*, inflation will ensure that the exposure increases over the policy-year. Furthermore there may be seasonal factors (for example heavier winter weather claims). Some holiday policies (cancellation risk apart) have no exposure in the period leading up to the holiday.

In practice, adjustments for uneven incidence of risk are very rarely found and a broad brush approach may be sufficient. But these adjustments are more significant for lump-sum premium business, where the period of exposure can extend for long periods: five years is quite common (e.g. for extended warranties), twenty years or more is possible (e.g. for mortgage guarantee) and some much longer periods are not unknown, albeit obscure (e.g. for issue risks). Sometimes the period is not known in advance (contractors all risks, for example) and is extendable; in addition exposure increases over the lifetime of the contract as the insurable value increases with a project nearing completion. On the other hand, in an inflationary environment the mortgage guarantee exposure rapidly diminishes, and indeed may be non-existent (subject to the need for an additional reserve for unexpired risk). Extended warranty business is an infamous example of improper assessment of the exposure to risk, with some insurers beguiled by a strong cash inflow in the first year of a policy's life.

18.3 INSURANCE PROFIT IN PRACTICE

It is possible to calculate the insurance profit as the discounted value of the cash-flow from an accident-year, underwriting-year, or any other suitable cohort (subject to the estimating caveats already described). But great care must be taken in identifying real cash-flows rather than mere accounting entries. For instance, cash-flows in reinsurance are substantially affected by the retention of deposits by ceding companies and by delays in the transmission of money from brokers. Further care must be taken in establishing the correspondence of underlying assumptions, for example between inflation and the rate of discount used. This cash-flow view may be modified when the cost of tying up shareholders' resources as contingency margins is taken into account. This aspect is discussed later.

Some insurance companies, at least in the United Kingdom, would like to present a fairer picture of the profits arising from their insurance activities than the one shown as underwriting profit. They are, however, restricted by the guiding accounting principles. A company reporting on a one-year basis can take the underwriting result of Table 18.2 and add on some of its investment return arising on the assets covering its technical reserves (not all of which may be investible). In so doing it leaves the balance of investment earnings as attributable to shareholder reserves. This simple desire to give a fairer picture gives rise to practical problems of interpretation and construction. These problems arise, first, from the fact that most accounts are built on accounting principles which contain an element of prudence, and secondly from the fact that investment return consists of income and a highly volatile capital appreciation element.

If the accounting principles allowed year-end reserves to be set up on a discounted basis, and if we could further assume that all future outgo and income was known and provided for with absolute precision, then the profit indicated by the one-year accounts would coincide with that of the accident-year cohort for that year. But by not discounting, and by prudent reserving, the company can hold the profit up. Indeed in the first year the establishment of non-discounted reserves may result in a financial strain. Thus one can think of an accident-year cohort as making a contribution to profit (or loss) over a number of years, and the reported profits for a given year as consisting of contributions from a number of accident-years (or alternatively underwriting years). If there is consistency of reserving from one year to the next, and if the rate of growth or diminution of the business is not too large, then the reported insurance profits for the year may not be too divergent from the insurance profits for the corresponding accident-year. However with the recent substantial fluctuations in inflation rates and inconsistent reserving associated with liability classes (where reserves did not anticipate late reportings such as those connected with asbestosis) there may be little correlation between the reported results and the actual profit arising from the business written in the year. Nevertheless the reported profits are the major factor in determining attitudes and providing feedback into the decision-making process. Underwriting cycles are normally described in terms of reported profit.

Where the reported insurance profit has been calculated by attributing investment earnings to the technical reserves, the results must be carefully interpreted. An example may help: an insurance company may normally have expectations of an insurance profit of 6 per cent of premiums, earns 10 per cent per annum on its assets and has shareholders' capital of 50 per cent of premiums. Assume that for one year an 'exceptional' large liability arises, equal to 10 per cent of premiums, and stays unpaid for several years. In the year the extra liability arises, the insurance 'profit' would be a 4 per cent loss, although an investment apportionment system based on mean technical reserves would result in an interest credit, so that the insurance loss would be $3\frac{1}{2}$ per cent. In the following year, a full year's interest on the higher claim reserve would be credited so that the insurance business is more profitable. In effect the accounting system, through its non-discounting, overstates the loss in the year it arises and overstates the subsequent profit.

The reported insurance profit may be based on investment earnings attributed at a notional rate on the investible technical reserves, or it may be based on an apportionment of actual investment earnings. Actual investment earnings consist of an income stream which is incorporated into reported profits, and capital appreciation which, with the possible exception of some realised appreciation, is not. The investment earnings may be a *pro rata* element of the insurer's total investment earnings or it may have regard to a notional segregation of assets regarded as backing the technical reserves. Whatever the chosen system, there may be problems of consistency from one year to another: for example, varying market values would imply, *ceteris paribus*, shifting levels of attributed investment income to technical reserves as the ratio of technical to shareholder reserves varies.

All forms of reporting insurance profit are suspect to some degree, and the appropriateness of the measure depends on the use to which it is put. In a historical context, reference to actual investment earnings are obviously highly relevant. The use of notional investment earnings may, however, be a more practical tool for decision-making and would allow for further refinements. For instance, the standard calculation depends on attributing investment earnings to the mean technical reserves for the year. The value of these reserves depends on past growth rates and so on. One technique which has been developed has been to estimate, for each class of business, the average period that the insurer holds its premium income: investment earnings are then estimated by reference to this period. This overcomes many of the problems but, like most of the problems of establishing profit in general insurance, depends on a trade-off between using facts and using estimates.

18.4 RATIO ANALYSIS OF PERFORMANCE

The essence of the performance of an insurer's general insurance business is the extent to which its premium income exceeds claim and expense outgo, having made suitable allowance for the investment earnings on the cash generated. The two ratios normally constructed (before considering investment income) are claim ratios and expense ratios. When investment income is considered, then either the claim ratio and expenses ratio must be adjusted to a discounted basis or a third ratio is added: the investment income ratio. Note that the denominator of all ratios is premium income.

The claim ratio can be for an underwriting- or policy-year, or an accident-year, or a revenue account year. The first two are estimated at the end of each calendar year. The revenue account ratio is a 'fact' once the accounts have been established. If the year 1987 is taken and policies were assumed to be evenly distributed throughout that year, the 1987 policy-year would include policies written on 31 December 1987. On average the ratio would refer to policies written on 1 July 1987. If claims were also evenly distributed, the average claim would occur six months after the policy was written, that is, on 1 January 1988. The policy-year claim ratio thus relates to a point of time which is six months later than that for the 1987 accident-year. On the other hand, around half the claims (those arising in 1988) have not yet been incurred. It would be normal to assess the 1987 policy-year for the first time at the end of 1988 (unless all policies had a January inception date) for it to have the same degree of accuracy as the 1987 accident-year ratio (which has a different type of estimating problem in the attribution of exposure). Normally policy-year ratios are produced a year later than accident-year ratios, relating to a point of time only six months later, but with slightly greater accuracy.

Expense ratios may be subject to the same consideration as claims ratios. The problems are different in degree, and the concept of attributing expenses to a given underwriting- or accident-year is rather esoteric. However a basis for identifying acquisition and claim-handling costs normally exists. More often than not, an expenses ratio is calculated on a policy-year basis, with all expenses except claim handling considered payable at the outset of the policy. This ratio is normally calculated straight from the revenue accounts as the ratio of expenses payable to written premiums.

It is quite common to see a policy-year expense ratio added to an accident-year (or more frequently revenue account) claim ratio to form an operating index or combined ratio. The fact that these two ratios have different denominators is not relevant if one accepts the fact that reported profits and operating indices are both broad brush indicators of profitability. An operating index of 100 might be regarded as an underwriting break-even (whatever that may mean). However, if business is growing throughout the year, it might also lead to a small reported underwriting loss in a revenue account which provided for unexpired risks on a prudent basis. As previously explained it is not usual to see claim reserves on a discounted basis. It is equally unusual to see claim ratios based on discounted claims.

The ratio of investment earnings to premium income is but a crude indicator and reflects the interpretational problems of Section 18.3. In a run-off situation, where the company was closed to new business, this income would still carry on for several years even with no premium income, so that obvious distortions can arise. A useful device might be to estimate the income which would have accrued if all investments had been placed on deposit in the short-term money market. The difference between this income and actual investment earnings would represent the contribution derived from the adoption of a more volatile investment profile.

18.5 THE NEED FOR SOLVENCY MARGINS

The simplified balance sheet of Table 18.1 showed shareholders' reserves as the excess of assets over liabilities, which may also be referred to as the solvency margin. For one insurer the value of this solvency margin at a given point of time will vary, depending on the basis chosen for calculating the value of assets and liabilities. An insurance supervisor is usually concerned with the continued solvency of a company so that, if it goes into liquidation, it will have sufficient surplus assets after the liabilities to policyholders have been met. Supervisors may require assets and liabilities to be valued as if they were on or near a 'break-up' basis. Shareholders, on the other hand, may want a more realistic assessment of assets and liabilities, on a 'going-concern' basis. These ideals are not always met in practice. Quantification of a solvency margin is to some extent in the eye of the beholder and will depend on a number of factors. However, even though this quantification may be subjective, it exists.

All companies, whether transacting insurance business or not, require working capital. The purpose of an insurance company's solvency margin is to provide sufficient assets, surplus to policyholder and other liabilities, to meet, with a sufficiently high probability, all the various adverse contingencies that may happen (if not already covered by the technical reserves). As it is always possible to think of some contingency which could exhaust an insurer's solvency margin, an insurer is only conditionally solvent. These contingencies are normally grouped into three categories: those arising from the technical insurance side, those relating to assets, and those relating to other risks. Further discussion can be found in Daykin *et al.* (1984), section 9.

In essence the adverse events arising from the technical nature of insurance business are all to do with having charged premiums which, in retrospect, turn out to be insufficient to provide an insurance profit. The primary reasons for this are fluctuations in claim ratios which arise from the randomness of the claim process and from catastrophe risk. Recently there has been an emphasis on the need to cover the lean years of an underwriting cycle and the probability that such cycles are getting longer. Losses can of course arise from bad management, lack of expense control and unfortunate positioning in terms of market mix. In addition there are contingencies arising from the inadequacy of the data. Where estimates are made, there is always the possibility that they are, with hindsight, imprudent.

The second contingency arises because the market value of an insurer's assets may fall. When a solvency margin is assessed using assets at market value, then the margin will exhibit considerable volatility as the stock market valuation of the assets moves up and down. The margin should be sufficient to cover fluctuations in these values. Where the insurer transacts foreign business, there will be a currency risk where liabilities are not covered by matching assets.

The third type of contingency relates mainly to the security of the insurer's reinsurance coverage. An insurer may reinsure a substantial part of its business, or it may reinsure little in premium terms yet have expectations of significant recoveries in the event of major claims arising from a risk or event. There may be doubts as to the ability of the reinsurers to pay and such bad debts would be met from the solvency margin, as would other bad debts.

There may be other reasons for the non-payment of expected reinsurance recoveries, for example from badly designed contracts or interference from foreign governments 'protecting' their currency. In addition there are other risks arising from the employees themselves, either through deliberate fraud or going beyond their limits of authority (for example, in accepting business) or by setting up inadequate reinsurance arrangements.

For some or all of these reasons, a supervisor may establish minimum standard levels for the solvency margin. With these in place the insurer has to decide on the extent to which it wants to maintain surplus margins in excess of the statutory minimum. Where there may already be a two-tiered structure, as in the EC, this introduces the third tier of a company standard. A complicating feature may arise with large international insurance groups where the solvency minimum standards relate to an insurer authorised in a given territory. The insurer may be a subsidiary of a holding company which is not an insurance company but whose prime purpose is to hold insurance subsidiaries in different countries. The consolidated accounts of these holding companies contain a solvency margin which may have a very different look to that of an individual subsidiary. The holding company should give careful consideration to the solvency margin which each subsidiary should retain and the ease with which these backing assets can be moved from one subsidiary to another. Many of these groupings contain life companies or even composites. In the United Kingdom, for example, there are composites with a considerable life fund and an attaching value to the life fund which is not shown in standard accounting presentations, although embedded values for the life business are now appearing in some balance sheets.

In addition to the established solvency margin an expanding company will need to have excess surplus assets to cover its expansion. The requirement arises because solvency margin requirements are often linked to premium or other volume indicators and because some of the new products may have an initial financing strain.

The solvency margin is augmented by the extent to which the technical reserves and future investment earnings exceed the actual outgo on the unexpired risks and claims outgo. The rules established by supervisors have, of necessity, steered a course towards practical rules which may be considered an over-blunt instrument. More theoretically satisfactory rules can normally be devised, although these are often of increased complexity and additional cost. Even with these more complex systems there is no guarantee of sufficiently discriminating between those insurers with adequate reserves and those without.

Minimum solvency margin levels may be prescribed by regulation, and there may be much debate within the industry on the adequacy of these minimum levels. Where a company is quoted on a stock market, there may be an investor perception as to what constitutes an adequate level of solvency margin. This might include a maximum level as well as a minimum, following considerations of the most efficient use of the company's money. The management of a company may wish to develop its own views on the adequacy of its capital and, with the greater volume of data available to it, may be able to develop a more refined view than that of the supervisor. A review of the major issues in the debate on solvency can be found in Kastelijn and Remmerswaal (1986).

18.6 MEASURES OF PROFITABILITY AND SOLVENCY

The preceding sections have outlined some of the problems in interpreting insurance company accounts; although no specific description has been given of the accounts of Lloyd's syndicates, these differ mainly in terms of presentation. This section assumes that these problems have been sufficiently resolved (with the appropriate warning notices registered) and that due regard has been paid to the guiding accounting principles.

Several versions of the profit from a year's activity exist:

(a) Gross or net of tax reported profits.
(b) Dividends paid plus the increase in the shareholder reserves (net of any capital injection) as in the balance sheet of Table 18.1 (and adjusted for market values). This could be referred to as the increase in reported added value.
(c) As for (b), but with adjustments to the shareholder reserves to allow for any prudency in the technical reserves and goodwill attaching in the stream of existing business and to a stream of possible new business (i.e. the appraised value added).
(d) Dividends paid plus the increase in the market value of the company, as determined by the market.

It could be argued that (c) and (d) would be coincident, with the stock market determining the value of the goodwill. However, as buyers and sellers of insurance companies have been prepared to pay a substantial premium over the 'price before the bid', this is not necessarily the case.

An accounting rate of return on capital can be computed as the ratio of the increase in reported added value to the shareholders' reserves at the beginning of the year. There are a number of variants on the calculation of an accounting rate of return, none of which is entirely satisfactory. The use of this rate is subject to the same constraints more generally applicable to accounting rates of return in other industries. Results must be treated with caution, owing to the inaccuracies in calculating outstanding liabilities, attributing profit to a period and identifying the capital in the first place.

Having said that, the concept of accounting rate of return is useful in exploring relationships. Let S_0 be the shareholders' reserves at the start of an accounting period, and let P_1 and P_0 be the written premiums in the current and previous years. Assume that the insurance profit is x per cent of the written premiums, and the investment return is i per cent. The accounting return on capital is then

$$\frac{i \cdot S_0 + x \cdot P_1}{S_0} = \left(i + x \cdot \frac{P_1}{S_0} \right)$$

This second term can be interpreted as showing that, in addition to the normal investment return, an incremental return is achieved which is geared up by the premium to shareholders' reserves ratio (that is, the reciprocal of the solvency margin to premium ratio). This ratio is normally found to be somewhere in the range 1 to 5.

In theory the return on capital ought to be commensurate with the attaching risk. However views vary as to quite what 'risk' means in these circumstances. It is easy to observe that the risk arising from insufficient capital decreases for a given insurance company as its solvency margin increases. The higher the solvency margin, the lower the accounting rate of return. However the higher solvency margin may increase the risk of the company being accused of an inefficient use of its capital. Risk is sometimes measured in a statistical way through the volatility of past experience (for example, standard derivation of claim ratios). Whatever the measure, it is unlikely that two insurers with different mixes of business will have the same attaching risk arising from the volatility of the profit from the attaching insurance business. If the insurers have similar margins, one insurer should be setting a higher target insurance profit to achieve the return which is commensurate with the risk. Alternatively the insurer should be operating on a higher margin for the same target profit. In practice the difficulties of quantifying both risk and return means that most insurance markets probably operate on a basis where risk is not always commensurate with return.

In the same way one insurer with a similar mix of insurance business but a higher solvency margin than another may take a more volatile investment stance. The extra return from this policy would increase the return on capital, possibly resulting in the two insurers having similar returns on capital.

In practice one of the more useful items to identify is the maximum growth rate of premium income, g, which can be achieved without recourse to fresh finance (where g is given by $P_1 = P_0 \cdot (1 + g)$). It would be normal to assume a desire to maintain a constant solvency margin ratio, say s per cent of premiums. The increase in the solvency margin as a result of growth g is given by $sP_0 \cdot (1 + g) - sP_0 = sP_0g$.

If no additional finance is to be required, this increase must be equal to retained profits, which in turn are given by:

$$\text{Retained Profits} = i\, S_0 + x \cdot P_1 - D$$

where i and x are as previously defined (net of tax) and D is the dividend paid. Equating the increased solvency margin with retained profits gives:

$$sP_0g = iS_0 + x \cdot P_1 - D$$

This shows the basic relationship between growth, solvency, profit and distribution policy. If the dividend paid were equal to the net investment return on the shareholders capital $(i{\cdot}S_0)$ then we get:

$$sP_0g = xP_1$$

If the growth rate x is low, then P_0 and P_1 are approximately equal, and we obtain $sg = x$, so that the maximum growth rate is approximately the net insurance profit margin geared up by the ratio of premium to shareholder reserves. Other assumptions can be made, leading to variations on a result. Simple models of insurance companies of this kind are helpful in creating an understanding of the interrelationships, but are easily capable of being abused.

References

Daykin, C.A., E.R. Devitt, M.R. Khan and J.P. McCaugham (1984) 'The Solvency of General Insurance Companies', *Journal of the Institute of Actuaries*, vol. III, pp. 279–336.

Kastelijn, W.M. and J.C.M. Remmerswaal (1986) 'Solvency', *Surveys of Actuarial Studies, No. 3* (Rotterdam: Nationale-Nederlanden N.V.) May.

19 Profit, Surplus and Reserves in a Life Office

Sidney Benjamin

19.1 ACTUARIAL RESERVES AND SURPLUS

Introduction

The actuarial concepts of profit, surplus and reserves as applied in life insurance underwent change in the nineteenth century with development of different bonus systems, and fundamental developments have taken place since the end of the Second World War. Actuaries work with algebra and are often described as 'mathematicians', but a closer analogy would be a comparison with physicists or engineers, because it is the numerical result in the real world which is the object of the work. As a result, ideas are most easily explained with simplified numerical examples and the reader is invited to follow the arithmetic as each idea and its numerical consequences are illustrated.

The examples chosen are not meant to be numerically realistic but the effects described are very real, as are the extra complications met with in practice. Many of the examples (except those involving with-profits policies) can also be interpreted in the context of general insurance. In the simpler examples, the interest earned on invested money is ignored, to avoid unnecessary complications.

An introduction to reserving and the emergence of surplus

Consider a group of three-year non-profit policies where the best estimate (based on forecast mortality experience) of claims in the three successive years is 100, 200 and 600. Office premiums are charged on a level annual basis and are assumed to be paid in each of the three years on 1 January, while claims are paid on 31 December. If interest is ignored, an office premium of 300 per annum would be levied, and the long-term insurance fund would be as shown in Table 19.1.

Suppose that competition allows the insurer to add a profit margin of 20 per cent to the premium rate (in order to produce profits for shareholders and bonuses for policyholders): there are now three annual office premiums of 360. When should the profit on this with-profits policy be recog-

Table 19.1 A simple insurance fund

Policy year	*1*	2	*3*
(a) Fund b/f	0	200	300
(b) Office premium	300	300	300
(c) Total income (a) + (b)	300	500	600
(d) Claims	100	200	600
(e) Fund c/f (c) – (d)	200	300	0

nised? This is a major question with important financial consequences.

An *actuarial reserve* is that amount which should be set aside so that, together with future premiums and any other income, it is sufficient to pay the claims and any other outgo. In practice 'other income' would include investment returns and 'other outgo' would include expenses and commission, but these complications are omitted at this stage. The future premiums used in the calculation of the actuarial reserve are usually termed *valuation premiums*; we will see in Tables 19.3 and 19.4 that these may be either 'net' or 'gross'. By definition, the reserve plus future income equals future outgo, so that the reserve is equivalent to future outgo less future income. The latter relationship shows why the reserve is often referred to as the 'net liability'.

The reserve of 31 December of the second policy year is such that:

reserve + third year valuation premium = third year claims;

in other words, the reserve at the end of the second policy year is future claims less future premiums (i.e. 600 − 360 = 240).

However before the analysis is continued suppose that no credit is taken for the profit loading of 60 in the valuation premium so that only the 'net premium' of 300 is used. In this case, the reserve at the end of second policy year equals 600 less 300 (i.e. 300). Similarly, the reserve of 200 at the end of the first policy year is given by future claims (i.e. 200 + 600) less future valuation (net) premiums (300 + 300). The corresponding accounts are shown in Table 19.2: these demonstrate that a surplus of 60 is released in line (g) as 'earned' each year.

This is the basic approach used by actuaries to control the emergence of surplus on a portfolio of conventional with-profits policies; it has a 'natural' look about it.

Distribution of bonuses

If the surplus were given as a cash bonus to policyholders, Table 19.2

Table 19.2 The emergence of surplus on a with-profits policy

Policy year	*1*	*2*	*3*
(a) Reserve b/f	0	200	300
(b) Office premium income	360	360	360
(c) Total income (a) + (b)	360	560	660
(d) Claims	100	200	600
(e) Reserve c/f	200	300	0
(f) Total outgo (d) + (e)	300	500	600
(g) Surplus (c) – (f)	60	60	60

would adequately explain the process. However, typically in the United Kingdom, 90 per cent of the surplus is declared as a bonus to policyholders and 10 per cent transferred from the life fund to the profit and loss account for the shareholders.

In order to illustrate the mechanics of declaring three yearly bonuses within the terms of a simplified three-year self-contained example, assume that a valuation of the group of policies takes place on 30 December, just before the year's claims are paid on the 31 December, using a valuation net premium of 300. As before, the claims paid in the three successive policy years amount to a total of 900 (that is, 100 in the first year, 200 in the second and 300 in the third). The results are illustrated in Table 19.3. The bonus which is then declared as a result of the valuation is added to the claims payable at the year-end. In practice the sequence of events is different; claims are paid as they arise, together with previously declared bonuses.

The *first* column of Table 19.3 is identical to that of 19.2 up to and including the emergence of a surplus of 60 in line (g). By definition, 90 per cent of this surplus is to be distributed among all existing with-profits policyholders: the total bonus of 54 is then divided *pro rata* according to the benefits to be paid (that is, one-ninth (6) at the end of the first year, two-ninths (12) in the second year, and six-ninths (36) after the third). The claim benefits due to be paid in the three policy years are thus increased to 106, 212, and 636 respectively. Consequently, after the valuation and bonus declaration, 'Claims including bonus' in line (h) becomes 106, and 'Reserve c/f' in line (i) is 248 (which is given by future claim benefits (212 + 636) less future valuation net premiums (300 + 300)).

In the *second* column of Table 19.3, 'claims' in line (d) have been increased by the first bonus declaration to 212, and the 'Reserve c/f' (line (e)) to 336 (which equals 636 less 300). Again a surplus of 60 is released in line (g), and 54 of this will be distributed to policyholders receiving benefits in the second and third years (in proportion to those benefits, that is

Table 19.3 The declaration of bonus (with a valuation net premium of 300)

	Policy year	*1*	*2*	*3*
	Income			
(a)	Reserve b/f	0	248	376.5
(b)	Office premium income	360	360	360.0
(c)	Total income (a) + (b)	360	608	736.5
	Before valuation and bonus declaration			
	Outgo			
(d)	Claims	100	212	676.5
(e)	Reserve c/f	200	336	0
(f)	Total (d) + (e)	300	548	676.5
(g)	Surplus (c) – (f)	60	60	60
	to shareholders 10%	6	6	6
	to policyholders 90%	54	54	54
	After valuation and bonus declaration			
	Outgo			
(h)	Claims including bonus	106	225.5	730.5
(i)	Reserve c/f	248	376.5	0
(j)	Total outgo (h) + (i)	354	602.0	730.5
(k)	Surplus transferred to shareholders (c) – (j)	6	6	6

two-eighths in year 2 (13.5) and six-eighths in year 3 (40.5)). After the valuation and bonus declaration, 'Claims including bonus' becomes 225.5 (i.e. 212 + 13.5) while 'Reserve c/f' is 376.5 (i.e. 636 + 40.5 – 300).

In the *third* column, the entire bonus of 54 is available to policyholders with benefits payable in Policy Year 3, so that the final 'Claims including bonus' becomes 730.5 (i.e. 676.5 + 54).

The emergence of surplus

In Table 19.3, although the full office premium of 360 was included as income in the revenue account (i.e. line(b)), the reserve calculation only allowed for valuation net premiums of 300 per annum (i.e. excluding the profit loading of 60). Suppose we had taken credit for the full 360 per annum in the valuation premiums (which would then be termed the valuation gross premium): the reserve at the end of the first year but before the bonus declaration would then be 80 (given by future claims (i.e. 200 + 600) less valuation gross (i.e. 360 + 360)). This is substantially lower than the earlier figure of 200 using valuation net premiums (in line (e) Table 19.3).

Table 19.4 The emergence of surplus (with a valuation gross premium of 360)

	Policy year	*1*	*2*	*3*
	Income			
(a)	Reserve b/f	0	224	348
(b)	Office premium income	360	360	360
(c)	Total income (a) + (b)	360	584	708
	Before valuation and bonus declaration			
	Outgo			
(d)	Claims	100	236	708
(e)	Reserve c/f	80	348	0
(f)	Total (d) + (e)	180	584	708
(g)	Surplus (c) – (f)	180	0	0
	to shareholders	18	0	0
	to policyholders	162	0	0
	After valuation and bonus declaration			
	Outgo			
(h)	Claims including bonus	118	236	708
(i)	Reserve c/f	224	348	0
(j)	Total outgo (h) + (i)	342	584	708
(k)	Surplus transferred to shareholders (c) – (j)	18	0	0

The consequences of using valuation gross premiums are illustrated in Table 19.4, where the figures are calculated in exactly the same manner as before (except that valuation premiums of 360 instead of 300 are utilised in the calculation of 'Reserve c/f').

A comparison of Tables 19.3 and 19.4 shows that the total surpluses over the three-year period for shareholders and for policyholders are 18 and 162 respectively in both cases. This illustrates the actuarial point that the reserving basis does not affect the total surplus; it merely changes the emergence of the surplus.

Table 19.5 illustrates the basic point that the weaker the valuation base, the earlier is the emergence of surplus. The equivalent statement when interest earnings are not ignored is that the capitalised, or discounted, present value of emerging surplus is unaffected by the valuation reserving basis used if the discounting is at the same rate as is earned on the life fund's investments.

The working in Table 19.4 shows that the valuation premium brought into the valuation reserving formula – and hence taken credit for in lines

Table 19.5 The emergence of surplus on with-profit policies

	From Table 19.3 (valuation net premiums)			
Policy year	*1*	*2*	*3*	*Total*
Shareholders	6	6	6	18
Policyholders	54	54	54	162
Total	60	60	60	180
	From Table 19.4 (valuation gross premiums)			
Policy year	*1*	*2*	*3*	*Total*
Shareholders	18	0	0	18
Policyholders	162	0	0	162
Total	180	0	0	180

(e) and (i) – should normally exclude the specific loading for bonus. Otherwise future profit loadings are capitalised into surplus in the first year of the policy and, as a result, too much surplus is paid out too early to shareholders and too much bonus is declared to the earlier generations of policyholders. This latter point is particularly important in practice, where life offices will have overlapping 'generations' of policyholders.

A further practical point arises if the example is made more realistic by assuming that an additional loading of 20 per cent on the premium is charged to cover expenses. The estimate of future expenses will normally be cautious, and the intention will be that any profit obtained by keeping actual expenses less than the loading in the premium should be used to give bonuses. It would then be imprudent to capitalise that future profit too early before the actual experience demonstrates that expenses have in fact been held below the premium loading.

The sources of surplus

It would complicate the examples to no purpose to bring in the other main items which contribute to surplus in practice. If the reserving assumptions are cautious, surplus will arise in several ways:

(a) *Mortality* The actual deaths may be fewer than assumed for life insurance or more than assumed for annuities.
(b) *Withdrawals* Reserves are established to cover the liabilities on the assumption that all contracts are held to termination, but in practice policyholders lapse and surrender their policies, and the surrender values may contain a margin.
(c) *Investment* In practice investments may produce a higher rate of interest than that assumed in the calculation of reserves.

(d) *Expenses* As described above, expenses may differ from the margins in the premiums.
(e) *Tax* An example of what can be a very complicated situation is as follows: the life fund is usually taxed on its interest income and receives relief of tax on its expenses up to the amount of interest income. In a young company, the expenses may exceed the interest income and the actuarial calculations may assume that none or very little of the future expenses will obtain tax relief, where in time the situation may well reverse and produce surplus.
(f) *Reinsurance* There are three sources of surplus in connection with life reinsurance. First, in a small company, the actuary may feel obliged to set aside money (that is, set up special reserves and hence hold back the release of surplus) in order to cover fluctuations in the mortality and claims experience. At the cost of paying reinsurance premiums, the reinsurer may enable the release of the special reserves into surplus. Secondly, the tax position of the life reinsurer may be different from that of the ceding company and advantage may be taken of this to a limited extent. Finally, the heavy outgo in initial commission and expenses which the office incurs on the issue of a policy may be relieved by receiving a commission in return from the reinsurer. On the understanding that nothing is obtained for nothing, the reinsurer's commission will be repaid inside the future reinsurance premiums, so the ceding company's future annual surpluses over the term of the policy will each be reduced slightly.

Because there are many sources of surplus it used to be a common working rule of thumb that, if an office premium is loaded to cover approximately one-half of the bonus rate which it is intended to declare, other sources of surplus will approximately supply the rest.

19.2 NET PREMIUM METHOD OF VALUATION

Introduction

The analysis which illustrated the advisability of using a valuation premium (in line (e) of Tables 19.3 and 19.4) of 300 rather than the full 360 leads to a dilemma in practice. In the estimation of the valuation premiums, should one start from the full office premium of 360 and make specific deductions for future expenses and profits as in Table 19.4, or should one use a net premium based on the benefits alone (i.e. 300) and allow the margin of 60 to emerge to cover future expenses and profits as in Table 19.3? The former method of reserving is known as the gross premium method of valuation, the latter as the net premium method. Because of the danger of

Table 19.6 The effect of renewal expenses (with a valuation net premium of 285)

	Policy year	*1*	*2*	*3*
	Income			
(a)	Reserve b/f	0	230	315
(b)	Premium income	315	315	315
(c)	Total income (a) + (b)	315	545	630
	Outgo			
(d)	Claims	100	200	600
(e)	Expenses	15	15	15
(f)	Reserve c/f	230	315	0
(g)	Total outgo	345	530	615
(h)	Surplus (c) – (g)	–30	15	15

capitalising future surpluses too easily under the gross premium method, the net premium method (as illustrated in Table 19.3) has found favour internationally for the purpose of statutory statements to supervisory authorities.

The net premium method of valuation acts as a benchmark but it often needs modification in practice to allow for renewal expenses, the possibility of negative reserves, and initial expenses. The effects of these modifications are demonstrated in the following sections.

Modification for renewal expenses

The margin between the valuation net premium and the full office premium may not be large enough to cover estimated future expenses, particularly in the case of non-profit policies where there is no bonus loading in the office premium. For example, non-profit policies may have been issued at total office premium of 315, allowing a 5 per cent margin for renewal expenses on the basic pure premium of 300, but caution in the valuation may require that a margin of at least 10 per cent (i.e. 30 per annum) should be allowed for expenses. The valuation premium brought into the reserving formula to calculate 'Reserve c/f' will then be 285 (= 315 – 30) instead of 300. Assuming that the original estimate for renewal expenses was correct (i.e. 15 per annum) the revenue accounts will be as illustrated in Table 19.6.

As before, in the first policy year the opening reserve in line (a) is zero; the closing reserve of 230 in line (f) is computed by deducting future valuation net premiums (285 + 285) from future claims payable of 800. Although the total surplus of line (h) summed across all three years is nil (so that the office premium exactly covers the benefits and expenses) the valuation has caused a negative surplus of −30 in the first year (i.e. a valuation strain of 30). This implies that not enough money was set aside at the outset; the actuary should therefore have set up an opening reserve of 30 instead of zero in line (a) of year 1. (The money comes from the shareholders' profit and loss accounts or from other surplus.) That would have produced nil surplus (and nil strain) in the first year; the surplus of 15 in each of the second and third years would then have repaid the 30 'borrowed' for the first year.

Modification for negative reserves

We have seen that restricting the valuation premium to allow a sufficiently prudent margin from the office premium produces higher reserves and delays the emergence of surplus. The opposite effect occurs if margins are reduced and it is then possible for the reserve to be reduced below zero. As an illustration, suppose the with-profit policies were issued with a 50 per cent loading for bonuses (that is, an annual office premium of 450). If the full office premium is brought into the reserve then the reserve at the end of the first year becomes:

Future claims	= 200 + 600 =	800
Future valuation premiums	= 450 + 450 =	900
Reserve		= −100

This negative reserve of −100 would represent an asset of 100 obtained by capitalising future margins, but this 'asset' would disappear if the policyholder were to allow his policy to lapse. It is therefore generally agreed that, where the reserve on a policy is negative, it should be taken as zero.

Modification for initial expenses (Zillmerisation)

The third modification to a net premium valuation is generally known as Zillmerisation, although in the United States the term 'modified net premium valuation' is used. The modification is aimed at compensating for the uneven effect on revenues of the heavy incidence of commission and expenses at the commencement of a policy. In practice initial commission and initial expenses can each be as high as 50 per cent of an annual office premium or even higher, whereas renewal commission and expenses are often as low as 2 1/2 per cent and 5 per cent respectively of an annual premium.

Let us return to the three-year without-profit policies of Table 19.1, where expected claims were 100, 200 and 600. Suppose that initial expenses (and commissions) are 90 in total and renewal expenses of 30 are incurred

Table 19.7 The effect of initial expenses (with a valuation net premium of 300)

	Policy year	*1*	*2*	*3*
	Income			
(a)	Reserve b/f	40	200	300
(b)	Premium income	350	350	350
(c)	Total income	390	550	650
	Outgo			
(d)	Claims	100	200	600
(e)	Expenses	90	30	30
(f)	Reserve c/f	200	300	0
(g)	Total outgo	390	530	630
(h)	Surplus (c) – (g)	0	20	20

for each of the two subsequent renewals. This gives a total office premium of 350 per annum, since

$$(100 + 200 + 600 + 90 + 30 + 30)/3 = 350$$

If a valuation net premium of 300 was utilised in the calculation of 'Reserves c/f' with 50 per annum left to cover the total expenses of 150, then the revenue accounts would be as illustrated in Table 19.7.

In line (a) of the first policy year, it has been necessary to introduce an opening reserve of 40 (known as the 'new business strain'). This is necessary because otherwise a negative surplus (of −40) would have been obtained at the end of the first year (line (h)). The sequence of surpluses in the three years is then 0, 20, 20 and the 'loan' of 40 can be repaid.

The opening new business strain of 40 in line (a) of Table 19.7 is unwelcome and can be eliminated by modifying the valuation net premium used in line (f). The excess of first year expenses over renewal years (i.e. 90 − 30 = 60) can be spread over the three-year term of the policies (i.e. 20 per annum) to produce a modified valuation net premium of 300 + 20 = 320 which is then utilised to calculate the 'Reserve c/f' in line (f). The revenue account of Table 19.8 shows no strain or surplus. The amount of 60 is known as the *Zillmer adjustment*. It may be that the Zillmered valuation premium will produce negative reserves which will have to be eliminated. In practice the circumstance which commonly prevents full Zillmerisation is that the margin left between the office premium and the increased Zillmered premium looks insufficient to cover future renewal expenses on a prudent basis. The result is a valuation strain where the fund built up from the income from premiums (and investment) less outgo is insufficient to cover the valuation reserve.

Table 19.8 The effect of Zillmerisation on initial expenses (with a valuation net premium of 320)

	Policy year	*1*	*2*	*3*
	Income			
(a)	Reserve b/f	0	160	280
(b)	Premium income	350	350	350
(c)	Total income	350	510	630
	Outgo			
(d)	Claims	100	200	600
(e)	Expenses	90	30	30
(f)	Reserve c/f	160	280	0
(g)	Total outgo	350	510	630
(h)	Surplus (c) – (g)	0	0	0

19.3 'ADEQUATE' RESERVING AND THE ESTATE IN A WITH-PROFIT OFFICE

Introduction

Even in the case of profitable policies it is common to find a valuation strain when a policy is first written, followed by surpluses in the later years. In life insurance it is generally agreed that a valuation reserving basis (that is, the set of assumptions made about the future) should be sufficiently cautious to make it extremely unlikely that further capital will be required at any future time during the course of a policy, once the initial 'new business strain' has been supported (either by surplus from other policies or by a transfer into the life fund from the shareholders' capital). This has come to be known as a standard of 'adequacy', as opposed to mere solvency.

To illustrate this point, suppose that over the next three years claims of 100, 200 and 600 are anticipated on a best estimate basis (this will be termed an 'anticipated actual' experience). Suppose that, if we ignore expenses, the market allows an office annual premium of 315 (i.e. a 5 per cent margin for profit). However a cautious view of the future might well require a 10 per cent uplift from 'anticipated actual' claims; the cautious reserving basis could assume future claims of 110, 120, and 660 in the calculation of 'Reserve c/f'.

Ideally the valuation net premium should also be increased to 330, but this value is unacceptably high because it exceeds the office premium of 315. So, within the terms of the example, 315 represents highest valuation

Table 19.9 An 'adequate' standard of reserving (with a valuation net premium of 315)

	Policy year	*1*	*2*	*3*
	Income			
(a)	Reserve b/f	35	250	345
(b)	Premium income	315	315	315
(c)	Total income	350	565	660
	Outgo			
(d)	Claims	100	200	600
(e)	Reserve c/f	250	345	0
(f)	Total outgo	350	545	600
(g)	Surplus (c) – (f)	0	20	60

premium for which we can take credit. Table 19.9 shows what will happen if the actual experience follows the 'anticipated actual'.

In line (a) of the first policy year, it has been necessary to counter new business strain by introducing an opening reserve of 35 (in order to avoid a negative surplus of −35 in line (g)). The 'Reserve c/f' in line (e) is obtained by deducting valuation net premiums from future claims computed on the valuation basis: in the first policy year this produces a reserve of 250, being future claims (220 + 660) less valuation net premiums (315 + 315). Provided the experience follows the 'anticipated actual' experience, the total surplus of 20 + 60 = 80 repays the initial new business train of 35 and leaves the total profit margin of 45. In practice the capital required to meet the new business strain of a conventional life office has been provided by the surplus it has retained during the course of its business. The accumulated retained surplus is known as the *estate*.

With-profit policies and the estate

The estate built up by a traditional life office writing with-profit business arises from retained surplus over and above that which is distributed to with-profit policyholders and shareholders. The example illustrated in Table 19.10 shows how, through the use of a cautious valuation basis, a retained surplus of 68.31 is built up over a period of three years from a total office premium of 1080; a further 12.17 is also paid to shareholders (representing 11.3 per cent of the total distributed surplus), with the remaining 999.52 being returned to policyholders in the form of claims including simple bonuses. As usual the impact of investment income is ignored, as is the existence of initial and renewal expenses and commissions.

Table 19.10 A simple bonus distribution and retained surplus (with a valuation net premium of 330)

	Policy year	*1*	2	3
	Income			
(a)	Surplus b/f	0	10.27	21.37
(b)	Reserve b/f	0	244.00	375.18
(c)	Premium income	360	360.00	360.00
(d)	Total income	360	614.27	756.55
	Valuation before bonus declaration			
(e)	Reserve	330	574.00	705.18
(f)	Surplus (d) – (e)	30	40.27	51.37
	to policyholders 90%	27	36.24	46.23
	to shareholders 10%	3	4.03	5.14
	After bonus declaration			
(g)	Claims paid	102.73	213.69	683.10
(h)	Reserve c/f	244.00	375.18	0
(i)	Surplus c/f	10.27	21.37	68.31
(j)	Transfer to shareholders	3.00	4.03	5.14
(k)	Total outgo	360.00	614.27	756.55

Assume that the life office is writing with-profit policies with 'anticipated actual' claims of 100, 200 and 600 and premiums of 360 per annum. Using a cautious valuation basis we assume claims will be 10 per cent higher at 110, 220 and 660 with a valuation net premium of (110 + 220 + 660)/3 = 330 (this is an acceptable valuation premium leaving a margin of 30 on the office premium of 360). The development of bonus distribution and retained surplus over three years is given in Table 19.10; the table also serves to sum up the preceding discussion on valuation and distribution in a conventional with-profit office.

The first column of Table 19.10 is straightforward up to the calculation of the 'Reserve' in line (e) where the figure of 330 is obtained by deducting valuation net premiums of 660 from future claims (as estimated from the cautious valuation basis, i.e. 990 = 110 + 220 + 660). Line (f) shows a surplus of 30 in the first policy year, 27 of which is available for distribution to with-profit policyholders.

In Table 19.3, the bonus was distributed in proportion to the 'anticipated actual' claims (which total 900); however it would be wrong to do so in this case because we have assumed in the valuation basis that claims could be 10 per cent higher (so that the possible payments in the three policy years may be 110, 220 and 660): sharing the surplus of 27 in proportion to claims as per valuation basis raises these respective benefits to 113, 226 and 678, an increase of 2.727 per cent. Suppose it transpires that actual claims in year 1 follow the 'anticipated actual' of 100; payments are then increased by the bonus rate of 2.727 per cent to give 102.73 in line (g); the 'Reserve c/f' in line (h) is then recalculated to allow for the impact of the bonus declaration on future claims (i.e. 244 = future claims (226 + 678) less valuation net premiums (660)). Finally, because the cost of the first-year claims (102.73) is less than those anticipated under the cautious valuation basis (113), the balance of 10.27 is carried forward as surplus (line (i)).

In the second policy year, the calculations proceed as before with the reserve of 574 in line (e) reflecting the increase in future claims as per the valuation basis (i.e. 574 = 226 + 678 − 330). Line (f) shows a surplus of 40.27, of which 90 per cent (36.24) is available for distribution to policyholders. The bonus rate for a *simple bonus* system is then obtained by dividing the policyholders' surplus of 36.24 by the future benefits on the original valuation basis (i.e. 220 + 660) excluding bonuses already declared, to give a simple bonus rate of 4.118 per cent. Applying this rate to claims per valuation basis (again excluding existing bonus) for the second and third policy years gives simple bonuses of 9.06 (which equals 4.118 per cent of 220) and 27.18 (4.118 per cent of 660). By then adding the bonus already declared in the first year, we obtain claims as per valuation basis with simple bonuses included of 235.06 (which equals 220 + 6 + 9.06) and 705.18 (i.e. 660 + 18 + 27.18) for the second and third years respectively. If the actual claims in year 2 follow the 'anticipated actual' of 200, then 'Claims paid' in line (g) amount to 213.69 (that is, 200 + 2.727 per cent + 4.118 per cent). The 'Reserve c/f' in line (h) reflects the impact of existing simple bonus declaration on claims expected as per valuation basis in year 3 (i.e. 705.18): the reserve is then obtained by deducting valuation net premiums of 330. As in the first year, because the actual cost of claims (at 213.69) is less than those anticipated under the valuation basis (235.06) the balance of 21.37 in line (i) is carried forward as surplus.

Exactly the same procedure is followed in the third year, to produce a final bonus of 7.005 per cent and a 'Surplus c/f' of 68.31 which then serves to strengthen the estate.

The example of Table 19.10 shows how the estate is increased by surpluses retained; in contrast the estate can be depleted by paying, for competitive reasons, bonuses which are greater than the profits being earned. The estate does not commonly appear in published accounts because, over the years, it has been used to strengthen the valuation basis and to maintain a strong valuation basis on expanding business by carrying the burden of new business strain.

The bonus system illustrated in Table 19.10 was that of a *simple* bonus, where the bonus rate was calculated by expressing policyholders' surplus as a percentage of future benefits as per the valuation basis, excluding bonus already declared. This bonus rate was then applied to the 'anticipated actual' claims for each year, again excluding existing bonuses accrued. In the case of a *compound* bonus the bonus rate is calculated by expressing policyholders' surplus as a percentage of future benefits on the valuation basis, including previous bonuses. This will then have been applied to the 'anticipated actual' claim plus existing bonuses.

Matching assets and liabilities

We have dissected the financial anatomy of insurance by using simplified examples. These examples have assumed that a zero rate of interest is earned on the investments of insurance companies. As explained in Section 16.1, the introduction of interest earnings certainly affects the operation of a company and much of the profit for shareholders and policyholders alike is derived from the investments, but the examples would have been complicated with little extra compensating benefit of explanation.

The effect of investment is modelled in actuarial calculations by the use of a rate of interest, but this implies that, if investments have to be sold or moneys invested or reinvested in the future, the future yields at which those transactions will take place will be the same as now. If a liability to pay £1 in 20 years' time is matched by an asset of £1 payable in 20 years' time then the rate of interest in the meanwhile is irrelevant. The effect of the mismatching which occurs in practice is allowed for in the valuation reserving basis by taking a margin on the rate of interest used in that basis.

In the case of investment in non-matching assets, a balance needs to be struck between the holding back of surplus because of the necessary margin in the valuation reserving basis, and the expectation of a better 'anticipated actual' investment result. One development designed to allow for the greater volatility of equities, for example, has been the introduction of 'final' or 'terminal' bonuses which can be quite large but are guaranteed for one year only. The limitation on the guarantee means that the promise need not be reflected in the valuation reserving basis (for example by a 'mismatching reserve' or other margin).

19.4 NON-PROFIT POLICIES AND SHAREHOLDERS' CAPITAL

Introduction

The description given so far of the method of actuarial control of a life office, and the emergence of its surplus, relates to methods which worked well within the context of a traditional UK life office where most of the business was with-profit endowment and whole life policies. The premiums with their bonus loadings were usually sufficiently large to make questions of solvency unimportant; the problem was much more a question of an equitable bonus system and equity between different generations of policyholders. Once the 'estate' of the office had been built up, there was no question of requiring more capital to support the writing of new business and its valuation strain.

In contrast, the method of 'discounted future profits' is particularly useful in the context of a proprietary company which writes only non-profit policies – a situation which is common in the United States and increasingly so in the United Kingdom (with the rising popularity of non-profit unit-linked policies). The central feature of the discounted future profits method is the rate of return required by shareholders as compensation for the commitment of their capital. In general, shareholders require an expected risk yield on their money which is greater than they could obtain by straight investment on the stock exchange.

Suppose, for example, that this rate is 15 per cent per annum net of tax. In the revenue accounts of Table 19.9 capital of 35 was required at the outset to cover the new business train, and annual surpluses then emerged of 0, 20, and 60 in the three policy years. From the shareholders' point of view the cash-flows are:

Policy year	0	1	2	3
Cash-flow	−35	0	20	60

The discounted present value to the shareholders of this cash-flow is therefore

$$-35 + 0/1.15 + 20/1.15^2 + 60/1.15^3 = 19.57.$$

An alternative interpretation is that the internal rate of return is 35 1/2 per cent per annum, since

$$0/1.355 + 20/1.355^2 + 60/1.355^3 = 35.$$

Thus, to write this policy, or group of policies, requires initial capital of 35 and gives an expected internal risk rate of return of 35 1/2 per cent per annum. The company could thus expand its new business (on that contract) at the rate of 35 1/2 per cent per annum without requiring more capital, provided the shareholders took no money from the company.

However, if a shareholder is to leave money in the insurance business, his or her desired risk rate of return must be higher than the rate earned on the relatively risk-free assets of the life fund. Hence the weaker the valuation basis, and thus the earlier the emergence of surplus, the greater the value of the policies written to the shareholders. The restraining feature in life insurance is the agreement of a standard of 'adequacy' within the actuarial profession, the industry and the supervisory authorities, and the open publication by the actuary of his valuation basis of reserving. No

Table 19.11 Non-profit premium calculation (with a valuation net premium of P)

Policy year	*1*	*2*	*3*
Income			
(a) Reserve b/f	980–3P	880–2P	660–P
(b) Premium income	P	P	P
(c) Total income	980–2P	880– P	660
Outgo			
(d) Claim	100	200	600
(e) Reserve c/f	880–2P	660–P	0
(f) Total outgo	980–2P	860–P	600
(g) Surplus (c) – (f)	0	20	60

similar feature exists in general insurance in the United Kingdom or elsewhere, however.

Calculating a premium

Consider the design of a policy using the approach of discounted future profits where the premium is an amount of money which we shall call *P*. The revenue accounts are given in Table 19.11: future claims are taken on the same basis as Table 19.9 and an initial capital injection of 980 − 3P is required to support the policy and cover the new business strain.

From the shareholders' point of view, the cash-flows generated in Table 19.11 are:

Policy year	0	1	2	3
Cash-flow	980–3P	0	20	30

If the shareholders' desired rate of return on capital is 35 1/2 per cent per annum, then the premium must be 315, since:

$$980 - 3P = 0/1.355 + 20/1.355^2 + 60/1.355^3 = 35.$$

If, however, competition in the market allows a premium of only 314 then the yield to shareholders will be *i*, where

$$980 - (3 \times 314) = 0/(1 + i) + 20/(1 + i)^2 + 60\ (1 + i)^3$$

which gives $i = 0.315$ (i.e. 31 1/2 per cent per annum). If this is not acceptable to the shareholders the contract will have to be redesigned.

The use of a shareholders' desired yield implies that shareholders are indifferent to the use of capital, provided they earn that rate. However, in practice, further capital cannot be raised easily so policy designs have aimed at producing a second year surplus in order to recover the inevitable first year strain and rotate the working capital as far as possible.

19.5 THE VALUE OF A LIFE COMPANY

Valuation by discounted future profits

The value of a life insurance company is made up of three main elements: the value of shareholders' assets, the present value of future profits generated by in-force business, and the goodwill arising from the expectation of future new business.

The shareholders' assets and the value of the in-force policies represent the value if the company were to cease writing new business and become a closed fund. The goodwill arises from the on-going business of the company. An acceptable method of approaching a valuation of goodwill is to assume that the company's current level of new business represents the 'momentum' it has developed, to take credit for this level as a perpetuity, and to imply that any increase from that level in future must come from the efforts of the new shareholders.

Consider the value of a company writing ten-year unit linked policies in 1988. The surpluses generated over the next ten years from contracts written at the start of 1988 are as follows:

Year start	1988	+1	+2	+3	+4	+5	+6	+7	+8	+9
Surplus	−20	40	2	2	2	2	2	2	2	2

If we assume the shareholders' required risk rate of return is 15 per cent per annum then the capitalised (present value) at the start of 1988 of the future profits generated by these contracts is 22.6 (which is given by $-20 + 40/1.15 + 2/1.15^2 \ldots\ldots + 2/1.15^9$). Typically this value is around one-quarter of one year's annual premium.

If these policies had been written at the start of 1987, the effects of the initial new business strain can be ignored, and the present value of future profits in 1988 (that is one year after inception) is 49.0 (given by $40 + 2/1.15 + 2/1.15^2 + \ldots\ldots + 2/1.15^8$). In the same way the capitalised profits in 1988 from new business written in 1986 is 10.3 (which is given by $2 + 2/1.15 + \ldots + 2/1.15^7$).

If we assume for the moment that the level of new business over the last ten years has been constant, we can obtain the present value at the start of 1988 of the future profits to be generated by all in-force contracts as follows:

Year of inception	1988	1987	1986	1985	1984	1983	1982	1981	1980	1979
Value	22.6	49.0	10.3	9.6	8.7	7.7	6.6	5.3	3.7	2.0

We now assume that past new business has actually increased at 20 per cent per annum with no lapses, so that the present value of 1987 business, for example, is 49.0/1.20; the value of the total business in-force at the start of 1988 is then:

$$49.0/1.20 + 10.3/1.20^2 + \ldots + 2.0/1.20^9 = 65.8$$

The value of goodwill is a perpetuity of 22.6 per annum at the required yield of 15 per cent, which capitalises at 150.7 (= 22.6/0.15).

If we take the value of the shareholders' assets at 20 the total value for the company is 236.5, as follows:

Shareholders' assets	20.0
In-force business	65.8
Goodwill	150.7
Total	236.5

The assessment of the value of a life office by the present value of its future profits is not so clear-cut when with-profit policies are considered. Referring to the example in Table 19.10, the surpluses paid to shareholders as a result of the bonus system (3, 4.03 and 5.14) and the shareholders' proportion of the estate (11.3 per cent of 68.31) can be valued as:

$$3/1.15 + 4.03/1.15^2 + 5.14/1.15^3 + 11.3 \text{ per cent} \times 68.31/1.15^3 = 14.1.$$

In practice there may be a new business strain or later financing strain if bonus rates are higher than can be sustained by the premium levels and there may be a subtle effect in operation: the estate may be reducing because of new business but the value of emerging surpluses to shareholders before the estate runs out may be increasing because of that same new business.

If the value of the company (i.e. 236.5 at the start of 1988) is recalculated each year on a consistent basis, it forms a good guide to the progress of the company. The annual increase in the value will normally be positive and gives a useful measure of progress. If, however, the company has written a large amount of new business, the new business strain may well be larger than the surplus released from earlier business, causing a net strain to be covered by a transfer from shareholders' profit and loss account into the life fund. This transfer is called a 'loss' in the published accounts and is the cause of much misunderstanding. On the other hand, the new business is normally intrinsically profitable and increases the value of the company.

Generally accepted accounting principles

The fact that the surplus shown in the published accounts of a life office can be a poor or misleading indication of the profitability of the company has led to a requirement by the accounting profession in the United States that life insurance accounts should be restated according to Generally Accepted Accounting Principles (GAAP). Unfortunately, the method adopted is not compatible with the approach described earlier, where the value of an asset is given by the discounted capitalised value of future net income from the asset, and the measure of the year's progress or 'earnings' is then the change in that value. GAAP starts with the concept of 'earnings' for the year; it assumes:

(a) that the office premium is built from an 'anticipated actual' of assumptions, together with a margin of profit which is a constant proportion of the premiums;
(b) that, if the actual experience follows the premium basis, the margin for profit should emerge levelly as surplus each year in order to give a 'truer and fairer view' of the financial working;
(c) that the valuation-reserving basis should be the same as the premium basis, thus releasing the margins as surplus in level annual amounts; and
(d) that, as the actual experience varies from the premium (and valuation) basis, so the variations in the resulting emerging surpluses give a truer and fairer view of the financial results.

As has been illustrated earlier, this approach is workable for the smooth operation of bonuses under a with-profit system where the bonus system has been designed with that operation in mind and where the operation of the bonus system is unhampered by problems of solvency and capital resources. Ironically, in the United States, with-profit policies are issued by the mutual companies and non-profit policies are issued by the proprietory companies, and GAAP was produced for the latter.

The result is that GAAP 'profits' bear no relationship to surplus as shown in the accounts and bear no relationship to the increase in value of the company. The restrictions caused by the cautious valuation basis of reserving are fundamental to the financial working of the company and determine its value. If two hypothetical companies are identical in the policies they issue and in their actual experience, but the first uses a weaker reserving basis, then, as explained in Section 19.4, the first has greater value to its shareholders. However, under GAAP, the two companies would have the same value because both are valued on the premium bases and the actual published reserving basis is ignored.

Recommended reading

Benjamin, S. (1970) 'Profit and Other Financial Concepts in Insurance', *Journal of the Institute of Actuaries*, 103.

de Vylder, F., Goovaerts, M. and Haezendonck, J. (1984) *Premium Calculation in Insurance* (Dordrecht: D. Reidel Publishing Company).

Wilkie, A.D. (1984) 'Some Notes On The Methods of Calculation of Life Assurance Premiums in the United Kingdom', in de Vylder *et al.* (1984) pp. 519–32.

Index